ACTS

Activating the **C**hurch with the **T**rue Gospel and **S**piritual Power

Wendy Bowen

ACTS

Copyright © 2015 Wendy Bowen

ALL RIGHTS RESERVED WORLDWIDE

Manifest International, LLC

MANIFEST
PUBLICATIONS

ISBN: 978-0-692-40510-9

Please note that the names and references to God are capitalized to acknowledge and worship His deity. In contrast, the names and other references to satan are not capitalized, even to the point of violating grammatical rules, so as to equally acknowledge his position of defeat.

Cover Design by Don Patton

Theological Review by Dr. Sidney Bradley

Proofreading by Susan Williams

DEDICATION

This book is wholly dedicated to the Lord Jesus Christ
and to every member of His Body who has impacted my walk with Him.

CONTENTS

ACTS
Introduction

Welcome to **ACTS**! ACTS is a study on the Bible's Book of Acts focused on <u>A</u>ctivating the <u>C</u>hurch with the <u>T</u>rue Gospel and <u>S</u>piritual power. The aim of this study is to empower believers today to do the things that Jesus did, the way that He did them, and the way the first followers of Christ did in the Book of Acts. ACTS incorporates both the historical account and personal application to our lives as Christ followers today.

This study has been entirely birthed by the prompting of the Lord and, in fact, it wasn't even my idea! I was recently at a conference where God was moving powerfully. In a time of surrendered prayer and listening to the Holy Spirit, the Lord shared His heart with me. It was as if, from within, I could hear Him crying out with deep sorrow and weeping, "My people, My people! They do not know Me. Help them to know Me." His weeping became my weeping as I was moved to the depths of my heart for His people, His Church, His Bride. Along the same lines, I believe that Christians today are hungry and thirsty for more of God, for a deeper walk with Christ, and for more of the work of the Holy Spirit in their lives. Therefore, my hope is that this study will help you to know God better than you did before. Through deeper knowledge of Him, I believe that you will be more like Jesus. By being more like Christ, my prayer is that you will do more of the things that He did by the power of the Holy Spirit. This is what ACTS is all about.

Historical Background of Acts

Author: Luke   **Date Written**: between 63-70 AD   **Addressed to**: Theophilus or *lovers of God*
Location: Jerusalem, Judea & Samaria, the ends of the earth

The Book of Acts is a major turning point in the Scriptures and also in world history. Acts was written by Luke as continuation of the Book of Luke, which details the life and ministry of Jesus, as a historical account of the life and ministry of the first Christ followers. Acts reveals the birth of a new people and the birth of the Church. From the start of Acts, we observe that the resurrection of Jesus Christ from the dead has changed everything because Jesus has been proven to be the Messiah of Israel. We hear Jesus' last words before He ascended to heaven, promising to return at a God-appointed time and promising the outpouring of the Holy Spirit:

> *{Act 1:7-8} 7 He said to them: "It is not for you to know the times or dates the Father has set by his own authority. 8 But you will receive power when the Holy Spirit comes on you; and you will be my witnesses in Jerusalem, and in all Judea and Samaria, and to the ends of the earth."*

In a dynamic explosion of heaven meeting earth, we see that the Holy Spirit is poured out as promised so that followers of Christ can continue the work that Jesus did in the Gospels. Whereas the Gospels tell us what "Jesus began to do and to teach" (see Acts 1:1) proclaiming the Kingdom of God with a demonstration of God's power, the Book of Acts shows us that the very same power of God has now been transferred to those who believe Jesus. In fact, this is where the Book of Acts derives its name. The word *acts* in Greek is *praxeis* which is all about *doing*, a *mode of acting*, *things done*, the *doings of*, the *works*, the *deeds*, the *actions*, and it is typically used to denote the works of extraordinary men. This said, the "extraordinary men" doing great works of God in the Book of Acts are actually just ordinary people like you and me. Therefore, we are going to learn in this study how to do acts of God today the same way that they did.

From the standpoint of the Scriptures, in the Book of Acts, the Old Testament and New Testament kiss in a beautiful prophetic fulfillment of all that God had promised, with the best still yet to come. Believers then did not have the New Testament yet, so their study of Christ was entirely from the Old Testament Scriptures. Accordingly, in this study we will highlight Old Testament foreshadowing of Christ and what He accomplished so that we enter into the Scriptures the way that they did.

From the standpoint of world history, the Book of Acts takes place over a span of more than 30 years. In Chapters 1-15, Luke, a brilliant man and trained physician, wrote with extraordinary attention to accuracy based on actual eyewitness events. In Chapters 16-28, Luke himself is a participant in the story which we know from his use of "we." Acts is the birth of Christianity as we know it today. News of King Jesus was on its way to the ends of the earth. Riots rose up in opposition to the enormous cultural changes which the Gospel message brings and world rulers were confronted with conflicts when their own people pledged allegiance to the King above all kings. Here are a few different ways of breaking down the Book of Acts from a historical standpoint:

Outline 1:	Chapters 1-12:	Founding of the Church
	Chapters 13-28:	Spreading of the Church
Outline 2:	Chapters 1-7:	Jerusalem (2 years)
	Chapters 8-12:	Judea & Samaria (13 yrs)
	Chapters 13-28:	Ends of the earth (15 yrs)
Outline 3:	Chapters 1-7:	Consolidated Church
	Chapters 8-9:	Persecuted Church
	Chapters 10-12:	Church Extended
	Chapters 13-15:	Paul's first journey (1 yr, 5 months)
	Chapters 16-18:	Paul's second journey (2 yrs, 5 months)
		Wrote 1 & 2 Thessalonians
	Chapters 19-23:	Paul's third journey (4 yrs)
		Wrote 1 & 2 Corinthians, Romans, Galatians
	Chapters 24-26:	Paul's trials (2 yrs)
	Chapters 27-28:	Paul's Imprisonment (2 yrs)
		Wrote Ephesians, Colossians, Philemon, Philippians
		Note: 1 & 2 Timothy and Titus were written after the Book of Acts

Outline 4:   Timeline (accurate within two year cushion):

- Year 30 AD: Founding of the Church in Jerusalem (Acts 1-2)
- 34:   Stephen martyred (Acts 7)
- 33/35:   Paul's conversion (Acts 9)
- 34/37:   Paul's first visit to Jerusalem (Acts 9:26)
- 45/46:   James martyred (Acts 12:2)
- 46/47:   First missionary journey begins (Acts 13-14)
- 48:   Jerusalem Council (Acts 15)
- 48-51:   Second missionary journey begins (Acts 15:26-18:22)
- 50:   Paul at Corinth (Acts 18)
- 53:   Third missionary journey begins (Acts 19)
- 54-57:   Paul at Ephesus (Acts 19)
- 57-58:   Paul in Greece (Acts 20)
- 58:   Paul in Jerusalem (Acts 21)
- 58-60:   Paul imprisoned in Caesarea (Acts 24-26)
- 60-61:   Paul appeals to Caesar, voyage to Rome (Acts 27)
- 61-62:   Paul imprisoned in Rome (Acts 28:30)
- 65:   Paul martyred (not recorded in Scripture)

My personal belief is that we, too, live in a dynamic turning point of world history. I believe that followers of Christ will experience more and more of the types of things we see in the Book of Acts in the days leading up to Christ's return. Therefore, we are not going to approach this study solely as a theological review or from strictly a historical perspective. Rather, we are going to study ACTS so that we are empowered to be the Church which Christ has called and chosen us to be. This is what the first disciples of Christ demonstrate so beautifully in the Book of Acts.

Outline for ACTS

I believe that the Lord has led me to structure this study with four main focus areas: The Gospel, the Holy Spirit, Community, and Opposition. These areas of study are as significant for us today as they were for the first followers of Christ. Each focus area has what I'm calling a "Primer" which lays the groundwork for understanding what they believed so that we can apply the Scriptures to our lives in the way that they did. Think of it like putting a coat of primer on a wall before painting it so that the paint color shows up as it should. While we will flow somewhat historically as we start, we will quickly move into highlighting significant topics within each category and draw from all chapters of the Book of Acts on that topic. This is what the outline for ACTS looks like according to category.

THE GOSPEL	HOLY SPIRIT	COMMUNITY	OPPOSITION
1. Primer: The Gospel	2. Primer: Holy Spirit	3. Primer: Communion	4. Primer: Trials
5. Old to New	6. Pentecost	9. Fellowship	11. Persecution
8. Rend Your Heart	7. Kingdom	12. Devotion	15. Yeast
13. Types & Shadows	10. Miracles	14. My Witnesses	
	16. God's Guidance		

You can read the chapters in their numerical order, by category, or in whatever order the Lord leads you to read them. There is some progression of information through the chapters and the categories and there is some cross-referencing between chapters to avoid redundancy but, basically, each chapter can stand on its own. So jump in however the Holy Spirit directs you.

Revelation

While I hope that this study challenges you to new levels in your walk with Christ, I know that there is only one Teacher, the Holy Spirit. Head knowledge is good, but revelation knowledge is permanent and empowers action. While I can encourage you, only God can direct you. While I can explain the Word of God and the work of Christ, only the Holy Spirit can reveal Him to you. I pray the Lord fills you with the spirit of wisdom and revelation (see Ephesians 1:17) as we go through this study together so that you grow in your understanding that Jesus Christ is all we need.

> *{Rom 1:16-17 KJV} 16 For I am not ashamed of* **the gospel of Christ**: *for it is* **the power of God unto salvation** *to every one that believeth; to the Jew first, and also to the Greek. 17 For therein is* **the righteousness of God revealed from faith to faith**: *as it is written, The just shall live by faith.*

The word for *salvation* in this verse is *soteria* which by its Greek definition includes *salvation, deliverance, healing, and sustenance.* Every time we place our faith in Jesus and what He accomplished for us for these things instead of anything else in heaven or on earth, we advance in our understanding of the righteousness of God. While the Scripture references in this study are from the New International Version (NIV) of the Bible, for this verse I use the King James Version because it clearly states *from faith to faith.* From faith to faith, to me, clearly articulates how one step at a time, one episode of faith at a time, one act of surrender and trust at time, we advance in our comprehension of the love of God for us in Christ Jesus and that He truly did finish the work of our salvation along with everything that it includes. We grow in our faith to spiritual maturity by receiving in our inmost being what has already been accomplished for us in Christ.

To illustrate this further, when Christ transferred us from the kingdom of darkness into the Kingdom of His marvelous light, it was a one-time full transfer. (see Colossians 1:13) We were permanently moved from one place to another. With the exception of denying Christ or renouncing Him, we do not become more transferred or less transferred because of what we do or do not do, nor do we become lighter or darker depending on how we are doing in our spiritual walk. Rather, as we grow in Christ, we are growing in our revelation knowledge, understanding, and ability to receive by faith the benefits of the transfer which has already taken place through the life, death, and resurrection of Jesus Christ. In another way of looking at it, the Holy Spirit dwelling in us gives us revelation knowledge from within and even the mind of Christ if we receive it by faith. (see 1 Corinthians 2:16) If the Holy Spirit has ever revealed anything to you in your walk of faith, then you know that it was like a lightning bolt went off in your brain and you finally understood something that you never comprehended before. This is usually rooted in the realization that Christ has already finished it. Additionally, it was most likely something so significant that it altered your beliefs and your behavior. This was the Holy Spirit speaking from your inmost being with an empowering certainty which gave you the supernatural ability to be changed. Every time this happens, we have moved from faith to faith. The more we allow this to happen in every area of our lives, the more we become like Jesus and do the things He did.

Therefore, whenever you encounter something in your walk with Christ which challenges you or does not quite fully make sense to you yet, don't worry about it. If there is a "stickiness" to a point of truth which you somehow know is true even though you can't quite fully grasp it yet, don't agonize. The Holy Spirit is the best Teacher in the world and, in due course, according to your journey with Jesus and God's plan for your life, everything you need to know will be revealed to you. It's already done so you can't mess it up. Seek the Lord and ask Him to give you revelation of the truth. Jesus is the truth, God's Word is the truth, and the Holy Spirit will lead you in all truth. Don't strive for what you already have – just surrender and receive it. Don't belabor – just believe. Your lightning bolt of revelation will be right on time.

Repent for the Kingdom of God is at Hand

The resounding message of Jesus' ministry, starting with His forerunner John the Baptist, was, *"Repent for the Kingdom of Heaven is at hand!"* This was the same message believers in the Book of Acts continued to proclaim in Jesus' name. To repent means *to change one's mind*, typically with abhorrence of the old way of thinking. True repentance is proper remorse over the things that we have believed or done, coupled with a humbling of ourselves before God and returning to Him and His ways. In the Old Testament, people demonstrated repentance externally by clothing themselves in sackcloth, tearing their clothing, and covering themselves in dust and ashes. This symbolized their internal mourning over their humanity. However, Jesus did not come to judge but to save. (see John 3:17) Therefore, His approach was not one of condemnation for sin but invitation to grace. Accordingly, our approach to repentance does not need to get stuck in mourning or self-abhorrence. Though there will be times when we will feel this way as Jesus changes our minds about things we believe and do, we must also press on to receive the clear consciences that Jesus' blood paid for us to have. (see Hebrews 9:14) Our sin has been fully paid for and we spiritually reside in heaven, righteous before God because of Jesus. Acknowledging this fact is the truest form of humility.

Additionally, as believers in Jesus, the Kingdom of Heaven now dwells within us. (see Luke 17:21) The more our minds change from focusing on sin to focusing on heaven, the more the Kingdom of God manifests in our lives. Therefore, the emphasis of my teaching is more geared towards revealing the finished work of Christ and how to receive it to the fullest in our lives. My approach tends to be pro-Christ and His righteousness rather than anti-sin. Think of it like promoting a candidate in an election through emphasis on positive aspects of the contender rather than highlighting negative aspects of the opponent. I believe Jesus died for us to be Christ-conscious not sin-conscious so that we are free to worship and serve Him as instruments of righteousness. (see Romans 6:13) This reflects the way that Jesus went about His ministry when He walked on the earth, and it is my personal experience of His dealings with me as His disciple. Christ's sacrifice is all sufficient. God's grace is not an excuse for sin but an empowerment for genuine holiness. Grace is how we are transformed and this is how we bring the Kingdom of Heaven to earth.

> *{Rom 12:2} 2 Do not conform to the pattern of this world, but **be transformed by the renewing of your mind**. Then you will be able to **test and approve what God's will is--his good, pleasing and perfect will.***

> *{Mat 6:10} 10 **your kingdom come, your will be done, on earth as it is in heaven.***

Engage with God

As you go through this study, I encourage you to engage with God through the Holy Spirit. Before you begin, I invite you to cast all of your cares on Jesus. (see 1 Peter 5:7) This could be through prayer or even writing down the things which are causing anxiety in your life. Then crumple up the list and throw it to the other side of the room, trusting that Jesus will take care of your cares.

Before you read, invite the Holy Spirit to come and guide your time. Ask Him for new insight into the finished work of Christ and ask for ways of applying truth to your life. As you go, don't be afraid to stop and seek the Lord or meditate on something that He reveals to you. Commit your time to God and receive as much from Him as you can.

My prayer is that this study blesses you, increases your faith, and empowers you to take action for Christ in ways that you never have before. In Jesus name, I declare a supernatural release of the Holy Spirit into your life right now as we embark on this journey together.

CHAPTER 1
Primer: The Gospel

The life, death, and resurrection of Jesus Christ occurred right before the Book of Acts begins. In fact, the Book of Acts starts with resurrected Jesus revealing that He is alive from the dead and then ascending to heaven. Before ascending, Jesus used the writings of Moses, the Psalms, and the Prophets (see Luke 24:44) to explain to His followers all of the things that had been accomplished by God's power through His resurrection. Through this Primer, you will have the same basic understanding which those believers had as we enter into the Book of Acts.

Simple Statement of the Gospel

Jesus Christ, the one and only Son of God, was born of a virgin into the lineage of King David of Israel. He was crucified, died and was buried, He descended into hell and was resurrected from the dead on the third day by the power of God. He ascended into heaven and is now seated at the right hand of God with all power and authority in heaven and on earth and under the earth. After ascending to heaven, He poured out the Holy Spirit into all who believe in Him so that Jesus Christ now dwells in us by faith. He is coming back to avenge all evil to restore all things to God's original design.

The Gospel is more than just Good News. The Gospel changes everything. Through the life, death, and resurrection of Jesus Christ, God established a new people in a right-standing relationship with Him. To know how something has changed, we need to know how it began. So let's start at the beginning.

Adam in Eden (see Genesis 1-2)

In the beginning, God created everything: the heavens, the earth, and every living thing. Then, God made man in His own image, like a son bears the image of his father so that man could rule over everything that He had created. In Hebrew, the word for *man* is *Adam*. God formed Adam out of dust. Adam was not born, he was formed as a grown man in the same way that a potter or an artist forms something of clay. Then, God breathed the breath of life into Adam's nostrils, and he became a living being. Adam lived in paradise, and there was only one rule.

> *{Gen 2:16-17} 16 And the LORD God commanded the man, "You are free to eat from any tree in the garden; 17 **but you must not eat from the tree of the knowledge of good and evil, for when you eat from it you will certainly die.**"*

While Adam was still alone, the Lord commanded him not to eat of the tree of the knowledge of good and evil. But it was not good for Adam to be alone. He needed a helper for ruling over God's creation, so God put Adam into a deep sleep and made a woman from his rib. Adam's wife was not born, she was built out of Adam's rib in the same way that a building or a temple is built from raw materials. Adam could tell that this woman was made just like him.

> {Gen 2:23} 23 *The man said,* **"This is now bone of my bones and flesh of my flesh***; she shall be called 'woman,' for she was taken out of man."*

Adam and his wife were completely innocent, unashamedly naked, and shared unhindered fellowship with each other and with God. They were one flesh – male and female of the same kind of species on the earth. They lived in paradise, in perfect bodies, in a perfect creation, where everything worked exactly as God designed it. God's purpose for creating the human race was for them to rule over His creation as God's appointed king and queen.

> {Gen 1:28} 28 *God blessed them and said to them,* **"Be fruitful and increase in number; fill the earth and subdue it. Rule over** *the fish in the sea and the birds in the sky and over every living creature that moves on the ground."*

In Hebrew, the word used for *subdue* in this passage is the word *kabash*. It means *to tread with the feet, to put into subjection, to make subservient*. You may have heard the expression *put the kabash on it* pertaining to getting a situation under control, or according to Urban Dictionary, *To squash something from a position of strength*. So to paraphrase, God told the man and his wife to fill the earth with people like them and *put the kabash* on all of creation. Moreover, the word for *rule over* in this passage also means *to tread with the feet* or *to have dominion*. In no uncertain terms, God was telling them that He had given them all authority over everything that He had created. Because of their innocence, they wouldn't abuse this authority and because they had an unhindered relationship with God, they would rule things exactly the way God wanted them. At least this was the plan.

Adam's Disobedience (see Genesis 3)

But along came the serpent, who is the Devil, (see Revelation 20:2) a part of God's creation which Adam and his wife had complete authority over. The serpent deceived the woman and she ate from the tree of the knowledge of good and evil, even though she knew that God had said not to eat of this tree. She then handed some to Adam who also ate. As soon as Adam ate from the forbidden tree, everything changed. By not exerting their God-given authority over the serpent, they became subject to him. When explaining to God what they had done, the woman admitted that the serpent had deceived her. The Hebrew word for *deceived* in this passage means *to put into debt, to become a creditor, to lend with interest and usury*, stemming from a Hebrew root word for deceptive practices. Essentially, like being trapped by a loan shark with astronomical interest rates, Adam and his wife were now slaves to the devil (see Proverbs 22:7) with no hope of paying their way out.

Adam sinned by disobeying the one command God had given him. The consequence was exactly what God had said from the beginning – death. This did not mean instantaneous death of the body as we would think of it but more an explanation of death coming about. In the expression *you will surely die*, die or death is the same expression that would be used to say that someone is *dying of thirst* except in this case, Adam and his wife are dying of sin. Their sin was more than just eating the wrong tree, it was turning their hearts from one master to another. Through disobedience, they separated themselves from fellowship with God, who is the source of life. Now, because of their sin their spirits were dead within them. Therefore, their bodies would eventually die because of this internal condition. This death also denotes premature death, something that was not originally intended or, like the example of dying of thirst, could be remedied if only a drink of water were available. The bottom line is that because of their sin and without a God-given remedy, physical death was going to happen to both of them and everyone who descends from them, which includes all of us.

I say again, as soon as Adam ate from the forbidden tree, everything changed. They had ingested poisonous forbidden food, their eyes were opened, and their entire consciousness was changed from innocence to shame. They immediately knew that they were naked, and they tried to hide from each other and from God. There was no remedy for what had happened, there was no drink of water for this thirst, there was no way to escape the oppression of sin and shame and death, and there was no way for them to pay their way out of debt to the evil one. They were stripped of their authority in the earth because they had now become the subjects of a new master. They lost their position of unhindered fellowship in the presence of God, and they and all of their descendants were now under a curse. Instead of freedom, authority and life, there was fear, subjection, and death. Adam's nature and way of thinking and doing things, his "operating system" so to speak, changed from good to evil, from righteous to sinful, and from blameless to rebellious.

Furthermore, Adam was cursed to return to the dust out of which God had formed him. In fact, because of Adam's error, all of creation was placed under a curse. Every problem that we know of in the world today – war, famine, sickness, strife, pain, grief, and all disasters in creation – are a result of Adam's disobedience. However, in spite of all this, we do see the first glimmer of some good news to come. Because the serpent had deceived the woman, God cursed the serpent and promised that someday in the future the offspring of the woman would crush him forever.

> *{Gen 3:15} 15 And I will put enmity between you and the woman, and between your offspring and hers; **he will crush your head**, and you will strike his heel."*

Jesus' Obedience

Fast forward to the days of Jesus. Jesus was not formed by God like Adam, and He was not built by God like Adam's wife. Rather, He was born of a woman, a descendant of Adam's wife, just like you and me. Accordingly, in the days of His ministry, Jesus' favorite way to refer to Himself was the Son of Man. Since the word for man in Hebrew is Adam, Jesus called Himself the son of Adam. After Jesus was born, He grew from infancy, to boyhood, to manhood in the same way that you and I grow up. However, He was not conceived by a man of natural descent or in the natural way. Rather, He was conceived by the power of the Holy Spirit of God. Therefore, His very nature from conception in His mother's womb was the perfect nature of God Himself. His "operating system" was the same as God's because He was the Son of God. By the miracle working power of God, Jesus was both the Son of Man and the Son of God in one package.

> *{Luk 1:30-35} 30 But the angel said to her, "Do not be afraid, Mary; you have found favor with God. 31 You will conceive and give birth to a son, and you are to call him **Jesus**. 32 He will be great and will be called the **Son of the Most High**. The Lord God will give him the **throne of his father David**, 33 and he will reign over Jacob's descendants forever; **his kingdom will never end**." 34 "How will this be," Mary asked the angel, "**since I am a virgin?**" 35 The angel answered, "The **Holy Spirit will come on you**, and the power of the Most High will overshadow you. **So the holy one to be born will be called the Son of God**.*

Furthermore, Jesus was born to a young woman named Mary who was a virgin, betrothed to marry a man named Joseph. Both Mary and Joseph could trace their family lineage directly back to King David of Israel. This means that Jesus was Jewish, born into the nation of Israel who were the only people on earth with a relationship with the one true God who created everything in the beginning. The Jewish people all have one common ancestor, a man named Abraham. God promised Abraham that He would make a special nation out of Abraham's descendants and that they would own a special land. This is the same land which we know of today as the land of Israel. In spite of the fact that even one descendant was totally unlikely because his wife was barren, Abraham believed God. Then, God did exactly what He promised, and Abraham's wife gave birth to a son named Isaac. Isaac was the only son of Abraham who inherited God's special promise. In due course, Isaac had a son named Jacob, and Jacob inherited God's promise of a nation made of his descendants. Jacob proceeded to have twelve sons, and after that, God changed Jacob's name to Israel. Jacob's sons had families which became tribes and were collectively known as the twelve tribes of Israel. After a while, there was famine in the land, so they moved to Egypt. (see Genesis 12–50) Over the course of time, all the people of Israel became subjected to harsh and oppressive slavery by the Egyptians and this went on for about four hundred years. But God appointed a man named Moses, an Israelite from the tribe of Levi, to confront the king of Egypt and lead the people of Israel to freedom. After they were freed from the Egyptians, Israel had become a nation of people descended from Abraham, just as God had promised. (see Exodus 1–15) At that time, God gave Moses and the nation of Israel His perfect standard of conduct and obedience which He required for maintaining a right relationship with Him. Israel was the only nation on earth with God's Law and commands which, if obeyed, resulted in God's abundant blessing. In fact, the promises obtained through obedience to these laws are righteousness, blessing, and life from God. See the following excerpts from the Law of God:

> *{Deu 6:25} 25 And **if we are careful to obey all this law before the LORD our God**, as he has commanded us, **that will be our righteousness**."*

> *{Deu 11:26-28} 26 See, I am setting before you today a blessing and a curse-- 27 **the blessing if you obey the commands of the LORD your God** that I am giving you today; 28 the curse if you disobey the commands of the LORD your God and turn from the way that I command you today by following other gods, which you have not known.*

*{Deu 30:19} 19 This day I call the heavens and the earth as witnesses against you that I have set before you **life and death, blessings and curses**. Now choose life, so that you and your children may live*

*{Deu 28:1-14} 1 **If you fully obey the LORD your God and carefully follow all his commands** I give you today, the LORD your God will set you high above all the nations on earth. 2 All these blessings will come on you and accompany you **if you obey the LORD your God**: 3 You will be blessed in the city and blessed in the country. 4 The fruit of your womb will be blessed, and the crops of your land and the young of your livestock--the calves of your herds and the lambs of your flocks. 5 Your basket and your kneading trough will be blessed. 6 You will be blessed when you come in and blessed when you go out.   7 The LORD will grant that the enemies who rise up against you will be defeated before you. They will come at you from one direction but flee from you in seven. 8 The LORD will send a blessing on your barns and on everything you put your hand to. The LORD your God will bless you in the land he is giving you. 9 The LORD will establish you as his holy people, as he promised you on oath, if you keep the commands of the LORD your God and walk in obedience to him. 10 Then all the peoples on earth will see that you are called by the name of the LORD, and they will fear you. 11 The LORD will grant you abundant prosperity--in the fruit of your womb, the young of your livestock and the crops of your ground--in the land he swore to your ancestors to give you. 12 The LORD will open the heavens, the storehouse of his bounty, to send rain on your land in season and to bless all the work of your hands. You will lend to many nations but will borrow from none. 13 The LORD will make you the head, not the tail. **If you pay attention to the commands of the LORD your God that I give you this day and carefully follow them**, you will always be at the top, never at the bottom. 14 Do not turn aside from any of the commands I give you today, to the right or to the left, following other gods and serving them.*

*{Deu 32:47} 47 They are not just idle words for you--**they are your life**. By them you will live long in the land you are crossing the Jordan to possess."*

Unfortunately, no one in history has ever been able to live up to this perfect standard. Why? Because, regrettably, ever since Adam rebelled against God way back in the beginning, his rebellious nature has been inherited by all of his descendants, meaning all of mankind, including even Abraham and his descendants. This inherited rebellious nature of Adam, which we are all born with, is completely opposed to the Law of God. This nature from our common ancestor has underlying evil desires which throughout the course of history have lured each and every one of us into sin. Nobody has ever been able to obey God's Law perfectly, and everyone has fallen short of God's perfect standard. (see James 1:14; Romans 3:23)

However, recall that Jesus was born by the power of the Holy Spirit and because of this, Jesus had the nature of God within Him. Therefore, everything Jesus thought and all of His actions were a perfect reflection and demonstration of the thoughts and actions of God Himself. Because of this, Jesus lived a life of perfect obedience to God's standard as expressed in God's Law for His special people Israel. Jesus was never lured into sin because He did not have any evil desires because He did not have the nature of Adam. Although His divine nature was tested in every possible way, Jesus never sinned. He did everything the way that God wanted it done. He lived up to the perfect standard of God's Law.

> *{Mat 4:1} 1 Then Jesus was led by the Spirit into the wilderness to be **tempted** by the devil. (See also Mark 1:13; Luke 4:2)*

> *{Heb 4:15} 15 For we do not have a high priest who is unable to empathize with our weaknesses, but we have one who has been **tempted in every way, just as we are--yet he did not sin**.*

> *{1Pe 2:22} 22 "**He committed no sin**, and no deceit was found in his mouth."*

> *{1Jo 3:5} 5 But you know that he appeared so that he might take away our sins. And **in him is no sin**.*

Jesus did many things which proved that He was sent by God and the Son of God living in human flesh. He performed many miracles that no one on earth had ever performed. He had God-given authority over all creation. He healed the sick, opened the eyes of the blind and the ears of the deaf, He caused the lame to leap, He cast demons out of people, and every funeral that He attended, He raised the dead. He even commanded the weather and the seas. Everything about Him brought life, peace, wholeness, and restoration. He taught the Word and the ways of the one true God, who created heaven and earth, with authority and demonstrated the power of God through miracles. Jesus demonstrated the perfect will of God and the life which God had intended for all of mankind to have when He created Adam way back in the beginning. You could say that it was as if He was bringing heaven to earth.

Jesus' Suffering and Death

In spite of this, the religious leaders of Israel and the rulers of the world in that day rejected Jesus. Without going into the whole story now, because we'll touch on it more later, they planned and plotted and arrested Jesus because of false accusations, and sentenced Him to death through an illegitimate trial for a crime that He did not commit. They crucified Him.

Jesus knew in advance that this would happen, and He told His followers many times that He would have to suffer and die. In fact, this had been God's design since before the earth was even formed. (see Revelation 13:8) This means that Jesus' life was not taken from Him because neither man nor the devil had any power or authority over Him. Jesus laid His life down willingly in order to fulfill the Scriptures concerning the Messiah of Israel and to do the will of God. This was the only way to remedy the problem that Adam had created at the beginning. Jesus, the only one who had earned through obedience the right to righteousness, blessing, and life, would instead willingly suffer exile, curse, and death.

> *{Mat 16:21} 21 From that time on Jesus began to explain to his disciples that **he must go** to Jerusalem and **suffer many things** at the hands of the elders, the chief priests and the teachers of the law, and that **he must be killed** and on the third day be raised to life.(see also Mark 8:31-9:1; Luke 9:21-27)*

*{Mat 20:18-19} 18 "We are going up to Jerusalem, and the Son of Man will be delivered over to the chief priests and the teachers of the law. **They will condemn him to death** 19 and will hand him over to the Gentiles **to be mocked and flogged and crucified**. On the third day he will be raised to life!" (see also Mark 10:32-34; Luke 18:31-34)*

*{Jhn 10:17-18} 17 The reason my Father loves me is that **I lay down my life**--only to take it up again. 18 No one takes it from me, but **I lay it down of my own accord**. I have authority to lay it down and authority to take it up again. This command I received from my Father."*

*{Jhn 19:11} 11 Jesus answered [Pilate], "You would **have no power over me** if it were not given to you from above. Therefore the one who handed me over to you is guilty of a greater sin."*

*{Jhn 14:29-31} 29 I have told you now before it happens, so that when it does happen you will believe. 30 I will not say much more to you, for the prince of this world [the devil] is coming. **He has no hold over me**, 31 but he comes so that the world may learn that I love the Father and do exactly what my Father has commanded me. "Come now; let us leave.*

*{Mat 26:53-54} 53 **Do you think I cannot call on my Father**, and he will at once put at my disposal more than twelve legions of angels? 54 But how then would the **Scriptures be fulfilled** that say it must happen in this way?"*

*{Mat 21:42} 42 Jesus said to them, "**Have you never read in the Scriptures**: " 'The stone the builders rejected has become the cornerstone; the Lord has done this, and it is marvelous in our eyes'? (see also Mark 12:10; Luke 20:17; Psalm 118:22)*

God's standard required an unblemished sacrifice without any defects to pay for sin. Without going into too much detail, the Law required an animal sacrifice of a bull, a lamb, or birds, depending on what the person could afford. Through the shedding of blood, sin was forgiven. The sacrifice of an innocent life restored an individual person or the whole community of Israel to right standing with God. Through Jesus' perfect, unblemished life, He was completely without defect by God's standard, and He offered Himself as a sacrifice to pay for our sin. He offered a sacrifice of the highest value, far beyond the value of an animal sacrifice. Jesus sacrificed human life, the life of a Son of Man, which has more value than a bull or a goat and the life of the Son of God which has infinite inexplicable worth. Therefore, through His incalculable sacrifice, He paid our debt and created a way for every individual and the whole world to be restored to right standing with God.

*{Jhn 1:29} 29 The next day John saw Jesus coming toward him and said, "Look, the **Lamb of God, who takes away the sin of the world!***

*{Lev 22:20} 20 **Do not bring anything with a defect**, because it will not be accepted on your behalf.*

*{Heb 9:22} 22 In fact, the law requires that nearly everything be cleansed with blood, and **without the shedding of blood there is no forgiveness [of sin.]***

{Lev 17:11} 11 *For the life of a creature is in the blood, and I have given it to you to make atonement for yourselves on the altar; it is the **blood that makes atonement for one's life**.*

{1Pe 1:18-19} 18 *For you know that it was not with perishable things such as silver or gold that you were redeemed from the empty way of life handed down to you from your ancestors, 19 but with the **precious blood of Christ, a lamb without blemish or defect.***

{Heb 10:5-10} 5 *Therefore, when Christ came into the world, he said: "Sacrifice and offering you did not desire, but **a body you prepared for me**; 6 with burnt offerings and sin offerings you were not pleased. 7 Then I said, 'Here I am--it is written about me in the scroll-- I have come to do your will, my God.' " 8 First he said, "Sacrifices and offerings, burnt offerings and sin offerings you did not desire, nor were you pleased with them"--though they were offered in accordance with the law. 9 Then he said, "Here I am, I have come to do your will." He sets aside the first to establish the second. 10 And by that will, **we have been made holy through the sacrifice of the body of Jesus Christ once for all***.

But that's not all. Jesus also came to fulfill the Scriptures which pointed to the promised Messiah of Israel, the one who would sit on David's throne and rule eternally with a Kingdom that has no end. We'll go into that in more detail throughout this study. The truth is that the Scriptures from the Old Testament all point to Jesus and are a shadow or a type or an example to demonstrate God's purpose for and through His one and only Son. (see Colossians 2:17; Hebrews 8:5, 10:1; Romans 5:14; John 5:39) In fact, Jesus used the Scriptures to explain to His followers in advance exactly what God was doing through His suffering and death. Then, He went on to fulfill them in exact accordance with God's plan and design. For example:

{Jhn 3:13-17} 13 *No one has ever gone into heaven except the one who came from heaven--the Son of Man. 14 **Just as Moses lifted up the snake in the wilderness**, so the **Son of Man must be lifted up**, 15 **that everyone who believes may have eternal life in him**." 16 For God so loved the world that he gave his one and only Son, that whoever believes in him shall not perish but have eternal life. 17 For God did not send his Son into the world to condemn the world, but **to save the world through him**.*

In this passage, Jesus referred to an incident from the Old Testament which His fellow Jewish countrymen who were listening would have known very well from their history. In the historical account, the Israelites were rebelling against Moses' authority and growing impatient on their long journey through the wilderness between Egypt and the Promised Land. They grumbled and complained, and even said that it would be better for them to go back to Egyptian slavery than to continue believing God and following Moses. They had turned their hearts away from God and this was made obvious through their rebellion against the leader that God had appointed for them. Jesus was referencing this passage:

{Num 21:4-9} 4 *They traveled from Mount Hor along the route to the Red Sea, to go around Edom. But the people grew impatient on the way; 5 **they spoke against God and against***

*Moses, and said, "Why have you brought us up out of Egypt to die in the wilderness? There is no bread! There is no water! And we detest this miserable food!" 6 Then the LORD sent venomous snakes among them; they bit the people and many Israelites died. 7 The people came to Moses and said, "**We sinned when we spoke against the LORD and against you**. Pray that the LORD will take the snakes away from us." So Moses prayed for the people. 8 Then the LORD told him, "**Make a replica of a poisonous snake and attach it to a pole**. All who are bitten will live if they simply look at it!" 9 So Moses made a snake out of bronze and attached it to a pole. Then anyone who was bitten by a snake could **look at the bronze snake and be healed!***

The Jewish people were in a very similar situation when Jesus was with them on the earth. They were growing impatient waiting for their Messiah to bring in the Kingdom that God had promised them. Then when that leader showed up, meaning Jesus, they grumbled against Him because their hearts had turned away from God. This was made obvious when they rejected and crucified their King. However, in fairness, the problem wasn't just with the Israelites and the Jews were not the only ones who crucified Jesus. The real problem went all the way back to Adam, who was the first to turn his heart away from God and God's leadership when he submitted himself to another master, the devil. When Jesus was lifted up on the cross of His crucifixion, which is what He meant when He said *the Son of Man is lifted up*, God addressed the issue which has plagued humanity since Adam.

In the historical reference, the Lord told Moses to make an exact replica of the poisonous snake, the very thing which afflicted them and caused them to die. Moses lifted up the replica of the enemy on a pole, and anyone who looked at the replica was healed and did not die. Therefore, Jesus meant that when He was lifted up on the cross, He became an exact replica of the very thing which has afflicted mankind since Adam's disobedience – sin. More than just becoming sin, He became the very nature of sin. He became the snake on the pole. He became the enemy.

> *{2Co 5:21} 21 God made him who had no sin **to be sin** for us, so that in him we might become the righteousness of God.*

But that's not all. By hanging on a tree, according to God's Law, Jesus also became a curse. The curse of God's Law is written out in great detail in Deuteronomy 28:15-68 and Leviticus 26:14-46. The curse includes every form of sickness and disease, every kind of lack and hunger, all relational problems between people and nations, all forms of oppression by every kind of enemy, and separation or exile from God. On the cross, Jesus received the full punishment and consequence for every disobedient act of all of mankind throughout the course of history.

> *{Gal 3:13} 13 Christ redeemed us from the curse of the law **by becoming a curse** for us, for it is written: "Cursed is everyone who is hung on a pole."*

> *{Deu 21:22-23} 22 If someone guilty of a capital offense **is put to death and their body is exposed on a pole**, 23 you must not leave the body hanging on the pole overnight. Be sure to bury it that same day, **because anyone who is hung on a pole is under God's curse**. You must not desecrate the land the LORD your God is giving you as an inheritance.*

But that's not all. When Jesus died, we also died with Him. In another passage Jesus said:

{Jhn 12:32-33 KJV} 32 *And I, if I be lifted up from the earth,* **will draw all [men] unto me**. *33 This he said, signifying* **what death he should die**.

Although this passage is written in Greek, let's consider what Jesus, who was a Hebrew, was really saying. Remembering that *man* in Hebrew translates as *Adam*, so when Jesus said *I will draw all men unto me*, He meant that He drew all of Adam, meaning every single one of Adam's descendants, the whole of mankind onto Himself on the cross. This includes me, you, and everyone that we know who has been afflicted by our inherited sinful nature, which is everyone on earth. He was the Son of Man, i.e. the son of Adam, embodying each and every one of us in His death. Like a giant magnet, Jesus drew the soul of every person ever born to Himself and into His death with Him. Like pin-the-tail on the donkey, every descendant of Adam was pinned onto Jesus in this miraculous working of God's power.

{Rom 6:6} 6 *For we know that our* **old self was crucified with him** *so that the body ruled by sin might be done away with, that we should no longer be slaves to sin--*

{Gal 2:20} 20 **I have been crucified with Christ and I no longer live**, *but Christ lives in me. The life I now live in the body, I live by faith in the Son of God, who loved me and gave himself for me.*

{Col 2:20} 20 *Since* **you died with Christ** *to the elemental spiritual forces of this world, why, as though you still belonged to the world, do you submit to its rules:*

{Col 3:3} 3 **For you died**, *and your life is now hidden with Christ in God.*

{2Co 5:14} 14 *For Christ's love compels us, because we are convinced* **that one died for all, and therefore all died**.

Needless to say, there was a lot going on when Jesus was crucified. Let's take a look at two important passages which describe in more detail exactly what was happening while Jesus was on the cross. On the following pages, you will find Isaiah 53 and Psalm 22. Both of these passages point to Jesus' crucifixion. In fact, the first and last verse of Psalm 22 are the "bookends" of Jesus' utterances when He was on the cross: *Why have you forsaken me?* and *It is finished* or *He has done it, finished it, accomplished it*, depending on which translation you are reading. Similarly, Isaiah 53's description of the Lord's Suffering Servant doing the will of the Lord begins with the very phrasing Jesus used to describe to His followers the way He would suffer and die. Jesus' words were:

{Mat 27:46} 46 *About three in the afternoon Jesus cried out in a loud voice, "Eli, Eli, lema sabachthani?" (which means* **"My God, my God, why have you forsaken me?"**) *(see also Mark 15:34)*

{Jhn 19:30} 30 *When he had received the drink, Jesus said,* **"It is finished."** *With that, he bowed his head and gave up his spirit.*

*{Jhn 8:28} 28 So Jesus said, "When you have **lifted up** the Son of Man, then you will know that I am he and that I do nothing on my own but speak just what the Father has taught me.*

Now read Isaiah 53 and Psalm 22 all the way through while thinking of Jesus on the cross.

The Lord's Suffering Servant – Isaiah 52:13-53

52:13 See, my servant will act wisely; he will be raised and lifted up and highly exalted.

14 Just as there were many who were appalled at him-- his appearance was so disfigured beyond that of any human being and his form marred beyond human likeness —

15 so he will sprinkle many nations, and kings will shut their mouths because of him. For what they were not told, they will see, and what they have not heard, they will understand.

53:1 Who has believed our message and to whom has the arm of the LORD been revealed?

2 He grew up before him like a tender shoot, and like a root out of dry ground. He had no beauty or majesty to attract us to him, nothing in his appearance that we should desire him.

3 He was despised and rejected by mankind, a man of suffering, and familiar with pain. Like one from whom people hide their faces he was despised, and we held him in low esteem.

4 Surely he took up our pain and bore our suffering, yet we considered him punished by God, stricken by him, and afflicted.

5 But he was pierced for our transgressions, he was crushed for our iniquities; the punishment that brought us peace was on him, and by his wounds we are healed.

6 We all, like sheep, have gone astray, each of us has turned to our own way; and the LORD has laid on him the iniquity of us all.

7 He was oppressed and afflicted, yet he did not open his mouth; he was led like a lamb to the slaughter, and as a sheep before its shearers is silent, so he did not open his mouth.

8 By oppression and judgment he was taken away. Yet who of his generation protested? For he was cut off from the land of the living; for the transgression of my people he was punished.

9 He was assigned a grave with the wicked, and with the rich in his death, though he had done no violence, nor was any deceit in his mouth.

10 Yet it was the LORD's will to crush him and cause him to suffer, and though the LORD makes his life [soul] an offering for sin, he will see his offspring and prolong his days, and the will of the LORD will prosper in his hand.

11 After he has suffered, he will see the light of life and be satisfied; by his knowledge my righteous servant will justify many, and he will bear their iniquities.

12 Therefore I will give him a portion among the great, and he will divide the spoils with the strong, because he poured out his life unto death, and was numbered with the transgressors. For he bore the sin of many, and made intercession for the transgressors.

Psalm 22

1 My God, my God, why have you forsaken me? Why are you so far from saving me, so far from my cries of anguish?

2 My God, I cry out by day, but you do not answer, by night, but I find no rest.

3 Yet you are enthroned as the Holy One; you are the one Israel praises.

4 In you our ancestors put their trust; they trusted and you delivered them.

5 To you they cried out and were saved; in you they trusted and were not put to shame.

6 But I am a worm and not a man, scorned by everyone, despised by the people.

7 All who see me mock me; they hurl insults, shaking their heads.

8 "He trusts in the LORD," they say, "let the LORD rescue him. Let him deliver him, since he delights in him."

9 Yet you brought me out of the womb; you made me trust in you, even at my mother's breast.

10 From birth I was cast on you; from my mother's womb you have been my God.

11 Do not be far from me, for trouble is near and there is no one to help.

12 Many bulls surround me; strong bulls of Bashan encircle me.

13 Roaring lions that tear their prey open their mouths wide against me.

14 I am poured out like water, and all my bones are out of joint. My heart has turned to wax; it has melted within me.

15 My mouth is dried up like a potsherd, and my tongue sticks to the roof of my mouth; you lay me in the dust of death.

16 Dogs surround me, a pack of villains encircles me; they pierce my hands and my feet.

17 All my bones are on display; people stare and gloat over me.

18 They divide my clothes among them and cast lots for my garment.

19 But you, LORD, do not be far from me. You are my strength; come quickly to help me.

20 Deliver me from the sword, my precious life from the power of the dogs.

21 Rescue me from the mouth of the lions; save me from the horns of the wild oxen.

22 I will declare your name to my people; in the assembly I will praise you.

23 You who fear the LORD, praise him! All you descendants of Jacob, honor him! Revere him, all you descendants of Israel!

24 For he has not despised or scorned the suffering of the afflicted one; he has not hidden his face from him but has listened to his cry for help.

25 From you comes the theme of my praise in the great assembly; before those who fear you I will fulfill my vows.

26 The poor will eat and be satisfied; those who seek the LORD will praise him-- may your hearts live forever!

27 All the ends of the earth will remember and turn to the LORD, and all the families of the nations will bow down before him,

28 for dominion belongs to the LORD and he rules over the nations.

29 All the rich of the earth will feast and worship; all who go down to the dust will kneel before him-- those who cannot keep themselves alive.

30 Posterity will serve him; future generations will be told about the Lord.

31 They will proclaim his righteousness, declaring to a people yet unborn: He has done it!

There is far too much in these two passages to go into great detail of every verse. Therefore, for our purposes, we're going to stay focused on the workings of God through the crucifixion of Christ by drawing out some important elements which we've already identified about what Jesus accomplished through His suffering and death. (For more on this see also Matthew 27; Mark 15; Luke 23; and John 19.)

> **He was a man, born in human flesh**: He grew up, He was a man of suffering, brought out of the womb, from birth was a worshiper of God – see Isaiah 53:2, 3; Psalm 22:9, 10.

> **He was an unblemished sacrifice for sin**: He was pierced for our transgressions, crushed for our iniquities, the Lord laid on Him the iniquity of us all, He was like a lamb for slaughter, He had committed no sin, no violence and had never told a lie, His life and soul were an offering for sin, He bore our iniquities – see Isaiah 53:5, 6, 7, 9, 11, 12.

> **He became sin**: He was marred beyond human likeness, He said, *I am a worm (serpent) and not a man*, He was the replica of the enemy – see Isaiah 53:14; Psalm 22:6.

> **He became a curse::** We considered Him punished by God (i.e. cursed) stricken, afflicted, our punishment and sickness was on Him, He was punished for our transgression, taken away by oppression and judgment, He was surrounded by bulls, lions, dogs, villains (which are symbolic of powerful oppressors, kings of the earth, religious leaders, troops and people of the world, evildoers, and evil spirits) and subject to the sword (which symbolizes death) – see Isaiah 53:4, 5, 8; Psalm 22:12, 13, 16.

> **He died:** He was cut off from the land of the living, assigned a grave with the wicked, He poured His life out unto death, He was laid in the dust of death – see Isaiah 53:8, 9, 12; Psalm 22:15.

But that's not all. Here is the best part! In both Isaiah 53 and Psalm 22, there is a shift from suffering to praise. Why? Because this has all been God's plan from the beginning and in spite of the most upside down looking circumstances, the will of the Lord is being put into effect! My favorite translation of Psalm 22 verse 21 is the New King James version because it shows the abrupt transition of the sufferer, who all of a sudden comes into full assurance that His prayer has been heard by God. Have you ever prayed something and then had a sense of peace wash over you because you simply knew beyond a shadow of a doubt that it is going to happen, that God has heard you, that there is no need for concern or doubt or worry because you knew that it was a done deal? This is what is happening here.

> {Psa 22:21 NKJV} 21 *Save Me from the lion's mouth And from the horns of the wild oxen!* **You have answered Me.**

Jesus knew that God had accepted His sacrificial offering and had heard His cry for help. From verse 21 to the end of the Psalm, there is nothing but praise and declaration of the glory of God. Similarly, Isaiah 53 verse 12 shifts from describing the suffering itself to describing what is going to happen after the suffering. The sufferer will see the light of life, He will live again and declare the work of God to people who seek the Lord, and they will all live forever. He will have a people who are just like Him, justified before God, righteous and in right standing with God because of Him. They are a whole new kind of people who are yet to be born, a new generation. They are His, and they all worship God together with Him as their leader and King.

Resurrection and Ascension

At His death, the soul of Jesus, the Son of Man descended into the pit of Hell and His whipped, beaten, and mutilated body went into the grave. However, on the third day, God's power worked the most spectacular event in human history. God had indeed accepted Jesus' sacrifice and went on to fulfill what had been written: He raised Jesus from the dead.

> {Act 2:24, 32} 24 But **God raised him from the dead**, *freeing him from the agony of death, because it was impossible for death to keep its hold on him. ... 32* **God has raised this Jesus to life**, *and we are all witnesses of it.*

> {Act 13:33-34 KJV} 33 *God hath fulfilled the same unto us their children, in that he hath raised up Jesus again; as it is also written in the second psalm,* **Thou art my Son, this day have I begotten thee**. *34 And as concerning that he raised him up from the dead, [now] no more to return to corruption, he said on this wise, I will give you the sure mercies of David.*

> {Rom 1:4} 4 *and who through the Spirit of holiness was* **appointed the Son of God in power by his resurrection from the dead**: *Jesus Christ our Lord.*

In resurrection, Jesus was not formed out of dust like Adam, and He was not born of a woman as He had been before. When God raised Jesus from the dead, Jesus was begotten by God, meaning He was born by God like a Father fathering a child. If you read various translations of genealogies, you will read things like "Abraham begot Isaac," meaning Isaac was Abraham's son, but here God begot Jesus as His Son. In truth, God had declared Jesus to be His Son several times throughout the Gospels before His death. (see Matthew 3:17, 17:5; Mark 1:11, 9:7; Luke 3:22, 9:35) But this time, instead of being born by God, Jesus was born again by God out of the pit of Hell and by God's miracle working power. His first birth had been miraculous as the Holy Spirit impregnated a virgin. But now, the Holy Spirit, the breath of life entered into His soul, His soul returned to His body, and the life giving power of the Spirit of holiness transformed His perishable body to an incorruptible body which would never perish. He walked out of the grave and showed Himself to hundreds of people to demonstrate that He was alive. He declared the marvelous work of God! Through this, it was proven that everything that He had said about Himself during His life was true, including that He is the King and Messiah of Israel who sits on David's throne and rules His Kingdom forever and ever.

But that's not all. Through His death and resurrection, Jesus crushed the head of the serpent. Recall the promise God made to Adam's wife back in the beginning. Ever since our ancestor's deception, all of mankind has lived in the fear of death because we have been subjected to the devil who has the power of death. However, the resurrection proves that the cruel oppressor could not keep Jesus captive and, therefore, the evil one has been conquered and stripped of his power. Jesus stomped on the serpent's head, trampled him with His feet, and *put the kabash* on him. Jesus is now alive eternally, never to die again. Death has been overcome and the enemy has been defeated.

Then, after forty days of revealing that He had indeed been raised from the dead, clouds encompassed Jesus, and He was lifted into heaven where He is seated at the right hand of God. Having crushed the head of the serpent, Jesus was now given all power and authority, even over death and the grave, to rule, reign, *put the kabash* on all of God's creation, and to be it's King forever.

> *{Mar 16:19} 19 After the Lord Jesus had spoken to them, **he was taken up into heaven** and he sat at the right hand of God. (see also Luke 24:51; Acts 1:9)*

> *{Phl 2:9-11} 9 Therefore **God exalted him to the highest place and gave him the name that is above every name**, 10 that at the name of Jesus every knee should bow, in heaven and on earth and under the earth, 11 and every tongue acknowledge that Jesus Christ is Lord, to the glory of God the Father.*

A New Adam

Again, Jesus is up in heaven and is King of all creation. But if this is all there is, then why did Jesus praise God from the cross because a whole new people were going to be born, not just His rebirth through resurrection? And since all of Adam's descendants were crucified with Christ and died with Him, where does this leave us now? I'm so glad you asked. Here is where things become interesting!

If you do not believe that Jesus Christ is Lord, then spiritually speaking, you are still dead, in the darkness of the pit of Hell, and separated from God. Whether you believe it or not, your soul was included with Jesus in His death on the cross and, when He died, you died. But this is where it ends for you. You are still part of the generation of the first Adam who ate from the wrong tree and will suffer the eternal consequences for it. There is no form of religious observance or spirituality which can give you access to the one true God who created heaven and earth or give you right standing with Him.

Let's look back again to Isaiah 53 where we see *who has believed?* (v.1) and *to whom has it been revealed?* and *through knowledge of Him* (v.11) many are justified and restored to right-standing before God. Additionally, Psalm 22 says *those who seek the Lord* (v.26) will have hearts that live forever, and *a people just like Him* (v.30) from the same seed as Him will serve Him, and that there is a whole new people who are *yet to be born.* (v.31) Also, from the example of Moses and the Israelites, it was only the people who looked at the serpent on the pole who were healed and did not die. The sacrificial death of Jesus on the cross is only extended to those who believe that Jesus is Lord and who place their faith in this miraculous work of God. When we believe in our hearts that Jesus Christ is Lord and that God raised Him from the dead, then we become part of a new people, a new generation, a new creation, a second Adam who is Christ Jesus. *(Note: For you theologians out there, yes, God knows who are His from before the foundation of the earth.)*

This means that on the earth today, there are only two kinds of people: First Adam's and Second Adam's. The only possible exception to this is the Jewish people who do not believe Jesus as Messiah. They are enemies of the Gospel but beloved of God because of their forefathers Abraham, Isaac and Jacob. (see Romans 11:28) We will talk a little bit more about this later in this study.

When we believe that Jesus is Lord and that God raised Him from the dead, we are born again, begotten again by God who is now our Father in the same way that Jesus was begotten again by God who is His Father. When He died, we died with Him. We were with Him in the pit of hell, the dominion of darkness, under the oppression of the devil, and in death. But, we were also with Him when He was raised and when He ascended into heaven. When we believe, we are spiritually transferred to heaven and to the kingdom of light where Jesus sits at the right hand of God. When we are baptized, we demonstrate what we believe in our hearts, and we are symbolically entering into the death and resurrection of Christ, being born again, and being begotten again by God.

> *{Jhn 1:12-13} 12 Yet to all who did receive him, to those who believed in his name, he gave the right to **become children of God**-- 13 children born not of natural descent, nor of human decision or a husband's will, but **born of God**.*

> *{Jhn 3:3-6} 3 Jesus replied, "Very truly I tell you, no one can see the kingdom of God unless they are **born again**." 4 "How can someone be born when they are old?" Nicodemus asked. "Surely they cannot enter a second time into their mother's womb to be born!" 5 Jesus answered, "Very truly I tell you, no one can enter the kingdom of God unless they are **born of water and the Spirit**. 6 Flesh gives birth to flesh, but the Spirit gives birth to spirit.*

> *{1Pe 1:3, 23 KJV} 3 Blessed [be] the God and Father of our Lord Jesus Christ, which according to his abundant mercy **hath begotten us again** unto a lively hope **by the resurrection of Jesus Christ** from the dead, ... 23 **Being born again**, not of corruptible seed, but of incorruptible, by the word of God, which liveth and abideth for ever.*

> *{1Jo 5:1} 1 Everyone who believes that Jesus is the Christ **is born of God**, and everyone who loves the father loves his child as well.*

> *{Jas 1:18} 18 He chose to **give us birth** through the word of truth, that we might be a kind of firstfruits of all he created.*

> *{Rom 6:4} 4 We were therefore **buried with him through baptism into death** in order that, just as Christ was raised from the dead through the glory of the Father, **we too may live a new life**.*

> *{Col 2:12-13} 12 having been **buried with him in baptism**, in which you were also **raised with him through your faith in the working of God**, who raised him from the dead. 13 When you were dead in your sins and in the uncircumcision of your flesh, **God made you alive with Christ**. He forgave us all our sins,*

> *{Col 3:1} 1 Since, then, **you have been raised with Christ**, set your hearts on things above, where Christ is, seated at the right hand of God.*

> *{Eph 1:3} 3 Praise be to the God and Father of our Lord Jesus Christ, who has **blessed us in the heavenly realms with every spiritual blessing in Christ**.*

> *{Col 1:13}* *13 For he has rescued us from the dominion of darkness and* **brought us into the kingdom of the Son he loves,**

But that's not all. There are some obvious realities that haven't been addressed yet. For example, we still live in bodies, and these bodies die. We still live on earth, not in heaven. We still sin, mess up and fall short of God's perfect standard. And, undoubtedly, evil continues in the world. We're going to examine all of these things now and throughout the rest of this study.

After Jesus ascended into heaven, He poured out the Holy Spirit into everyone who believes in Him. Through our faith in Jesus, the Holy Spirit dwells in our hearts and becomes our new nature. In the same way that Jesus functioned in flesh like ours but with the operating system of God's nature, we now have the Holy Spirit in us as our new operating system even though we are still in our earthly bodies. When we allow the Holy Spirit to direct our lives, we live the way that Jesus did when He was in the flesh. Through faith and obedience to the Holy Spirit within us as our new operating system, we can live in constant and unbroken communion and communication with God, and we can demonstrate the perfect will of God. In fact, as believers, we have been given authority in the same way that Jesus had authority when He was on the earth. The Holy Spirit gives us power to do miracles, heal the sick, cast out demons, raise the dead, and command creation the same way that Jesus did when He was on the earth. You could even say that, through the power of the Holy Spirit within us, we can bring heaven, where we are already spiritually with Christ, to earth where our bodies still live.

> *{Act 2:33}* *33 Exalted to the right hand of God, he has received from the Father* **the promised Holy Spirit and has poured out** *what you now see and hear.*

> *{2Pe 1:4}* *4 Through these he has given us his very great and precious promises, so that through them* **you may participate in the divine nature,** *having escaped the corruption in the world caused by evil desires.*

> *{1Jo 3:9}* *9 No one who is born of God will continue to sin,* **because God's seed [the Holy Spirit] remains in them; they cannot go on sinning,** *because they have been born of God.*

> *{Mat 6:10}* *10 your kingdom come,* **your will be done,** *on earth as it is in heaven.*

> *{Jhn 14:12}* *12 Very truly I tell you, whoever believes in* **me will do the works I have been doing, and they will do even greater things than these,** *because I am going to the Father.*

Think of it this way: God formed the first man out of dust and breathed life into him – a natural Adam – and his wife was in him when he was formed. Then, God built Adam's wife out of his rib to be just like him, to be one flesh with him, and to help him fulfill God's purpose in the earth. When Jesus was born again in resurrection, God breathed again the breath of life (the Holy Spirit) into Him, forming a whole new type of Adam – a spiritual Adam – and his wife, which is us who believe, was in Him when He was born again. Now, God is building Jesus' wife, which is the Church, out of His own spiritual substance, His Body, to be just like Him, to be one flesh with Him, male and female of the same kind of species, to help Him fulfill God's purpose in the earth. Everyone who believes that Jesus is Lord is a new species, a born again species, a spiritual species, a heavenly species. God formed the first Adam like a potter or artist forms a vessel of clay, and the first Adam's wife was taken out of him. God made the second Adam like an artist or a poet creating a masterpiece, and we who believe are part of this new creation.

> *{Eph 2:4-10} 4 But because of his great love for us, God, who is rich in mercy, 5 **made us alive with Christ** even when we were dead in transgressions--it is by grace you have been saved. 6 And God **raised us up with Christ and seated us with him in the heavenly realms** in Christ Jesus, 7 in order that in the coming ages he might show the incomparable riches of his grace, expressed in his kindness to us in Christ Jesus. 8 For it is by grace you have been saved, through faith--and this is not from yourselves, it is the gift of God-- 9 not by works, so that no one can boast. 10 For **we are God's handiwork**, created in Christ Jesus to do good works, which God prepared in advance for us to do.*

> *{2Co 5:17} 17 Therefore, **if anyone is in Christ, the new creation has come**: The old has gone, the new is here!*

But, let's be real. We all still sin and make mistakes and fall short of perfection. Yes, this is true, but this is where the news gets really good! Through faith in what Jesus did on our behalf, we receive His perfect record as if we had never sinned. The blood of Jesus purifies us through faith and the Holy Spirit seals us in Christ with His righteousness. By faith, we have been cleansed and we are perfect in God's sight which means that we are already holy.

> *{1Jo 1:7} 7 But if we walk in the light, as he is in the light, we have fellowship with one another, and **the blood of Jesus, his Son, purifies us from all sin**.*

> *{Col 1:22} 22 But now he has reconciled you by Christ's physical body through death **to present you holy in his sight, without blemish and free from accusation**--*

> *{Col 2:13-15} 13 When you were dead in your sins and in the uncircumcision of your flesh, God made you alive with Christ. He **forgave us all our sins**, 14 **having canceled the charge of our legal indebtedness, which stood against us and condemned us; he has taken it away, nailing it to the cross**. 15 And having **disarmed the powers and authorities**, he made a public spectacle of them, triumphing over them by the cross.*

> *{Heb 10:10, 14} 10 And by that will, **we have been made holy** through the sacrifice of the body of Jesus Christ once for all. ... 14 For by one sacrifice **he has made perfect forever those who are being made holy**.*

Therefore, no matter what we may have done in our past, no matter what we may have done an hour ago, no matter what we may do tomorrow or next week or five years from now, Jesus' blood and death has already paid for it. As a result of being included in His death, spiritually speaking, we are dead. The last time I checked, nobody takes a dead person to court even if they are guilty of a crime. In the same way, spiritually speaking, the charges against us for any wrongdoing that we may have done or are doing or will do are as useless against us as if we were dead. But since we have been made alive with

Christ through faith in His resurrection, we can go on living in right standing with God as if we had never sinned at all. There is no reason for us to ever hide from God as Adam and his wife did, there is no reason for shame, and there is nothing which can keep us from having unbroken fellowship with God who is our creator and our Heavenly Father.

Think of it this way: when God made the rule about eating from the wrong tree, it was a rule between Him and Adam when Adam was alone. Adam's wife had not been built yet. Adam's wife is the first one who ate from the wrong tree, but nothing actually changed for them until Adam ate it because God had made the rule with Adam. It was Adam's disobedience which caused the change in their position before God. In the same way, but reversing this error, Jesus re-established our right standing with God through His perfect obedience to God's Law. Therefore, in the same way that Adam's wife eating from the wrong tree did not change their status with God, our errors against the Law of God do not change our status with God. We stay in right relationship with God no matter how much we mess up because the rule was established between God and Jesus who never sinned.

That's really good news!

He's Coming Back

Jesus died to save us from death. He became a curse to save us from the curse. He became sin to save us from sin. He became man to save us from ourselves. He's coming back to save us from the wrath of God which is still yet to come.

> *{Heb 9:27-28} 27 Just as people are destined to die once, and after that to face judgment, 28 so Christ was sacrificed once to take away the sins of many; and **he will appear a second time, not to bear sin, but to bring salvation to those who are waiting for him**.*

When Jesus comes back, everyone who believes in Him will be clothed with an imperishable resurrection body just like His. Those whose bodies have already died will be raised from the grave, and those who are still alive when He returns will be instantly transformed. We will all be taken up into the air to meet Him and be with Him forever.

> *{1Co 15:52} 52 in a flash, in the twinkling of an eye, at the last trumpet. For the trumpet will sound, **the dead will be raised imperishable**, and we will be changed.*

> *{1Th 4:17} 17 After that, we who are still alive and are left will be **caught up together with them in the clouds to meet the Lord in the air**. And so we will be with the Lord forever.*

But those who do not believe will be subject to eternal judgment, condemnation, and hell. The wrath of God will be poured out on the earth to avenge all evil. We don't want anyone that we know to be subject to this. Importantly, we don't know when He is coming back. Therefore, we do everything that we can to share Jesus and the hope of salvation with everyone we know.

> *{2Co 5:10-11} 10 For **we must all appear before the judgment seat of Christ**, so that each of us may receive what is due us for the things done while in the body, whether good or bad. 11*

*Since, then, we know what it is to fear the Lord, **we try to persuade others**. What we are is plain to God, and I hope it is also plain to your conscience.*

*{2Pe 3:9-10} 9 The Lord is not slow in keeping his promise, as some understand slowness. Instead he is patient with you, **not wanting anyone to perish, but everyone to come to repentance**. 10 But the day of the Lord will come like a thief. The heavens will disappear with a roar; the elements will be destroyed by fire, and the earth and everything done in it will be laid bare.*

Jesus is not just for us. We must share the gift of salvation with everyone that we know so that they have the opportunity to believe and be part of God's people. Think of it this way: God told the first Adam and his wife to be fruitful and multiply in the natural way, through giving birth to natural children. Now, God through Jesus tells us to be fruitful and multiply in a spiritual way, through making disciples of Christ.

*{Mat 28:18-20} 18 Then Jesus came to them and said, "All authority in heaven and on earth has been given to me. 19 **Therefore go and make disciples** of all nations, baptizing them in the name of the Father and of the Son and of the Holy Spirit, 20 and **teaching them** to obey everything I have commanded you. And surely I am with you always, to the very end of the age."*

You may have noticed that, so far, I have not once referred to the original Adam's wife by her name. This is because she was not called Eve until after they had eaten from the wrong tree and had been separated from God. The name *Eve* means *life* or *living* because Eve was the one who gave birth to all of Adam's natural descendants. Interestingly, the Hebrew word for Eve stems from a root word which means *to proclaim* or *make known*. Therefore, Eve's God-given assignment as Adam's wife was to proclaim to everyone the promise of the Savior who would crush the head of the serpent. In the same way, before Jesus returns, we, the Church, are the Bride of Christ and have been given a similar assignment. We give spiritual birth by proclaiming and making known to everyone the work which Jesus Christ has already accomplished and that He is coming back to destroy the enemy forever. At that time, when Jesus totally reverses the wrong tree incident once and for all, our name will be changed and we will be called *Hephzibah* which means *my delight is in her*. (see Isaiah 62:4)

*{Eph 3:10-11} 10 His intent was that now, **through the church**, the manifold wisdom of God should be **made known** to the rulers and authorities in the heavenly realms, 11 **according to his eternal purpose that he accomplished in Christ Jesus our Lord**.*

But that's not all. God's command to Adam and his wife in their innocence was to rule over the earth, and maintain God's original order and design, trampling any enemies with their feet. Jesus came in the flesh the first time to partially fulfill the first Adam's assignment and Jesus is coming again to *put the kabash* on all evil for the rest of eternity. After that, all of creation will be restored to God's original design. Then, Jesus will reign in a Kingdom where there is no war, famine, sickness, strife, pain, grief, or chaos and we will be with Him. In that day, there will be only perfection, harmony, and peace. It will be like Eden all over again.

{Eph 1:22-23} 22 *And God placed all things **under his feet** and appointed him to be head over everything **for the church**, 23 which is his body, the fullness of him who fills everything in every way.*

{Psa 110:1} 1*The LORD says to my lord: "Sit at my right hand until I make your **enemies a footstool for your feet.**"*

{1Co 15:25-26} 25 *For he must reign until he has put **all his enemies under his feet**. 26 The last enemy to be destroyed is death.*

{Rev 21:1-8} 1 *Then I saw **"a new heaven and a new earth,"** for the first heaven and the first earth had passed away, and there was no longer any sea. 2 I saw the Holy City, the new Jerusalem, coming down out of heaven from God, prepared as a bride beautifully dressed for her husband. 3 And I heard a loud voice from the throne saying, "Look! God's dwelling place is now among the people, and he will dwell with them. They will be his people, and God himself will be with them and be their God. 4 'He **will wipe every tear from their eyes. There will be no more death'** or mourning or crying or pain, for the old order of things has passed away."* 5 *He who was seated on the throne said, "**I am making everything new!**" Then he said, "Write this down, for these words are trustworthy and true." 6 He said to me: "It is done. I am the Alpha and the Omega, the Beginning and the End. To the thirsty I will give water without cost from the spring of the water of life. 7 **Those who are victorious will inherit all this**, and I will be their God and they will be my children.** 8 But the cowardly, the unbelieving, the vile, the murderers, the sexually immoral, those who practice magic arts, the idolaters and all liars--they will be consigned to the fiery lake of burning sulfur. This is the second death."*

We want everyone we know and love to be with us in heaven and on the new earth in the age to come. Through faith in the name of Jesus, we have been given all power and authority to work miracles which prove that Jesus is who He says He is. Therefore, until Christ returns, we have an assignment. We take the Gospel of Jesus Christ to the ends of the earth with signs and wonders following so that everyone may believe and receive this inheritance, just like they did in the Book of Acts.

Ok, that's all… for now.

Invitation

I know that we just covered a lot of ground including all of God's plan for history from the beginning to the end. But, even though it can seem very complex, walking with God does not have to be complicated. In fact, it is actually quite simple. It starts with a single step of faith in your heart, just believing that Jesus is who He says He is, even if you don't understand it all.

When I first came to faith in Jesus, I was completely ignorant. I did not know a thing about His life, the crucifixion, the resurrection, or what it all meant. I just knew in my heart that He was true. While I was praying to God to take my first step of faith in Christ, I remember saying, "I'll believe Jesus, even though

I don't understand." That was enough for God. He accepted my prayer, and my life has been forever changed.

If you have not yet placed your faith in Jesus Christ as your Lord and Savior and you desire to be included in the salvation you've just learned about, then all that you need to do is believe. If you are ready for the Gospel to change everything in your life, then pray this prayer out loud and from your heart.

God,

I am by nature a sinner and I believe that you died for my sins,

I believe that you are the Son of God and that God raised you from the dead,

I repent of my sins and I make you my Lord and Savior.

Send your Holy Spirit into my heart and make me who You designed me to be.

In Jesus' name, Amen.

Welcome friend! The journey has only just begun.

CHAPTER 2
Primer: Holy Spirit

At the beginning of the Book of Acts, Jesus promised to send the Holy Spirit to His disciples. He had taught them about the Holy Spirit while He was walking with them, before His crucifixion and resurrection. Then, prior to His ascension to heaven, Jesus told them to wait for the Holy Spirit before they did anything in His name. In fact, all of the things which Christ followers did throughout the rest of the Book of Acts were dependent upon them receiving the Holy Spirit. Therefore, let's familiarize ourselves with what Jesus taught about living and walking with the Holy Spirit so that we are empowered to do the things that His first followers did in the Book of Acts.

Christ in You

From the beginning, it was God's design to have intimate fellowship with mankind and for us to do things on earth the way that He intended. We've already covered the fact that Adam messed this up by eating from the wrong tree. But now, because of the resurrection of Jesus Christ, Christ followers have the Holy Spirit dwelling within us so that we remain constantly connected to Him at all times and know His will. Through faith in Jesus, we have been born again as a new type of people on the earth who have the very nature of God within us so that we can carry out His purposes on the earth as they are in heaven. The Holy Spirit dwelling in us is the mystery which God kept hidden since before Adam's error but which He has now revealed to those who place their faith in Christ. (see Colossians 1:26-27) It is only through divine nature dwelling within us that we are able to victoriously overcome trials and temptations such as, metaphorically, eating from the wrong tree. Additionally, it is only through our anointing from Christ that we are able to do the works of God.

> *{Col 1:27} 27 To them God has chosen to make known among the Gentiles the glorious riches of this mystery, which is **Christ in you, the hope of glory**.*

> *{2Pe 1:4} 4 Through these [God's power, glory, and goodness] he has given us **his very great and precious promises**, so that through them **you may participate in the divine nature**, having escaped the corruption in the world caused by evil desires.*

The word *Christ* means *Anointed* or *Anointed One*. To *anoint* means *to smear*, typically with oil, and it is symbolic of consecration or being set apart for a special assignment from God. The word *Christ* is the Greek equivalent used to express that Jesus is the *Messiah*, or anointed King, of Israel. Appropriately, to be a Christian is to be a follower and subject of God's anointed King. Fortunately, our King loves us and shares His anointing with us. I like Thayer's Greek Lexicon definition of Christ: *who by His holy power and Spirit lives in the souls of His followers, and so moulds their characters that they bear His likeness giving them a mind conformed to the mind of Christ*. In the same way that Jesus was God's Anointed One, now, we are His anointed ones. He has anointed us with the Holy Spirit. Our King does not just rule over us, and He does not just smear us and send us, our King rules in us and through us because He has shared Himself with us by living inside of us.

As descendants of Adam, in our human minds, we can never figure out what Jesus would do and, even if we could, it would not be in our nature to do it. God knew this and knew the solution. He made a promise which He fulfilled in Christ and which He fulfills for us when we believe Christ.

> *{Eze 36:26} 26 I will **give you a new heart** and put a **new spirit in you**; I will remove from you your heart of stone and give you a heart of flesh.*

> *{Eze 11:19} 19 I will **give them an undivided heart** and put a **new spirit in them**; I will remove from them their heart of stone and give them a heart of flesh.*

> *{Jer 24:7} 7 I will **give them a heart to know me, that I am the LORD**. They will be my people, and I will be their God, for they will return to me with all their heart.*

The Holy Spirit is the *new spirit* which God has placed within us and the *new heart* which God has given us. It is an *undivided heart* which knows the will of God and desires to do it. The Holy Spirit dwells in our inmost being, guiding us in the will of God, giving us the very life of God in our mortal bodies, and giving us the same power which raised Christ from the dead. Because of this, when we follow the guidance of the Holy Spirit, we are like Jesus, and we do the things that He did as our own genuine response in whatever situation we face. Again, it doesn't happen instantaneously, but the more we follow the Holy Spirit, the more our new heart takes over.

If you are a believer and you want to know where the Holy Spirit is, position your hand at the place where your left and right rib cage form an upside down V. My old ballet teacher used to metaphorically say, "Put a lemon in your ribs and squeeze," because, if that place between our ribs was firm, it gave us tremendous balance and stability and there was almost nothing we couldn't do. When we believe Christ, the Holy Spirit and the power of God reside in that very same spot. Jesus Christ is right inside of us. Spiritually speaking, when we are strong there, nothing is impossible.

Let's take a deeper look at the Spirit of the Lord which dwells inside of us.

> *{Isa 11:2-3a} 2 The Spirit of the LORD will rest on him-- **the Spirit of wisdom and of understanding**, the Spirit of **counsel and of might**, the Spirit of the **knowledge and fear of the LORD**-- 3 and he will **delight in the fear of the LORD**.*

> *{2Ti 1:7} 7 For **the Spirit God gave us** does not make us timid, but **gives us power, love and self-discipline**.*

> *{Rom 8:15} 15 The Spirit you received does not make you slaves, so that you live in fear again; rather, **the Spirit you received brought about your adoption to sonship**. And by him we cry, "Abba, Father."*

The Holy Spirit gives us *wisdom and understanding* so that we know what to do and how to do it in every situation we face. The Holy Spirit gives us *counsel and might* so that we have God's guidance to know and the *power* to do God's will whether that is supernaturally empowered *self-discipline* for virtuous conduct or power for working a miracle, depending on the situation. The Holy Spirit gives us *knowledge* of God, without which we perish. (see Hosea 4:6) The Holy Spirit also teaches us *knowledge* of God's ways and the things which are to come so that we perceive with a higher level of intelligence – the intelligence of the Creator of all things and the author of all truth. The Holy Spirit gives us *the fear of the Lord* so that we are reverent towards the One who has all power in heaven and on earth so that we sincerely aim to live lives which are pleasing to Him. Most importantly, the Holy Spirit fills us with LOVE. We have in us the love of God for us, who did not spare His most precious Son so that we could *be His children and call Him Father.* We have the love of Christ for us, who loved us enough to die for us. And, because of this, love flows in us and through us to others so that we love them the way that Christ loves us.

Therefore, because the Holy Spirit is within us, we do not have to wonder what Jesus would do. Rather, when we allow ourselves to be guided by the Holy Spirit, we know for ourselves what Jesus is doing right NOW because Jesus is in us right NOW, and He is doing it right NOW through us in the very situation that we are facing. But this is not through our own logic and reasoning but by listening and being led by the Holy Spirit. This said, living our lives by the indwelling Holy Spirit does not happen overnight, and it cannot be rushed, forced, or faked. In fact, it seems that the more we try to rush, force, and fake it, the worse things go for us. Living by the guidance of God through the Holy Spirit is not about doing what we think Jesus would do in a situation or rationally doing whatever the most godly thing seems to be. By standards of logic and common sense, Jesus was completely unpredictable, and God's ways often seem like foolishness. (see 1 Corinthians 1:18) Instead, we must set our hearts to seek God's guidance above all else and allow Him to correct and guide us along with way, trusting that He will. This requires faith that He is who He says He is and trust that He is a gentle Shepherd, not a harsh master. (For more on this see Psalm 23; Matthew 25: 14-30) The more we listen, the more He will guide us.

> *{Mar 4:24-25 NLT} 24 Then he added, "Pay close attention to what you hear.* **The closer you listen, the more understanding you will be given--and you will receive even more.** *25* **To those who listen to my teaching, more understanding will be given.** *But for those who are not listening, even what little understanding they have will be taken away from them." (see also Matthew 25:29; Luke 8:18)*

When I was a little girl, I watched a children's television show where one of the popular puppets named Grover was having his reflexes tested at the doctor. The doctor tap-tap-tapped on Grover's right knee, and Grover kicked his left leg high up in the air. Apparently, this demonstrates excellent puppet reflexes. Soon after watching this, I went to the doctor where I had my reflexes tested. The doctor tap-tap-tapped on my right knee, and I kicked my left leg high up in the air, just like I had seen Grover do. This is what I thought I was supposed to do because I had seen Grover do it. Unfortunately, while left leg kicking was the correct reflex response to right knee tapping for Grover the puppet, it was the absolute wrong response to right knee tapping for a human. Needless to say, the doctor looked at me with a very quizzical look and said, "Why did you do that?" You see, I should have just relaxed and allowed a genuine response instead of doing what I thought I should be doing. Unfortunately, this is how a lot of us are trying to follow Jesus. We read about Him, imagine the way that we think He is or how we think He would handle a situation, and then we do it that way. We do what we think we should be doing rather than actually seeking Him and waiting for Him to tap-tap-tap on our hearts and responding genuinely to His prompting. Basically, we all just need to relax into the guidance of the Holy Spirit within us and allow Him to guide us.

Here's another way to think about it: Picture two fuel tanks side by side, each full of fuel. One fuel tank has the finest and best quality, highest grade, purest fuel available. When this fuel runs through a machine, it cleans the machine as it goes, and the exhaust it creates is a pleasant fragrance of purity. The other fuel tank is lowest grade fuel which has not been well filtered, and even has a few particles left in it. When this fuel runs through a machine, it clogs it up with junk that shouldn't be there and eventually the machine sputters and coughs and gasps its last breath and dies, leaving a stench of wreckage. This is an example of the choice that we have between following the Holy Spirit's guidance verses following our own thoughts, desires, and passions, which are the desires of our flesh.

> {Rom 8:5-6} 5 *Those who live according to the flesh have their minds set on **what the flesh desires**; but those who live in accordance with the Spirit have their minds set on **what the Spirit desires**. 6 The **mind governed by the flesh is death**, but the **mind governed by the Spirit is life and peace**.*

Along these lines, I heard a well respected man of God say that the most important things to do when serving Jesus are #1: Show up and #2: Be empty-headed. Showing up means being where God wants you to be and being empty-headed means letting go of your preconceived notions of what you are supposed to do and say and to whom you are supposed to do and say these things. Shortly after hearing him say this, I was on an online conference call of ministry leaders. One person's online name was *Kingdum*. I was about to judge this person for their obvious misspelling of the word Kingdom, but the Lord stopped me. The Lord reminded me what the man of God had said about showing up empty-headed, which by human standards seems pretty dumb, or even *dum*. I knew that the Lord wanted me to rely more on Him and be a little more King-dum myself, trusting King Jesus' guidance over my own smarts. It's my aim to be *Kingdum* from now on!

> {Pro 3:5-6} 5 **Trust in the LORD** *with all your heart and* **lean not on your own understanding**; *6 in all your ways* **submit to him**, *and he will make your paths straight.*

To be clear, I am not suggesting that God desires us to be stupid people or discard the capacities which He has given us. Rather, I am saying that, as we make decisions, we should choose to follow the guidance of the Holy Spirit, even if it does not seem to measure up with our common sense or a logical way of approaching things. Even if we are the smartest person on the planet, God is still smarter. His wisdom is beyond that of any human and He has placed that wisdom within us. God knows how to guide us on the path which is best for us if we will only listen to Him and place more importance on His direction than anything else in our lives. Actually, living by the Holy Spirit gives us the highest intelligence available!

> *{1Co 1:25} 25 For the foolishness of God is **wiser than human wisdom**, and the weakness of God is **stronger than human strength**.*

> *{1Jo 2:20, 27} 20 But you have an **anointing from the Holy One [the Holy Spirit]**, and all of you **know the truth**. ... 27 As for you, the anointing [the Holy Spirit] you received from him remains in you, **and you do not need anyone to teach you**. But as **his anointing [the Holy Spirit] teaches you about all things** and as that anointing is real, not counterfeit--just as it has taught you, **remain in him**.*

The Tree of Life

When Adam and his wife were banished from the Garden of Eden, they were forbidden from accessing the Tree of Life and since then, all of mankind has been yearning to access it again. But now through Christ, God has given us access to the Tree of Life again. Biblical references to the Tree of Life can only be found in the book of Genesis, which is the beginning, the book of Revelation, which is the end, and the book of Proverbs, which is a collection of God's wisdom right in the middle. In the beginning, God gave humans full access to the Tree of Life and in the end, after God has judged the earth and restored it, we will again have full access to the Tree of Life. In His grace, even though we are right in the middle between these two, God has made a way for us to partake.

> *{Pro 3:18} 18 **She [wisdom] is a tree of life** to those who take hold of her; those who hold her fast will be blessed.*

> *{1Co 1:30} 30 It is because of him that **you are in Christ Jesus, who has become for us wisdom from God**--that is, our righteousness, holiness and redemption.*

> *{Pro 13:12} 12 Hope deferred makes the heart sick, but a **longing fulfilled is a tree of life**.*

God's wisdom is a Tree of Life. Jesus Christ dwelling in us and us in Him is the wisdom of God. Therefore, we are a part of the Tree of Life and the Tree of Life is within us! Moreover, this fulfills the longing of our hearts by connecting us again with God, who is the source of life. The word for *life* in *Tree of Life* is *zoe* which means the actual *life of God* and the *vitality* of the giver of life Himself. When we remain in Christ and follow the Holy Spirit, it is as if we are eating of the Tree of Life.

But there was another tree in the Garden, wasn't there? Unfortunately, the Tree of the Knowledge of Good and Evil was side by side with the Tree of Life. The Tree of the Knowledge of Good and Evil was very appealing for many reasons, but it had no ability to give life and, in fact, brought only death. Every day, figuratively speaking, we can choose to eat from the Tree of Life by obeying and abiding in Jesus by following the Holy Spirit, or we can choose to eat from the Tree of the Knowledge of Good and Evil by following our own inclinations, desires, and fleshly passions. Even when we do Good things, they can be wrong things when they are not God-directed things. Our aim is not to be Good but to be like Jesus and to do the things that Jesus did. Jesus never did anything because it was a Good thing to do. Jesus never did anything because it was an Evil thing to do. Jesus did not spend a moment of His time debating between Good and Evil in order to be right before God or be a Good person. Jesus was entirely directed by God's leading through the Holy Spirit. Therefore, everything He did was a Life-giving thing to do because Life-giving is the perfect and pleasing will of God. For certain, Jesus could discern Good and Evil very clearly, but He did not base a single one of His actions on whether they were Good or Evil. All of His actions were based on God's will and guidance because Jesus always had open communication with God and was listening to all God told Him to do.

Fortunately, unlike Adam in the original garden, if we eat from the wrong tree we do not lose our access to the Tree of Life. This is because Jesus' sacrifice was sufficient for us to make mistakes and to learn and grow without losing our right standing with God, even when we sin or err. Because of Christ's righteousness within us, we have the same open communication with God that Jesus had so that we can listen and serve Him freely with clear consciences as if we had never eaten from the wrong tree. This is God's amazing grace and kindness towards us!

> *{Heb 9:14} 14 How much more, then, will the blood of Christ, who through the eternal Spirit offered himself unblemished to God, **cleanse our consciences from acts that lead to death, so that we may serve the living God**! (see also Hebrews 9:26; Hebrews 10:10; Peter 3:18; Romans 6:10)*

In spite of this tremendous freedom, why would we want such a bad diet? When we have a bad spiritual diet, we do not grow into spiritual maturity, we are motivated by Good and Evil rather than discerning it, and we tend to become confused and frustrated because we are always searching for the next great teaching that is going to fix our lives. Moreover, when we follow our own inclinations or try to be Good rather than following the Holy Spirit, we cannot do the things that Jesus did.

> *{Heb 5:14 NASB} 14 But **solid food is for the mature**, who because of practice have their senses trained to **discern good and evil**.*

> *{Eph 4:13-14} 13 until we all reach unity in the faith and in the knowledge of the Son of God and **become mature**, attaining to the whole measure of the fullness of Christ. 14 Then we will **no longer be infants, tossed back and forth by the waves, and blown here and there by every wind of teaching and by the cunning and craftiness of people in their deceitful scheming**.*

However, when we have a good spiritual diet, we not only eat from the Tree of Life, we become a Tree of Life. Through the right spiritual diet, we become like Jesus, even doing the things that He would do and saying things the way that He would say. We grow into spiritual maturity, which is to be like Him or, in a word, *Christlike*. We become branches of Christ and the Tree of Life and we produce Life-giving fruit which nourishes others.

> *{Pro 11:30} 30 **The fruit of the righteous is a tree of life**, and the one who is wise saves lives.*

> *{Pro 15:4} 4 **The soothing tongue is a tree of life**, but a perverse tongue crushes the spirit.*

Listening and Abiding

Living by the guidance of the Holy Spirit does not have to be complicated. It starts with simply trusting that you do indeed hear His voice. Sometimes at first, it doesn't seem like a voice speaking. Actually, it seems more like an inner knowing about something, usually about something that you have no rational way of knowing but somehow, you just know. You might call it an impression or a sense of what is really happening underneath the surface of a situation or of what you are supposed to do about something. We begin living by the Holy Spirit by trusting that this inner knowing is, in fact, the voice of God. Begin by trusting that Jesus does speak to you because you are His disciple. Then, once you have received wisdom from the Holy Spirit, believe that you have heard God and stand firm in what you have heard.

> {Jhn 10:14, 27} 14 "*I am the good shepherd; I know my sheep and **my sheep know me**-- ... 27 **My sheep listen to my voice**; I know them, and **they follow me**.*

> {Jas 1:5-8} 5 *If any of you lacks wisdom, you should ask God, who gives generously to all without finding fault, and it will be given to you. 6 But when you ask, **you must believe and not doubt, because the one who doubts is like a wave of the sea, blown and tossed by the wind**. 7 That person should not expect to receive anything from the Lord. 8 Such a person is double-minded and unstable in all they do.*

There are three primary ways that we will be tempted to doubt the guidance of the Holy Spirit and doubt that we have heard God. Depending on what the Lord has said, these three ways can happen almost in an instant, or they can happen over time if what the Lord has said is slow in coming to pass. (There are various scenarios given at the end of this chapter.) Jesus told the Parable of the Four Soils about a farmer who sowed seeds on 4 different kinds of soils. (see Matthew 13:1-23; Mark 4:1-24; Luke 8:4-18) In this parable, the seed represents God's word, and the soil represents the condition of our hearts to trust what God has said. We do not have time to dig fully into the Parable of the Four Soils but, instead, we're going to use it as a template for understanding how to stand firm in the Holy Spirit's guidance. The first way that we are tempted to doubt what God has said to us is through the enemy. Yes, we do have an enemy who does not want us to obey the Holy Spirit. The same serpent who tempted Adam and his wife to eat from the wrong tree in the Garden of Eden by saying to them, *Did God really say...?*, will say the same thing to us. Of course, I am not referring to a literal serpent but a spiritual one who has a voice very similar to the Holy Spirit but who is constantly contradicting or twisting what God did indeed say. In fact, it seems that whenever God truly has said something, that contrary voice is right there saying, *Did God really say...?*, to get us to doubt and abandon God's guidance. Be alert for this, and don't allow the enemy to snatch away your confidence. The second way that we are tempted to doubt what God has said to us is through others misunderstanding us and trials which arise between the time that God gives a promise and the time when the promise or purpose is fulfilled. We set out to obey God, and then everything seems to go wrong or our friends abandon us or pick on us or tell us that we've lost our mind to be doing such a thing. It's just another way of causing us to question, *Did God really say...?* Be ready for this and be prepared to stand on God's promises through trials and misunderstandings, all the while expecting that God will be faithful in what He has said. The third way that we are tempted to doubt what

God has said to us is through our desire for other things, usually temporal things like comfort, money, status, or security. We set out to obey God and then, somehow, God's way just seems too hard, or it seems that we could have our desires fulfilled faster if we did it our own way, or we convince ourselves that God wants to bless us in ways that are, in truth, a distraction. When temptation comes, we find ourselves asking, *Did God really say…?* This is why it is important to keep our hearts set on Christ and His Kingdom and things of eternal value so that these temporal things hold less value in our lives. All of this said, there is a fourth soil in this parable and that is the soil that stands firm and endures through the questions, trials, confusion, and temptations all the way to receiving the promised outcome. This is the person who has remained or abided, in God's word and the things that He has promised.

> *{Jhn 15:4-12} 4* **Remain in me, as I also remain in you***. No branch can bear fruit by itself; it must remain in the vine. Neither can you bear fruit unless you remain in me. 5 "***I am the vine; you are the branches***. If you remain in me and I in you, you will bear much fruit;* **apart from me you can do nothing***. 6 If you do not remain in me, you are like a branch that is thrown away and withers; such branches are picked up, thrown into the fire and burned. 7* **If you remain in me and my words remain in you, ask whatever you wish, and it will be done for you***. 8 This is to my Father's glory, that you bear much fruit, showing yourselves to be my disciples. 9 "As the Father has loved me, so have I loved you.* **Now remain in my love***. 10 If you keep my commands, you will remain in my love, just as I have kept my Father's commands and remain in his love. 11 I have told you this so that my joy may be in you and that* **your joy may be complete***. 12 My command is this:* **Love each other as I have loved you***.*

The word for *remain* here means to *abide*, to *not depart*, to *continue*, to *endure*, to *keep*, to *wait for*, and to *not become different*. When we place our faith in Jesus and when we hear His voice, we are to stay and not depart from what He said. We are to continue, endure, and wait for Him to prove Himself faithful and not turn our hearts away from what He said. (see Hebrews 3:7) Jesus instructed His followers to stay constantly connected to Him, listening to His voice at every moment, trusting that He is faithful to fulfill everything He promises, and not giving up or giving in when trials and temptations come along. While abiding can be difficult, it is not strenuous or strained. Staying connected to Jesus is as natural as a branch staying connected to a vine. The branch does not try to be a branch, it just is. The branch does not try to produce fruit, it just does. The branch does not ask itself, *Am I really a branch?, Am I a good enough branch?, Have I done enough branching today?, Does the vine approve of me?, Will I ever produce fruit?* or *Are there better vines across town?* No. The branch is a branch because that's what it has been made to be. A branch simply cannot live without the vine. The branch receives all of its sustenance and life from the vine and all the branch has to do is allow the vine to fill it with sap and receive all that the vine has to give it. Then, the branch can't help but produce fruit – much fruit. Then, the vine and the gardener receive praise because the branch has fulfilled its purpose.

One time, I was trusting God in a very difficult situation, and I was feeling highly overextended in my faith. You could say that every possible way of forcing me to ask, *Did God really say…?* was going full force in my life. I cried out to the Lord in desperation, saying, "Jesus, I really feel like I am out on a limb here." He responded, "Wendy, you are my limb," and pointed me to the vine and branch passage above. What a relief to know that we are connected to Him! We are never beyond His reach! On that day, I came to know what being a branch was really all about. Branch life is about trusting God through faith in Jesus and following the Holy Spirit no matter what. As long as our hearts are set in this way, we have nothing to worry about. Jesus is our vine, and He knows just what we need.

Furthermore, as we remain in this trusting relationship with Jesus, we can ask for anything, and it will be done for us. Throughout Scripture, we see many promises of God which speak of blessings, wholeness, and restoration to God's design or even better. Jesus, through His perfect life, earned every single promise of God in the Scriptures for us. When we go to God asking Him to fulfill a promise of Scripture to us, He says *Yes* to us because of what Jesus did. Therefore, we say *Amen* to receive the promises that Christ has obtained for us. The word *amen* is not just a casual phrase tagged onto the end of our prayers. Amen means *so be it* and is a wholehearted expression of absolute trust, faith, and confidence that what has been promised will come to pass. As an example, in the Old Testament, God enumerated both blessings and curses in His Law – blessings for obedience and curses for disobedience. When the people of Israel crossed into the Promised Land, the Levites, who were the ministers serving God, were instructed to stand on a mountain and shout certain curses to the people so that everyone understood and agreed with what would happen if they disobeyed God's Law. The people were to unanimously shout back by saying, *Amen*. In one case, the Levites shouted, "Cursed is anyone who leads a blind person astray on the road," and the people shouted back, "Amen!" They essentially agreed that this was right and *so be it* as God had said. Furthermore, they fully expected that anyone who led a blind person astray on a road would undoubtedly be cursed by God. (see Deuteronomy 27:11-26) When Jesus came and lived the perfectly obedient life under the Law of God, He maintained right standing with God at all times, which was proved by His resurrection. Jesus' right standing with God entitles Him to every blessing God ever promised and nullified the curse of the Law by overcoming it. This said, Jesus did not keep all of those blessings to Himself and is not selfishly hoarding them all. Instead, He poured His Spirit into us who believe so that we may benefit from His right standing with God and the blessings that He rightfully earned. Accordingly, when we see a promise of God in the Scriptures, we know that it is rightfully ours because of what Jesus did for us. Therefore, we shout out *Amen!* from our hearts meaning this is right and *so be it* as God has promised. We can confidently believe that we will be blessed and receive our rightful blessing!

> *{2Co 1:20} 20 For no matter how many **promises God has made, they are "Yes" in Christ**.*
> *And so through him the "Amen" is spoken by us to the glory of God.*

In fact, this is the work that Christ has for us – believing Jesus. When Jesus walked on earth, He knew that He had, or would receive, whatever He asked for from God because He always asked according to God's will. (see 1 John 5:14) Jesus had perfect faith to believe that God was able to do it. Jesus brought heaven to earth because He believed God, and the only people who received from Jesus were the ones who believed Him. As an illustration of this, the only place where Jesus' work seemed stunted was Nazareth, His hometown, where He could do very few miracles because of their unbelief. (see Matthew 13:57; Mark 6:4;

Luke 4:24) In another instance, when Jesus' disciples asked Him what they had to do for God and how they could do the same miraculous works that Jesus did, He made it very simple.

> {Jhn 6:29 NLT} 29 Jesus told them, "**This is the only work God wants from you: Believe in** the one he has sent."

Jesus is the One God sent. Jesus is the vine that we abide in as branches. When we believe that Jesus is who He says He is and remain connected to Him, we can ask for anything, and He will give it to us. When we believe what He did for us, all things are possible.

> {1Co 2:2, 5} 2 For **I resolved to know nothing** while I was with you **except Jesus Christ and him crucified.** ... 5 so that your faith might not rest on human wisdom, but on God's power.

Walking as Jesus Walked

The Biblical writer who best expressed this abiding relationship of us in Christ and Christ in us through the Holy Spirit was John. John emphasized Jesus' teaching about His relationship with God the Father and our relationship with Christ through the Holy Spirit. These are a mirror image of one another. When we are truly following Christ and living by the guidance of the Holy Spirit, we walk on the earth in the same way that Jesus walked on the earth by God's guidance. We even say the same things He said and do the same things He did. It is only through this abiding relationship that we are empowered to carry out God's purposes in the earth. Let's take a look at the parallels between Jesus' relationship with His Father and our relationship with Christ now that He has ascended to heaven and poured the Holy Spirit into our hearts.

God did not leave Jesus alone – *mirrors* – Jesus does not leave us alone as orphans:

> {Jhn 8:29} 29 The one who sent me **is with me**; he has **not left me alone**, for I always do what pleases him."

> {Jhn 14:16-18} 16 And I will ask the Father, and he will give you another advocate to help you and **be with you forever**-- 17 **the Spirit of truth.** The world cannot accept him, because it neither sees him nor knows him. But you know him, for **he lives with you and will be in you.** 18 **I will not leave you as orphans;** I will come to you.

God taught Jesus, showed Jesus what to do and what to say, and Jesus obeyed God's commands – *mirrors* – Jesus teaches us all that He knows, shows us what to do and what to say, and we keep His commands

> {Jhn 8:28-29} 28 So Jesus said, "When you have lifted up the Son of Man, then you will know that I am he and that **I do nothing on my own but speak just what the Father has taught me.** 29 The one who sent me is with me; he has not left me alone, for **I always do what pleases him.**"

> {Jhn 12:49-50} 49 For **I did not speak on my own, but the Father who sent me commanded me to say all that I have spoken.** 50 I know that his command leads to eternal life. So **whatever I say is just what the Father has told me to say.**"

{Jhn 14:15, 21, 23, 26, 31} 15 "If you love me, keep my commands. ... 21 Whoever has my commands and keeps them is the one who loves me. The one who loves me will be loved by my Father, and I too will love them and show myself to them." ... 23 Jesus replied, "Anyone who loves me will obey my teaching. My Father will love them, and we will come to them and make our home with them. ... 26 But the Advocate, the Holy Spirit, whom the Father will send in my name, will teach you all things and will remind you of everything I have said to you. ... 31 but he comes so that the world may learn that I love the Father and do exactly what my Father has commanded me. "Come now; let us leave.

{Jhn 15:3, 10, 15} 3 You are already clean because of the word I have spoken to you. 10 If you keep my commands, you will remain in my love, just as I have kept my Father's commands and remain in his love. ... 15 I no longer call you servants, because a servant does not know his master's business. Instead, I have called you friends, for everything that I learned from my Father I have made known to you.

{Jhn 16:13, 15} 13 But when he, the Spirit of truth, comes, he will guide you into all the truth. He will not speak on his own; he will speak only what he hears, and he will tell you what is yet to come. ... 15 All that belongs to the Father is mine. That is why I said the Spirit will receive from me what he will make known to you."

{1Jo 2:20, 27} 20 But you have an anointing from the Holy One, [the Holy Spirit] and all of you know the truth. ... 27 As for you, the anointing you received from him remains in you, and you do not need anyone to teach you. But as his anointing teaches you about all things and as that anointing is real, not counterfeit--just as it has taught you, remain in him.

God was in Jesus and Jesus was in God – *mirrors* – Christ is in us and we are in Christ:

{Jhn 10:38} 38 But if I do them, even though you do not believe me, believe the works, that you may know and understand that the Father is in me, and I in the Father."

{Jhn 14:10-11, 17, 20, 23} 10 Don't you believe that I am in the Father, and that the Father is in me? The words I say to you I do not speak on my own authority. Rather, it is the Father, living in me, who is doing his work. 11 Believe me when I say that I am in the Father and the Father is in me; or at least believe on the evidence of the works themselves. ... 17 the Spirit of truth. The world cannot accept him, because it neither sees him nor knows him. But you know him, for he lives with you and will be in you. ... 20 On that day you will realize that I am in my Father, and you are in me, and I am in you. ... 23 Jesus replied, "Anyone who loves me will obey my teaching. My Father will love them, and we will come to them and make our home with them.

{Jhn 15:4-7} 4 Remain in me, as I also remain in you. No branch can bear fruit by itself; it must remain in the vine. Neither can you bear fruit unless you remain in me. 5 "I am the vine; you are the branches. If you remain in me and I in you, you will bear much fruit; apart from me you can do nothing. 6 If you do not remain in me, you are like a branch that is thrown away and

withers; such branches are picked up, thrown into the fire and burned. 7 If you remain in me and my words remain in you, ask whatever you wish, and it will be done for you.

Jesus could do nothing by Himself, only what He saw the Father doing – *mirrors* – We can do nothing apart from Him and our flesh profits nothing:

> *{Jhn 5:19-20} 19 Jesus gave them this answer: "Very truly I tell you, the **Son can do nothing by himself; he can do only what he sees his Father doing**, because whatever the Father does the Son also does. 20 For **the Father loves the Son and shows him all he does**. Yes, and he will show him even greater works than these, so that you will be amazed.*

> *{Jhn 6:63} 63 **The Spirit gives life; the flesh counts for nothing**. The words I have spoken to you--they are full of the Spirit and life.*

> *{Jhn 15:5} 5 "I am the vine; you are the branches. If you remain in me and I in you, you will bear much fruit; **apart from me you can do nothing**.*

Jesus' teaching was not His own but God's – *mirrors* – Our teaching is not our own but Christ's:

> *{Jhn 7:16} 16 Jesus answered, "**My teaching is not my own. It comes from the one who sent me**. ...*

> *{Jhn 14:24, 26} 24 Anyone who does not love me will not obey my teaching. **These words you hear are not my own; they belong to the Father who sent me**. ... 26 But the Advocate, **the Holy Spirit**, whom the Father will send in my name, **will teach you all things and will remind you of everything I have said to you**.*

> *{Jhn 15:15} 15 I no longer call you servants, because a servant does not know his master's business. Instead, I have called you friends, **for everything that I learned from my Father I have made known to you**.*

> *{Mat 28:19-20} 19 **Therefore go and make disciples of all nations**, baptizing them in the name of the Father and of the Son and of the Holy Spirit, 20 and **teaching them to obey everything I have commanded you**. And surely I am with you always, to the very end of the age."*

Jesus is the Son of God – *mirrors* – We are the children of God:

> *{Jhn 3:16} 16 For God so loved the world that **he gave his one and only Son**, that whoever believes in him shall not perish but have eternal life.*

> *{Jhn 10:36} 36 what about the one whom the Father set apart as his very own and sent into the world? Why then do you accuse me of blasphemy because I said, '**I am God's Son**'?*

> *{Jhn 1:12} 12 Yet **to all who did receive him**, to those **who believed** in his name, he gave the right to **become children of God**--*

Jesus is the light of the world – *mirrors* – We are the light of the world:

*{Jhn 1:4} 4 In him was life, and that life was **the light of all mankind**.*

*{Jhn 9:5} 5 While I am in the world, **I am the light of the world**."*

*{Jhn 8:12} 12 When Jesus spoke again to the people, he said, "**I am the light of the world**. Whoever **follows me** will never walk in darkness, but will **have the light of life**."*

*{Jhn 12:36, 46} 36 Believe in the light while you have the light, so that you may **become children of light**." When he had finished speaking, Jesus left and hid himself from them. ... 46 **I have come into the world as a light**, so that no one who believes in me should stay in darkness.*

*{Mat 5:14} 14 "**You are the light of the world**. A town built on a hill cannot be hidden.*

Jesus had life in Him – *mirrors* – We have life in us:

*{Jhn 1:4} 4 **In him was life**, and that life was the light of all mankind.*

*{Jhn 5:26} 26 For as the Father has life in himself, so he has granted **the Son also to have life in himself**.*

*{Jhn 6:40, 47-48, 54, 57} 40 For my Father's will is that everyone who looks to the Son and **believes in him shall have eternal life**, and I will raise them up at the last day." ... 47 Very truly I tell you, the one who **believes has eternal life**. 48 **I am the bread of life**. ... 54 Whoever eats my flesh and drinks my blood **has eternal life**, and I will raise them up at the last day. ... 57 Just as the living Father sent me and **I live because of the Father**, so the one who feeds on me **will live because of me**.*

*{Jhn 11:25 } 25 Jesus said to her, "**I am** the resurrection and **the life**. The one who **believes in me will live**, even though they die;*

*{Jhn 14:6,19} 6 Jesus answered, "I am the way and the truth and the life. No one comes to the Father except through me. 19 Before long, the world will not see me anymore, but you will see me. **Because I live, you also will live**.*

Jesus did not sin – *mirrors* – We will not sin:

*{1Jo 3:5-6, 9} 5 But you know that he appeared so that he might take away our sins. **And in him is no sin**. 6 **No one who lives in him keeps on sinning.** No one who continues to sin has either seen him or known him. ... 9 **No one who is born of God will continue to sin**, because God's seed remains in them; **they cannot go on sinning**, because they have been born of God.*

*{1Jo 5:18} 18 We know that **anyone born of God does not continue to sin**; the One who was born of God keeps them safe, and the evil one cannot harm them.*

God loves Jesus – *mirrors* – Jesus loves us:

*{Jhn 5:20} 20 For **the Father loves the Son** and shows him all he does. Yes, and he will show him even greater works than these, so that you will be amazed.*

> *{Jhn 14:21} 21 Whoever has my commands and keeps them is the one who loves me.* **The one who loves me will be loved by my Father, and I too will love them** *and show myself to them."*

> *{Jhn 15:9} 9 "**As the Father has loved me, so have I loved you.** Now remain in my love.*

Therefore We Go

Jesus was sent into the world by His Father, God. Now, because we can hear His voice through the indwelling Holy Spirit, Jesus sends us out into the world to be like Him and to do the things He did.

> *{Jhn 6:38} 38 For* **I have come down from heaven** *not to do my will but to do the will of him who sent me.*

> *{Jhn 12:45} 45* **The one who looks at me is seeing the one who sent me.**

> *{Jhn 14:9} 9 Jesus answered: "Don't you know me, Philip, even after I have been among you such a long time?* **Anyone who has seen me has seen the Father.** *How can you say, 'Show us the Father'?*

> *{Jhn 13:20} 20 Very truly I tell you,* **whoever accepts anyone I send accepts me; and whoever accepts me accepts the one who sent me.**"

> *{Mat 28:19-20} 19 Therefore* **go and make disciples of all nations,** *baptizing them in the name of the Father and of the Son and of the Holy Spirit, 20 and* **teaching them to obey everything I have commanded you.** *And surely* **I am with you** *always, to the very end of the age."*

> *{Mar 16:15-18} 15 He said to them, "**Go into all the world and preach the gospel to all creation.** 16 Whoever believes and is baptized will be saved, but whoever does not believe will be condemned. 17 And* **these signs will accompany those who believe***: In my name they will drive out demons; they will speak in new tongues; 18 they will pick up snakes with their hands; and when they drink deadly poison, it will not hurt them at all; they will place their hands on sick people, and they will get well."*

> *{Jhn 14:12} 12 Very truly I tell you,* **whoever believes in me will do the works I have been doing, and they will do even greater things than these,** *because I am going to the Father.*

Let's pull this all together with a few practical examples.

Scenario 1: Hypothetically speaking, let's say that, on three separate occasions, you pass by three different beggars, and they are each asking you for money as you drive by. In the Scriptures, Jesus said, *Give to everyone who asks of you* (see Luke 6:30) so you know that giving to the poor is a Good thing to do. Rather than doing something because it is Good, you quickly listen for the Lord's guidance in your heart from the Holy Spirit. For the first beggar, the Lord may say, *Give them everything in your wallet;* for the second beggar, the Lord may say, *Tell them about Jesus;* and for the third beggar, the Lord may say *Lock your doors*. Now, let's be clear, this is no excuse for not giving to the poor. If you are locking your doors every time, there is probably something wrong with your spiritual ears. However, what I am emphasizing is that the Lord guides us in each situation with what He wants us to do in that moment. As a matter of fact, when I first began devoting my life to following the Holy Spirit's guidance, I was shocked at all the Good things that God didn't actually want me to do just because they were Good. Our aim is not to be Good but to be obedient to His promptings. His focus is our heart of willingness to do anything He asks – our focus is on His heart and doing what He directs.

Scenario 2: Hypothetically speaking, let's say that the Lord instructs you to go lay hands on a sick person and pray for them. After you have sensed the Lord's prompting, the first thing that will happen is you'll hear an alternate voice saying, *Was that really God, or is that just me?* or *Who do I think I am?* followed by *What will people think of me if I do that?* or *What if I can't?* followed by *What if I'm humiliated?* or *It would be easier not to,* or *I have somewhere else to be.* In one moment, you have just experienced the three attacks of *Did God really say…?* This is normal. Rise above it and trust that you have heard the Lord speak to you. Be empowered by the Holy Spirit to do what He says.

Scenario 3: Hypothetically speaking, let's say the Lord tells you there is a call on your life to serve Him and be used powerfully by Him for His Kingdom. The first thing that will happen is you will hear an alternate voice saying, *Was that really God, or is that just me?* or *Who do I think I am?* If you proceed to move in faith towards what God has said to you, you will then begin to experience other people's lack of support for what you are doing, even voicing your worst fears that God could not have possibly said what He said to you. At the same time, as you set out to serve the Lord with all your heart, things in your life will start to crumble around you in strange ways that don't make much sense at all. Most likely, you will also do several things that you think you should do because they seem like Good things to do. Unfortunately, because God did not tell you to do these Good things, they will undoubtedly fall apart before your eyes, and this is discouraging. If you proceed past this and continue to move in faith towards what God has said to you, you will then begin to encounter temptation from *get-blessed-now* ideas, or you will be drawn to do or not do things because of money or lack thereof. If God does not seem to be providing for you in accordance with your standards of lifestyle, you will be tempted to do things for money which are actually a distraction from God's path for you. Regardless of your lifestyle, you will be tempted to be motivated into doing things purely because they are more profitable rather than because they are what God has said. Simultaneously, certain things in your life or relationships will become strained because of the course that you are taking for the Lord, and your pride or dignity may be squashed. You will be tempted to prioritize those things, including your pride and dignity, over continuing on the path that the Lord has set for you. All of these experiences are the attacks of *Did God really say…?* This is normal. Persevere and endure through these struggles and temptations, listen diligently to the Holy Spirit's continual guidance, and follow God's path. Then, you will be and do everything that He has promised and called you to be and to do.

Scenario 4: While we are here on earth, we all have to decide once and for all if we truly believe that Jesus is Lord, that He is who He says He is, and that He did what He said He did. The desire of every human heart, whether they know it or not, is to be pleasing to God and to be approved of by Him. Therefore, we desire to be Good for Him and to be a Good person, not an Evil one. We experience the question of *Is Jesus really the truth?* and we may wonder if His sacrifice was truly enough no matter how Good or Evil we have been in our past. Once we place our faith in Jesus, we may experience rejection from friends and loved ones because of Christ, we may be mocked and ridiculed for believing Jesus, and things may not always go perfectly in our lives. We may find ourselves wondering, *Is He really the only way?* Then, as we proceed with faith in Jesus, we may experience temptation to succeed in the world's way rather than God's way, or to take the easy road of least resistance rather than God's path. We may even be pressed into situations where we are pushed to deny Christ at the expense of something valuable to us, even ultimately our lives. We may question, *If I deny Him, will I still be ok?* All of these are the attacks of *Did God really say...?* All of these questions are normal. But deep down, we know that Jesus is the truth, that Jesus is the only way, and that we cannot deny Him because He truly is Lord. He is worthy of our devotion above everything else in our lives, and even life itself. We must stand firm and be empowered by the Holy Spirit and endure in our faith. Then, we will receive heaven and eternal life with Jesus on the new earth in the age to come.

All of these scenarios express aspects of why the Holy Spirit has been given to us. Only through the Holy Spirit can we hear the voice of God Himself and be guided by Him to fulfill His purpose for our lives. Only through the Holy Spirit in us, directing us, empowering us, and strengthening us, will we become like Jesus. Then we will walk like He walked, talk like He talked, do the things that He did, and endure through the trials of life in order to receive everything that God has promised... just like the first Christ followers in the Book of Acts.

CHAPTER 3
Primer: Communion

The Book of Acts is the history of the beginning of the Church – a community of people who follow Christ as their Lord and King. What started with only 120 people in Jerusalem now includes billions of people across the globe. Let's examine the very special and common bond believers have with one another in Christ, the way that believers would have understood it in the Book of Acts.

A Nation Born in a Day

A long time ago, a whole new nation was born in a day, delivered from their bondage, oppression, and enemies so that they could freely worship their God, the one true God who created heaven and earth. If you know your history and your Bible, this will immediately remind you of the birth of the nation of Israel. God delivered them from Egyptian slavery on the night of Passover by walking them through the parted waters of the Red Sea into the wilderness of Sinai to worship Him. But this also describes the Church, including everyone who believes that Jesus is Lord and that God raised Him from the dead. In a parallel of events and even on the anniversary of Passover over one thousand years later, a whole new nation of people was born in a day. Through the death and resurrection of Jesus, we who believe have been delivered from our bondage to sin and death and from our old way of life so that we can worship God freely. In spite of the fact that we are scattered all over the ends of the earth, we are bound together as a special people like a nation of people united under the same King. God is our God, Jesus is our King, and we are His people.

In order to gain a better understanding of what God accomplished in birthing the Church, we're going to look at the original Passover which is a foreshadow of Christ's resurrection. In the original Passover, Israelites had been subjected to harsh and cruel Egyptian slavery for several hundred years. It had been an iron-smelting furnace of affliction where they were ruthlessly treated by their oppressors. (see Deuteronomy 4:20) Then, God appointed Moses as their leader and gave him instructions on how to lead the people of Israel to freedom. In the events which followed, God made a distinction between the people who were His and the people who were not. He dealt favorably with His own. (see Exodus 8:22-2; Exodus 9:4, 26) Read the following excerpts from Exodus Chapters 12 through 14:

> *{Exo 12:3, 5-14, 23} 3 "Tell the whole community of Israel that on the tenth day of this month each man is to take a lamb for his family, one for each household… 5 The animals you choose must be year-old males without defect, and you may take them from the sheep or the goats. 6 Take care of them until the fourteenth day of the month, when all the members of the community of Israel must slaughter them at twilight. 7 Then they are to **take some of the blood and put it on the sides and tops of the doorframes** of the houses where they eat the lambs. 8 That same night*

*they are to **eat the meat** roasted over the fire, along with bitter herbs, and **bread made without yeast**. 9 Do not eat the meat raw or boiled in water, but roast it over a fire--with the head, legs and internal organs. 10 Do not leave any of it till morning; if some is left till morning, you must burn it. 11 This is how you are to eat it: with your cloak tucked into your belt, your sandals on your feet and your staff in your hand. Eat it in haste; **it is the LORD's Passover**. 12 "**On that same night I will pass through Egypt and strike down every firstborn** of both people and animals, and I will bring judgment on all the gods of Egypt. I am the LORD. 13 **The blood will be a sign for you on the houses where you are, and when I see the blood, I will pass over you. No destructive plague will touch you when I strike Egypt**. 14 "**This is a day you are to commemorate**; for the generations to come you shall **celebrate it as a festival to the LORD--a lasting ordinance**... 23 **When the LORD goes through the land to strike down the Egyptians, he will see the blood on the top and sides of the doorframe and will pass over that doorway, and he will not permit the destroyer to enter your houses and strike you down**.*

*{Exo 12:29-31} 29 At midnight the LORD struck down all the firstborn in Egypt, from the firstborn of Pharaoh, who sat on the throne, to the firstborn of the prisoner, who was in the dungeon, and the firstborn of all the livestock as well. 30 Pharaoh and all his officials and all the Egyptians got up during the night, and there was loud wailing in Egypt, for there was not a house without someone dead. 31 During the night Pharaoh summoned Moses and Aaron and said, "**Up! Leave my people, you and the Israelites! Go, worship the LORD as you have requested**.*

*{Exo 12:47-49} 47 The whole community of Israel must celebrate it. 48 "**A foreigner residing among you who wants to celebrate the LORD's Passover must have all the males in his household circumcised; then he may take part like one born in the land. No uncircumcised male may eat it**. 49 The same law applies both to the native-born and to the foreigner residing among you."*

*{Exo 14:21-31} 21 Then Moses stretched out his hand over the sea, and all that night the LORD drove the sea back with a strong east wind and turned it into dry land. The waters were divided, 22 and **the Israelites went through the sea on dry ground**, with a wall of water on their right and on their left. 23 The Egyptians pursued them, and all Pharaoh's horses and chariots and horsemen followed them into the sea. 24 During the last watch of the night the LORD looked down from the pillar of fire and cloud at the Egyptian army and threw it into confusion. 25 He jammed the wheels of their chariots so that they had difficulty driving. And the Egyptians said, "Let's get away from the Israelites! The LORD is fighting for them against Egypt." 26 Then the LORD said to Moses, "Stretch out your hand over the sea so that the waters may flow back over the Egyptians and their chariots and horsemen." 27 Moses stretched out his hand over the sea, and **at daybreak the sea went back to its place**. The Egyptians were fleeing toward it, and the LORD swept them into the sea. 28 The water flowed back and covered the chariots and horsemen-- the entire army of Pharaoh that had followed the Israelites into the sea. Not one of them survived.*

*29 But the Israelites went through the sea on dry ground, with a wall of water on their right and on their left. 30 **That day the LORD saved Israel** from the hands of the Egyptians, and Israel saw the Egyptians lying dead on the shore. 31 And when the Israelites saw the mighty hand of the LORD displayed against the Egyptians, the people feared the LORD and put their trust in him and in Moses his servant.*

*{Exo 13:14-16} 14 "In days to come, when your son asks you, 'What does this mean?' say to him, '**With a mighty hand the LORD brought us out of Egypt, out of the land of slavery**. 15 When Pharaoh stubbornly refused to let us go, the LORD killed the firstborn of both people and animals in Egypt. **This is why** I sacrifice to the LORD the first male offspring of every womb and redeem each of my firstborn sons.' 16 **And it will be like a sign on your hand and a symbol on your forehead that the LORD brought us out of Egypt with his mighty hand**."*

To recap: On the tenth day of the month, every family was ordered to select an unblemished lamb from their flock and bring it into their home. Then, on the fourteenth day of the month, they were to slaughter that lamb at twilight, paint the blood of the lamb on the doorpost of their home, and eat the lamb with unleavened bread. They did all of this as God had commanded through Moses, and then God did exactly what He said He was going to do and sent the destroyer to bring judgment on Egypt. God *passed over* the doors which were marked with the blood of the lamb so that the destroyer did not and could not touch the faithful Israelites. The Passover was for the Israelites only, no foreigner was allowed to participate in it unless they were circumcised because circumcision was the symbol of the Israelite's special relationship with God and had been ever since God's covenant with their ancestor Abraham. In the middle of the night, they began walking out of Egypt and away from their lives as slaves. Then, on the third day, God parted the waters of the Red Sea and the Israelites walked through on dry ground, and, as a side note, even after over 400 years of oppressive slavery, nobody was sick or feeble as they left Egypt. (see Psalm 105:37) Finally, the waters closed back up to separate them from their enemies forever. This was the birth of their nation. There were most likely about two million of them, and they all made it through the waters of the Red Sea unscathed. This was a day that they were to remember and celebrate forever what God had done for them and how He had been faithful to deliver them from their enemies. In fact, this is the one event which is most frequently remembered in the Scriptures as the most significant day in their history as God's people.

Fast forward to the week of the Passover celebration in the last days of Jesus' life on earth. On the tenth day of the month, Jesus rode into Jerusalem presenting Himself as the unblemished Lamb who would be sacrificed. (see Matthew 21:1-11; Mark 11:1-11; Luke 19:28-44; John 12:12-19) Then, on the fourteenth day of the month, He was arrested and sentenced to be crucified. While He was on the cross being slaughtered, judgment was passed on Him in our place. Every enemy of mankind was placed upon Him including every sin, curse, sickness, punishment, and every oppression of the devil. The destroyer was allowed to destroy Jesus on the cross. He shed His blood and died, and He descended into the eternal fiery inferno, the pit of hell. (see Matthew 27; Mark 15; Luke 23; John 19) But then on the third day, God raised Him from the dead. At daybreak, He walked out of the tomb in an imperishable resurrection body to live forever. He was once and for all separated from His enemies. This was the birth of a whole new kind of people: a spiritual people, an eternal people who will never die. The stone of the tomb had been rolled away just like the waters of the Red Sea had been for the people of Israel. Jesus walked out of the grave and all of us who believe were included with Him. This is the event we remember every time we take communion to celebrate forever what God has done for us and how Jesus delivered us from all of our enemies.

> *{Jhn 1:29} 29 The next day John saw Jesus coming toward him and said,* **"Look, the Lamb of God, who takes away the sin of the world!**

> *{1Pe 1:18-19} 18 For you know that it was not with perishable things such as silver or gold that you were redeemed from the empty way of life handed down to you from your ancestors, 19 but with the* **precious blood of Christ, a lamb without blemish or defect**.

> *{1Co 5:7b} 7b.* **For Christ, our Passover lamb, has been sacrificed**.

The New Covenant

Knowing in advance that all of this was going to happen, Jesus explained and demonstrated the observance of this new eternal Passover celebration, which we know of today as communion. On the very night that Jesus was betrayed and handed over to be crucified, which was the night of Passover, He showed His disciples the way to remember and celebrate the New Covenant which would be established through His death and resurrection.

> *{Mat 26:26-28} 26 While they were eating,* **Jesus took bread**, *and when he had given thanks, he broke it and gave it to his disciples, saying,* **"Take and eat; this is my body."** *27 Then* **he took a cup**, *and when he had given thanks, he gave it to them, saying, "Drink from it, all of you. 28* **This is my blood of the covenant**, *which is poured out for many* **for the forgiveness of sins***. (see also Mark 14:17-25; Luke 22:14-30; John 13:21-30)*

A covenant is a legally binding agreement between two or more parties where one or the other or all of them are obligated to fulfill certain stated conditions. A covenant is an agreement of highest value, sealed with blood to symbolize that any party who does not meet the expressed terms will pay with their own blood, usually meaning they must be put to death. Covenants are serious business which should not be taken lightly. In Jesus' day, all of Israel was expectantly waiting for their Messiah to arrive to institute a New Covenant which was better than the covenant of the Law. In this New Covenant, they would know God and His ways in their own hearts, God would forgive all of their sins perpetually forever. Moreover, because their sins were forgiven, God would delight to bless them and deal with them as if they had never sinned. Their King would keep them constantly in God's good graces, and they would always be in right standing with God.

> *{Jer 31:31-34} 31 "The days are coming," declares the LORD, "when I will make a* **new covenant** *with the people of Israel and with the people of Judah. 32 It will not be like the covenant I made with their ancestors when I took them by the hand to lead them out of Egypt, because they broke*

*my covenant, though I was a husband to them," declares the LORD. 33 "**This is the covenant** I will make with the people of Israel after that time," declares the LORD. "**I will put my law in their minds and write it on their hearts. I will be their God, and they will be my people**. 34 No longer will they teach their neighbor, or say to one another, 'Know the LORD,' because **they will all know me**, from the least of them to the greatest," declares the LORD. "For **I will forgive their wickedness and will remember their sins no more**."*

*{Jer 32:40-41} 40 I will make **an everlasting covenant** with them: I will **never stop doing good to them**, and I will inspire them to fear me, so that they will never turn away from me. 41 **I will rejoice in doing them good** and will assuredly plant them in this land **with all my heart and soul**.*

*{Jer 33:15-16} 15 " 'In those days and at that time I will make a **righteous Branch sprout from David's line**; he will do what is just and right in the land. 16 In those days Judah will be saved and Jerusalem will live in safety. This is the name by which it will be called: **The LORD Our Righteousness**.'*

Jesus fulfilled these promises and established the New Covenant. He is the Righteous One born in the line of David who gives us right standing with God because of His righteousness. Through His sacrifice in our place, our sins are forgiven, and God deals with us as if we had never sinned and because of this, we are perpetually positioned for God's favor and good graces. Moreover, through the Holy Spirit, God's Laws are written upon our hearts and we can each know God for ourselves.

*{Heb 9:15} 15 For this reason **Christ is the mediator of a new covenant**, that those who are called may receive the promised eternal inheritance--now that **he has died as a ransom to set them free from the sins** committed under the first covenant.*

*{Heb 10:16-18} 16 [Quoting Jeremiah 31:31-34] "**This is the covenant** I will make with them after that time, says the Lord. **I will put my laws in their hearts, and I will write them on their minds**." 17 Then he adds: "**Their sins and lawless acts I will remember no more**." 18 And where these have been forgiven, **sacrifice for sin is no longer necessary**.*

Of course, Jesus knew in advance that the New Covenant would be established by the breaking of His body through suffering and death and the shedding of His blood on the cross. At an earlier point in His earthly ministry, He had explained more about the significance of His body and His blood to those who believe Him.

*{Jhn 6:35, 48-58} 35 Then Jesus declared, "**I am the bread of life.** Whoever comes to me will never go hungry, and whoever believes in me will never be thirsty... 48 **I am the bread of life**. 49 Your ancestors ate the manna in the wilderness, yet they died. 50 But here is the bread that comes down from heaven, which **anyone may eat and not die**. 51 **I am the living bread** that came down from heaven. **Whoever eats this bread will live forever. This bread is my flesh**, which I will give for the life of the world." 52 Then the Jews began to argue sharply among themselves, "How can this man give us his flesh to eat?" 53 Jesus said to them, "Very truly I tell you, **unless***

> *you eat the flesh of the Son of Man and drink his blood, you have no life in you. 54* ***Whoever eats my flesh and drinks my blood has eternal life****, and I will raise them up at the last day. 55* ***For my flesh is real food and my blood is real drink. 56 Whoever eats my flesh and drinks my blood remains in me, and I in them****. 57 Just as the living Father sent me and I live because of the Father, so* **the one who feeds on me will live because of me.** *58 This is the* **bread that came down from heaven.** *Your ancestors ate manna and died, but* **whoever feeds on this bread will live forever.***"

When we eat the bread and drink the wine of communion, we eat Jesus' body and drink His blood and, therefore, we have the life of Christ in us. The word for *life* here is *zoe* which means the actual *life of God* and the *vitality* of the giver of life Himself and we are, indeed taking into ourselves His resurrection life through faith. Unfortunately, this was one of, if not the most, controversial teachings that Jesus taught. In fact, many people who had followed Him up to this point deserted Him after He taught this. Why? Because His Jewish countrymen who were listening to Him say these things would have been deeply offended at drinking blood and eating flesh, both of which were strictly prohibited by their Laws. They knew the significance of blood in God's sight, and they knew the value of human life by God's decrees. (see Genesis 9:5-6; Leviticus 17:11-12) But unlike Jesus, they were not anticipating His death and resurrection, and they were not expecting that the promised New Covenant would be established by the blood of their King.

The Blood of Jesus

On the night of Passover and the Last Supper with His disciples, Jesus lifted the cup of wine and told them that it was His blood, shed for the forgiveness of sins. In truth, God places a high value on blood. This is because God is the author of life, and life is in the blood. Every significant act of God with man since Adam and his wife's error in Eden has involved blood, and blood is the only currency which can pay the way for a sinful person to have access to God. Moreover, every covenant God entered into with man was sealed with blood, and people throughout history who understood the significance of blood in God's sight demonstrated their worship through blood sacrifice.

> *{Lev 17:11} 11 For* **the life of a creature is in the blood***, and I have given it to you to make atonement for yourselves on the altar;* **it is the blood that makes atonement for one's life.**

After Adam and his wife ate from the wrong tree, it was God who shed the first blood on earth in order to cover their nakedness and relieve their shame. (see Genesis 3:21) Abel made a blood sacrifice to God, and it was accepted. (see Genesis 4:4) God made a covenant with Noah when he landed on dry ground after the flood. Noah sealed this by offering blood sacrifices to God of every kind of clean animal which was a magnificent offering considering that he was drawing from the small remnant of all living things. (see Genesis 8:20) God made a covenant with Abraham through a blood sacrifice of a bull, a goat, a ram, a turtle dove, and a pigeon, guaranteeing Abraham that a nation of people would descend from Him. (see Genesis 15:7-21) When God made a covenant with His people Israel, which is the Law of God, it included detailed regulations for carrying out blood sacrifices in order to maintain their right standing with Him.

(see Leviticus 1-17) When David brought the Ark of the Covenant into Jerusalem with the priests and Levites, he offered a sacrifice of blood after every six steps. (see 2 Samuel 6:13) When Solomon dedicated the Temple of God, he offered 22,000 oxen and 120,000 sheep. (see 1 Kings 8:63) That's a lot of blood.

Blood has a voice. After Cain killed Abel, God heard Abel's blood crying out from the ground pleading to be avenged for the injustice against him. (see Genesis 4:10) The blood of covenants says, *I promise.* The blood of sacrifices offered to God cries out for God's mercy. Jesus' blood also has a voice, but Jesus' blood cries out something altogether different. While Jesus shed His blood on the cross, He said, *Father, forgive them, for they know not what they are doing.* (see Luke 23:34) This is still what the blood of Jesus cries out for us today.

> *{Heb 12:24} 24 to Jesus the mediator of **a new covenant**, and to the **sprinkled blood that speaks a better word than the blood of Abel**.*

The blood of Jesus purchased us, redeemed us, covers over and forgives our sins, makes us holy, and purifies us continually:

> *{Act 20:28} 28 Keep watch over yourselves and all the flock of which the Holy Spirit has made you overseers. Be shepherds of the church of God, which **he bought with his own blood**.*

> *{Rom 3:25a} 25 God presented Christ as **a sacrifice of atonement, through the shedding of his blood**--to be received by faith.*

> *{Heb 13:12} And so Jesus also suffered outside the city gate to **make the people holy through his own blood**.*

> *{1Jo 1:7} But if we walk in the light, as he is in the light, we have fellowship with one another, and **the blood of Jesus, his Son, purifies us from all sin**.*

> *{Rev 1:5} and from Jesus Christ, who is the faithful witness, the firstborn from the dead, and the ruler of the kings of the earth. To him who loves us and has **freed us from our sins by his blood**,*

> *{Rev 5:9} And they sang a new song, saying: "You are worthy to take the scroll and to open its seals, because you were slain, and **with your blood you purchased for God persons from every tribe and language and people and nation**.*

The blood of Jesus gives us a clean record before God and right standing with Him, gives us peace with God, and brings us near to God:

> *{Rom 5:9} 9 Since we have now been **justified by his blood**, how much more shall we be saved from God's wrath through him!*

> *{Eph 1:7} 7 In him we have **redemption through his blood, the forgiveness of sins**, in accordance with the riches of God's grace*

> *{Col 1:20} 20 and through him to reconcile to himself all things, whether things on earth or things in heaven, **by making peace through his blood**, shed on the cross.*

> *{Eph 2:13} 13 But now in Christ Jesus you who once were far away have been **brought near by the blood of Christ**.*

The blood of Jesus cleanses our conscience and gives us confidence to enter God's presence:

> *{Heb 9:14} 14 How much more, then, will the **blood of Christ**, who through the eternal Spirit offered himself unblemished to God, **cleanse our consciences** from acts that lead to death, **so that we may serve the living God!***

> *{Heb 10:19} Therefore, brothers and sisters, since **we have confidence to enter the Most Holy Place by the blood of Jesus**,*

The blood of Jesus gives us victory over every enemy:

> *{Rev 12:11} They **triumphed over him by the blood of the Lamb and by the word of their testimony**; they did not love their lives so much as to shrink from death.*

Jesus also consecrated the heavenly Temple with His blood (which is worth more than the blood of 120,000 sheep) so that we can enter into the very throne room of God. We don't have time to get into this fully in this study but you can read more about it in Hebrews 9–10.

The Body of Christ

On the night of Passover with His disciples, Jesus first took bread and broke it in the same way that His body was about to be broken through death. Being Passover, He broke unleavened bread, made without yeast, which was a reminder for the Israelites of how they fled out of Egyptian slavery in such a hurry that their bread did not have time to rise. Biblically speaking, yeast symbolized sin, defilement, uncleanness, false religious teaching, and worldliness. Jesus knew from the beginning that His body was prepared especially by God to be offered as an unblemished sacrifice for all of mankind and was of infinitely higher value than any animal sacrifice. He was holy and without sin so that, metaphorically speaking, His life and character were completely unleavened or without yeast. Through His suffering, His physical body was punished with all of our punishment and was made sick with all of our sicknesses. Through the death of His physical body, we are reconciled to God, we are made holy, and we are freed from the Law of God, from sickness, and from death. Through faith in Christ, we stand before God as if we are perfect and without sin.

> *{Heb 10:5-7} 5 Therefore, when Christ came into the world, he said: "Sacrifice and offering you did not desire, but **a body you prepared for me**; 6 with burnt offerings and sin offerings you were not pleased. 7 Then I said, 'Here I am--it is written about me in the scroll-- **I have come to do your will, my God.**' "*

> *{Heb 10:10} And by that will, we have **been made holy through the sacrifice of the body of Jesus Christ** once for all.*

{Rom 7:4} So, my brothers and sisters**, you also died to the law through the body of Christ***, that you might belong to another, to him who was raised from the dead, in order that we might bear fruit for God.*

{Col 1:22} But now he has **reconciled you by Christ's physical body** through death **to present you holy in his sight, without blemish and free from accusation**

{1Pe 2:24} **"He himself bore our sins"** in his body on the cross*, so that we might die to sins and live for righteousness;* **"by his wounds you have been healed."**

But there's more. We've described what Jesus accomplished through His physical body which was crucified and resurrected but now that He is ascended to heaven and poured out the Holy Spirit, everyone who believes is a member of His spiritual Body, which is the Church.

{Col 1:18} And **he is the head of the body, the church***; he is the beginning and the firstborn from among the dead, so that in everything he might have the supremacy.*

{Eph 5:29-30} After all, no one ever hated their own body, but they feed and care for their body, just as Christ does the church-- **for we are members of his body***.*

{Eph 4:15} 15 Instead, speaking the truth in love, we will grow to become in every respect **the mature body of him who is the head, that is, Christ***.*

{Eph 1:22-23} And God placed all things under his feet and appointed him to be head over everything for **the church, which is his body***, the fullness of him who fills everything in every way.*

{Col 3:15 } Let the peace of Christ rule in your hearts, since **as members of one body** you were called to peace. And be thankful.*

Spiritually speaking, His Body was broken and is now in many pieces. When Jesus broke the bread on Passover night, He broke one loaf of bread and handed one piece to each person at the table with Him. In the same way, each of us as believers hold one piece of Jesus, and each one of us is one piece of the one loaf which is His spiritual Body in the earth.

{1Co 12:12-14} 12 Just as a body, though one, has many parts, but **all its many parts form one body, so it is with Christ***. 13 For we were all baptized by one Spirit* **so as to form one body**-- *whether Jews or Gentiles, slave or free--and we were all given the one Spirit to drink. 14 Even so* **the body is not made up of one part but of many***.*

{Rom 12:4-5} 4 For just as each of us has one body with many members, and these members do not all have the same function, 5 so **in Christ we, though many, form one body***, and each member belongs to all the others.*

{1Co 10:16-17} 16 Is not the cup of thanksgiving for which we give thanks a participation in the blood of Christ? And is not the **bread that we break a participation in the body of Christ***?*

*17 Because **there is one loaf, we, who are many, are one body, for we all share the one loaf.***

Think of a loaf of unleavened bread for a moment which is perfectly intact. Now, in your mind, take it and break it into as many pieces as you possibly can, all the way to crumbs. Is there any difference between one crumb and another? I didn't think so. This is the same way it is with us in the Body of Christ. Each one of us is a crumb from the same loaf. There is no difference between one crumb and another, and all crumbs are of equal importance in the whole loaf. How can there be any superiority from one cracker to another? There isn't. So when a fellow believer sins against us, we can have mercy on them and pray *Forgive them, God, they're just a cracker!* We are all just crackers from the same loaf of bread. Accordingly, no matter what our race, heritage, nationality or social status may be, and no matter what past we come from or what we may have done or not done, we are the same in Christ. We are a whole new people group. We are Christians.

> {Gal 3:28} 28 ***There is neither Jew nor Gentile, neither slave nor free, nor is there male and female**, for you are all one in Christ Jesus.*

> {Rom 3:22} 22 *This righteousness is given through faith in Jesus Christ to all who believe. **There is no difference between Jew and Gentile**,*

> {1Co 12:13} 13 *For we were all baptized by one Spirit so as to form one body--**whether Jews or Gentiles, slave or free**--and we were all given the one Spirit to drink.*

One New Man

On the anniversary of Israel's birth as a nation, at the same time that they had walked through the Red Sea, Jesus walked out of the tomb and gave birth to a whole new species of humanity. Through our faith in Him, we who believe are a new creation, a new species in the earth, a new generation, a new nation born through the resurrection of Christ. Under the Old Covenant, only the nation of Israel had a relationship with God, and everyone else (collectively referred to as Gentiles, foreigners, and strangers) was completely excluded from the covenant and its blessings unless they were circumcised. But now, in Christ, there is no separation between Jews and Gentiles and no difference between one believer and another. In the New Covenant, we are spiritually circumcised because our old Adamic nature has been rolled away. When we place our faith in Christ, we change from being the generation of the first Adam who sinned, to being the generation of the second Adam, who is Jesus, the perfect Son of God. Through faith, we are transformed from being an old type of humanity to being a new type of humanity, and we become born again sons and daughters of God. We are a new creation and baptism symbolically expresses our rebirth into this new species of humanity.

> {Eph 2:15-19} 15 *by setting aside in his flesh the law with its commands and regulations. **His purpose was to create in himself <u>one new humanity</u> out of the two, thus making peace, 16 and in one body to reconcile both of them to God through the cross, by which he put to death their hostility**. 17 He came and preached peace to you who were far away and peace to those who were near. 18 For **through him we both have access to the Father by one Spirit**.*

*19 Consequently, **you are no longer foreigners and strangers, but fellow citizens with God's people and also members of his household**,*

*{Col 2:11-12} 11 **In him you were also circumcised** with a circumcision not performed by human hands. **Your whole self ruled by the flesh was put off when you were circumcised by Christ**, 12 having been buried with him in baptism, in which you were also raised with him through your faith in the working of God, who raised him from the dead.*

In fact, in the same way that Israel is different from every other nation on earth under the Old Covenant because of their special relationship with God, now through the New Covenant, the whole Body of Christ is a different type of people than everyone else on earth because of our relationship with God through Christ. The word for Church in Greek is *ekklesia* which literally means *a called out people*. God has called us out, or chosen us, from every nation and background and ethnicity to participate in this new people in Christ. We collectively are appointed to worship Him, serve Him, and be blessed by Him. In the same way that God made a distinction between the people of Israel and the people of Egypt at the original Passover because of the blood of the lamb, God now makes a distinction between those who believe in Christ and those who do not believe based on their faith in the blood of Jesus.

*{Rev 5:9-10} 9 And they sang a new song, saying: "You are worthy to take the scroll and to open its seals, because you were slain, and **with your blood you purchased for God persons from every tribe and language and people and nation**. 10 You have made them to be **a kingdom and priests to serve our God**, and they will reign on the earth."*

*{1Pe 2:9-10} 9 But you are **a chosen people, a royal priesthood, a holy nation**, God's special possession, that you may declare the praises of him who called you out of darkness into his wonderful light. 10 Once you were not a people, but **now you are the people of God**; once you had not received mercy, but now you have received mercy.*

I do not express this difference to be superior or exclusionary because Christ died for all mankind, and it is God's desire for everyone to be included and saved through Him. I say all of this to express what we in the Body of Christ have in common with each other and that this commonality is eternally more significant than any other human bond, loyalty, ethnicity, or nationality. In Christ we are one, from one loaf of bread, we all have the same heart – the Holy Spirit, the same King - Jesus, and the same Father – God. This *oneness* is so important that Jesus passionately prayed for us as believers to function in unity with one another. This harmony among us is one of the ways by which those who do not know Christ as their Savior may be drawn in to know Him.

*{Jhn 17:20-23} 20 "My prayer is not for them alone. I pray also for those who will believe in me through their message, 21 **that all of them may be one**, Father, just as you are in me and I am in you. May they also be in us so that the world may believe that you have sent me. 22 I have given them the glory that you gave me, **that they may be one as we are one**-- 23 I in them and you in me--**so that they may be brought to complete unity**. Then the world will know that you sent me and have loved them even as you have loved me.*

Additionally, the word for fellowship in Greek is *koinonia* which means *association, community,* or *communion* with each member holding an essential piece of the whole. The magnitude of *koinonia* is not just casual come and go and getting together. Rather, it is fellowship where the whole is not whole if a single piece is missing. Recall the loaf of bread which was broken down to the crumbs. If a single crumb of that loaf is missing, it is not the whole loaf. In the same way, every believer is essential to the Body of Christ and if one person is missing, then the Body is not whole. We don't have a lot of time to dig deeper into this so for further study, see Romans 12 and 1 Corinthians 12.

> {1Co 12:27} 27 Now **you are the body of Christ**, and **each one of you is a part of it**.

> {Rom 12:4-5} 4 For just as each of us has one body with many members, and these members do not all have the same function, 5 so in Christ we, though many, **form one body, and each member belongs to all the others**.

Lastly, the word most often used in the New Testament to address the people of the Church, is *brethren* which is also translated *brothers and sisters*. This word indicates people who *came out of the same womb* and signifies people of the *same bloodline, ancestor, or people group*. Because we have been born again through faith in Christ, believers all come out of the same womb (the tomb of Christ) and we are brothers and sisters and children of God. Because of the blood of Christ, believers all share the same bloodline which is Jesus' blood, shed for the forgiveness of our sins. Because His body was broken for us, believers all belong to a new people group that has been called out from every nation on the earth. This connects us to one another in a profoundly significant and eternal bond.

Communion

The Jews observe Passover every year to remember and celebrate the most significant event in their history as God's people, when God delivered them from bondage and slavery to freedom. In the same way, we take communion as often as we like in order to remember and celebrate what Jesus Christ accomplished for us through His death and resurrection. We remember that, through the breaking of His body and the shedding of His blood, He delivered us from the bondage of sin and death to absolute freedom through faith in Him. More than that, He made us to be a special people of God.

> {1Co 11:23-26} 23 For I received from the Lord what I also passed on to you: The Lord Jesus, on the night he was betrayed, took bread, 24 and when he had given thanks, he broke it and said, **"This is my body, which is for you; do this in remembrance of me."** 25 In the same way, after supper he took the cup, saying, **"This cup is the new covenant in my blood; do this, whenever you drink it, in remembrance of me."** 26 For whenever you eat this bread and drink this cup, you proclaim the Lord's death until he comes.

When we are assembled together, we eat the broken bread to remember that Christ's body was a sacrifice for us and we partake knowing that each one of us is a part of the Body of Christ. We drink the cup to remember that Christ's blood was shed for the forgiveness of our sins while believing that this gives us a perfect record before God no matter what we have or have not done. It is a cup of blessing, thanksgiving, and celebration of the New Covenant which Jesus Christ established for us. (see 1 Corinthians 10:16) It does not have to be somber and in fact, we should rejoice! We are encouraged to *examine ourselves* before partaking communion to be certain that we are believing and receiving in our hearts the fullness of all that Christ accomplished for us through His sacrifice. When we take communion, we remember that, even at our worst, Christ accepted us, died in our place, and included us in His Body not because of anything we have done to deserve it and not because of our piety or worthiness but, because of His love for us.

What was your life like before you knew Jesus as your Lord and Savior? How has your life changed since you placed your faith in Jesus? How many times has He rescued you from situations which seemed hopeless? The truth is that all of us in Christ were once dead in our sins, oppressed and enslaved by fears, insecurities, addictions, torments, and ailments, and all of us in Christ have been rescued by Him time and time again. He delivered us from ourselves just like He delivered the Israelites from Egypt. He delivered us, healed us, set us free, gave us peace, and unconditionally continues to love us, even when we were at our worst. More than that, we remember that Jesus' body was broken for what we are going through today and that we are never alone. We remember that His blood was shed for anything that is hindering us or ailing us today. His broken body and shed blood are just as effective today as they were when we first began in faith. Through faith in Jesus, we have been made new, and we are made new again and again. Hallelujah!

Therefore, if you are a believer in Jesus Christ as your Lord and Savior, then no matter what is ailing or afflicting you and no matter what sin you may have in your life, receive God's forgiveness afresh through Jesus' sacrifice and come and take communion. In fact, all the more so if you have afflictions, ailments, and sins, then you need communion to help you remember what Jesus accomplished for you. Take communion knowing that, until He returns, His sacrifice is sufficient for you, His mercies for you are new every morning, and you are a part of His very special people. Remember. Receive it. And rejoice!

CHAPTER 4
Primer: Trials

In the Book of Acts, followers of Christ encountered various forms of intense opposition to the Gospel message. In truth, during His ministry, Jesus warned His followers that this antagonism would arise so that trials would not lead them astray from the true faith. Let's take a look at what Jesus taught about these hostilities so that we are empowered to respond the way that the first disciples of Christ did in the Book of Acts.

Living Sacrifice

Every trial we face as followers of Christ is about one thing – it is a test of whether we really believe that God loves us and that His plans for us are good. Every time things happen in our lives which could cause us to doubt God's love for us in Christ, it is a new opportunity to believe afresh that Jesus truly is who He says He is, that His sacrifice was sufficient for all that we face, and that He will faithfully fulfill everything that He has promised. Undoubtedly, all of us will endure all sorts of suffering in our lives. However, when we hear the heart of God asking us through these trials and the pain *Do you believe that I am good?*, *Do you believe that I love you?*, *Do you believe that I am enough?*, *Do you believe what I have promised you?*, and *Do you believe that I have finished it?* let us keep our eyes on Jesus and our minds on heaven and resoundingly answer back to Him, *Yes!*

> *{1Pe 1:6-7} 6 In all this you greatly rejoice, though now **for a little while you may have had to suffer grief in all kinds of trials**. 7 These have come **so that the proven genuineness of your faith**--of greater worth than gold, which perishes even though refined by fire--**may result in praise, glory and honor when Jesus Christ is revealed**.*

We serve a King who came willingly to lay down His life as a sacrifice to God so that we could be with Him for eternity. Now, He tells us to go and do likewise for others so that they may be with us in heaven and in the age to come.

> *{Rom 12:1} 1 Therefore, I urge you, brothers and sisters, in view of God's mercy, **to offer your bodies as a living sacrifice**, holy and pleasing to God--**this is your true and proper worship**.*

> *{2Ti 2:10} 10 Therefore I **endure everything for the sake of the elect, that they too may obtain the salvation** that is in Christ Jesus, with eternal glory.*

This said, I am not writing this to encourage anybody to recklessly throw themselves in the face of danger, and I certainly do not want to inspire any martyr complexes. Rather, I believe that it is important for all of us as Christ followers to be prepared and strengthened to follow Him to the fullest, no matter the cost. Nobody is willing to suffer or even die for something or someone that they do not truly believe.

For this reason, trials simply serve as a test of what we do truly believe by revealing how we respond when push comes to shove.

Different Purpose

Before we go even one step further, let us clarify one major difference between Jesus' suffering and death and what we do when we offer ourselves as living sacrifices to God. Jesus is the only One appointed by God who could ever suffer and die for our sins and accomplish God's plan of salvation. You and I cannot suffer and die to pay for the sins of ourselves or others. We may suffer for Christ, and some of us may even be martyred for our faith in Jesus, but our wounds and our death have no sacrificial atoning value. God appointed Jesus exclusively for this task, and He completed it. He came the first time to provide the way of salvation through faith in Him, and He is returning to collect all of us who have believed Him and spare us from the wrath of God which is still yet to come.

> {Heb 10:14} 14 For **by one sacrifice** he has made perfect forever those who are being made holy.

> {Heb 9:27-28} 27 Just as people are destined to die once, and after that to face judgment, 28 so **Christ was sacrificed once to take away the sins of many;** and he will appear a second **time**, not to bear sin, but to **bring salvation to those who are waiting for him**.

Think of it this way: back in the first several generations of man when God knew that He had to wash all creation by a massive flood because of the sin of mankind, He appointed a man named Noah to build a humongous boat called an Ark so that those who believed and were on the boat with Noah would be spared from the flood. When Jesus came the first time, metaphorically speaking, He built the Ark through His life, death, and resurrection to rescue all of us who place our faith in Him. Now, as believers in Christ, we are appointed by Him for our own task. He sends us out to tell everyone to, figuratively, get on the boat through faith in Him in order to be spared from the judgment to come, which will not be by water but by fire.

> {2Pe 3:6-7} 6 By these waters also the world of that time was deluged and destroyed. 7 By the same word the **present heavens and earth are reserved for fire,** being kept for the **day of judgment** and **destruction of the ungodly**.

Even though our task is slightly different than what Jesus was sent by God to do, we are sent by Jesus to do our task by being like Him and doing the things He did. This means that our purpose is similar enough to His that we can expect to face the same type of opposition that He faced. Fortunately, the way He endured through trials gave us an example which demonstrated righteousness and love in the face of the most horrific antagonism.

> {Jhn 15:18-21} 18 "If the world hates you, **keep in mind that it hated me first.** 19 If you belonged to the world, it would love you as its own. As it is, you do not belong to the world, but I have chosen you out of the world. That is why the world hates you. 20 Remember what I told you: '**A servant is not greater than his master**.' If they persecuted me, **they will persecute you**

*also. If they obeyed my teaching, they will obey yours also. 21 **They will treat you this way because of my name**, for they do not know the one who sent me.*

*{1Pe 4:1} 1 Therefore, **since Christ suffered** in his body, **arm yourselves also with the same attitude**, because whoever suffers in the body is done with sin.*

*{1Pe 2:21} 21 To this you were called, because Christ suffered for you, **leaving you an example, that you should follow in his steps**.*

Ok, now that we've clarified this, we can keep going.

Suffering for Doing Right

Before we look at Jesus' example for persevering through trials, let's clear out a few more things. Jesus was without sin, He always spoke the truth, and His life was a demonstration of perfect love. Therefore, He was not crucified for being a bad person, for deceit or trickery, or because He deserved it. He came to carry out God's fore-ordained purpose for Him, and He laid down His life in perfect submission to God, the God-appointed religious leaders, and the governing powers in the world. Accordingly, He did not suffer for doing wrong but for doing right. In contrast, we will be far more likely to do wrong things than Jesus ever could have. However, suffering for doing wrong or for not submitting to the governing authorities is not quite the same as suffering for doing right.

*{1Pe 2:19-20} 19 For it is commendable if someone bears up under **the pain of unjust suffering because they are conscious of God**. 20 But how is it to your credit if you **receive a beating for doing wrong and endure it**? But if you suffer for doing good and you endure it, **this is commendable before God.***

*{1 Pe 3:17} 17 For it is better, if it is God's will, to **suffer for doing good than for doing evil**.*

*{1Pe 4:15, 19} 15 **If you suffer, it should not be as a murderer or thief or any other kind of criminal, or even as a meddler**. ... 19 So then, those who suffer according to God's will should commit themselves to their faithful Creator and **continue to do good**.*

Furthermore, unless the governing authorities demand that we renounce our faith in Christ in order to submit to them or to their laws, we cannot use our faith as an excuse for breaking the law. As an example, Jesus was perfectly obedient to the God-appointed governing powers in the world in His day and paid His taxes to Caesar. (Matthew 22:21; Mark 12:17; Luke 20:25) He did not have to do this because He is the King above all kings and the One who appoints all rulers in the world, meaning that He paid His taxes to someone under His authority. Additionally, Jesus paid the Temple tax to the God-appointed religious authorities. He did not have to do this because He was the Son of God, not a Temple servant, meaning that He paid "rent" to His Father's tenants. (Matthew 17:24-27) Even though Jesus did not have to do these things, He did them willingly in order to not offend the governing authorities or incite any form of doctrinal rebellion among His followers. He did not come to start a political or religious insurgence but to usher in the Kingdom of God.

> *{Rom 13:1} 1 Let everyone* **be subject to the governing authorities**, *for there is no authority except that which God has established. The* **authorities that exist have been established by God**.

> *{1Pe 2:13-14} 13* **Submit yourselves for the Lord's sake to every human authority***: whether to the emperor, as the supreme authority, 14 or to governors, who are sent by him to punish those who do wrong and to commend those who do right.*

Moreover, Jesus did not suffer because He followed some perverse or bizarre religious teaching or for unduly subjecting Himself to suffering for the sake of attaining favor with God. He obeyed the Law of God perfectly because He was His Father's Son and reflected His Father's character, not due to religious observance. Jesus suffered at the hands of men while remaining true to His Father's purpose, no matter the cost.

All of this is to say that, when we suffer for righteousness' sake, our suffering will be like Christ's, not for doing wrong but for doing right. Jesus suffered because He willingly laid down His life as the ultimate expression of selfless love. Accordingly, as we lay our lives down as living sacrifices, we demonstrate the love of Christ in our hearts.

> *{Jhn 15:13} 13* **Greater love has no one than this: to lay down one's life for one's friends***.*

> *{Gal 5:6b} 6b The only thing that counts is* **faith expressing itself through love***.*

The Example Jesus Set

Jesus responded righteously to every trial that He faced. He did so because He lived by the abiding direction of the Holy Spirit which always led Him in the will of God. Before Jesus began His ministry, He was led by the Holy Spirit into the wilderness to be tempted by the devil for 40 days. (see Matthew 4:1-11; Mark 1:12-13; Luke 4:1-13) The word for *tempt* can also be translated *test* and, during this time, the devil tested Jesus with many tests. We can safely assume that these tests included every form of *Did God really say…?* in addition to every possible provocation to sin and ungodliness. Through all of this testing, Jesus never sinned. He was empowered by the nature of God within Him, the Holy Spirit, and He declared the Scriptures as a weapon of truth against the lies of the enemy. Although the enemy was attempting to prove that Jesus was not the Son of God, instead these tests proved Jesus to be the Son of God, perfect, holy, blameless and without sin.

> *{Heb 4:15} 15 For we do not have a high priest who is unable to empathize with our weaknesses, but we have one who* **has been tempted [tested] in every way***, just as we are--***yet he did not sin***.*

Throughout His ministry, Jesus was hated by the religious leaders who constantly attempted to trap Him into error or deception because they were offended by Jesus and jealous of Him. They did not understand how He could possibly be the promised Messiah so they challenged Him, tested Him, and attempted to kill Him several times. Even though they studied the Scriptures extensively, they could not wrap their minds around the ways of God when their promised Messiah was walking right in front of them. Jesus simply but strongly rebuked the religious leaders for their error. He did not respond to them at their level but at a much higher level while continuing in perfect submitted obedience to God's true standard of holiness. The religious leaders, in contrast, were rendered incapable of answering His questions.

> *{Pro 26:4-5}* 4 **Do not answer a fool** *according to his folly, or you yourself will be just like him.* 5 **Answer a fool according** *to his folly, or he will be wise in his own eyes.*

> *{Jhn 3:10}* 10 *"You are Israel's teacher," said Jesus, "and* **do you not understand these things?**

> *{Jhn 5:39-40}* 39 **You study the Scriptures diligently** *because you think that in them you have eternal life.* **These are the very Scriptures that testify about me**, *40 yet you refuse to come to me to have life.*

> *{Mat 22:46}* 46 **No one could say a word in reply**, *and from that day on* **no one dared to ask him any more questions.**

Additionally, Jesus pointed out how far the religious leaders had strayed from the heart and purpose of God. In the passages of John Chapters 9 and 10, religious people were on a sin-hunt to discover the sin-based reason behind why a man had been born blind. Based on their religious upbringing, they figured that the blind man must be cursed by God for something he did or generationally cursed because of something his parents did. They believed that sickness was God's will for this man and that God had allowed it because of something that he had done. Jesus, on the other hand, healed the blind man in love and compassion, regardless of the reason for his condition. This infuriated the religious leaders because, if it was God's will for this man to be ill, then Jesus had defied the will of God by healing him. To add insult to injury, it was a Sabbath, so this was a double whammy of rebellion in their view. Notably, religious teaching is always condemning rather than life-giving and always looks to blame the sufferer rather than help or show compassion. The *thief* Jesus spoke of in this passage is the religious teachers and their false teachings. Religion *steals* our fellowship with God, *kills* us through condemnation, and *destroys* our lives through shame and dejection. In contrast, Jesus came with compassion and grace so that we may be reconnected with God, He came not to judge us but to save us, and He took our shame and humiliation upon Himself on the cross.

> *{Jhn 10:10}* 10 **The thief comes only to steal and kill and destroy; I have come that they may have life, and have it to the full.**

Jesus also rebuked the religious leaders for the hypocrisy revealed by the importance that they placed on their own traditions. The ordinances which they had put in place took higher precedent for obedience and observance than the actual Law of God. In fact, the religious leaders considered their man-made rules and traditions to be equal with God's Law.

> *{Mar 7:6-9}* 6 *He replied, "Isaiah was right when he prophesied about you hypocrites; as it is written: " 'These people honor me with their lips, but their hearts are far from me. 7 They worship me in vain; their teachings are merely human rules.' 8* **You have let go of the commands of**

God and are holding on to human traditions." 9 And he continued, "You have a fine way of setting aside the commands of God in order to observe your own traditions!

Lastly, when the religious leaders demanded a sign from Jesus, He refused to indulge their requirement. He knew that, even though He had performed many miraculous signs, no sign would be enough to convince them. Additionally, when they questioned His authority and where it came from, He refused to answer.

> *{Mat 12:39} 39 He answered, "A wicked and adulterous generation asks for a sign!* **But none will be given** *it except the sign of the prophet Jonah. (see also Mark 8:12; Luke 11:29)*

> *{Luk 16:31} 31 "He said to him, 'If they do not listen to Moses and the Prophets,* **they will not be convinced even if someone rises from the dead.'** *"*

> *{Luk 20:8} 8 Jesus said, "***Neither will I tell you by what authority** *I am doing these things."*

During His ministry, Jesus was also surrounded by people who wanted to believe Him, but somehow they could not quite get fully onboard in their faith. In gentleness and mercy, Jesus' most common expression to followers like these was *O, you of little faith,* which chided them for their unbelief. He also made comments here and there about their hard hearts or the fact that they were slow to believe. On a few occasions, with a sigh of exasperation, Jesus asked *Do you still not believe?* To anyone who proclaimed their undying loyalty and devotion, Jesus always raised the bar to the ultimate price. He made it clear in no uncertain terms that following Him costs everything and that His followers should *count the cost* before declaring allegiance. (see Luke 14:25-33) When He taught things like this, which were difficult for His followers to comprehend, many people said that He had lost His mind, accused Him of being evil, or deserted Him. He did not defend Himself or demand their loyalty or submission. Instead, He let them go their own way. Jesus always let the Scriptures and the works of God defend Him. In fact, He knew from the start that, when the time came for His greatest trial, everyone would reject and abandon Him because they did not understand God's ways.

> *{Jhn 10:37-38} 37* **Do not believe me unless I do the works of my Father.** *38 But if I do them, even though you do not believe me,* **believe the works,** *that you may know and understand that the Father is in me, and I in the Father." (see also John 5:36, 10:25, 14:11)*

> *{Luk 7:22-23} 22 So he replied to the messengers, "Go back and report to John* **what you have seen and heard:** *The blind receive sight, the lame walk, those who have leprosy are cleansed, the deaf hear, the dead are raised, and the good news is proclaimed to the poor. 23* **Blessed is anyone who does not stumble on account of me."** *(see also Matthew 11:6)*

> *{Jhn 6:60-61, 66-67} 60 On hearing it, many of his disciples said, "This is a hard teaching. Who can accept it?" 61 Aware that his disciples were grumbling about this, Jesus said to them, "***Does this offend you?** *... 66 From this time* **many of his disciples turned back and no longer followed him.** *67 "You do not want to leave too, do you?" Jesus asked the Twelve.*

> *{Mat 26:31} 31 Then Jesus told them, "This very night **you will all fall away on account of me, for it is written**: " 'I will strike the shepherd, and the sheep of the flock will be scattered.' (see also Mark 14:27, John 16:32, quoting Zechariah 13:7)*

In His greatest trial, Jesus was betrayed by a close friend, turned over to the religious authorities, offered up to the governing world powers, given a mock trial which scarcely complied with any form of order or legal standards, and was sentenced to death at the hands of the very people that He came to save. The time had come for Jesus to fulfill the Scriptures written about His suffering and death so He did not rebuke or resist, nor would He allow any of His followers to do so. (see Matthew 26:52; John 18:11) After intense prayer in the Garden of Gethsemane where He petitioned God for any other way for His wrath (the cup of God's wrath) to be satisfied, Jesus submitted Himself to the cross and crucifixion. In order to fulfill God's purpose, Jesus willingly allowed the religious system, the world powers, and the evil one himself to have dominion and rulership over Him. He offered Himself as a sacrifice.

> *{Luk 22:42, 44, 52-53} 42 "Father, if you are willing, **take this cup from me; yet not my will, but yours be done**." ... 44 And being in anguish, he prayed more earnestly, and his sweat was like drops of blood falling to the ground. ... 52 Then Jesus said to the chief priests, the officers of the temple guard, and the elders, who had come for him, "Am I leading a rebellion, that you have come with swords and clubs? 53 Every day I was with you in the temple courts, and you did not lay a hand on me. **But this is your hour--when darkness reigns**."*

Jesus was led like a lamb to the slaughter and did not open His mouth. (see Isaiah 53:7) Throughout His illegitimately conducted arrest and trial, when Jesus stood before the religious leaders, before Pilate, before Herod, and before the people of Israel and the masses of the world, He never defended Himself.

> *{Mat 27:12} 12 When he was accused by the **chief priests and the elders, he gave no answer**.*

> *{Mar 15:5} 5 But **Jesus still made no reply**, and **Pilate** was amazed.*

> *{Luk 23:8-9} 8 When **Herod** saw Jesus, he was greatly pleased, because for a long time he had been wanting to see him. From what he had heard about him, he hoped to see him perform a sign of some sort. 9 He plied him with many questions, but **Jesus gave him no answer**.*

> *{Mat 27:25} 25 **All the people** answered, "His blood is on us and on our children!"*

Jesus willingly allowed darkness to have its glory for a moment and He took upon Himself all of the wrath, punishment, curse, sickness, and evil oppression of the world. He did so because He knew the promises of God pertaining to His resurrection to eternal life and His eternal rewards. He knew the will of God from before the foundation of the earth.

> *{Rev 13:8} 8 All inhabitants of the earth will worship the beast--all whose names have not been written in the Lamb's book of life, **the Lamb who was slain from the creation of the world**.*

> *{Phl 2:6-8} 6 Who, **being in very nature God**, did not consider equality with God something to be used to his own advantage; 7 rather, **he made himself nothing** by taking the very nature of a*

*servant, being made in human likeness. 8 And being found in appearance as a man, **he humbled himself by becoming obedient to death-- even death on a cross!***

*{Heb 12:2b} 2b **For the joy set before him he endured the cross**, **scorning its shame**, and sat down at the right hand of the throne of God.*

Jesus counted the cost before leaving the comforts of Heaven to fulfill His task from God, just as He told His followers to do. He counted the cost of laying down His own life before going to the cross and He *scorned the shame*. In the Greek, *scorned* means *to think little of*, meaning that Jesus knew the cost and thought it was a small price to pay in order to complete the work of God and receive the promised eternal rewards. Jesus demonstrated perfect faith because He believed the promises from the Scriptures that God would be faithful to resurrect Him on the third day. He also demonstrated perfect love and blameless compassion because He prayed for His enemies, for those who persecuted Him, and for the very ones who were murdering Him. He blessed them without animosity or contention.

*{Luk 23:34a} 34a Jesus said, "**Father, forgive them, for they do not know what they are doing**."*

Most importantly, through all of this and culminating in His cry of *It is finished!* Jesus did not doubt God's love for Him. He did not doubt His Father's ability to do all that He had promised and planned. Jesus knew God was worthy of His submission, His hope, His faith, His love, and His sacrifice. By the power of the Holy Spirit, Jesus was empowered to respond rightly throughout every trial and test, even unto death. This perfect demonstration of love proved that Jesus is the Son of God, made in the likeness of God, who is love. (see 1 John 4:8) Moreover, Jesus, the Son of Man, endured through His trials in perfect faith and right conduct in human flesh like ours. Praise God that we have such a compassionate High Priest! (see Hebrews 4:15) He learned obedience to God by following His divine nature, the indwelling Holy Spirit, rather than obeying His flesh and what it desired. (see Hebrews 5:7-8) Therefore, as we follow Jesus, not by outward imitation but by the inward leading of the Holy Spirit, we can anticipate that the Holy Spirit will guide us to respond rightly no matter what we face.

Types of Testing

There are two primary types of testing which we will encounter as Christ followers. The first is a *negative test* in which the thing being tested is expected to fail and may even be tested in increasing levels of severity until it fails. The second is a *positive test* for genuineness in which the thing being tested is expected to be proven true. In the New Testament Greek, the words for this are *peirazo* and *dokimazo*, respectively.

God never tests us negatively. (see James 1:13) Trials of life *negatively test* us through hardship, and the enemy *negatively tests* us through provocation to sin, through lies, and through deception, distraction, and accusation. For example, when Jesus was in the wilderness being tested by satan, He was being *negatively tested* [*peirazo*] in every possible way and yet proved genuine in character and faith. Another example of *negative testing* is when Jesus warned Peter that satan had asked to *sift him like wheat*. (see Luke 22:31) This was an expression used for the *negative testing* that the enemy conducts, defined as *an inward agitation to try one's faith to the verge of overthrow.* We are not going to go into that whole story because it was before the resurrection and before the Holy Spirit was poured out. The point is that when we endure *negative testing* by the enemy, his aim is to lure us into failure in our character and our beliefs through all means available in increasing levels of pressure until failure is accomplished. Pre-Holy Spirit, Peter did, in fact, fail the test. However, post-resurrection and with the indwelling Holy Spirit, Peter went on to be one of the great strengtheners of the Church. He wrote 1 Peter, which addresses the various trials that we face from the world and unbelievers, and 2 Peter, which addresses the various trials that we face from false teachings within our midst.

When we are being *negatively tested*, the enemy launches attacks of every form of *Did God really say…?* into our lives. Through temptation, hardship, sickness, and seemingly unfulfilled promises of God, our faith and character are tested. Often it seems like this happens in increasing measures of difficulty and oppression or in many different areas of our lives at one time, pushing us beyond what we can endure on our own. Indeed, the enemy is trying to push us to the point of failure. At the same time, lies against God seem to multiply in our mind, particularly against His goodness, love, sufficiency, and promises. Mostly, the lies are against the fact that Christ completed the work of *salvation* including *salvation, deliverance, healing, and sustenance* on the cross and through His resurrection once and for all. Additionally, the enemy plants lies about ourselves in our own minds in order to weary us with discouragement, principally through thoughts of guilt, shame, and hopelessness, especially if we seem to be waiting a long time for God's promises to come to pass. Typically, these lies tell us that we deserve hardship because of something that we have done and are accompanied by thoughts that it is never going to be different for us because of something we are not doing. This said, when these *negative tests* and temptations happen in our lives we can respond rightly by following the direction of the Holy Spirit. In the same way that Jesus and Holy Spirit filled Peter responded to trials, when we live by the Holy Spirit's direction, our faith and character will be proven genuine.

> {1Co 10:12-13} 12 *So, if you think you are standing firm, be careful that you don't fall! 13 No* **temptation [peirasmos]** *has overtaken you except what is common to mankind. And God is faithful; he will not let you be* **tempted [peirazo] beyond what you can bear.** *But* **when you are tempted [peirasmos], he will also provide a way out so that you can endure it.**

In addition to that, we are exhorted to *positively test* ourselves to prove [*dokimazo*] that our faith is genuine. Jesus never had to do this kind of testing because He was the genuine article. However, this type of *positive testing* is encouraged in order to prove the character of anyone nominated to be a deacon of the Church – they must demonstrate that they are the real deal. (see 1 Timothy 3:10) More significantly, before we partake of communion, ingesting the very blood and body of Jesus *because we believe* that He is Lord, we are encouraged to *positively test* or examine [*dokimazo*] ourselves to see if we are truly believing all that He has accomplished for us. (see 1 Corinthians 11:28-30) In fact, some believers were experiencing weakness, sickness, and even death because they were not fully perceiving the body and blood of Jesus and believing all that Christ had accomplished for them. This could also mean that, perhaps, some of the trials that we experience are because we are not fully perceiving and believing what Jesus accomplished for us through His life, death, and resurrection. Therefore, we should *positively test* ourselves. Is our faith the genuine article?

Interestingly, these two types of testing can also be beautifully coupled together as we grow in the knowledge of God's grace towards us. Unlike Jesus, when we are *negatively tested*, sometimes we fail. There are times when we give into temptation or we stumble into sin or error. It is exactly at these times when we may repent and return again to Jesus. He cried out, *It is finished!* meaning that His sacrifice was sufficient to cover all of our stumbling. Accordingly, we can continue to press on in His purposes for us in spite of our failures. This is not a flippant or casual returning but a deep inner working in our hearts when we recognize that, even when we have been *negatively tested* to the point of personal catastrophe, God's grace is still unquestionably extended to us through faith in Jesus and what He did for us. Then, we have the opportunity to *positively test* ourselves and ask ourselves afresh if we really believe that Jesus finished it and that we are accepted by God because of Jesus in spite of our stumbling.

For instance, I was already deep into my walk of faith with Jesus and was experiencing much *negative testing* in every area of my life including relationships, finances, health, purpose, and reputation. Lies against me and against God's character were abounding. (see the Book of Job) Without offering you any excuse, I admit that I was pressed to the point of failure. It was as if the enemy placed a giant banana peel on my spiritual path and, even though I saw it, I stepped on it, slipped, did a gigantic whoop-de-do back-flip and landed flat on my face. While I was still metaphorically on my face, I knew I had royally messed up and fallen short of God's standard. I was deeply sorry for what I had done. In this same moment, the Lord spoke to me through the Holy Spirit reminding me that *There is now therefore no condemnation for those who are in Christ Jesus.* (see Romans 8:1) My heart was filled again with God's acceptance of me in spite of my sin. By God's mercy and grace, I was able to get back up, dust myself off, remove myself from the situation, and continue on in the Lord's purpose for me. I knew that God was not holding this incident against me in any way, that my sin had not restricted my access to Him, had not changed His purpose for my life, and that I would not suffer consequences from Him because of what I had done. Because of Jesus, God is for us at all times and not against us even though we mess up. (see Romans 8:31) I knew this truth all over again to the depth of my being. Through this, my faith was proven genuine in Christ and, as a side note, I have not stumbled in that way again.

In fact, this is the whole purpose of every trial. Whether *positive testing* or *negative testing* and whether a test of character or steadfastness, the genuineness of our faith is proven. At the same time, we are drawn to spiritual maturity as we grow in the knowledge of God's ever-abounding grace and the completed work of the cross of Christ. Moreover, as we endure hardships and trials, we can be confident that God is using them to train us as His children in righteousness – in responding rightly – in responding the way that Jesus, His Son, responded.

> *{Jas 1:2-4} 2 Consider it pure joy, my brothers and sisters, **whenever you face trials of many kinds**, 3 because you know that the **testing of your faith** produces perseverance. 4 Let perseverance finish its work **so that you may be mature and complete, not lacking anything**.*

*{2Ti 2:1} 1 You then, my son, **be strong in the grace that is in Christ Jesus**.*

Training in Righteousness

Every disciple of Christ knows that Jesus said to love others as He loved us. Accordingly, we set out to be like Him and bring the love of God to the whole world. Then, it happens. Someone whom we are loving with all this love that we have received from Jesus turns around and mocks us, rejects us, or is intensely mean to us. They may also accuse us of having lost our mind, being evil, and they may attempt in various ways to destroy us or our work for God. How do we respond? Do we respond like ourselves in self-defense, with a counter-mock, with retorted insults, or with equalizing rejection? Or do we respond like Christ, with love and more love, with compassion, with kindness, with forgiveness, and with self-sacrifice? Let the training in righteousness begin!

Trials are not punishment from God because Jesus took all of our punishment upon Himself and God does not test us negatively. (see Isaiah 53:3; James 1:13) Rather, as situations arise, God chastises or trains us in right conduct and right beliefs, helping us to respond rightly as we listen to Him through the indwelling Holy Spirit. Think of it like a loving heavenly Father training His children about how to defend themselves from a big schoolyard bully. The devil, the world and its ways, and our own fleshly desires intimidate and terrorize us while we live in this playground called the world. But our loving heavenly Daddy whispers to us through the Holy Spirit about how to handle all of these bullies the way that His beloved Son Jesus did. Accordingly, as we follow the guidance of the Holy Spirit when we encounter tests and trials, we are learning from God how to respond the way that Jesus would respond, no matter what we encounter. Through this specialized boot camp for character and faith, which often includes much waiting, patience, and endurance, God brings us to spiritual maturity so that we are like His perfect Son.

> *{Heb 12:7-8, 11} 7 **Endure hardship as discipline; God is treating you as his children**. For what children are not disciplined by their father?... 11 No discipline seems pleasant at the time, but painful. Later on, however, it **produces a harvest of righteousness and peace** for those who have been trained by it.*

As an illustration, a friend of mine serves on the local Police force. When he joined the Police Academy, the first item on the training agenda was for a boot-camp bad guy (a fellow officer) to punch him in the face. Why? Because being punched in the face is shocking and this shock can stunt an officer's response if he is not expecting it. Also, being punched in the face is a most likely occurrence in the life of an officer out in the field doing their job. The Police Academy is designed to train officers to be able to do their job in real life scenarios no matter what attacks are launched at them. Similarly, as we set out to follow Jesus and do the things that He did, every trial feels like a spiritual, emotional, and often humiliating punch in the face. Trials can be as simple as being mocked for our faith or as intense as severe persecution. Tests can be those of lack when nothing is going our way or of abundance when everything seems to be going our way. Trials can be inward emotional torment or actual physical beatings because of our faith in Christ. Tests can be sacrificing our simple needs and preferences or even paying the ultimate price of dying for Christ as the definitive proof of our faith. We should not be shocked but rather rejoice when testing and trials come because we know that we are being trained by the Holy Spirit in the *Jesus Academy*. His righteous training through real life scenarios teaches us to love others the way that He loves us and to carry out His purposes in spite of the attacks which are launched against us.

> *{1Pe 4:12-13} 12 Dear friends,* **do not be surprised at the fiery ordeal that has come on you to test you,** *as though something strange were happening to you. 13* **But rejoice** *inasmuch* **as you participate in the sufferings of Christ,** *so that you may be overjoyed when his glory is revealed.*

For example, the Lord asked me to live in a way that appears odd to people, including other Christ followers. I set out towards the purpose of God and poured my heart into laying my life down for whatever the Lord asked me to do. For a while, it was fun for me and everyone around me to watch Him move miraculously in my life. However, after a while, it made people very uncomfortable. I was rejected by almost every person that I knew who did not believe Jesus and even by many other believers. Soon enough, false accusations began to spring up about me. Anything that I did which others deemed not up to their standards was magnified through gossip and exaggeration. Every time I obeyed the prompting of the Holy Spirit, someone would tell me I wasn't hearing God or that I was a false prophet. Lies spread around about me, and many people believed what they heard. I knew that God had commissioned me to spread the Good News but, instead, my accusers warned others that I was bad news. As this continued to the point of culmination, even though the false accusers couldn't get their stories to line up, a key member of the leadership team of my church believed the lies and I thought I might be asked to leave. I was not kicked out of my church but I was blacklisted by the very ones that I had poured my life into. They also told me that God must be punishing me, that I must have unconfessed sin in my life, that I did not have enough faith, that I had enough faith but I did not have enough love, that I had lost my mind, and that I was in absolute error against the ways of God in addition to many other insults, accusations, much mockery, and excessive suspicion. I knew that Jesus had never defended Himself, so I did not utter a word of self-defense. In my agony, I desperately sought the Lord because the pain was so intense that I began to consider that maybe the false accusations were true. I read through the Book of Proverbs, and it was like a psychedelic experience. I could not tell anymore if I was the righteous or the wicked, the diligent or the sluggard, the wise or the foolish. But right there, in the middle of it all, the Lord met me and spoke with me about the meaning and value of sharing in His sufferings. He reminded me that His purpose for my life was to know Him and to be like Him. He re-fired my heart for Him and re-filled me with genuine love for others, even the ones who had crucified me. I forgave them because they did not know what they were doing. This happened years ago, and I still love them today.

> *{Phl 3:8-11} 8 What is more,* **I consider everything a loss because of the surpassing worth of knowing Christ Jesus my Lord, for whose sake I have lost all things. I consider them garbage, that I may gain Christ** *9 and be found in him, not having a righteousness of my own that comes from the law, but that which is through faith in Christ--the righteousness that comes from God on the basis of faith. 10* **I want to know Christ--yes, to know the power of his**

resurrection and participation in his sufferings, becoming like him in his death, 11 and so, somehow, attaining to the resurrection from the dead.

Truth be told, there are only two ways to respond to the trials we face: with our flesh which is our inherited sinful Adamic nature or, by the power of the Holy Spirit, with Christlikeness which is our new nature in Him. Selfishness and self-defense is always flesh. Trusting God and continuing to love is always Christlikeness. Our response to trials reveals what we really believe about God's love for us, God's goodness towards us, God's sufficiency in all things, and whether our hearts are focused on temporal or eternal rewards.

> *{Rom 12:19-21} 19* **Do not take revenge***, my dear friends, but leave room for God's wrath, for it is written:* **"It is mine to avenge; I will repay," says the Lord***. 20 On the contrary: "If your enemy is hungry, feed him; if he is thirsty, give him something to drink. In doing this, you will heap burning coals on his head." 21* **Do not be overcome by evil, but overcome evil with good***.*

For a Christian, the token mark of being *mature,* which is also translated as *being perfect,* is to do the very thing that Jesus did as He was being crucified. He loved His accusers and His enemies. He forgave and prayed for the very people who were murdering him. While our trials may be small by comparison, whatever we face, our response proves which "operating system" we are using to function. Jesus' right response to all things proved Him to be the Son of God and it is our right responses which prove us to be God's children.

> *{Mat 5:43-48} 43 "You have heard that it was said, 'Love your neighbor and hate your enemy.' 44 But I tell you,* **love your enemies and pray for those who persecute you***, 45* **that you may be children of your Father in heaven***. He causes his sun to rise on the evil and the good, and sends rain on the righteous and the unrighteous. 46 If you love those who love you, what reward will you get? Are not even the tax collectors doing that? 47 And if you greet only your own people, what are you doing more than others? Do not even pagans do that? 48* **Be perfect [mature], therefore, as your heavenly Father is perfect [mature].***

True perfection is the perfect love which Jesus demonstrated by laying down His life so that we could live. This said, true love is costly even when our lives are not on the line. Love costs us time and dignity, love costs us our own desires and our own way of doing things, love costs us our right to be right and our right to be mad and seek revenge. Love is not a feeling, it's a state of being which flows into action. The word for God's kind of *love* means *charity* – selfless and unconditional *giving* to and *serving* others without any expectation of repayment. This is the way Christ loves us. We were designed by God to receive His love and to love others as He loves us, no matter what attacks are launched against us.

> *{1Co 13:4-8a} 4 Love is* **patient***, love is* **kind***. It does* **not envy***, it does* **not boast***, it is* **not proud***. 5 It does* **not dishonor others***, it is* **not self-seeking***, it is* **not easily angered***, it keeps* **no record of wrongs***. 6 Love does* **not delight in evil but rejoices with the truth***. 7 It always*

*protects, **always trusts**, **always hopes**, **always perseveres**. 8 Love **never fails**. (see also Romans 12:9-21)*

We will also face internal trials in our minds and hearts which reveal whether we are obeying the Holy Spirit or our fleshly desires. We all have yearnings from within for things other than what we have. These cravings may be totally ungodly or may seem harmless enough but, whether good or bad, they are not God's will for our lives. Our flesh lures us by temptation and the enemy whispers excuses to enable us to indulge our lusts. In contrast, the Holy Spirit whispers to us in purity, truth, and holiness while reminding us that, because Jesus' sacrifice covered over all of our sins, the enticement and allure of the forbidden has been nullified. God's grace is so sufficient that all things are permitted, meaning that we are totally and absolutely free in Christ. This said, not all things are beneficial, good for us, or worth doing because they do not reflect the nature of Christ within us and are unloving towards others. (see 1 Corinthians 6:12, 10:23) We have the same divine nature which strengthened Jesus in the wilderness against all of satan's temptations and testings within us to strengthen us as we are tested in these various ways so that we can respond the way that He did and pass the test.

> *{Jas 1:14-16} 14 but **each person is tempted** when they are dragged away **by their own evil desire** and enticed. 15 Then, after **desire has conceived**, it **gives birth to sin**; and sin, when it is full-grown, gives birth to death. 16 **Don't be deceived**, my dear brothers and sisters.*

> *{2Pe 1:3-4} 3 His divine power **has given us everything we need for a godly life** through our knowledge of him who called us by his own glory and goodness. 4 Through these he has given us his very great and precious promises, so that through them you may **participate in the divine nature**, having **escaped the corruption in the world caused by evil desires**.*

We will also encounter false religious teachings and teachers who go on sin-hunts of condemnation or who are attempting to enforce their code of conduct on disciples of Christ. Their teachings often impose requirements, blame believers for their problems, or demand a perfect life as a sign of God's favor rather than having compassion, teaching the perfection of Christ, and pointing believers to the absolute sufficiency of the finished work of the cross. In other instances, their teachings may compromise the truth in order to lessen or eliminate suffering for Christ, may support self-imposed suffering as a way of attaining perfection before God, or may be geared towards creating profit for themselves rather than glory for God. (We will examine different types of false teaching later in this study.) However, as we are guided by the Holy Spirit and Jesus' example, using the Scriptures as guardrails of truth, we will be able to discern good from evil and the truth from lies. (see John 16:13, 17:17; 1 Peter 2:21; Hebrews 5:14) As we are trained to be like Jesus, we will not argue or quarrel with religious people or false teachers, we will not yield to man-made regulations, and we will remain faithful to the truth without compromise.

> *{Mat 7:15 } 15 "**Watch out for false prophets**. They come to you in sheep's clothing, but inwardly they are ferocious wolves. (see also Matthew 24:22, 24; Mark 13:5-6, 22)*

*{2Pe 2:1} 1 But there were also **false prophets** among the people, just as there will be **false teachers** among you. They will **secretly introduce destructive heresies**, even denying the sovereign Lord who bought them--bringing swift destruction on themselves.*

*{2Co 11:3} 3 But I am afraid that **just as Eve was deceived by the serpent's cunning**, your minds may somehow be **led astray from your sincere and pure devotion to Christ**.*

*{Col 2:22-23} 22 These rules, which have to do with things that are all destined to perish with use, are **based on merely human commands and teachings**. 23 Such regulations indeed have an appearance of wisdom, with their **self-imposed worship**, their **false humility** and their **harsh treatment of the body**, but they lack any value in restraining sensual indulgence.*

*{Gal 6:12} 12 Those who want to **impress people by means of the flesh** are trying to compel you to be circumcised. The only reason they do this is **to avoid being persecuted** for the cross of Christ.*

*{2Ti 2:23} 23 **Don't have anything to do with foolish and stupid arguments**, because you know they produce quarrels.*

*{Tit 3:9} 9 But **avoid foolish controversies and genealogies and arguments and quarrels about the law**, because these are unprofitable and useless.*

*{1Ti 1:8-11} 8 We know that the law is good if one uses it properly. 9 We also know that **the law is made not for the righteous but for lawbreakers and rebels, the ungodly and sinful, the unholy and irreligious**, for those who kill their fathers or mothers, for murderers, 10 for the sexually immoral, for those practicing homosexuality, for slave traders and liars and perjurers-- **and for whatever else is contrary to the sound doctrine 11 that conforms to the gospel concerning the glory of the blessed God**, which he entrusted to me.*

The Holy Spirit will also guide us when trials come from earnest believers who desire to follow Jesus but who haven't fully grasped or embraced the cost of following Him. In love and patience, we will chide these types of people with great mercy but without blurring the truth of the price we pay to follow Christ to the fullest. As we are led by the Holy Spirit, we will reflect Jesus' approach.

*{Eph 4:15} 15 Instead, **speaking the truth in love**, we will grow to become in every respect the mature body of him who is the head, that is, Christ.*

*{2Ti 4:2} 2 Preach the word; be prepared in season and out of season; **correct, rebuke and encourage--with great patience and careful instruction**.*

*{Jde 1:22-23} 22 **Be merciful to those who doubt**; 23 **save others by snatching them from the fire**; to others show mercy, mixed with fear--hating even the clothing stained by corrupted flesh.*

Trials Will Come

The point of all of this is to say that, as Jesus warned us, trials will come. In no uncertain terms, He prepared His followers for trials, particularly in the times to come before His return. This is so that our faith does not fail and so that we can endure to the end, no matter the cost. He is with us in every trial to give us wisdom, strength, and courage to respond rightly, the way that He would respond if He were in our exact set of circumstances. God assured Jesus of eternal victory and Jesus believed Him. Now, because Jesus has already overcome the world, the flesh, and the devil, we are assured of our victory when our faith is in Him. He has not left us as orphans and He does not call us to lives of sacrifice without the promise of eternal rewards.

*{Luk 21:12-19} 12 "But before all this, **they will seize you and persecute you**. They will hand you over to synagogues and put you in prison, and **you will be brought before kings and governors**, and all on account of my name. 13 And so you will bear testimony to me. 14 But **make up your mind not to worry beforehand how you will defend yourselves**. 15 For I will give you words and wisdom that none of your adversaries will be able to resist or contradict. 16 You will be betrayed even by parents, brothers and sisters, relatives and friends, and **they will put some of you to death**. 17 **Everyone will hate you because of me**. 18 **But not a hair of your head will perish**. 19 **Stand firm, and you will win life**. (see Luke 21 and Matthew 24)*

*{Rom 8:35-39} 35 **Who shall separate us from the love of Christ?** Shall trouble or hardship or persecution or famine or nakedness or danger or sword? 36 As it is written: "For your sake we face death all day long; we are considered as sheep to be slaughtered." (quoting Psalm 44:11, 22) 37 **No, in all these things we are more than conquerors through him who loved us**. 38 **For I am convinced that neither death nor life, neither angels nor demons, neither the present nor the future, nor any powers**, 39 **neither height nor depth, nor anything else in all creation, will be able to separate us from the love of God that is in Christ Jesus our Lord.***

*{Rev 12:10-11} 10 Then I heard a loud voice in heaven say: "Now have come the salvation and the power and the kingdom of our God, and the authority of his Messiah. For the accuser of our brothers and sisters, who accuses them before our God day and night, has been hurled down. 11 **They triumphed over him by the blood of the Lamb and by the word of their testimony; they did not love their lives so much as to shrink from death**.*

*{Jhn 16:1-4a} 1 "**All this I have told you so that you will not fall away**. 2 They will put you out of the synagogue; in fact, **the time is coming when anyone who kills you will think they are offering a service to God**. 3 They will do such things because they have not known the Father or me. 4 **I have told you this, so that when their time comes you will remember that I warned you about them**.*

Again I say, through every trial and through all the pain, when we hear the heart of God asking, *Do you believe that I am good?*, *Do you believe that I love you?*, *Do you believe that I am enough?*, *Do you believe what I have promised you?*, and *Do you believe that I have finished it?* let us keep our eyes on Jesus and our minds on heaven and resoundingly answer back to Him, *Yes!*

CHAPTER 5

Old to New

In the first chapter of the Book of Acts, there were several events which clearly revealed a transition from an old way of doing things to a new way of doing things. As we said before, the Gospel had changed everything. Jesus' life, ministry, and death were completed and new life through His resurrection was just beginning for His followers. Let's take a look at some clear demonstrations of this old-to-new transfer so that we can be sure that we are functioning in our faith as New Covenant believers.

Law to Grace

> *{Act 1:1-4} 1 In my former book, Theophilus, I wrote about all that Jesus began to do and to teach 2 until the day he was taken up to heaven, after giving instructions through the Holy Spirit to the apostles he had chosen. 3 **After his suffering, he presented himself to them and gave many convincing proofs that he was alive.** He appeared to them over a period of forty days and **spoke about the kingdom of God.** 4 On one occasion, while he was eating with them, he gave them this command: "**Do not leave Jerusalem, but wait for the gift my Father promised, which you have heard me speak about.***

Jesus Christ had presented Himself as alive from the grave, which proved that He is indeed the Son of God and the Messiah of Israel. (Romans 1:4) For forty days, He presented proof of the resurrection as He showed hundreds of people that He was alive from the dead. For example, Mary Magdalene saw Jesus at the side of the tomb and Jesus called specifically to meet with Peter and the other disciples. (see Matthew 28:1-10; Mark 16:1-11; Luke 24: 1-12; John 20:1-18) Jesus appeared to His followers on several more occasions, including Thomas who would not believe unless He saw Jesus' scars, two disciples who were travelling on the road to Emmaus, a special breakfast with His disciples by the Sea of Galilee, and a meeting with believers in Jerusalem. (see John 20:19-25; Mark 16:12-14; Luke 24:13-49) The apostle Paul later recounts these events:

> *{1Co 15:3-6} 3 For what I received I passed on to you as of first importance: that Christ died for our sins according to the Scriptures, 4 that he was buried, that he was **raised on the third day** according to the Scriptures, 5 and that he **appeared to Cephas, and then to the Twelve.** 6 After that, he **appeared to more than five hundred of the brothers and sisters at the same time**, most of whom are still living, though some have fallen asleep.*

Jesus spent this time explaining from the Scriptures, which we know of as the Old Testament, particularly the writings of Moses, the Psalms, and the Prophets, to reveal what had been accomplished by God's power through His suffering, death, and resurrection. Jesus spoke about the Kingdom of God and told His followers to wait until the Holy Spirit gave them power from heaven which would institute a whole new way of doing things. (Luke 24:49) Jesus revealed to them that through His life, death, and resurrection, He had fulfilled the Old Covenant. (see Matthew 5:17) and had established and sealed the New Covenant with His blood. This constituted a transfer from the old way of the Law, which required measuring up to God's standard in order to earn right standing with or access to God, to the new way of God's grace through faith in Jesus Christ, by which believers receive right standing with and access to God (along with everything that entails) as a free gift. In other words, when we believe in our hearts that God raised Jesus from the dead, we are no longer required to measure up to God's standard because Jesus measured up for us. Through faith in the New Covenant of Christ, we are not blessed or cursed because of our obedience or observances of piety, or lack thereof. We are blessed by God because of Christ's obedience which fulfilled the Old Covenant completely. When we believe Jesus as Lord and Savior, we are transferred from the kingdom of darkness (the evil one's dominion) into the Kingdom of light, which is the Kingdom of God and also the Kingdom of Heaven. (see Colossians 1:13) Moreover, the Kingdom of Heaven is exactly what it sounds like – heaven! In heaven, every blessing of God flows freely without hindrance according to God's original design and there is *no death, mourning, crying or pain*. (see Revelation 21:4) Spiritually speaking, we stand boldly before God because our record is as clear as Adam and his wife's record before the wrong tree incident. The charges against us have been cancelled by the cross of Christ. (see Colossians 2:14) Therefore, we have access to God's favor so that we can freely receive every blessing from above. (see Ephesians 1:3; Deuteronomy 28:1-14; Leviticus 26:1-13)

> *{Rom 5:1-2}* 1 *Therefore, since* **we have been justified through faith***,* **we have peace with God through our Lord Jesus Christ***,* 2 *through whom* **we have gained access by faith into this grace** *in which we now stand. And we boast in the hope of the glory of God.*

Think of it this way: have you ever parked your car in a parking garage where there is a fee for parking? If so, then you know that there is a difference between when you have to pay to leave the parking garage and when you have visited the right person who can offer parking validation. When your parking ticket is validated, you do not have to pay because your ticket has been stamped PAID by the person you visited. This is what happens through faith in Jesus. Everyone since Adam has had an un-payable parking fee and has been stuck in the oppressive and miserable "parking lot" of the evil one's domain. Under the Old Covenant, the Law was the fee schedule for paying our way out of the parking garage and perfect obedience was the only way be released. Nobody in all of history had ever been able to pay the fee and leave. However, through the New Covenant in Christ, we receive a PAID stamp on our lives because Jesus' perfect obedience PAID the fee for everyone who will believe. Therefore, we are free to leave the "parking garage" of the evil one's control over our lives once and for all. Jesus PAID for our freedom forever from all oppression of any sort including everything we may have done in our past, bad circumstances, sickness, poor relationships, poor self-image, all demonic oppression through evil spirits, and everything else included in the curse of the Law of God. (see Deuteronomy 28:15-68; Leviticus 26:15-39) We stand justified before God as if we never had a parking fee at all because our ticket is stamped PAID. We are totally free in Christ.

I also call this transfer from Law to grace graduating from Romans chapter 7 to Romans chapter 8. In Romans 7, the apostle Paul described how, when he lived under the Law, the Law invoked in him an uncanny war between what he knew was the right thing to do and what he actually did. It seemed that the more he tried to do what was right, the more wrong he did. He said, in effect, *I do what I don't want to do, and I don't do what I do want to do.* Finally, in exasperation, he gave up and denounced himself as a wretched man. (see Romans 7:15-24) I call this getting stuck in the *do do,* pronounced *doo doo.* For those of you who don't know, in my culture *doo doo* is an expression used for excrement, like the kind from a dog that we might accidentally step in from time to time. Getting stuck in the *do do* is no fun for anyone much like life under the Law because we can never measure up by what we *do do.* But Paul used this demonstration from his own life to guide us into the glorious freedom from the Law which we now have through faith in Christ. He graduated from Law-mindedness in Romans 7 to grace and Holy Spirit-mindedness in Romans 8. He then boldly declared that those who have placed their faith in Christ are not in the *do do* anymore. Why? Because we no longer live as those who are measured by what we *do* but as those who have direct access to God because of what Jesus *did.* Accordingly, we no longer strive to obey God's Law to be good or to measure up through our conduct. Rather, now we strive to rest in Jesus' perfect obedience on our behalf and to obey the Holy Spirit which God has placed within us.

> *{Rom 8:1-2} 1 Therefore, there is now **no condemnation for those who are in Christ Jesus**, 2 because through Christ Jesus the law of **the Spirit who gives life has set you free from the law of sin and death**.*

Another old-to-new shift which has taken place is one of love. Under the Old Covenant, the Law commands us to *Love the Lord your God with all your heart with all your soul with all your mind and with all your strength and to love your neighbor as yourself.* (see Matthew 22:36-40; Mark 12:29-31; Luke 10:27; quoting Deuteronomy 6:4-5; Leviticus 19:18) However, Jesus gave us a new command in the New Covenant which is to love others as He has loved us. (see John 13:34; John 15:12,17; 1 John 3:23; 1 John 4:10) This transition moved us from working really hard to prove our love for God through good deeds for Him and others to resting and receiving Christ's love for us and then loving others the way that He loves us. Significantly, this also changes the way that we pray because of our grasp of what Christ accomplished for us. When we live according to the Law, the only thing to pray for is God's mercy because we can never and will never measure up. Typically, this leaves us looking for new methods or techniques of prayer or piety in order to attain what we seek and we are never quite sure of God's goodness or willingness to fulfill His promises. However, when we live established in the righteousness of the New Covenant, we live dependent on God's ever present mercy in Christ, and we pray boldly and confidently to bring His kingdom to earth *as it is in heaven* as an extension of God's grace, mercy, and fulfilled promises to everyone who will receive it by faith.

In short, if we are working to be good or to prove our love for God or for others, then we are not truly doing good works for Christ. In fact, if we are working with a motive of attaining right standing with God, it means that we are still operating under the old way of doing things rather than the new way which Christ established for us. Christ followers have been transferred from old to new, from the Old

Covenant to the New Covenant, from Law to grace, from darkness to light, and from hell to heaven. We live our lives by the power of the indwelling Holy Spirit so that we can conduct ourselves as Jesus did, love others the way that Jesus does, and have power from above to do the things that Jesus did.

Baptism into Christ

> {Act 1:5} 5 For **John baptized with water**, but in a few days you will be baptized with the Holy Spirit."

Another transition from chapter 1 of Acts is a shift from the baptism of John the Baptist to a new kind of baptism. While we will not go into too much depth here, there is a difference between John's baptism and water baptism in the name of Jesus. (We will cover baptism of the Holy Spirit in the next chapter.) John the Baptist was the last Old Testament style prophet of God, commissioned by God specifically as a forerunner for the Messiah. (see Matthew 3:1-12; Mark 1:1-8; Luke 3:1-18; Isaiah 40:3-5) John baptized people by submerging them in water as a demonstration that they had repented of their sins and were placing their faith in God's mercy and forgiveness. (see Luke 3:3; Acts 13:24-25) They were renouncing sin, meaning not doing things their own way anymore, and returning to God and His way of doing things. This washing of the body symbolized the washing away of sin and uncleanness and was culturally referred to as a *mikveh* in Hebrew. Ritual cleansing like this was required of priests before serving God, of common people after certain contaminating events so that the community of Israel remained clean before God, and of animal sacrifices before being offered to God on the altar. As a side note, our expression of *washing our hands* of a matter derives its meaning from this type of washing. (see also Psalm 26:6; Psalm 73:13) When we wash our hands of something, we disassociate ourselves from guilt and involvement with any contaminating aspects of the person, incident, or issue.

John baptized in water in order for the people to be ceremonially clean while they waited for the Messiah to come. This was so that when Jesus arrived as their Messiah, they would be ready to serve Him, stand before Him, and offer their lives to Him. This said, as soon as Jesus presented Himself to John, John immediately took second place to Jesus and pointed people exclusively to Him. (see John 3:27-30) Moreover, when John died, his baptism died with Him. While there was some confusion about this in Ephesus, which we will get into later, there should be no confusion about this today. Through the resurrection, Jesus proved to be the Messiah that people were waiting for. Due to this fact, baptism shifted from John's baptism to Jesus' baptism.

Outwardly the two baptisms seem similar because the baptism that we know today as the baptism of Jesus is also an outward sign of an inward change of heart. Believers repent, or change our minds about what we believe and do. However, baptism into the name of Jesus goes much deeper into symbolizing our inclusion in His death and resurrection. Through baptism in Jesus' name, we descend into a watery grave and rise again as new creations in Christ (see 2 Corinthians 5:17) which was something John's baptism did not entail. In John's baptism, people were washed and waiting but in Jesus' baptism, we are washed and transformed.

> *{Rom 6:3-4} 3 Or don't you know that all of us who were **baptized into Christ Jesus were baptized into his death**? 4 We were therefore **buried with him through baptism into death** in order that, just as Christ was **raised from the dead** through the glory of the Father, **we too may live a new life**.*

Think of it this way: the word for *baptize* in Greek was first used in a recipe for making pickles. If you *baptize* a cucumber in vinegar, it comes out as a pickle. It is not just a washed cucumber, it changes from an old state of being to a new state of being – it is now and forever more, irreversibly, a pickle. Similarly, when we are *baptized* into Christ, we go under the water as our old self with the nature of the first Adam, and we come out of the water as a new creation in the second Adam, who is Christ. We are permanently altered because of our inclusion in Him. Our entire state of being has been modified from old to new. The old has gone, and the new has come. (see 2 Corinthians 5:17) And, come to think of it, since Jesus is Jewish, I could say that it makes us like baby kosher dills but that might be taking it a little too far…

Jesus commanded His followers to go to the ends of the earth and baptize disciples in the name of the Father, the Son, and the Holy Spirit. (see Matthew 28:19) This way, Christ followers could serve Him, stand before Him purified from sin, and offer our lives to Him as living sacrifices. Additionally, repeating what John the Baptist had said, Jesus told His followers that they would not only be baptized with water but with fire, which we will address in the next chapter.

> *{Luk 3:16} 16 John answered them all, "I baptize you with water. But one who is more powerful than I will come, the straps of whose sandals I am not worthy to untie. **He will baptize you with the Holy Spirit and fire**. (see also Matthew 3:11; Mark 1:8)*

Earthly Kingdom to Heavenly Kingdom

> *{Act 1:6-8} 6 Then they gathered around him and asked him, "**Lord, are you at this time going to restore the kingdom to Israel?**" 7 He said to them: "It is not for you to know the times or dates the Father has set by his own authority. 8 But you will receive power when the Holy Spirit comes on you; and you will be my witnesses in Jerusalem, and in all Judea and Samaria, and to the ends of the earth."*

Christ's disciples were expecting Jesus to fulfill all of the Scriptures about the Messiah of Israel who rules over all nations for eternity. Now that Jesus had proven to be the Messiah of Israel through His resurrection, His followers thought that Jesus was going to establish His Kingdom in the earth. Moreover, since all of Israel at the time was under Roman authority, they were most likely expecting Jesus to lead them in political and military overthrow as He took eternal dominion and raised Israel above all other nations on the earth. Essentially, this was a reasonable expectation on their part because of Scriptures like this one:

> *{Dan 7:27} 27 Then the sovereignty, power and greatness of **all the kingdoms under heaven will be handed over to the holy people of the Most High. His kingdom will be an everlasting kingdom, and all rulers will worship and obey him**.'*

Assuredly, the day that they were anticipating is a day that will come. However, until that day, Jesus' Kingdom is not fully of this world yet. (see John 18:36) Jesus' Kingdom is the Kingdom of Heaven, and He establishes it in and through the hearts of those who believe until He returns to reign over the new heavens and a new earth for all of eternity. (see Luke 17:21; Revelation 21:1; Isaiah 65:17) Therefore, even though Jesus is the One appointed by God who rules and reigns forever, His purpose is not political rebellion but the salvation of souls. As a side note, starting on this very day with His first 120 disciples, people began to wonder and try to predict when Jesus will come back. But Jesus had already explained that He does not even know the hour that God has appointed for His return and that He will return unexpectedly, like a thief in the night. (see Matthew 24:32, 36; Mark 13:32; 1 Thessalonians 5:2; 2 Peter 3:10; Revelation 16:15)

Before the Holy Spirit was poured out, Christ's disciples asked their question with an earthly point of view – the old way of looking at things. But Jesus answered with a heavenly response – the new way of seeing things. His disciples had to wait for the Holy Spirit so that they, too, could have heaven's perspective and power from on high to usher in the Kingdom of Heaven by being like Christ and doing the things that He did the way that He had done them during His ministry years.

Transfer of Anointing

> *{Act 1:9-11} 9 After he said this,* **he was taken up before their very eyes, and a cloud hid him from their sight.** *10* **They were looking intently up into the sky as he was going,** *when suddenly two men dressed in white stood beside them. 11 "Men of Galilee," they said, "why do you stand here looking into the sky? This same Jesus, who has been taken from you into heaven, will come back in the same way you have seen him go into heaven."*

Next, Jesus ascended into heaven in a cloud of glory and His disciples watched it happen. This was reminiscent of another transfer from old to new which had occurred in the Old Testament as a prophetic foreshadow of this event. The Prophet Elijah had been taken up into heaven in a whirlwind while his successor Elisha watched and saw the fiery chariots and horsemen of Israel. (see 2 Kings 2:11-12) Elijah had been the world's most powerful prophet of the one true God. He did mighty works which proved his anointing from God. He even called down fire from heaven in a duel of truth against false religion and changed the weather through prayer. (see 1 Kings 18) However, after this, Elijah found himself in a cave thinking that he was the only one who truly believed God. There in the cave, God spoke to Elijah, and assured him that there were others who believed. As Elijah left the cave, he was instructed by God to do three things. The first was to anoint Elisha as his successor, which Elijah did. (see 1 Kings 19) Later, when the time came for Elijah's dramatic departure from this world, Elisha requested a double portion of Elijah's spirit (his anointing from God) in order to be his successor and carry out his work. Then, when Elijah was taken up into heaven right before Elisha's eyes, Elijah's cloak, also called his *mantle* (which symbolizes the glory of God upon him) fell down from above. Elisha received the cloak as his own. Those who saw this transaction take place even noted, *Elijah's spirit now rests upon Elisha!* (see 2 Kings 2:15) Elisha then proceeded to do twice as many mighty works of God as Elijah had done in addition to fulfilling the two other portions of God's post-cave assignment to Elijah.

Let's pause for a moment to take a look at the old-to-new transfer from Elijah to Elisha, as evidenced by the miraculous works that God did through them.

ELIJAH – 7 MIRACLES *(see 1 Kings 17-18, 2 Kings 1-2)*	**ELISHA – 14 MIRACLES** *(see 2 Kings 2-6, 13)*
Commanded the weather	Parted the Jordan River
Fed by birds	Purified bad water with a bowl of salt
Food supply during famine	Cursed mocking boys
Raised a widow's son from the dead	Water pooled without rain
Fire from heaven	Oil for a widow to pay her debts
Fire from heaven three more times	Raised a woman's son from the dead
Parted the waters of the Jordan River	Purified poisonous food with flour
	Food multiplication: 20 loaves feed 100 people
	Healed an incurable leper
	Discerned servant's lie and smote him
	Made a sunken ax head float in water
	Opened servant's spiritual eyes to see angels
	Blinded the enemy army
	Dead man raised to life

Again, this transfer from Elijah to Elisha prophetically foreshadowed the transfer of anointing from Jesus to His disciples after His ascension to heaven. Like Elijah, Jesus was the Anointed One of the one true God and did great and mighty works and miracles in the earth. Then, He found Himself in a cave called the grave as the only one who truly believed God, since everyone else had deserted Him. As Jesus stepped out of the grave, He knew God's purpose for Him included anointing His successors. For the next 40 days, He commissioned His disciples and told them about their assignment to be His witnesses to the ends of the earth. Then, He ascended to heaven in the clouds. Then, as we will dig into in the next chapter, Jesus sent down the Holy Spirit, which fell upon believers like Jesus' robe of righteousness and His mantle from God. The Spirit of Jesus would rest upon His disciples so that they could do the works that He did, proclaiming the Kingdom of God with signs and wonders following. This is what ACTS is all about.

No More Casting Lots

> *{Act 1:12-26} 12 Then the apostles returned to Jerusalem from the hill called the Mount of Olives, a Sabbath day's walk from the city. 13 When they arrived, they went upstairs to the room where they were staying. Those present were Peter, John, James and Andrew; Philip and Thomas, Bartholomew and Matthew; James son of Alphaeus and Simon the Zealot, and Judas son of James. 14 They all joined together constantly in prayer, along with the women and Mary the mother of Jesus, and with his brothers. 15 In those days Peter stood up among the believers (a group numbering about a hundred and twenty) 16 and said, "**Brothers and sisters, the Scripture had to be fulfilled in which the Holy Spirit spoke long ago through David concerning Judas,***

*who served as guide for those who arrested Jesus. 17 **He was one of our number and shared in our ministry.**" 18 (With the payment he received for his wickedness, Judas bought a field; there he fell headlong, his body burst open and all his intestines spilled out. 19 Everyone in Jerusalem heard about this, so they called that field in their language Akeldama, that is, Field of Blood.) 20 "For," said Peter, "**it is written in the Book of Psalms: "'May his place be deserted; let there be no one to dwell in it,'** (quoting Psalm Psalm 69:25) **and, " 'May another take his place of leadership.'** (quoting Psalm 109:8) 21 **Therefore it is necessary to choose one of the men who have been with us the whole time the Lord Jesus was living among us**, 22 **beginning from John's baptism to the time when Jesus was taken up from us.** For one of these must become a witness with us of his resurrection." 23 So they nominated two men: Joseph called Barsabbas (also known as Justus) and Matthias. 24 **Then they prayed, "Lord, you know everyone's heart. Show us which of these two you have chosen** 25 to take over this apostolic ministry, which Judas left to go where he belongs." 26 **Then they cast lots**, and the lot fell to Matthias; so he was added to the eleven apostles.*

This portion of Scripture always makes me laugh. I'm not laughing at the disciples, but I do delight in their humanity – they are just like you and me. Without the Holy Spirit, they were doing the best that they could to carry out what they perceived as God's purpose. In the same way that, in earlier verses, they knew the Scriptures pointed to a literal earthly Kingdom over which Jesus would rule and reign forever, they also interpreted the Scriptures to mean that they had to replace Judas as an apostle. While they were obediently waiting in Jerusalem for the Holy Spirit to come as Jesus had promised, they made themselves busy doing something else. They set out to bring God's will to pass through their own rationale. They came up with criteria that needed to be met for Judas' replacement and nominated two finalists who met their conditions. Then, they did the most spiritual thing that they could think of. They *cast lots*. In essence, this is a spiritual coin toss. To us this seems pretty silly but to them, it was a good, godly, completely Scripturally approved and proven methodology for settling differences. There are numerous Old Testament examples of casting lots which could be used to justify this course of action and assert its wisdom. The Lord commanded the casting of lots to segment Israel's assignments tribe by tribe, clan by clan, and family by family. (see Joshua 7:14; 1 Chronicles 24; Nehemiah 10:34) The sailors who took Jonah on board cast lots to see which person was the source of all of their problems and, in accordance with divine providence, the lots accurately pointed to Jonah. (see Jonah 1:7) Even Gentile kings cast lots as a form of seeking an omen, and the Lord exerted His control over lots cast in order to guide and direct the hearts of kings and the course of history. (see Ezekiel 21:21)

*{Pro 16:33} 33 The lot is cast into the lap, **but its every decision is from the LORD**.*

*{Pro 18:18} 18 **Casting the lot settles disputes** and keeps strong opponents apart.*

When the first believers cast lots, the lot fell on Matthias, who was appointed as an apostle. However, even after all of their hard work in qualifying the final candidates for apostleship, Matthias and Barsabbas (who may or may not be the same Barsabaas we read about in Acts 15) are never mentioned again in the Scriptures. Assuredly, they served the Lord Jesus sincerely but whether or not they were true apostolic candidates is subject to interpretation. More significantly, we never hear of another decision being made by casting lots. Why? Because, in the chapters to come, the Holy Spirit was poured out from heaven to give believers an internal guidance system which is better than casting lots could ever be.

Therefore, let us learn from their pre-Holy Spirit example and not do what they did. It can be tempting for us, even with the Holy Spirit, when we perceive and believe that we understand the will of God, to rush ahead and try to bring it to pass using our own way of doing things. This is especially true when we have good ways of doing things and even "Biblical" ways of approaching situations. However, our logical, practical, common sense methods may not be at all the way that God has designed to bring His will to pass. Like the first believers, there are times when God tells us to wait for Him and instead, we busy ourselves doing things that He did not ask us to do. There are times when we put all of our own criteria on something or someone even though that may or may not be the criteria that God has for that thing or person. There are times when, even though we are very prayerful, we are simply wrong because we are not waiting for God and listening for the Holy Spirit the way that we should. The disciples were told to wait for the Holy Spirit before they went anywhere or did anything for Jesus. In our walk with the Lord, we also must learn to wait for the Holy Spirit, both for His prompting and His power, before we go anywhere or do anything in Jesus name. Otherwise, we ourselves are no better than lot casters.

Because Jesus was raised from the dead, the old way of doing things was made obsolete. The Gospel had changed everything for Christ followers, including His original disciples and believers today. Christ's first 120 followers waited in Jerusalem for the Holy Spirit to come and impart the fullness of the New Covenant into their lives. They needed Jesus' mantle to fall upon them like Elijah's cloak fell to Elisha, and they needed a new guidance system which would lead them into all truth and show them what to do and how to do it. Let us, like them, wait for the direction of the Holy Spirit and power from heaven as we press onwards, out of the old way and into the new life that we have in Christ.

> {Zec 4:6b} 6b **'Not by might nor by power, but by my Spirit,'** *says the LORD Almighty.*

> {Jhn 6:63} 63 **The Spirit [new way] gives life; the flesh [old way] counts for nothing.** *The words I have spoken to you--they are full of the Spirit and life.*

CHAPTER 6
Pentecost

From the start of the second chapter of the Book of Acts, there was great anticipation and expectancy as the 120 disciples of the risen and ascended Lord Jesus waited for Him to send power from heaven. Their King had given them a global assignment but had told them to wait to be empowered by the Holy Spirit so that they could carry out their Kingdom task. In this chapter, we're going to examine the significance of the events of Pentecost and the inclusion of believers from all nations into Christ. We will also consider some dynamics of the Holy Spirit's workings in our lives, explore what being filled with the Holy Spirit really means, and discuss the significance of the gift of tongues. Then, in the next chapter, we will dig deeper into the heavenly empowerment we have been given as followers of Christ so that we can do the things that the first believers did in the Book of Acts.

More Old to New

On the day of Pentecost, God fearing Jews from every nation under heaven were gathered in Jerusalem. This was because there was an important Feast of God taking place which required all Israelite men to be there. In the Old Testament, Feasts of God serve as prophetic foreshadows of the work of Christ. (see Leviticus 23) Three of these Feasts were fulfilled through Jesus' crucifixion, resurrection, and the outpouring of the Holy Spirit. Here is a chart of them:

ISRAEL	FEAST OF GOD	FULFILLED IN CHRIST
Passover	Passover	Crucifixion
Red Sea	Feast of First Fruits	Resurrection
Law at Sinai	Feast of Weeks	Pentecost

We previously covered how the original *Passover* (see Exodus 12) was a prophetic shadow of what God fulfilled through the sacrifice of His Son Jesus, our eternal Passover Lamb. In the first Passover, Israelites who were enslaved in Egypt slaughtered a lamb and painted its blood on their doorposts so that the destroyer could not touch them. This was a picture of Jesus, the Lamb of God, whose blood was shed on the posts of the cross so that, by His blood, we who believe overcome the things that seek to enslave and destroy us, including the destroyer himself who is the devil. Jews observe the Passover every year to remember how God delivered them from slavery to freedom, and we observe communion to remember what Christ has done for us.

Three days after Passover, early in the morning, the Israelites walked through the Red Sea on dry ground and their enemies, the Egyptians, were overcome. (see Exodus 14) In the years that followed, after the Israelites entered into the Promised Land, every year on the anniversary of this historic event, early in the morning, the appointed priest would wave the first sheaf of the harvest, a bundle of grain from the first cutting, as an offering to dedicate the harvest to the Lord. This was an observance of the *Feast of First Fruits*. (see Leviticus 23:9-14) Through this, they dedicated the first and best portion to God and celebrated the harvest that was still to come. Early in the morning on the third day after Christ's crucifixion, Jesus walked out of the tomb, having conquered the enemies of sin and death. On the anniversary of the day that the waters of the Red Sea had been rolled away so that the Israelites walked on to freedom, the stone of Jesus' tomb was rolled away and He walked out to eternal life. Jesus is the first fruits of the resurrection, the first and best portion of the harvest, wholly dedicated to God. This means that we who believe and will be resurrected when He returns are the harvest that He celebrates.

> {1Co 15:23 NLT} 23 But there is an order to this resurrection: **Christ was raised as the first of the harvest; then all who belong to Christ will be raised when he comes back**.

Then, fifty days after the Israelites had walked through the Red Sea, God met with His people in power and with fire. Israel was to be dedicated to God as a kingdom of priests and a holy nation, God's very own special possession and treasure out of all the nations on the earth. Accordingly, God told Moses to consecrate the people for three days, meaning to have them wash themselves and their clothes and have them abstain from common activities while they waited to meet their God. (see Exodus 19:1-16) Then, on the fiftieth day after leaving Egypt, God descended on the mountain in a great pillar of fire with billowing smoke, thunder which shook the earth, and a great trumpet blast. All of the Israelites standing at the base of the mountain trembled at the power of their God. At Sinai, God wrote His Laws on tablets of stone, and the Israelites agreed to do everything that God commanded. (see Deuteronomy 9:10; Exodus 24:7) Unfortunately, because they were unable to obey the Laws of God, 3,000 people died. (see Exodus 32:28)

> {Exo 19:16-19} 16 On the morning of the third day [of consecration] there was thunder and lightning, with a thick cloud over the mountain, and a very loud trumpet blast. Everyone in the camp trembled. 17 Then Moses led the people out of the camp to meet with God, and they stood at the foot of the mountain. 18 **Mount Sinai was covered with smoke, because the LORD descended on it in fire. The smoke billowed up from it like smoke from a furnace, and the whole mountain trembled violently.** 19 As the sound of the trumpet grew louder and louder, Moses spoke and the voice of God answered him.

> {Exo 24:17} 17 To the Israelites **the glory of the LORD looked like a consuming fire** on top of the mountain.

In the years that followed, all Israelite men were required to gather in Jerusalem for the *Feast of Weeks*, which takes place on the anniversary of God's powerful Sinai visitation. This was a feast of celebration, a holy day for worshipping the Lord and rejoicing in the abundance of the Promised Land. Everyone was included in this feast, even foreigners, and the poor were remembered with mercy and grace. (see Deuteronomy 16:1-17; Leviticus 23:15-22) After Christ's resurrection, He appeared to His disciples for forty days and then the disciples waited in Jerusalem for ten days. Then, the day of *Pentecost*, which means *fiftieth day* arrived on the anniversary of the day God descended to His people with fire power at

Sinai. Notably, leading up to this day, Christ's disciples had all been washed through water baptism, and they had devoted themselves to prayer while they waited for the Lord to pour out the Holy Spirit.

> *{Act 1:4-5, 8} 4 On one occasion, while he was eating with them, he gave them this command: "Do not leave Jerusalem, but wait for the gift my Father promised, which you have heard me speak about. 5 For John baptized with water,* **but in a few days you will be baptized with the Holy Spirit."** *... 8* **But you will receive power when the Holy Spirit comes on you;** *and you will be my witnesses in Jerusalem, and in all Judea and Samaria, and to the ends of the earth."*

> *{Act 2:1-4} 1* **When the day of Pentecost came,** *they [120 disciples of Christ] were all together in one place. 2 Suddenly* **a sound like the blowing of a violent wind came from heaven and filled the whole house** *where they were sitting. 3 They saw what seemed to be* **tongues of fire that separated and came to rest on each of them.** *4* **All of them were filled with the Holy Spirit** *and began to speak in other tongues as the Spirit enabled them.*

> *{Act 2:33} 33 [Jesus has been] Exalted to the right hand of God, he has received from the Father* **the promised Holy Spirit and has poured out what you now see and hear.**

The same fire power of God which descended on the top of Mount Sinai had now descended into the very hearts of Christ's disciples. The same gigantic fire which was on top of Mount Sinai was now divided into smaller segments and rested upon (and within) each of them. The fiery finger of God which had written His Laws on tablets of stone now wrote on hearts of stone and transformed them into hearts of flesh. (see Ezekiel 11:19, 36:26-27; Jeremiah 24:7) A new people was sealed for redemption and set apart to God as His very precious possession, His people, the Church. (see 2 Corinthians 1:22, 5:5) In fact, on the day of Pentecost, Peter delivered a speech (which we will discuss in depth in a later chapter) explaining Christ's resurrection and this fire power from heaven. That very day, 3,000 people received eternal life through faith in Jesus and were baptized into Christ.

These three feasts from the Old Testament, *Passover*, the *Feast of First Fruits*, and the *Feast of Weeks*, all served as prophetic shadows of the work of Christ. They also serve to demonstrate that the old has passed and the new has come. The Old Covenant (the Law) was given by the fire of God on the mountain, consisting of commandments which brought death, and 3,000 people died. The New Covenant (God's grace and eternal life through faith in Christ) gives believers the fire of God within us and, on the day of Pentecost, 3,000 were brought into everlasting life! All things have been made new!

> *{2Co 3:6-9} 6 He has made us competent as* **ministers of a new covenant**--*not of the letter but of the Spirit;* **for the letter kills, but the Spirit gives life.** *7 Now if the ministry that brought death, which was engraved in letters on stone, came with glory, so that the Israelites could not look steadily at the face of Moses because of its glory, transitory though it was, 8 will not the ministry of the Spirit be even more glorious? 9* **If the ministry that brought condemnation was glorious, how much more glorious is the ministry that brings righteousness!**

Inclusion in the Outpouring

In addition to this dramatic outpouring of the Holy Spirit upon Jews in Jerusalem on the day of Pentecost, similar events later in the Book of Acts demonstrate the inclusion of Samaritans, Gentiles, and disciples of John the Baptist who believed Jesus. Just like the *Feast of Weeks/Pentecost* was a Feast of God that included foreigners, as the Gospel spread to the ends of the earth, all people were included in the gift of the Holy Spirit.

For instance, by the eighth chapter of Acts, believers had been scattered out of Jerusalem due to persecution and Philip, an evangelist, went to Samaria and preached the Gospel of Jesus Christ. Many believed and were baptized into the name of the Lord Jesus.

> *{Act 8:4-6, 12} 4 Those who had been scattered preached the word wherever they went. 5* **Philip went down to a city in Samaria and proclaimed the Messiah there***. 6 When the crowds heard Philip and saw the signs he performed, they all paid close attention to what he said. ... 12 But* **when they believed** *Philip as he proclaimed the good news of the kingdom of God and the name of Jesus Christ,* **they were baptized***, both men and women.*

All of this is not as casual as it may seem. You see, Jews hated Samaritans and considered them half-breeds with illegitimate worship practices. This was because, way back in Israel's history, the twelve tribes of Israel were divided into two kingdoms after the reign of David's son Solomon. Ten tribes formed the *Northern Kingdom*, named *Israel*, and two tribes formed the *Southern Kingdom*, named *Judah*. The Southern Kingdom's capital was Jerusalem and God faithfully maintained His covenant with these people because of His promise to King David that the Messiah would come from his descendants. (see 1 Kings 11:26-40; 2 Samuel 7:1-17; 1 Chronicles 17:1-15) The Northern Kingdom's capital was Samaria which was set up almost like an imitation Jerusalem, a city on a different hill which had been purchased by King Omri and was named after the guy that he bought it from. Notably, the first king to reign from Samaria was Ahab who was married to Jezebel. Both of them did evil in the sight of the Lord and they were succeeded by king after king who reigned from Samaria in rebellion against God's ways. Finally in 722 BC, the Northern Kingdom was captured by invading Assyrians, and the people of Israel were sent into exile. (see 2 Kings 17:5-23) The Assyrians then sent their own people to live in and resettle the Israelite towns and cities that they had conquered. However, since these Assyrian foreigners did not worship the Lord properly in His land, God sent lions among them and people died. In response, the Assyrians brought back some of the exiled priests of Israel so that they could teach the new settlers how to worship the God of Israel so that the lions would leave. The priests taught these immigrants how to worship the one true God, but the people still persisted in worshiping their own gods at the same time, blending their worship practices. (see 2 Kings 17:24-41) This is why their descendants, who were the Samaritans of Jesus' day in the New Testament, were regarded as illegitimate half-breeds by the Jews.

Accordingly, at this stage in the story of Acts, it was controversial for the scorned Samaritans to be included in the gift of salvation through Jesus, the Messiah from David's lineage. In line with this, during His earthly ministry, Jesus told His disciples not to go to Samaritans but only to Israelites, indicating that even He made a distinction between Jews and Samaritans. (see Matthew 10:5) However, Jesus also had an encounter with a Samaritan woman, who was surprised that a Jewish man was talking to her because it was considered so forbidden and scandalous. This said, Jesus revealed to this most unlikely woman that He is the Messiah who came to bring living water, which is symbolic of the Holy Spirit, so that those who worship God, no matter where they come from, may worship Him in Spirit and in truth, even Samaritans! (see John 4:1-26, 7:38-39) Therefore, when the Samaritans believed Philip's preaching of Jesus and were baptized into His name, the apostles went to fill them with the Holy Spirit so that they could fully partake of this heavenly gift. Jews and Samaritans were both officially included in salvation through Christ and the gift of the Holy Spirit.

> *{Act 8:14-17} 14 When the apostles in Jerusalem heard that Samaria had accepted the word of God, they sent Peter and John to Samaria. 15 When they arrived, **they prayed for the new believers there that they might receive the Holy Spirit**, 16 because the Holy Spirit had not yet come on any of them; they had simply been baptized in the name of the Lord Jesus. 17 Then Peter and John placed their hands on them, **and they received the Holy Spirit**.*

Later, in the tenth chapter of the Book of Acts, a God-fearing Roman soldier named Cornelius (who always gave generously to the poor) had a vision from heaven. In this vision, an angel of the Lord instructed Cornelius to fetch the apostle Peter and told him where Peter could be found. (see Acts 10:1-8) Meanwhile, Peter also had a vision from the Lord. In this vision, which occurred three times in the same way, unclean foods descended from heaven in what appeared to be a great sheet, while the Lord said, *What God has made clean, do not call common.* Immediately after this, Peter was informed that Cornelius' men were waiting for him, and he went with them to Cornelius' house. (see Acts 10:9-33) Peter proceeded to preach the Gospel of Jesus Christ and, as he did, the Holy Spirit was poured out on Gentiles in a very similar fashion to how it was poured out on Pentecost.

> *{Act 10:44-48} **While Peter was still speaking these words, the Holy Spirit came on all who heard the message**. 45 The circumcised believers who had come with Peter were astonished that **the gift of the Holy Spirit had been poured out even on Gentiles.** 46 For they heard them speaking in tongues and praising God. Then Peter said, 47 "Surely no one can stand in the way of their being baptized with water. **They have received the Holy Spirit just as we have.**" 48 So he ordered that they be baptized in the name of Jesus Christ. Then they asked Peter to stay with them for a few days.*

Sharing the Gospel of Jesus Christ with Gentiles would have been even more controversial than sharing it with Samaritans. This is because, historically speaking, ever since God called Abraham out of Ur of the Chaldeans, all of Israel has been set apart from everyone else on earth as a special people. (see Genesis 12:1-3; Exodus 19:5; Deuteronomy 7:6, etc.) Since Abraham, Israelites have had exclusive rights to the one true God who created heaven and earth, and God-given rights to the land of Israel. No foreigners (all collectively referred to as Gentiles) were included in God's special people unless they were circumcised. Also, Jews knew from their history, particularly their exodus from Egypt, that God made a distinction between Jews and Gentiles. (see Exodus 8:22-2, 9:4, 26) Additionally, the Court of Gentiles at God's

Temple was the furthest away from the Most Holy Place where God's presence dwelt because Gentiles were not permitted to draw near to God. Notably, in Jesus' day, Jews had taken this separation from Gentiles a little too far and had turned the Gentile court into a marketplace rather than a welcoming room. The point is that, throughout history and right up to this point in the Book of Acts, there had been great animosity and hostility between Jews and Gentiles. (see Ephesians 2:11-22)

Needless to say, it was bizarre and offensive for God to break through these barriers and include Gentiles in salvation through Christ. During His ministry, Jesus had specifically told his disciples not to go to the Gentiles but only to Israelites. (see Matthew 10:5) Accordingly, given the fact that Jews were scattered to every nation of the earth, it would have been a reasonable assumption that Jesus was now sending His disciples to the ends of the earth to convert only scattered Jews to faith in Him as their Messiah. This said, there were only two people that Jesus praised for their great faith. These were a Syrophoenician woman who begged for her daughter's deliverance and a Roman Centurion who asked Jesus to heal his servant. Both were Gentiles but Jesus granted their requests because they believed Him. (see Matthew 8:5-13, 15:21-28; Mark 7:24-30; Luke 7:1-10) In line with this, as Peter preached at Cornelius' house, the Lord sovereignly poured the Holy Spirit upon them because they believed the word of Christ and His resurrection. The Holy Spirit came upon Gentiles without any interference from man, confirming their inclusion into the faith and into this heavenly gift.

> {Act 10:34-36, 43} 34 Then Peter began to speak: "**I now realize how true it is that God does not show favoritism 35 but accepts from every nation the one who fears him** and does what is right. 36 You know the message God sent to the people of Israel, announcing the good news of peace through Jesus Christ, **who is Lord of all.** ... 43 All the prophets testify about him that **everyone who believes in him receives forgiveness of sins through his name**."

Later, when Peter recapitulated the whole incident to fellow believers after traveling back to Jerusalem, they were quite upset with him at first. But Peter explained how God had clearly accepted Gentiles into faith in Jesus Christ.

> {Act 11:12-18} 12 **The Spirit told me to have no hesitation [make no distinction] about going with them**. These six brothers also went with me, and we entered the man's house. 13 He told us how he had seen an angel appear in his house and say, 'Send to Joppa for Simon who is called Peter. 14 **He will bring you a message through which you and all your household will be saved.**' 15 "As I began to speak, **the Holy Spirit came on them as he had come on us at the beginning**. 16 Then I remembered what the Lord had said: 'John baptized with water, but you will be baptized with the Holy Spirit.' 17 **So if God gave them the same gift he gave us who believed in the Lord Jesus Christ, who was I to think that I could stand in God's way?**" 18 When they heard this, they had no further objections and praised God, saying, "**So then, even to Gentiles God has granted repentance that leads to life.**"

Lastly, in the nineteenth chapter of Acts, there were men in Ephesus who had been baptized by John the Baptist. When the apostle Paul arrived in Ephesus, he quickly instructed them with updates about Jesus being the One to whom John the Baptist had pointed. The men were then baptized in the name of Jesus and received the Holy Spirit when Paul laid hands on them. This left no doubt that John the Baptist was the forerunner of the promised One but not the One and certainly not a competitor to the One. John the Baptist's disciples were unquestionably included in God's grace of salvation through Jesus Christ the Messiah.

> *{Act 19:1-7} 1 While Apollos was at Corinth, Paul took the road through the interior and arrived at Ephesus. There he found some disciples 2 and asked them, "**Did you receive the Holy Spirit when you believed?**" They answered, "**No, we have not even heard that there is a Holy Spirit**." 3 So Paul asked, "Then what baptism did you receive?" "John's baptism," they replied. 4 Paul said, "John's baptism was a baptism of repentance. He told the people to believe in the one coming after him, that is, in Jesus." 5 On hearing this, they were baptized in the name of the Lord Jesus. 6 When Paul placed his hands on them, **the Holy Spirit came on them**, and they spoke in tongues and prophesied. 7 There were about twelve men in all.*

All of these events confirm that Jews, Samaritans, Gentiles, and disciples of John the Baptist were forever included in salvation through faith in Christ. Of course, this also served to fulfill the promises and prophecies (of which there are many) of the Messiah of Israel who would save not only Israel but the Gentiles as well, in addition to a prophecy that was spoken over Jesus as an eight day old baby. For example:

> *{Isa 42:6} 6 "I, the LORD, have called you in righteousness; I will take hold of your hand. I will keep you and will **make you to be a covenant for the people and a light for the Gentiles**,*

> *{Isa 49:6} 6 he says: "It is too small a thing for you to be my servant to restore the tribes of Jacob and bring back those of Israel I have kept. **I will also make you a light for the Gentiles, that my salvation may reach to the ends of the earth**."*

> *{Luk 2:30-32} 30 For my eyes have seen **your salvation**, 31 which you have prepared in the sight of **all nations**: 32 **a light for revelation to the Gentiles, and the glory of your people Israel**."*

> *{Gal 3:14} 14 He redeemed us **in order that the blessing given to Abraham might come to the Gentiles through Christ Jesus**, so that by faith we might **receive the promise of the Spirit**.*

Long story short, receipt of the Holy Spirit is a deposit from heaven for all who place their faith in Christ. Through this, we have a guarantee of heaven and eternal life on the new earth to come where worshippers from all nations will praise the Lord together forever. (see Ephesians 1:13; Romans 8:23; 2 Corinthians 1:22, 5:5; Psalm 87; Revelation 5:9, 21:10-27)

Power from Above

Before Jesus ascended into heaven, He met with His disciples to commission them for Kingdom work. In order for His disciples to do the works that Jesus did, they needed power from above.

*{Jhn 14:12} 12 Very truly I tell you, **whoever believes in me will do the works I have been doing, and they will do even greater things** than these, because I am going to the Father.*

*{Jhn 20:21-22} 21 Again Jesus said, "Peace be with you! **As the Father has sent me, I am sending you.**" 22 And with that **he breathed on them and said, "Receive the Holy Spirit."***

*{Act 1:8} 8 **But you will receive power when the Holy Spirit comes on you; and you will be my witnesses** in Jerusalem, and in all Judea and Samaria, and to the ends of the earth."*

The words for *spirit* in Hebrew and Greek can both mean *breath*. God breathed the breath of life into Adam and God breathed the Holy Spirit into Jesus to raise Him from the grave. Jesus literally breathed on His disciples before His ascension to heaven. (see John 20:22) It is up for debate whether or not the disciples received a portion of the Holy Spirit when He did this or if this was a prophetically symbolic act on Jesus' part. Either way, when the disciples were gathered together in the upper room on the day of Pentecost, they heard the sound of a mighty rushing wind, the very breath of God, the Holy Spirit being poured out upon them.

*{Act 2:2-11} 2 Suddenly a **sound like the blowing of a violent wind came from heaven and filled the whole house where they were sitting**. 3 They saw what seemed to be tongues of fire that separated and came to rest on each of them. 4 All of them were filled with the Holy Spirit and **began to speak in other tongues as the Spirit enabled them**.   5 Now there were staying in Jerusalem God-fearing Jews from every nation under heaven. 6 When they heard this sound, a crowd came together in bewilderment, because **each one heard their own language being spoken**. 7 Utterly amazed, they asked: "Aren't all these who are speaking Galileans? 8 Then how is it that each of us hears them in our native language? 9 Parthians, Medes and Elamites; residents of Mesopotamia, Judea and Cappadocia, Pontus and Asia, 10 Phrygia and Pamphylia, Egypt and the parts of Libya near Cyrene; visitors from Rome 11 (both Jews and converts to Judaism); Cretans and Arabs--**we hear them declaring the wonders of God in our own tongues!**"*

Once the Holy Spirit was poured out, the believers in Jerusalem were supernaturally empowered by God. Immediately, they spoke in foreign languages unknown to them about the great wonders of God, most likely about the resurrection of Jesus Christ, the Messiah of Israel. Later, when the Holy Spirit was received by the Samaritan believers, they also manifested some supernatural ability, even though what they did is not mentioned specifically. (see Acts 8:18) When the Holy Spirit was poured out at Cornelius' house, the people spoke in tongues and praised God. (Acts 10:46) Lastly, when the Holy Spirit was given to believers in Ephesus, they spoke in tongues and prophesied. (see Acts 19:6) Clearly, when the Holy Spirit came upon believers, they received power from above.

We previously discussed the Old Testament example of the transfer from Elijah to Elisha. Elijah's cloak fell to Elisha and Elisha continued Elijah's work and did twice as many miracles. This was a prophetic example of what happened when Jesus ascended to heaven and poured the Holy Spirit into believers. Christ's disciples were now empowered to carry out His purpose and to work miracles the way that He did. (We will dig more into this anointing for the works of God in the next chapter.) There are a few other noteworthy Old Testament examples of God sharing His Spirit. First, in the days of Moses, Moses was the only one who was able to approach God to receive wisdom from Him in order to lead the people of Israel. (see Exodus 24:2) The workload of administering justice for the people became overwhelming so Moses, heeding the counsel of his father-in-law, appointed seventy elders to judge smaller disputes. (see Exodus 18:13-26) The Lord then told Moses to gather the elders of Israel together so that He could share the Spirit of the Lord, which was on Moses, with the elders. This way, they would be able to help in bearing Moses' burden because they were empowered by the same Spirit that Moses had so that they could do the works that Moses did. Then, when the Spirit of the Lord came upon the elders of Israel, they prophesied. (see Numbers 11:16-30) Moses was so delighted at this event that he uttered words that came to pass at Pentecost, *"I wish that all of the Lord's people were prophets and that the Lord would put His Spirit on them!"* Additionally, in the Book of Judges Othiniel, Gideon, Jephthah, and Samson each experienced the Spirit of the Lord *coming upon them, rushing upon them, clothing them,* or *stirring them* so that they were strengthened with power to do great exploits for God. They were particularly empowered for going to war against enemies in oftentimes seemingly impossible situations. (Judges 3:10, 6:34, 11:29, 13:25, 14:6, 19, 15:14) The Spirit of the Lord also came upon Saul, Israel's first anointed king. When this happened, Saul prophesied and even onlookers wondered aloud, *"Can anyone be a prophet? Even Saul?"* (see 1 Samuel 10:1-12) In another instance, the Spirit of the Lord came upon Saul in righteous anger over the way that enemies were treating the Israelites, and he led Israel to victory in battle. (see 1 Samuel 11:6) Lastly, the Spirit of the Lord came powerfully upon David, the next king of Israel. This anointing made David a brave warrior and a man of war with good judgment, able to slay giants and defeat all of Israel's enemies by God's power which was with him. (see 1 Samuel 16:10, 18) Moreover, this list does not include the experiences that the Prophets of the Old Testament had with the Spirit of the Lord, which we do not have time to get into in detail right now. Most significantly, even Jesus demonstrated this working dynamic of receiving power from Holy Spirit as power from above. After Jesus was baptized by John the Baptist, the Holy Spirit descended upon Him and rested upon Him like a dove. (see Matthew 3:16; Mark 1:10; Luke 3:22; John 1:32-33) Following this, Jesus began His ministry with power from heaven. In His first public speech, He announced that *the Spirit of the Lord was upon Him,* anointing Him to proclaim the Kingdom of God, to heal the sick, to cast out demons, to raise the dead, and to destroy the works of the devil who is the ultimate enemy of all mankind. (see Luke 4:14; 1 John 3:8)

> *{Luk 3:21-22} 21 When all the people were being baptized, Jesus was baptized too. And as he was praying, heaven was opened 22 and* **the Holy Spirit descended on him in bodily form like a dove.** *And a voice came from heaven: "You are my Son, whom I love; with you I am well pleased."*

> *{Luk 4:18-19} 18* **"The Spirit of the Lord is on me,** *because he has anointed me to* **proclaim good news to the poor.** *He has sent me to proclaim* **freedom for the prisoners** *and recovery of* **sight for the blind,** *to* **set the oppressed free,** *19 to proclaim the year* **of the Lord's favor."** *(quoting Isaiah 61:1-2)*

> *{Act 10:38} 38 how **God anointed Jesus** of Nazareth **with the Holy Spirit and power**, and how he went around **doing good** and **healing all who were under the power of the devil**, because God was with him.*

The word for *power* in Greek is *dynamis* from which we derive our word for *dynamite* and it certainly expresses explosive power. The word *dynamis* is technically defined as *great power or strength*, *power for performing miracles*, and the *power resting upon armies*. However, the word *dynamis* can also be translated as *virtue* or *moral power and excellence of soul*. These two meanings express two different dynamics of the Holy Spirit that Jesus clearly demonstrated in action. Because Jesus was born by the power of the Holy Spirit, He had the perfect nature of God within Him. This empowered Him from within for perfect conduct according to God's standard and, accordingly, He maintained right-standing with God at all times. This said, when the Holy Spirit descended on Jesus, He received dynamite power from heaven to do the works of God. The power of God was working both within Jesus for perfect character and resting upon Jesus to enable His works against the kingdom of darkness and all the enemies of mankind.

Think of it kind of like this: To the natural eye when a bolt of lightning strikes the earth, it appears that lightning is coming down from the clouds. However, technically speaking, it is not a one way transaction. In truth, electric current rises up from the earth to meet the power that is coming down from the heavens. Sometimes, we can even see this meeting of heaven and earth when the two bolts of lightning unite in midair in a dynamic explosion of electricity and then we hear its rumblings. This is like the power of God being both within Jesus and descending upon Jesus. Indwelling power for virtue gave Him righteousness, or right standing with God, which allowed Him to reach up in prayer to God in the throne room of heaven. Then, power from heaven descended down to meet these prayers. Without indwelling righteousness on the earth, God cannot be accessed. Without power from above, the works cannot be done. But when these two forces meet, heaven and earth kiss – *your Kingdom come, your will be done, on earth as it is in heaven.* The result is miracles – the very works of God.

Along these lines, after the Holy Spirit was poured out on the day of Pentecost, throughout the Book of Acts, believers were *full of the Holy Spirit* or *filled with the Holy Spirit*. In our language, these words appear to be the same. However, in the Greek they are different, and their difference expresses the exact dynamic that Jesus demonstrated. Being *full of the Holy Spirit* denotes *a permeation of the soul* and longevity of character. Believers who are *full of the Holy Spirit* exhibit Christ's character because they manifest the fruit of the Spirit, namely, love, joy, peace, patience, kindness, goodness, faithfulness, gentleness, self-control and self-sacrificing devotion to God. (see Galatians 5:22-23) Being *full of the Holy Spirit* is also what strengthens believers through various trials of life and opposition to the faith.

> *{Act 6:3-5} 3 Brothers and sisters, choose seven men from among you who are known to be **full of the Spirit** and wisdom. We will turn this responsibility over to them 4 and will give our attention to prayer and the ministry of the word." 5 This proposal pleased the whole group. They chose Stephen, a man **full of faith and of the Holy Spirit**; also Philip, Procorus, Nicanor, Timon, Parmenas, and Nicolas from Antioch, a convert to Judaism.*

*{Act 7:55} 55 But Stephen, **full of the Holy Spirit**, looked up to heaven and saw the glory of God, and Jesus standing at the right hand of God. [while being stoned to death]*

*{Act 11:24} 24 He [Barnabas] was a good man, **full of the Holy Spirit** and faith, and a great number of people were brought to the Lord.*

Being *filled with the Holy Spirit* indicates an immediate instance or surge for the moment, which passes when the moment is over. For example, this same word is used to describe being *filled with wonder* (see Acts 3:10) or *filled with jealousy,* (see Acts 5:17) neither of which last forever. Believers who were *filled with the Holy Spirit* were filled with power from above to prophesy, dream dreams, speak in other languages, proclaim the Gospel with boldness, heal the sick, cast out demons, and raise the dead.

*{Act 2:4} 4 All of them were **filled with the Holy Spirit** and began to speak in other tongues as the Spirit enabled them.*

*{Act 4:8, 31} 8 Then Peter, **filled with the Holy Spirit**, said to them: "Rulers and elders of the people!*

*{Act 4:31} 31 After they prayed, the place where they were meeting was shaken. And they were all **filled with the Holy Spirit** and spoke the word of God boldly.*

*{Act 9:17} 17 Then Ananias went to the house and entered it. Placing his hands on Saul, he said, "Brother Saul, the Lord--Jesus, who appeared to you on the road as you were coming here--has sent me so that you may see again and be **filled with the Holy Spirit**."*

*{Act 13:8-11} 8 But Elymas the sorcerer (for that is what his name means) opposed them and tried to turn the proconsul from the faith. 9 Then Saul, who was also called Paul, **filled with the Holy Spirit**, looked straight at Elymas and said, 10 "You are a child of the devil and an enemy of everything that is right! You are full of all kinds of deceit and trickery. Will you never stop perverting the right ways of the Lord? 11 Now the hand of the Lord is against you. You are going to be blind for a time, not even able to see the light of the sun." Immediately mist and darkness came over him, and he groped about, seeking someone to lead him by the hand.*

Today, it is no different for us. Because the Holy Spirit has been poured out, when we believe in Jesus, we are marked and indwelt by the Spirit of the Lord. The Holy Spirit within us molds and shapes us to be like Jesus, and we have righteousness, or right standing, with God and access to Him as a free gift because of what Jesus did. As we follow Jesus, we become *full of the Holy Spirit* as the Lord permeates more and more of our lives and character. Then, as we set out to do the works of God, meaning the same works that Jesus did in the Gospels and even greater works, we are *filled with the Holy Spirit* to give us power from above. Sometimes, we can even feel the palpable presence of God, like a weight in the air which presses down on us, or an atmosphere that is filled with love and hope or charged with power. Sometimes, we can feel God's power burning in our inmost being, or in our hands for healing, or giving us goose bumps or things like this. Regardless of what we experience or feel, we become, like Jesus, a conduit of God's grace, reaching up to heaven in righteousness and bringing heaven to earth to work miracles.

Speaking in Tongues

While we have already learned that there were some significant events taking place on the day of Pentecost, there is one more prophetic shadow that we have not yet discussed. A long long time ago after the flood of Noah's day but before the call of Abraham, all of humanity spoke the same language. They decided to build a tower in Babel (which later became Babylon) so that they could reach the heavens, make a name for themselves, and so that they would not be scattered all over the face of the earth. The tower was symbolic of human independence and self-sufficiency. Building it was rooted in the concept that, as long as everyone on earth was united together, nothing would be impossible, and therefore, a relationship with God was not required. God saw this and intervened. He multiplied their languages so that people could not communicate with one another and He scattered them all over the face of the earth so that they could not unite in their efforts to rule the world without Him. (see Genesis 11:1-9) *Babel* means *confusion* and, needless to say, human communication has been babel-ed ever since! However, on the day of Pentecost when the Holy Spirit was poured out, there were men from every nation under heaven in Jerusalem for the *Feast of Weeks*. When believers who had received the Holy Spirit began speaking, they proclaimed the glory of God in the languages of every person who was there to invite believers from every nation, tribe, and tongue into salvation through Jesus Christ. (see Revelation 5:9)

> *{Act 2:5-13} 5 Now there were staying in Jerusalem God-fearing Jews **from every nation under heaven.** 6 When they heard this sound, a crowd came together in bewilderment, because each one heard their own language being spoken. 7 Utterly amazed, they asked: "**Aren't all these who are speaking Galileans? 8 Then how is it that each of us hears them in our native language?** 9 Parthians, Medes and Elamites; residents of Mesopotamia, Judea and Cappadocia, Pontus and Asia, 10 Phrygia and Pamphylia, Egypt and the parts of Libya near Cyrene; visitors from Rome 11 (both Jews and converts to Judaism); Cretans and Arabs--we hear them declaring the wonders of God in our own tongues!" 12 Amazed and perplexed, they asked one another, "What does this mean?" 13 Some, however, made fun of them and said, "They have had too much wine."*

Effectively, the supernatural ability to speak in tongues represents the "reversal" of what God had done at Babel. Not a reversal by giving everyone the same language but by reversing the confusion of having different languages. One aspect of speaking in tongues is that believers are given the supernatural ability to speak a language that we don't naturally know so that we can proclaim the Gospel of Jesus Christ to all the nations of the earth. God gives us the supernatural ability to communicate with one another, enabling us to unite together and build ourselves up. Of course, we do not build a tower to ourselves and our self-sufficiency but a temple of God to worship Christ and the sufficiency of His sacrifice. (see 1 Corinthians 3:16; Ephesians 2:19-22) As an example of the gift of tongues in action, I was in a great big mega-store one day, and there was a man with a very distinct ethnic look. Out of nowhere, the Holy Spirit bubbled up a phrase within me to speak to him. (I could not repeat this phrase to you now if I tried.) Embarrassingly, I confess that I did not have the nerve on that occasion to speak to this man what the Holy Spirit had spoken to me. However, when I went home, I typed on the internet the phrase that the Holy Spirit had spoken to me in the store. The phrase translated *Blessed be the name of the Lord* and it was in a language that I do not speak. Praise God! I only wish that I had spoken out the phrase to him! If I'd had the nerve to say this to him in his native language, I'm sure that we both would have been encouraged.

Conversely, tongues is also a sign to unbelieving Jews who have not accepted Christ as their Messiah. The prophet Isaiah foretold long ago that God would speak to His own people through a different people who had a strange tongue and a foreign speech. (Isaiah 28:11) In the context of Isaiah's prophecy, the Jews complained that God was speaking to them like children, giving them the same thing again and again to the point of nausea. Of course, God was doing this because they were not really listening to Him, which is why He had to repeat Himself over and over again. Similarly, in the days of Jesus, the Jews looked and searched the Scriptures while awaiting their Messiah. But when Jesus their Messiah came, they did not even recognize Him because they did not understand what God was saying to them. (see John 5:39-40) In accordance with Isaiah's prophecy, on the day of Pentecost, God began to speak to His people through a language that was not their own, which would have been horribly offensive. Furthermore, as the Gospel spread to include Gentiles, the thought that heathens could claim to know and worship the one true God of Israel would be a preposterous idea to any Jew who had not accepted Jesus as Savior and Lord. Therefore, an unbelieving Jew might presume that someone speaking in tongues must be drunk, just like the Jews in Jerusalem on the day of Pentecost. Notably, the apostle Paul clearly linked speaking in tongues with this Isaiah prophecy which anticipated this response from the Jews. (see 1 Corinthians 14:21)

Additionally, as a side note, this inclusion/exclusion pattern of communication was also demonstrated by Jesus. During His earthly ministry, Jesus did not speak foreign languages, but He uttered the mysteries of the Kingdom of God through the use of parables. He explained (or translated) His parables to His disciples who believed Him but to those who did not believe Him, the parables made no sense whatsoever, and their hearts were hardened more in unbelief. (see Matthew 13:11-17; Mark 4:11-12; Luke 8:9-10) Speaking in tongues has a similar inclusionary/exclusionary effect of including those who believe and excluding those who do not.

Speaking in tongues is also a gift that edifies believers through prayer and builds up our faith. The gift of tongues is the supernatural ability to speak to God in prayer in the language of heaven which we ourselves do not understand. As the Holy Spirit enables us to speak the languages of men and angels, we utter the mysteries of God in accordance with His perfect will. (see 1 Corinthians 13:1) Especially in circumstances in which we do not know how to pray, when we pray in tongues, our minds are able to disengage. This helps us not to lean on our own understanding but on the finished work of Christ and God's perfect and pleasing will. (see Proverbs 3:5-6; Romans 12:2) Our faith increases because we are praying perfect prayers, even things that our minds may not yet fully understand.

> *{1Co 14:2} 2 For **anyone who speaks in a tongue does not speak to people but to God**. Indeed, no one understands them; **they utter mysteries by the Spirit**.*

{Rom 8:26-28} 26 In the same way, the Spirit helps us in our weakness. **We do not know what we ought to pray for, but the Spirit himself intercedes for us through wordless groans.** *27 And he who searches our hearts knows the mind of the Spirit, because* **the Spirit intercedes for God's people in accordance with the will of God.** *28 And we know that in all things* **God works for the good of those who love him, who have been called according to his purpose.**

{1Co 14:14} 14 **For if I pray in a tongue, my spirit prays, but my mind is unfruitful.**

{Jde 1:20-21} 20 But you, dear friends, by **building yourselves up in your most holy faith and praying in the Holy Spirit***, 21 keep yourselves in God's love as you wait for the mercy of our Lord Jesus Christ to bring you to eternal life.*

The apostle Paul, who was probably used by God more than anyone else in history besides Jesus, praised God that he spoke in tongues more than anyone else. (see 1 Corinthians 14:18) It was his sincere desire for everyone to have the gift of tongues because he clearly understood its edifying value. (see 1 Corinthians 14:5) This said, he also made it clear that not everyone has the gift of tongues and that speaking in tongues will be over when the perfect comes, meaning at the return of Christ when He restores all things to their pre-sin condition. (see 1 Corinthians 12:8, 30) Therefore, if you do not have or never receive the gift of tongues, do not worry about it, and do not feel neglected or like you are missing out. Pursue love and earnestly desire spiritual gifts but trust that God knows what you need. (see 1 Corinthians 14:1)

As for me, I began praying in tongues many years ago and I must admit, it felt very strange at first. Then, I heard some false teachings about tongues, which gave me reservations about using the gift. Consequently, I allowed it to go dormant. For a few years, I would only pray in tongues if I was in a real predicament, and I did not let anyone know that I was doing it or that I had the gift. After a while, the Lord had brought me into deeper knowledge of the Scriptures, and He encouraged me to begin praying in tongues again. Now, when I pray in tongues, I sense the peace of God with me because I know that I am praying His perfect will into my life and the lives of those for whom I am praying. Additionally, whenever I minister in ways different from my ordinary day to day activities, I pray in tongues almost exclusively to prepare my heart and mind for the task of God. As a side note, I also believe that we can *pray in the spirit* in our own native language if we have fully surrendered our minds to the Holy Spirit's leading.

Lastly, tongues is a gift that can edify the Church in corporate worship when spoken publicly. Paul made it clear that tongues should not be forbidden but also gave some guidelines about how this gift works in a communal setting. If anyone prays in tongues publicly in corporate worship, then the tongue spoken must be interpreted into the language of the people who are listening. Remember, the gift of tongues is for the purpose of *including* foreigners in the faith and *communicating* with people so that they are able to understand. For example, if an English-speaking person were to go to Russia, the Lord may give them the supernatural ability to speak Russian so that they are able to proclaim the Gospel in a language that the hearers understand, hence, including them in the love of Christ. However, if God gives someone who is among English-speaking people a prayer that is in Russian, or any other language, it must be interpreted so that the English-speaking listeners can know what is being spoken and be encouraged in the Lord. Otherwise, everyone will just think we are crazy. (See 1 Corinthians 14 for more on this subject.) One of my first experiences with the gift of tongues was in a corporate setting. It was my first time at a church that believed in the gift of tongues, and the Spirit of the Lord was moving powerfully. On this day (even though it did not happen every time) as the pastor began to lead us, everyone spontaneously began to groan in their spirit and speak in tongues quietly. As the pastor spoke in tongues, he also interpreted what was being said. These were messages from the Lord for the purpose of strengthening our faith. I thought that it was the coolest thing that I'd ever seen... or heard!

The Baptism of the Holy Spirit

There are two ends of the theological spectrum concerning what we hear about as the *baptism of the Holy Spirit.* I don't mean to be difficult, but I tend to disagree with both sides of the debate. Let me get right to it and say that when it comes to the Lord Jesus and the Holy Spirit, it's not about an experience, it's about today. Think of it this way: You can ask someone, *Did you have a wedding?* and they could very well have had a wedding but be divorced today. They could have had a wedding many years ago but have a marriage which is in shambles or a spouse who has passed away. Asking about a wedding or a particular experience is not the right question – asking about the state of things today is.

Let's keep it simple. If you believe Jesus Christ is Lord and that God raised Him from the dead, then you received the Holy Spirit when you believed. (see Ephesians 1:13) If you do not believe Jesus, then you do not have the Holy Spirit in you, and you do not belong to Christ. (see Romans 8:9) Followers of Jesus are baptized with the Holy Spirit and with fire – purifying fire to burn sin out of our character and fire power to do the works of God. (see Matthew 3:11; Mark 1:8; Luke 3:16) This said, just because you have the Holy Spirit dwelling within you does not mean that the Holy Spirit is always upon you. And, just because you were filled with the Holy Spirit on a certain occasion does not mean that you are full today. Therefore, if you want more of Jesus, ask for more, ask to be *full* of the Holy Spirit and commit to living your life by following His direction. The Holy Spirit will guide you, shape you, and mold you to be like Jesus. Then, as God sends you to do Kingdom tasks for Him, whether that is praying for people, giving prophetic words, or working miracles, ask to be *filled* with the Holy Spirit and allow the power of God to come upon you as you carry out great exploits in the name of Jesus and for His glory.

Personally, I was water baptized in the Gulf of Mexico, and it is a day that I will remember forever. I was the first one dunked, and then I stood to the side, still in the water while other people were being baptized. As we waited, someone began to become very agitated because there was a crab crawling around our feet. Very calmly, I said to them, "Don't worry, it's on my foot." It was, but I didn't care, and I wasn't afraid in the slightest because the peace of God was with me. About a year later, I had become frustrated with certain situations in my life and, one night while I was taking a bath, I decided to re-baptize myself and re-dedicate myself to the Lord. I like to be thorough, so I dunked myself three times, once for the Father, once for the Son, and once for the Holy Spirit – no need to imitate me in this. When I came out of the water the third time, I was speaking a few words in tongues, not a lot, just a few. I experienced some significant breakthroughs in my life after that, and I somehow knew that it was connected to this new type of prayer. Since then, I have experienced many peaks and valleys in my life and walk of faith. There are days when I feel full of the Spirit and days when I feel not-so-full. There are times when I am filled and feel the power of God coming upon me like a weight of glory or a fire burning within me, and there are times when I do not feel anything at all, but God is still working. It is not about a feeling or an experience – it is all about Jesus. Therefore, no matter what I am feeling or experiencing, I always ask for more.

> *{Luk 11:9-13} 9 [Jesus speaking]* "**So I say to you: Ask and it will be given to you; seek and you will find; knock and the door will be opened to you.** *10 For everyone who asks receives; the one who seeks finds; and to the one who knocks, the door will be opened. 11 "Which of you fathers, if your son asks for a fish, will give him a snake instead? 12 Or if he asks for an egg, will give him a scorpion? 13 If you then, though you are evil, know how to give good gifts to your children,* **how much more will your Father in heaven give the Holy Spirit to those who ask him!**"

Let the cry of our hearts always be: *We want more of you, Lord Jesus! More of you, God! Come Holy Spirit!*

CHAPTER 7
Kingdom

We interrupt our previously scheduled programming for a special message from our sponsor – Heaven. Once the Holy Spirit was poured out on the day of Pentecost, believers in the Book of Acts were empowered and authorized to do the works that Jesus did. The transfer of mission and anointing from Jesus to His disciples had taken place, just like the transfer from Elijah to Elisha had prophetically symbolized. Let's dig deeper into the power and authority that Christ followers have been given so that we can do the things that the first believers did in the Book of Acts.

Jesus' Anointing

In the Bible, people's names often indicate their personality or purpose. The name *Jesus* means *God saves*, and this is certainly descriptive of God's purpose for Him. When Jesus described His mission on the earth, He described it like this:

> *{Jhn 3:17} 17 For God did not send his Son into the world to condemn the world, but* **to save the world through him**.

> *{Jhn 12:47} 47 "If anyone hears my words but does not keep them, I do not judge that person. For* **I did not come to judge the world, but to save the world**.

> *{Luk 19:10} 10 For the Son of Man came* **to seek and to save the lost**.*"*

Clearly, Jesus came for the purpose of saving the whole world, meaning every person in the human race who has been separated from God since the sin of Adam. This includes all of us, everyone we know, and everyone that we will ever meet. The word used to describe Jesus' purpose to *save* is *sozo* which means *to rescue from peril, to keep safe and sound,* and *to rescue from danger and destruction*. This includes imminent afflictions and oppressions and the peril of eternal damnation. Another way of saying it would be:

> *{Luk 4:18-19} 18* **"The Spirit of the Lord is on me**, *because he has* **anointed me** *to* **proclaim good news to the poor**. *He has sent me to proclaim* **freedom for the prisoners** *and* **recovery of sight for the blind**, *to* **set the oppressed free**, *19 to proclaim the* **year of the Lord's favor**.*"*
> *(quoting Isaiah 61:1-2)*

Jesus was anointed to *save*, [*sozo*] which is why we call Him our *Savior*. He is the Savior of all people, and it is not His will that anyone should not be saved. (see 1 Timothy 2:4, 4:10; 1 John 4:14; 2 Peter 3:9) This *salvation*, [*soteria*] includes *salvation, deliverance, healing,* and *sustenance* and is also technically defined as *deliverance from the molestation of all enemies*, is a free gift offered to everyone who will receive it by faith. To show you just how closely all of this is linked together, the word *Savior* is *soter* which stems from the word *sozo* and is the root word for *soteria*. I know it is silly to say it this way, but essentially, all of this means that the Gospel covers all aspects of Jesus' work of salvation [*soteria*] as our Savior [*soter*] who came to save [*sozo*] all who will believe.

> {1Ti 1:15} *15 Here is a trustworthy saying that deserves full acceptance:* **Christ Jesus came into the world to save [sozo] sinners--of whom I am the worst**.

> {Rom 1:16} *16 For I am not ashamed of* **the gospel, because it is the power of God that brings salvation [soteria] to everyone who believes**: *first to the Jew, then to the Gentile.*

> {1Jo 4:14} *14 And we have seen and testify that* **the Father has sent his Son to be the Savior [Soter] of the world**.

God gave Jesus all *power* and *authority* over everything in order to carry out His purpose. *Power is strength or ability*, as in being stronger than an opponent. We previously learned that the word for *power* in Greek is *dynamis,* like dynamite. On the other hand, *authority is rank and the right to do something*, as in being the boss and having your way. The word for authority is *exousia* and is defined as *the power of choice* or *the liberty to do as one pleases*, including *the power of rule or government*, or *jurisdiction*. Within Jesus' territory, which included all of creation, He had all *dynamis* and *exousia*.

This said, in order to save us so that we can receive the benefits of salvation through faith in Him, Jesus had to *overpower* the sin problem that Adam created back in the beginning. To recap, Adam and his wife lived on earth as God originally designed it. They had perfect bodies which never experienced sickness or even pain. There was no death, decay, or even the slightest diminishing of their strength. It was paradise and what we now know to be God's perfect will as it is in heaven. (see Revelation 21:4) However, the evil serpent, the devil, preyed on man's weakness and enticed him to sin, which put all of mankind in exorbitant and unpayable sin-debt. Sin led to a curse, the curse led to sickness and death, and we've all been plagued ever since because the devil *overpowered* us. What a mess. Then, Jesus entered into human weakness but, strengthened by divine nature, lived a sinless life. But on the cross, Jesus willingly allowed sin, the curse, and sickness to *overpower* Him to the point of death. For three days it seemed that evil was able to triumph. But God raised Jesus from the dead on the third day which proved that His *power* is stronger than every enemy of mankind, even the evil one. He demonstrated the *power* of an indestructible life and *overpowered* death and everything which causes it! (see Hebrews 7:16) Hallelujah!

> {Gal 3:13} *13* **Christ redeemed us from the curse** *of the law by becoming a curse for us, for it is written: "Cursed is everyone who is hung on a pole."*

> {1Pe 2:24} *24* **"He himself bore our sins"** *in his body on the cross, so that we might die to sins and live for righteousness;* **"by his wounds you have been healed."**

> {2Ti 1:10} *10 but it has now been revealed through the appearing of* **our Savior, Christ Jesus, who has destroyed death** *and has brought life and immortality to light* **through the gospel**.

> {1Jo 3:5, 8} *5 But you know that* **he appeared so that he might take away our sins**. *And in him is no sin. ... 8 The one who does what is sinful is of the devil, because the devil has been*

*sinning from the beginning. **The reason the Son of God appeared was to destroy the devil's work.***

Through His life, death, and resurrection, Jesus paid our otherwise unpayable sin debt and bought us back from sin and all of its effects and from subjection to the enemy. No matter the cost, Jesus paid it all. Moreover, Jesus did not just buy us, He bought us back so that through faith in Him, we can be restored to God's original design – the way that it was before Adam's error, and the way that it is in heaven. (see Ephesians 1:7; Colossians 1:14; 1 Timothy 2:6; Romans 3:24-25, 12:2) Notably, this is also why we call Christ our *Redeemer*. During the course of His earthly life, Jesus performed miracles by faith, trusting that God would raise Him from the dead on the third day, according to the Scriptures. In fact, we could say that He banked on it. Think of it like charging something on a credit card that you know you are going to pay in full at the end of the billing cycle. Better still, technically speaking, since the Lamb was slain from before the creation of the world, (see Revelation 13:8) it was more like a prepaid card with guaranteed assurance of available funds. Effectively, Jesus had purchasing *power* and with every miracle, when anyone came to Him in faith, He said to God, *Put their sin debt on My account.* He bought believers back from the oppression of the devil due to sin, curse, sickness, and death.

Additionally, God's original design was one which reflected His love for mankind, and He put man in charge of keeping it that way. God gave Adam and his wife all *authority* in the earth in their state of purity and innocence and they had God-given command over all creation including the animals, fish, birds, and plants. All they had to do was speak the word, and all of creation had to obey. For example, Adam could say to the birds, *Come here,* or to the clouds, *Move from here to there,* and the birds and clouds had to obey because they were subject to Adam's rule. Furthermore, before the wrong-tree incident, man outranked the devil and all Adam had to say to the serpent was, *No,* even though, unfortunately, he didn't. When Jesus walked on the earth, He had the same type of God-given authority over all creation that Adam had in the beginning. As God's Son, this authority was Jesus' birthright. He could do anything that He pleased, and all creation had to obey. Unlike Adam, Jesus maintained His rank over the devil even when the evil one tested Him for forty days in the wilderness by saying, in essence, *No.* Jesus' divine nature always led Him in purity so that He used His God-given authority to restore people to their pre-sin condition. Jesus also had authority from God to forgive sin, something only God can do and which inherently releases people from the devil's subjection. In line with all of this, the signs and wonders and works of God that followed Jesus' ministry proved that He is the boss of everything and the God-appointed King of all.

> *{Mar 1:27} 27 The people were all so amazed that they asked each other, "What is this? **A new teaching--and with authority! He even gives orders to impure spirits and they obey him.**" (see also Luke 4:36)*

> *{Luk 5:23-24} 23 Which is easier: to say, 'Your sins are forgiven,' or to say, 'Get up and walk'? 24 **But I want you to know that the Son of Man has authority on earth to forgive sins.**" So he said to the paralyzed man, "I tell you, get up, take your mat and go home." (see also Matthew 9:1-8, Mark 2:5-11)*

*{Mat 8:27} 27 The men were amazed and asked, "What kind of man is this? **Even the winds and the waves obey him!"***(see also Mark 4:41)*

All of this is to say that Jesus' miracles testified to Jesus' absolute *power* and *authority* over all creation and revealed a loving God's perfect and pleasing will *on earth as it is in heaven*. Think of it this way: Imagine a bad teenage babysitter who abuses the child that they are supposed to be caring for. The babysitter is stronger than the child and is temporarily the person in charge. Even if the child was somehow able to overpower the babysitter, the babysitter would still technically be the person in authority. The father of the child is a grown man, stronger than the teenage babysitter, and is also the one who is truly the boss of the child. As soon as the father of the child returns, the babysitter's power and authority are totally usurped and nullified. The father banishes the babysitter so that they cannot abuse or oppress the child anymore, and the father comforts the child to undo any and all damage done by the bad babysitter. In a similar way, ever since Adam's sin, all of mankind has had a really bad babysitter, namely, sin and the devil which we have been unable to conquer in our own strength and have been subject to. But then Jesus came as a representative of our heavenly Father, God. Jesus was stronger than sin, the curse, sickness, and the devil, meaning that He was able to *overpower* them in addition to the fact that He was truly the boss who had all *authority*. (see Matthew 12:29; Mark 3:27) Basically, when Jesus showed up, the power and authority of sin and the devil were totally usurped and nullified for anyone who placed their faith in Christ. Jesus' miracles attest to this, and each act of love and compassion had a way of saying, *Daddy's home.*

Previously, we listed Elijah's miracles in order to examine how his purpose and anointing from God were transferred to Elisha. Now, God's purpose and anointing for Jesus, as evidenced through His miracles, have been transferred to us as Christ followers. The Holy Spirit was poured out in order to give us the same power and authority that Jesus had during His ministry so that we can fulfill his mission and do the works that He did.

*{Jhn 14:12} 12 Very truly I tell you, **whoever believes in me will do the works I have been doing, and they will do even greater things than these***, because I am going to the Father.*

See the chart of Jesus' miracles on the next page...

THE MIRACLES OF JESUS	ADDITIONAL SCRIPTURES
Healing the Sick Blood issue: Matthew 9, Mark 5, Luke 8 Paralytic: Matthew 9, Mark 2, Luke 5 Leper: Matthew 8, Mark 1, Luke 5 Fever: Matthew 8, Mark 1, Luke 4 Near Death: Matthew 8, Luke 7 Mute: Matthew 9 Deaf and Mute: Mark 7 Swelling/Dropsy: Luke 14 Ten Lepers: Luke 17 Ear Restored: Luke 22 Very Sick: John 4 Lame 38 years: John 5 Hand Restored: Matthew 12, Mark 3, Luke 6 **Blind Receive Sight** Bartimaeus: Matthew 20, Mark 10, Luke 18 2 Men: Matthew 9 Man: Mark 8 Man born blind: John 9 **The Dead Raised** Jairus' Daughter: Matthew 9, Mark 5, Luke 8 Widow's Son: Luke 7 Lazarus: John 11 **Casting Out Demons and Evil Spirits** Insanity: Matthew 8, Mark 5, Luke 8 Seizures: Matthew 17, Mark 9, Luke 9 Torment: Matthew 15, Mark 7 Evil Spirit: Mark 1, Luke 4 Mute: Matthew 12, Luke 11 Crippled: Luke 13 **Feeding the Masses** 5,000 men: Matthew 14, Mark, 6, Luke 9, John 6 4,000 men: Matthew 15, Mark 8 **Power Over Creation** Turning Water into Wine: John 2 Calming Storm: Matthew 8, Mark 4, Luke 8 Walking on Water: Matthew 14, Mark 6, John 6 Cursing a Fig Tree: Matthew 21, Mark 11 Coin in Fish's Mouth: Matthew 17 Miraculous Fish Catch #1: Luke 5 Miraculous Fish Catch #2: John 21	*{Mat 12:15} 15 Aware of this, Jesus withdrew from that place. A large crowd followed him, and **he healed all who were ill**.* *{Mat 4:23} 23 Jesus went throughout Galilee, teaching in their synagogues, proclaiming the good news of the kingdom, and **healing every disease and sickness among the people**.* *{Luk 9:11} 11 but the crowds learned about it and followed him. He welcomed them and spoke to them about the kingdom of God, and **healed those who needed healing**.* *{Luk 7:21} 21 At that very time **Jesus cured many who had diseases, sicknesses and evil spirits, and gave sight to many who were blind**.* *{Luk 6:19} 19 and the people all tried to touch him, **because power was coming from him and healing them all**.* *{Mat 11:5} 5 **The blind receive sight, the lame walk, those who have leprosy are cleansed, the deaf hear, the dead are raised**, and the good news is proclaimed to the poor.* *{Mat 8:16} 16 When evening came, many who were demon-possessed were brought to him, and **he drove out the spirits with a word and healed all the sick**.* *{Mar 1:32-34} 32 That evening after sunset the people brought to Jesus **all the sick and demon-possessed**. 33 The whole town gathered at the door, 34 and Jesus **healed many who had various diseases**. He also **drove out many demons**, but he would not let the demons speak because they knew who he was.* *{Mar 1:39} 39 So he traveled throughout Galilee, preaching in their synagogues and **driving out demons**.* *{Jhn 20:30} 30 **Jesus performed many other signs** in the presence of his disciples, which are not recorded in this book.* *{Act 10:38 } 38 how God anointed Jesus of Nazareth with the Holy Spirit and power, and how he went around doing good and **healing all who were under the power of the devil, because God was with him**.*

The Gospel is the Power

The Gospel is the power of God. (see Romans 1:16) God is not the power, Jesus is not the power, and the anointing of the Holy Spirit is not the power – the Gospel is the power. Again, *power is strength or ability*. Think of it this way: Hypothetically, if we are all deathly allergic to bee stings then when we are stung by a bee, we know that we are going to die. That bee sting has *power* over us because, as the bee venom permeates our being and kills us, it proves to be stronger than we are. However, if we possess the anti-venom to bee stings, then all bee stings are rendered powerless and have no effect. Similarly, sin is like a bee sting, and the Law is like the bee venom enforcing consequences of the sting which pervade our being until we perish. (see Romans 6:23) Christ's resurrection proves that Jesus is stronger than sin and death so, therefore, the Gospel is like the anti-venom that renders sin powerless, nullifies its effects and, by faith, grants us immunity from stings that lead to death for all eternity.

> {1Co 15:55-57} 55 *"Where, O death, is your victory? Where, O death, is your sting?"* 56 *The* **sting of death is sin**, *and the* **power of sin is the law**. *57 But thanks be to God! He* **gives us the victory through our Lord Jesus Christ**.

> {Heb 2:14-15} 14 *Since the children have flesh and blood, he too shared in their humanity so* **that by his death he might break the power of him who holds the power of death--that is, the devil**-- *15 and free those who all their lives were held in slavery by their fear of death.*

Accordingly, when Jesus' disciples asked Him how they should pray, He responded with a simple answer:

> {Mat 6:9-13} 9 *"This, then, is how you should pray: " 'Our Father in heaven, hallowed be your name, 10* **your kingdom come, your will be done, on earth as it is in heaven**. *11* **Give us today our daily bread**. *12 And* **forgive us our debts**, *as we also have* **forgiven our debtors**. *13 And lead us not into temptation, but* **deliver us from the evil one**.'

This prayer is a simple request to use the anti-venom against sin and put a charge on the account of the Lamb of God. Just like Jesus went around metaphorically saying, *Put their sin-debt on My account*, Jesus sends out His followers to proclaim the Gospel by saying, *Put your sin-debt on Jesus' account* and by charging everyone's sins on the prepaid account of the cross of Jesus Christ. Jesus came to save the world. Now, He sends us for the very same purpose, and He has given us power through the Gospel to do it. This prayer is not the Gospel, but it engages the Gospel through faith. What, then, is the Gospel?

> {1Co 15:2-4} 2 **By this gospel you are saved**, *if you hold firmly to the word I preached to you. Otherwise, you have believed in vain. 3 For what I received I passed on to you as of first importance: that* **Christ died for our sins** *according to the Scriptures, 4 that* **he was buried**, *that he was* **raised on the third day** *according to the Scriptures,*

Through His life, death, and resurrection, Jesus paid for all of our sins and, therefore, the effects and consequences of sin have absolutely no legal right to our lives. Think of it this way: if we owed money to a creditor, then they would have the legal right to pursue us for the debt owed to them. This could include sending bills, calling relentlessly, seizing some of our assets, or even putting us in prison. However, if the debt was paid in full, then the creditor would have no more right to pursue us. Similarly, all of mankind is in debt to the devil because of sin and, until this debt is paid, he has the legal right to hunt us down with curses, sickness, oppression, and death. However, since Jesus paid our sin-debt in full, the devil has no more right to impose any of these consequences. The charges against us have been cancelled through the cross of Christ. Through faith in the Gospel of Jesus Christ, we have been made holy, as if we are without sin, have always been without sin, and will always be without sin. This gives us the right to blessing, health, and life – also known as God's will *on earth as it is in heaven*.

> {Col 2:13-14} 13 When **you were dead in your sins** and in the uncircumcision of your flesh, God made you alive with Christ. He forgave us all our sins, 14 **having canceled the charge of our legal indebtedness**, which stood against us and condemned us; he has **taken it away**, **nailing it to the cross**.

> {Heb 10:10} 10 And by that will, **we have been made holy** through the sacrifice of the body of Jesus Christ **once for all**.

In another way of looking at it, the curse of God's Law is the presiding standard of retribution for our sin and stumbling and, without Christ, it has the right to enforce its consequences in our lives. However, when we believe Jesus, we are no longer subject to the Law or its curse.

CURSE OF THE LAW (see also *Leviticus 26*)	**CHRIST OUR REDEEMER** (see many many other Scriptures)
Lack: Deut 28:15-19, 23-24, 26, 38-42, 48, 63 **Sickness:** Deut 28:21-22, 27-28, 34-35, 58-62 **Defeat:** Deut 28:25-26, 29-33, 43-44, 48-57 **Unholiness:** Deut 28:15, 25 , 37, 45-47, 53-58 **Enmity with God:** Deut 28: 34, 36, 48, 61, 65-67 **Wandering:** Deut 28:29, 32, 63-68 **Sinfulness:** Deut 28:15, 45-47, 53-58 **Exiled from God:** Deut 28:32, 36-37, 41, 63-68	{Rom 8:32} 32 He who **did not spare** his own Son, but **gave him up** for us all--how will he not also, along with him, **graciously give us all things?** {1Pe 2:24} 24 "He himself bore our sins" in his body on the cross, so that we might die to sins and live for righteousness; "**by his wounds you have been healed**." {Col 2:15} 15 And having disarmed the powers and authorities, he made a public spectacle of them, **triumphing over them by the cross**. {Heb 10:14} 14 For by one sacrifice he has **made perfect forever those who are being made holy**. {Col 1:20} 20 and through him to reconcile to himself all things, whether things on earth or things in heaven, **by making peace through his blood, shed on the cross**. {1Pe 2:25} 25 For "you were like sheep going astray," **but now you have returned to the Shepherd and Overseer of your souls**. {Eph 1:7} 7 In him we have redemption through his blood, **the forgiveness of sins**, in accordance with the riches of God's grace {Eph 2:13} 13 But now in Christ Jesus you who once were far away **have been brought near by the blood of Christ**.

No matter how much we stumble, Jesus took it all upon Himself. This profound exchange is the Gospel. Jesus Christ, who never sinned, had all of our sins imputed to Him, charged against Him, and placed on

His account. Through faith, we, who are incapable of righteousness, (see Romans 3:9, 23; James 3:2; Isaiah 64:6) have all of Jesus' righteousness imputed to us, credited to our account, and given to us as a free gift. He became sin. We become the righteousness of God. (see 2 Corinthians 5:21) Accordingly, anything which is outside of God's perfect and pleasing will for us *as it is in heaven* has no legal grounds to be in our lives.

In short, Jesus *overpowered* all of our enemies through His life, death, and resurrection and the Gospel renders all sin, the curse, the devil, and even death *powerless* against everyone who believes Christ. Therefore, the Gospel of Jesus Christ is the answer to all of our problems and every affliction and oppression facing everyone that we know. This said, the power of the Gospel is only accessed through faith. When Jesus' first followers asked Him what God required of them, His answer was simple: *believe*.

> *{Jhn 6:28-29} 28 Then they asked him, "**What must we do to do the works God requires?**" 29 Jesus answered, "**The work of God is this: to believe in the one he has sent**."*

It is only through faith in Christ that we receive all of the benefits of His salvation and do the works that He did. He sends us out to proclaim the Gospel, which is the power of God to work miracles, signs, and wonders, so that we receive and reveal God's will *on earth as it is in heaven*.

Authority in Christ

Jesus' *authority* over all creation was His birthright as the Son of God, and He used it to serve those whose lives had been damaged by the effects of sin. (see Philippians 2:6-7) While He was on the earth, He shared this *authority* with His disciples when He sent them out to proclaim the Kingdom of Heaven and to do the works that He had been doing, namely, miracles. Notably, He cautioned His followers to remain focused on what was truly significant – not their authority in Jesus' name but that they knew Him and were known by Him.

> *{Mat 10:1, 7-8} 1 Jesus called his twelve disciples to him and **gave them authority to drive out impure spirits and to heal every disease and sickness**... 7 As you go, **proclaim this message: 'The kingdom of heaven has come near.' 8 Heal the sick, raise the dead, cleanse those who have leprosy, drive out demons**. Freely you have received; freely give. (see also Mark 6:7-13; Luke 9:1-6, 10:1-23)*

> *{Luk 10:19-20} 19 **I have given you authority** to trample on snakes and scorpions and **to overcome all the power of the enemy; nothing will harm you**. 20 However, do not rejoice that **the spirits submit to you**, but rejoice that **your names are written in heaven**."*

After His resurrection, Jesus commissioned His disciples into their Kingdom assignment. Because we who believe were included with Christ in His resurrection, His *authority* has become our born-again birthright as sons and daughters of God. (see 1 Peter 1:3; John 1:12) Post-resurrection, our *authority* in Christ is not just an assignment, it is part of who we have become.

> *{Mat 28:18-20} 18 Then Jesus came to them and said, "**All authority in heaven and on earth has been given to me. 19 Therefore go and make disciples of all nations**, baptizing them in*

*the name of the Father and of the Son and of the Holy Spirit, 20 and **teaching them to obey everything I have commanded you**. And surely I am with you always, to the very end of the age."*

*{Jhn 20:22-23} 22 And with that he breathed on them and said, "**Receive the Holy Spirit.** 23 **If you forgive anyone's sins, their sins are forgiven; if you do not forgive them, they are not forgiven.**"*

After Jesus ascended to heaven, He received all *authority* in heaven, on earth, and under the earth, both in this age and in the age to come. Jesus Christ is supreme over everything created and is seated at the right hand of God in the throne room of heaven. (see Colossians 1:15-20) We who believe were with Jesus when He ascended to heaven, and therefore, we are seated in Him in the throne room of God, and we have the same God-given *authority* that He has.

*{Phl 2:8-11} 8 And being found in appearance as a man, he humbled himself by becoming obedient to death-- even death on a cross! 9 Therefore **God exalted him to the highest place and gave him the name that is above every name**, 10 **that at the name of Jesus every knee should bow, in heaven and on earth and under the earth**, 11 and every tongue acknowledge that Jesus Christ is Lord, to the glory of God the Father.*

*{Eph 1:19-23} 19 and his incomparably great power for us who believe. That power is the same as the mighty strength 20 he exerted when he raised Christ from the dead and **seated him at his right hand in the heavenly realms**, 21 **far above all rule and authority, power and dominion, and every name that is invoked, not only in the present age but also in the one to come**. 22 And God **placed all things under his feet and appointed him to be head over everything for the church**, 23 **which is his body**, the fullness of him who fills everything in every way.*

*{Eph 2:6} 6 And God raised us up with Christ and **seated us with him in the heavenly realms in Christ Jesus**,*

In Christ and according to God's will, we have *authority* over creation, we outrank the devil and all of his cohorts, and we have the right to declare that sins have been forgiven in Jesus' name. God placed everything under subjection to Jesus so that through faith in Him, we can execute God's will in the earth and do the works that Jesus did. Through this we reveal Christ's victory over sin, death, and the devil and we make it known that Jesus has absolute *authority* over all.

*{Eph 3:10-11} 10 His intent was that now, **through the church, the manifold wisdom of God should be made known to the rulers and authorities in the heavenly realms**, 11 according to his eternal purpose **that he accomplished in Christ Jesus our Lord**.*

Additionally, when we are led by the indwelling Holy Spirit, we have knowledge of God's perfect and pleasing will *as it is in heaven.* (see 1 Corinthians 2:10) When we truly follow this divine nature, we inherently use our Christ-given authority to serve others. Jesus sends us not to judge but to *save* people who are suffering because of sin and its effects. Again, we previously examined how Elijah's anointing and mission became Elisha's anointing and mission and how Elijah's cloak and a double portion of his spirit equipped Elisha with everything that he needed to fulfill his task. Now that the Holy Spirit has been poured out, Christ's anointing and purpose has become the anointing and purpose of His disciples. He commissions His followers to proclaim the Kingdom of God to the whole world, and the anointing of the Holy Spirit equips us to do the works that Jesus did in the way that He did them. Read this verse again, but this time, read it as your own anointing and assignment from God.

> *{Luk 4:18-19} 18 "**The Spirit of the Lord is on ME**, because he has **anointed ME** to **proclaim good news to the poor**. He has sent **ME** to proclaim **freedom for the prisoners** and **recovery of sight for the blind**, to **set the oppressed free**, 19 to proclaim the **year of the Lord's favor**."*
> (emphasis added)

Doing the Works that Jesus Did

In order to do the works that Jesus did in the way that He did them, let us examine Jesus' ministry on earth to see what He did and how He did it. Jesus demonstrated the will of God to forgive, to heal, to deliver from oppression, and even to deliver from death – all revealing His purpose to *save*. Jesus' goodwill towards people was not hindered by their sins or anything that they had done. He did not inquire of anyone's worthiness or piety before healing or delivering them, and He did not go on religious sin-hunts to prove that the sufferer was suffering because of something that they had done to deserve it. Jesus knew that His sacrifice was totally sufficient to cover anything they may have done or not done and therefore, no matter what the problem was, when someone came to Him in faith, Jesus was moved with compassion and was willing and able to bring heaven to earth for them. He did not drone on with long flowery prayers quoting a lot of Scripture to be impressive. Rather, He freely and succinctly forgave even blatant sin without condemnation, and He exercised His *power* and *authority* over sickness, demons, creation, and even over death.

> *{Luk 7:48} 48 Then Jesus said to her, "**Your sins are forgiven**." (Jesus forgives immoral people.)*
>
> *{Jhn 8:11} 11 "No one, sir," she said. "**Then neither do I condemn you**," Jesus declared. "Go now and leave your life of sin." (Jesus forgives even egregious sin.)*
>
> *{Luk 4:39 } 39 **So he bent over her and rebuked the fever, and it left her**. She got up at once and began to wait on them. (Jesus commands sickness to leave.)*
>
> *{Jhn 9:3} 3 "Neither this man nor his parents sinned," said Jesus, "but **this happened so that the works of God might be displayed in him.** (Jesus heals without blaming the sufferer.)*
>
> *{Luk 5:12-13} 12 While Jesus was in one of the towns, a man came along who was covered with leprosy. When he saw Jesus, he fell with his face to the ground and begged him, "**Lord, if you are willing,** you can make me clean." 13 Jesus reached out his hand and touched the man. "**I am willing**," he said. "**Be clean! [healed]**" And immediately the leprosy left him. (Jesus is willing.)*

{Mar 9:22-23 NLT} *22 The spirit often throws him into the fire or into water, trying to kill him. Have mercy on us and **help us, if you can**." 23 **"What do you mean, 'If I can'?"** Jesus asked. "Anything is possible if a person believes."(Jesus is able.)*

{Mat 20:34} *34 **Jesus had compassion on them** and touched their eyes. Immediately **they received their sight** and followed him. (Jesus has compassion on the afflicted.)*

{Mat 8:31-32 } *31 The demons begged Jesus, "If you drive us out, send us into the herd of pigs." 32 **He said to them, "Go!"** So they came out and went into the pigs, and the whole herd rushed down the steep bank into the lake and died in the water. (Jesus commands demons with a single word.)*

{Mar 4:39 } *39 He got up, **rebuked the wind and said to the waves, "Quiet! Be still!"** Then the wind died down and it was completely calm. (Jesus commands creation.)*

{Jhn 11:25} *25 Jesus said to her, "**I am the resurrection and the life. The one who believes in me will live, even though they die**; (Jesus raises the dead.)*

Practically speaking, in order to do the works that Jesus did in the way that He did them, we cannot simply imitate what He did. We must do what He did. It is impossible to replicate the works of Jesus by any formula because He never did anything the same way twice. For example, in different episodes of giving sight to the blind, Jesus touched their eyes, spit on their eyes, or made mud to put on their eyes. In spite of these different methods, each one received sight. In every miracle that Jesus did, He did what He saw God doing, acting on God's command, and saying what God said. In the same way, as Jesus sends us out to do the works that He did, He shows us or tells us through the Holy Spirit exactly what we are supposed to do with the person right in front of us. We will lay hands on the sick, we will command body parts to be healed, and we will command unclean spirits to flee in Jesus' name. As we wait for His spiritual direction, in our minds eye we may see ourselves doing something such as laying hands on a person in a particular place, or we may experience a physical sensation somewhere in our bodies as an indication of where their pain is. In other instances, we may hear the Holy Spirit from our inmost being whispering to us, *foot pain* or *anxiety*, or we may experience a momentary onset of emotion to indicate how the person is feeling. As the Holy Spirit guides us, we may hear Jesus whispering things like, *Tell her I love her*, or *Tell her I am not ashamed of her*. When we watch and listen for Jesus' instructions and step out to obey His promptings, we do only what we see Him doing and say what He says. We will do the things that He did in the way that He did them.

In order to do these things, we must remain heavenly minded and abide in Christ. For a moment, I must ask you to grant me a little artistic license. At the beginning of Jesus' ministry, two of John the Baptist's disciples began to follow Jesus and ask Him, *Rabbi, where are you staying?* and Jesus responded, *Come and see.* (see John 1:38-39) They proceeded to walk with Jesus as He went on to perform many miracles, signs, and wonders. Yes, Jesus was staying in a literal place at this point in the Scriptures, but let's explore another aspect of where Jesus was staying. The word for *staying* is the same word that we talked about previously as *abiding* or *remaining* – in essence, they asked Jesus *where are you abiding?* At all times of His ministry, Jesus *abided* and *remained* in His Father. (see John 14:10-11, 20, 10:38, 17:21) Jesus *abided* and *remained* in heaven, doing only what He saw the Father doing. (see John 5:19, 30, 12:49) Technically speaking, even though He was on the earth, Jesus was a citizen of heaven. Jesus was sent by God as an ambassador to do God's will on the earth, the way it is in heaven. (see John 7:16, 14:24) Every miracle that He did had a way of saying, *This is how it is where I am staying.*

Similarly, we who believe have been made citizens of heaven, even though we are still on the earth. We are sent by Christ as His ambassadors to do His will on earth, the way it is in heaven. We *abide* and *remain* in Christ the same way that He *abided* in God and, when we do so, He says, *Ask whatever you wish, and it will be done for you.* (see John 15:1-17) In heaven, there is no lack, only abundance; there is no sickness, only health; there is no oppression, only freedom; there is no rejection, only acceptance; there is no depression, only joy; there is no stress, only peace. In heaven, there is no death, mourning, crying, or pain. (see Revelation 21:4) In order to bring heaven to earth, we must keep our minds in heaven and do only what we see Jesus doing. This way, when people ask us where we are staying, we can say, *Come and see,* and we can show them, *This is how it is where I am staying.*

> *{Rom 12:2 NLT} 2 Don't copy the behavior and customs of this world, but let God transform you into a new person by changing the way you think.* **Then you will learn to know God's will for you, which is good and pleasing and perfect***. (God's will as it is in heaven.)*

> *{Phl 3:20} 20 But* **our citizenship is in heaven***. And we eagerly await a Savior from there, the Lord Jesus Christ,*

> *{2Co 5:20} 20 We are therefore* **Christ's ambassadors***, as though* **God were making his appeal through us***. We implore you* **on Christ's behalf: Be reconciled to God***.*

> *{Eph 1:3} 3 Praise be to the God and Father of our Lord Jesus Christ,* **who has blessed us in the heavenly realms with every spiritual blessing in Christ***.*

> *{Phl 4:8} 8 Finally, brothers and sisters, whatever is* **true***, whatever is* **noble***, whatever is* **right***, whatever is* **pure***, whatever is* **lovely***, whatever is* **admirable***--if anything is* **excellent or praiseworthy***--think about such things.*

> *{Col 3:1-2} 1 Since, then, you have been raised with Christ,* **set your hearts on things above***, where Christ is, seated at the right hand of God. 2* **Set your minds on things above***, not on earthly things.*

Jesus gives us all *power* and *authority* to do the works that He did the way that He did them. When we believe that Jesus' sacrifice is greater than whatever affliction the person in front of us is dealing with, we engage the *power* of God through faith in the Gospel as our hearts cry out, *Jesus paid it all, Put this on Jesus' account,* and *It is finished.* We exercise our *authority* to do the works of God as we watch and listen to Jesus through the anointing of the Holy Spirit, and He reveals to us what He is doing and saying right now. Through all of this we effectively say, *Your will be done on earth as it is in heaven!* Hallelujah!

To All Who Believe

The good news of Jesus Christ and all of the benefits of His salvation are available to anyone and everyone who believes that Jesus Christ is Lord and that God raised Him from the dead. Does this sound too good to be true? Then let us recall for a moment the state that we ourselves were in before we believed Jesus. We were dead in our inherited and ongoing sin, obeying the devil, without hope, outsiders, and excluded from God and His benefits. (see Ephesians 2:1-3, 11-12) We were powerless, ungodly, sinners, and enemies of God. When we ourselves were in this horribly hopeless position, this is when Jesus Christ died for us. When we were in a spiritual state of death, Jesus restored us to right standing with God and gave us life.

> *{Col 1:21-23} 21 Once you **were alienated** from God and **were enemies** in your minds because of your evil behavior. 22 **But now** he **has reconciled** you by Christ's physical body through death **to present you holy in his sight, without blemish and free from accusation**-- 23 if you continue in your faith, established and firm, and do not move from the hope held out in the gospel. **This is the gospel** that you heard and that has been proclaimed to every creature under heaven, and of which I, Paul, have become a servant.*

> *{Rom 5:6-10 } 6 You see, at just the right time, **when we were still powerless**, **Christ died for the ungodly**. 7 Very rarely will anyone die for a righteous person, though for a good person someone might possibly dare to die. 8 But God demonstrates his own love for us in this: **While we were still sinners, Christ died for us**. 9 Since we have now been justified by his blood, how much more shall we be saved from God's wrath through him! 10 For if, **while we were God's enemies, we were reconciled to him through the death of his Son**, how much more, having been reconciled, shall we be saved through his life!*

However, even Jesus encountered people who did not believe Him and could not receive heaven on earth from Him. For example, in Nazareth, Jesus' boyhood hometown, people doubted His *power*. (see Matthew 13:53-58; Mark 6:1-6) They scoffed, believing that He was just like everybody else, and they were deeply offended by Him. I imagine that they believed things such as *this is the way things are in the world*, and *we get what we deserve*, and *Jesus is a good guy, but He is not able fix me*, or *my situation is too hard or impossible for Him*. Jesus could not do many miracles in Nazareth because they could not receive from Him. On the other hand, the religious leaders of the day had issues with Jesus' *authority*. At times, they questioned if Jesus had the right to do the things that He was doing, particularly His miracles. (see Matthew 21:23-27; Mark 11:27-33; Luke 11:1-8) Other times, they attributed Jesus authority to the devil or they demanded a miraculous sign from Jesus in order to prove that His authority was from God. (see Matthew 12:22-42, 16:1-4; Mark 3:23-30, 8:11-13) They believed that the Law of God was the ultimate authority and that the curse of the Law (i.e. all forms of suffering) was rightfully God's will for people living in sin. Therefore, in their view, freeing people from their afflictions was rebellion against God's will. Accordingly, when they saw Jesus exercising His authority, they thought *who does He think He is – God?* or *only God can do that, not this guy*. When they demanded a sign from Jesus, they required evidence of both His *power* and *authority*, treated God like their servant and refused to believe Jesus unless they received what they wanted, the way they wanted it. Jesus would not do any miracles for religious people because they would not receive from Him.

Similarly, as we set out to do the works that Jesus did in the way that He did them, we will also encounter resistance from people who need a miracle but are unable or unwilling to receive. We will meet people who do not believe in the *power* of God through the Gospel of Jesus Christ and therefore, do not experience it, just like the people of Nazareth when Jesus was in town. We will also come across people who do not believe that believers have the *authority* in Christ to do the works of Jesus and who will resist miracles or accuse us of working for the devil, just like the religious leaders in Jesus' day. We may encounter those who come to us for a miracle but, in their hearts, they are demanding a sign from God as proof rather than coming with a heart of faith. In my experience, when this is the case, the anointing of the Holy Spirit is absent because God has no need of proving Himself. Lastly, we should take note of something significant which Jesus asked a man who had been incapacitated for thirty-eight years: *Do you want to be well?* Though it may seem obvious that afflicted people want to be well, sometimes, they do not. We cannot force anyone to receive what Jesus died to give them.

The bottom line is that Jesus Christ died for the sins of the whole world. He did not come to judge but to save everyone who will believe. (see John 3:17, 12:47) The same salvation that was offered to us is available to every single person that we meet no matter what they have done. Jesus Christ destroyed death, bore our sickness, redeemed us from the curse, cancelled our sin-debt, and destroyed the works of the devil so that we could all be saved, healed, blessed, made holy, reign over the devil, and have eternal life in Him. Accordingly, as we go out into the world to proclaim the Gospel of Jesus Christ, we no longer view people from the perspective of their sin and unworthiness but as someone for whom Christ died.

> {2Co 5:14-19} 14 For Christ's love compels us, because we are convinced that **one died for all, and therefore all died**. 15 And **he died for all**, that those who live should no longer live for themselves but for him who died for them and was raised again. 16 **So from now on we regard no one from a worldly point of view**. Though we once regarded Christ in this way, we do so no longer. 17 Therefore, if anyone is in Christ, the new creation has come: The old has gone, the new is here! 18 All this is from **God, who reconciled us to himself through Christ and gave us the ministry of reconciliation**: 19 For God was in Christ, **reconciling the world to himself, no longer counting people's sins against them. And he gave us this wonderful message of reconciliation**.

> {1Jo 2:2 NLT} 2 He himself is the sacrifice that atones for our sins--**and not only our sins but the sins of all the world**.

> {Rom 2:11 NLT} 11 For **God does not show favoritism**.

> {1Ti 4:10} 10 That is why we labor and strive, because we have put our hope in the living God, who is **the Savior of all people, and especially of those who believe**.

> {2Pe 3:9} 9 The Lord is not slow in keeping his promise, as some understand slowness. Instead he is patient with you, **not wanting anyone to perish, but everyone to come to repentance**.

> {1Ti 2:4} 4 *who wants **all people to be saved and to come to a knowledge of the truth.*** *(Note: Jesus is the truth, see John 14:6)*

You are not the exception to the rule, and the person that you are praying for is not the exception to the rule. No matter where we are in our walk of faith, no matter what we have done or may be doing, and no matter what aspect of God's perfect will we are believing for, the *power* of God in the Gospel is not hindered, and the *authority* of Christ is supreme. Believe it and receive it by faith for yourself. Then, become it to everyone that you meet. In fact, the next time you read through the Gospels of Matthew, Mark, Luke, and John, instead of seeing yourself as the sinner in need of Jesus, see yourself as being in the role of Jesus. The works that Jesus did as the Son of God are the very same works that we are commissioned, authorized, and empowered to do as God's sons and daughters in Christ. He came to save. We go to save. Let's go!

Again, for emphasis:

> {Rom 1:16-17} 16 For **I am not ashamed of the gospel, because it is the power of God that brings salvation to everyone who believes:** *first to the Jew, then to the Gentile. 17 For **in the gospel the righteousness of God is revealed**--a righteousness that is by faith from first to last, just as it is written: "The righteous will live by faith."*

> {Mat 6:9-13} 9 *"This, then, is how you should pray:* **'Our Father in heaven,** *hallowed be your name,* 10 **your kingdom come, your will be done, on earth as it is in heaven.** 11 **Give us today our daily bread.** 12 **And forgive us our debts, as we also have forgiven our debtors.** 13 *And lead us not into temptation, but **deliver us from the evil one.'***

> {Luk 4:18-19} 18 *"**The Spirit of the Lord is on ME,** because he has **anointed ME** to **proclaim good news to the poor.** He has sent **ME** to proclaim **freedom for the prisoners** and **recovery of sight for the blind,** to **set the oppressed free,** 19 to proclaim the **year of the Lord's favor."** (emphasis added)*

And now we return to our scheduled programming – the Book of Acts!

CHAPTER 8
Rend Your Heart

On the day of Pentecost, when the Holy Spirit was poured out, certain prophetic promises from the Old Testament were fulfilled. Peter preached the Gospel in Jerusalem using Scriptures which would have been very familiar to the people of Israel and which called them to return to the heart of their God. Proving to them through God's Word that Jesus Christ is the Messiah of Israel and Lord of all, Peter cried out for everyone to repent and receive a new heart, the Holy Spirit, so that they would be spared from the wrath of God to come. Let's examine the speech that Peter gave on the day of Pentecost to see what relevance it has for our lives and our faith today.

Not Drunk

The scene in Jerusalem on the day of Pentecost included Jewish men from every nation under heaven who were gathered for the Feast of Weeks. The Holy Spirit was poured out on 120 followers of Jesus Christ, and these believers began to supernaturally declare the works of God in the languages of every person present. Perplexed by this supernatural event, onlookers wondered, *What can this mean?* Some even concluded that Christ's disciples must be drunk. But Peter stood up to explain what was happening and, filled with the Holy Spirit, gave a speech. He explained that what the people in Jerusalem were witnessing with their own eyes and ears was the fulfillment of the promises that God made to the Jewish people centuries before.

> *{Act 2:14-21} 14 Then **Peter stood up with the Eleven**, raised his voice and addressed the crowd: "**Fellow Jews and all of you who live in Jerusalem**, let me explain this to you; listen carefully to what I say. 15 **These people are not drunk**, as you suppose. It's only nine in the morning! 16 No, this is **what was spoken by the prophet Joel**: 17 "'In the last days, God says, **I will pour out my Spirit on all people**. Your **sons and daughters will prophesy**, your young men will see visions, your old men will dream dreams. 18 Even on my **servants, both men and women, I will pour out my Spirit in those days**, and they will prophesy. 19 I will show wonders in the heavens above and signs on the earth below, blood and fire and billows of smoke. 20 The sun will be turned to darkness and the moon to blood before **the coming of the great and glorious day of the Lord**. 21 And **everyone who calls on the name of the Lord will be saved.**' (quoting Joel 2:28-32)*

Peter quoted the Book of Joel which was written to the people of Judah in a time when they had turned their hearts away from God. No one is sure of the exact date that it was written, but its resounding message is one of repentance and returning to the Lord. Joel cried out to the people of Israel, summoning them to humble themselves before the Lord with fasting and prayer, to weep over their sin with genuine contrition, and to return to the Lord with their whole heart. Israelites were in the practice of tearing their clothing and wearing sackcloth and ashes as an outward sign of inward mourning over their sin but, through Joel, God appealed to His people to drop the outward show and come back to Him in sincere faith and heartfelt devotion. This genuine change of heart was so important because of the *day of judgment* to come, when God will administer justice in the earth against all evil and wickedness. This is the day when all those who do not acknowledge the Lord will be subjected to eternal damnation and only those with a total change of heart will be spared from God's wrath.

> *{Joe 2:1-3} 1 Blow the trumpet in Zion; sound the alarm on my holy hill. Let all who live in the land **tremble, for the day of the LORD is coming**. It is close at hand-- 2 **a day of darkness and gloom, a day of clouds and blackness**. Like dawn spreading across the mountains **a large and mighty army comes, such as never was in ancient times nor ever will be in ages to come**. 3 Before them **fire devours**, behind them a **flame blazes**. Before them the land is like the garden of Eden, behind them, a desert waste-- **nothing escapes them**.*

> *{Joe 2:12-13} 12 "Even now," declares the LORD, "**return to me with all your heart**, with **fasting and weeping and mourning**." 13 **Rend your heart and not your garments. Return to the LORD your God**, for he is gracious and compassionate, slow to anger and abounding in love, and he relents from sending calamity.*

Truth be told, a complete and total change of heart is only possible if God supplies it. Of course, this is exactly what God had promised to do. Through Joel, Isaiah, Jeremiah, Ezekiel, and Zechariah, God spoke of days when the Holy Spirit would be poured out in order to change people's hearts. (see Isaiah 32:15, 44:3; Jeremiah 24:7, 31:33; Ezekiel 11:17-20, 36:26-27, 37:14, 39:29; Zechariah 12:10) In each of their messages, God had addressed Israel's complacency, folly, worldliness, worship of other gods, and their resulting state of disgrace and distance from Him. But in each case, God also spoke of giving His people a *new heart and a new Spirit*, his very own Spirit, so that their hearts could be fully devoted to Him. God was going to write His Laws on people's hearts so that every believer could know Him and sincerely live by His ways.

Unfortunately, in the days of Peter's Pentecost speech, just as they had in the past, the Jewish people had again become religious in their outward demonstration of devotion without really meaning it in their hearts. They honored God with their lips but their hearts were far from Him, and they had become hypocrites. (see Isaiah 29:13; Matthew 15:8; Mark 7:6) When Jesus, the Messiah who their Scriptures pointed to had arrived, they had crucified Him. But God, in spite of all of this, is so rich in mercy and grace that on the day of Pentecost, He bestowed His Spirit upon His people to *rend their hearts* for them. Peter explained to the onlooking Jews that what the prophets of old had prophesied was what was happening – God was sharing His Spirit with His people. God poured out His Spirit on all people – sons, daughters, young men, old men, women, servants, and everyone who calls upon the name of the Lord Jesus.

Ever since Pentecost and even today, when we believe Jesus and receive the Holy Spirit, we are marked with a holy seal of redemption so that we are spared from the wrath of God on the *day of judgment*. Additionally, we become sons and daughters of God, adopted into His family as His very own children so that we can call Him *Father*. Moreover, through the Holy Spirit, God reveals His wisdom and even hidden mysteries to us just as a father confides important family information to his children. Through this, the Holy Spirit renews our mind and gives us the mind of God's Son, Jesus Christ.

> *{2Co 1:21-22} 21 Now it is God who makes both us and you stand firm in Christ. He **anointed us**, 22 **set his seal of ownership on us, and put his Spirit in our hearts as a deposit, guaranteeing what is to come**. (see also Ephesians 1:13-14, 4:30)*

> *{Rom 8:15} 15 The Spirit you received does not make you slaves, so that you live in fear again; rather, **the Spirit you received brought about your adoption to sonship. And by him we cry, "Abba, Father."** (see also Galatians 4:6)*

> *{1Co 2:9-13, 16} 9 However, as it is written: "What no eye has seen, what no ear has heard, and what no human mind has conceived"-- the things God has prepared for those who love him-- 10 **these are the things God has revealed to us by his Spirit**. The Spirit searches all things, **even the deep things of God**. 11 For who knows a person's thoughts except their own spirit within them? In the same way **no one knows the thoughts of God except the Spirit of God**. 12 What we have received is not the spirit of the world, but the **Spirit who is from God, so that we may understand what God has freely given us**. 13 This is what we speak, not in words taught us by human wisdom but in **words taught by the Spirit, explaining spiritual realities with Spirit-taught words**. ... 16 for, "Who has known the mind of the Lord so as to instruct him?" **But we have the mind of Christ**.*

Peter (and Joel) also connected this new heart and spirit from God with the ability to *prophesy*. By definition, to *prophesy* is to *declare the words of God to men* or *speaking by divine inspiration*. In the Old Testament, this ability was limited to a select few and was only given as needed for specific tasks and at specific times but now in the New Covenant, God has granted it to everyone who believes that Jesus is Lord. The Holy Spirit reveals the words and ways of God to us and then, when we speak the things that the Holy Spirit has revealed to us, we prophesy. Therefore, everyone who has the Holy Spirit is able to prophesy, dream dreams, and see visions, which we will cover in more depth in another chapter. Jesus speaks to and through His people and, as Christ's disciples, our prophesying points all people to the sufficiency and love of Jesus and His work of salvation.

> *{Jhn 15:26} 26 "When the Advocate comes, whom I will send to you from the Father--**the Spirit of truth** who goes out from the Father--**he will testify about me**.*

> *{Rev 19:10b} 10b At this I fell at his feet to worship him. But he said to me, "Don't do that! I am a fellow servant with you and with your **brothers and sisters who hold to the testimony of Jesus. Worship God! For it is the Spirit of prophecy who bears testimony to Jesus**."*

On the day of Pentecost, believers were so overwhelmed when the Holy Spirit came upon them that they prophesied in the languages of everyone present! They were definitely not drunk.

Believe the Works

After quoting the prophet Joel, Peter spoke about the works of Jesus. Peter pointed to the miracles, signs, and wonders that Jesus had done during His ministry as being evidence of His anointing from God. More significantly, Peter highlighted the resurrection of Jesus Christ from the dead, the ultimate miracle, sign, wonder, and proof that Jesus Christ is indeed the Messiah of Israel and God's Chosen One.

> *{Act 2:22-32} 22 "Fellow Israelites, listen to this: Jesus of Nazareth was a man **accredited by God to you by miracles, wonders and signs, which God did among you through him**, as you yourselves know. 23 This man was handed over to you **by God's deliberate plan and foreknowledge**; and you, with the help of wicked men, put him to death by nailing him to the cross. 24 **But God raised him from the dead**, freeing him from the agony of death, **because it was impossible for death to keep its hold on him**. 25 David said about him: "'I saw the Lord always before me. Because he is at my right hand, I will not be shaken. 26 Therefore my heart is glad and my tongue rejoices; my body also will rest in hope, 27 **because you will not abandon me to the realm of the dead, you will not let your holy one see decay**. 28 You have made known to me the paths of life; you will fill me with joy in your presence.' (quoting Psalm 16:8-11) 29 "Fellow Israelites, I can tell you confidently that the patriarch David died and was buried, and his tomb is here to this day. 30 But he was a prophet and knew that God had promised him on oath that he would place one of his descendants on his throne. 31 **Seeing what was to come, he spoke of the resurrection of the Messiah, that he was not abandoned to the realm of the dead, nor did his body see decay**. 32 **God has raised this Jesus to life**, and we are all witnesses of it.*

When Jesus walked on the earth and people did not believe in Him, He never defended Himself. He simply pointed to His miracles as proof that He had God's approval. Jesus told religious leaders who demanded a sign from Him that they would not receive any sign except the sign of Jonah. He was referring to the story of Jonah who was swallowed up into the belly of a fish and then spit back out to declare the mercy of God for those who would repent. (see the Book of Jonah) Jesus was also prophetically pointing to His resurrection from the grave which, at that point, was still yet to come. But, alas, He also knew that these religious leaders had turned their hearts so far away from God that they would not be convinced even when the grave spit Him out and He came back to life from the dead.

> *{Mat 12:39-40} 39 He answered, "A wicked and adulterous generation asks for a sign! But none will be given it **except the sign of the prophet Jonah**. 40 For as **Jonah was three days and three nights in the belly of a huge fish, so the Son of Man will be three days and three nights in the heart of the earth**. (see also Matthew 16:4; Luke 11:29-30)*

> *{Luk 16:31} 31 "He said to him, 'If they do not listen to Moses and the Prophets, **they will not be convinced even if someone rises from the dead.'** "*

Trust in God's victory over death is the type of faith that God has required since the beginning of His redemptive work of salvation through Abraham. God tested Abraham's faith by requesting that Abraham offer up his one and only son, Isaac, the very son through whom all the promises that God had made to Abraham were going to be fulfilled. Abraham willingly offered Isaac on the altar of sacrifice because he believed that God was able to raise the dead and that God would be faithful to fulfill every promise that He had made, regardless of how bizarre it seemed from a worldly point of view. Indeed, Abraham, who considered Isaac to be as good as dead, received him back from death because, just in time, God provided a ram in Isaac's place so that Abraham, though willing, did not have to sacrifice his son.

> {Heb 11:17-19} 17 **By faith Abraham**, *when God tested him,* **offered Isaac as a sacrifice.** *He who had embraced the promises was about to* **sacrifice his one and only son**, *18 even though God had said to him, "It is through Isaac that your offspring will be reckoned." 19* **Abraham reasoned that God could even raise the dead, and so in a manner of speaking he did receive Isaac back from death.** *(referring to Genesis 22:1-18)*

Abraham's faith was *credited to him as righteousness* meaning that, even though he was a man born with the rebellious nature of Adam just like me and you, Abraham had right standing with God because of his faith. His faith was *credited to Him* when He first believed God, but it was the test of his faith in God's power over death which proved the genuineness of his faith. Abraham is called the *father of the faithful* because everyone who has the faith of Abraham is considered to be his spiritual offspring. Accordingly, when we believe that God has raised Jesus Christ from the dead, we exhibit the faith of Abraham and God *credits our faith to us as righteousness*. This means that we have right standing with God and there is nothing hindering our relationship with Him, even in spite of our imperfect human condition.

> {Rom 4:16-17, 22-25} *16 Therefore, the promise comes by faith, so that it may be by grace and may be* **guaranteed to all Abraham's offspring**--*not only to those who are of the law but also* **to those who have the faith of Abraham. He is the father of us all**. *17 As it is written: "I have made you a father of many nations." He is our father in the sight of God, in whom he believed--***the God who gives life to the dead** *and calls into being things that were not... 22 This is why "***it was credited to him as righteousness.***" 23 The words "it was credited to him" were written not for him alone, 24 but also for us,* **to whom God will credit righteousness--for us who believe in him who raised Jesus our Lord from the dead**. *25 He was delivered over to death for our sins and was* **raised to life for our justification**.

> {Gal 3:6-9} *6 So also Abraham* **"believed God, and it was credited to him as righteousness."** *7 Understand, then, that* **those who have faith are children of Abraham**. *8 Scripture foresaw that God would justify the Gentiles by faith, and announced the gospel in advance to Abraham: "All nations will be blessed through you." 9* **So those who rely on faith are blessed along with Abraham, the man of faith.**

> *{Rom 10:9} 9 If you declare with your mouth, "Jesus is Lord," and **believe in your heart that God raised him from the dead,** you will be saved.*

All of this is to say that the resurrection of Jesus Christ from the dead is the absolute and essential cornerstone, foundation, and basis for our Christian faith. If Christ were not raised from the dead, then He was just a guy who was killed by an angry mob. The resurrection proves that Jesus is who He says He is – the Messiah of Israel and the one and only Son of God. Unlike Abraham, Jesus' righteousness was based upon His perfect obedience to the Law of God. This means that Jesus was an acceptable and unblemished offering for the sins of mankind. The resurrection proved that Jesus' obedience-based righteousness fulfilled God's holy and perfect standard and, on top of that, demonstrated God's acceptance of Jesus' sacrifice on behalf of us all. Therefore, it is only because of the resurrection that we have infallible assurance of God's approval of us when we place our faith in Christ.

> *{Rom 1:4 NLT} 4 and he was **shown to be the Son of God when he was raised from the dead** by the power of the Holy Spirit. He is Jesus Christ our Lord.*

> *{1Co 15:14, 17} 14 And if Christ has not been raised, our preaching is useless and so is your faith. ... 17 And **if Christ has not been raised, your faith is futile; you are still in your sins**.*

> *{Rom 4:25} 25 He was **delivered over to death for our sins** and was **raised to life for our justification**. (Justification means a clear record and right standing with God.)*

As Peter continued his Pentecost speech, he quoted Psalm 16. In this psalm, a suffering person entrusted themselves to God and declared God's goodness, even in the face of death. Let us take a moment and read Psalm 16 from the perspective of Jesus on the cross.

Psalm 16

1 Keep me safe, my God, for in you I take refuge.
2 I say to the LORD, "You are my Lord; apart from you I have no good thing."
3 I say of the holy people who are in the land, "They are the noble ones in whom is all my delight."
4 Those who run after other gods will suffer more and more. I will not pour out libations of blood to such gods or take up their names on my lips.
5 LORD, you alone are my portion and my cup; you make my lot secure.
6 The boundary lines have fallen for me in pleasant places; surely I have a delightful inheritance.
7 I will praise the LORD, who counsels me; even at night my heart instructs me.
8 I keep my eyes always on the LORD. With him at my right hand, I will not be shaken.
9 Therefore my heart is glad and my tongue rejoices; my body also will rest secure,
10 because you will not abandon me to the realm of the dead, nor will you let your faithful one see decay.
11 You make known to me the path of life; you will fill me with joy in your presence, with eternal pleasures at your right hand.

Leading us all by His example, Jesus was a man like us who entrusted Himself into the hands of His heavenly Father. With faith even greater than Abraham's, Jesus believed that God would raise Him from the dead and would fulfill every promise of His eternal inheritance. Jesus believed that God would not abandon Him and that His reward would be an eternal inheritance. Additionally, Jesus also had faith that God would complete His work of redeeming a people for His name by including all of us with Him in this supernatural transaction. (We talked about this in more depth in a prior chapter.) This means that we are not only saved by our faith in what Jesus did for us but we were also saved because of Jesus' faith in what God was accomplishing through His death and resurrection.

> *{Gal 2:20 KJV} 20 I am crucified with Christ: nevertheless I live; yet not I, but Christ liveth in me: and the life which I now live in the flesh I live* **by the faith of the Son of God** *[Jesus' faith],* **who loved me, and gave himself for me***.*

> *{Heb 12:1-2} 1 Therefore, since we are surrounded by such a great cloud of witnesses, let us throw off everything that hinders and the sin that so easily entangles. And let us run with perseverance the race marked out for us, 2* **fixing our eyes on Jesus, the pioneer** *[the one who sets the* **example and leads the way] and perfecter of faith. For the joy set before him he endured the cross, scorning its shame, and sat down at the right hand of the throne of God***.*

After death, Jesus' body was laid in the tomb. According to Jewish belief, a person is not considered fully dead until the third day. According to science, decay does not set in until after the third day. According to Scripture, Jesus was fully dead but His body, though mutilated and tortured, did not suffer any decay. Regardless of which stance you adopt, Jesus was officially dead. But Christ was raised from the dead on the third day before the effects of death, namely decay, had time to set in. His life proved to be indestructible (see Hebrews 7:16) because the righteousness, holiness, and perfection that He had attained while He was living prevented death and the grave from being able to hold Him. Therefore, the grave spit Him out, just like He had prophesied.

> *{Heb 2:14-15} 14 Since the children have flesh and blood, he too shared in their humanity* **so that by his death he might break the power of him who holds the power of death--that is, the devil***-- 15 and free those who all their lives were held in slavery by their fear of death.*

> *{2Ti 1:10} 10 but it has now been revealed through the appearing of* **our Savior, Christ Jesus, who has destroyed death and has brought life and immortality to light** *through the gospel.*

> *{1Co 15:55} 55 "Where, O death, is your victory? Where, O death, is your sting?"*

Through His death and resurrection, Jesus conquered death and revealed the path of life. Jesus is ALIVE! Peter, the apostles, and the 120 disciples who were there on the day of Pentecost had all seen Him with their own eyes. (1 Corinthians 15:3-8) God's work of redemption was completed by Jesus and is available to everyone who will believe!

Messiah Descended of David

Peter continued his speech by expounding on the promises of God concerning the Messiah of Israel.

> *{Act 2:29-36} 29 "Fellow Israelites, I can tell you confidently that the patriarch David died and was buried, and his tomb is here to this day. 30 But* **he was a prophet and knew that God had**

*promised him on oath that he would place one of his descendants on his throne. 31 Seeing what was to come, he spoke of the resurrection of the Messiah, that he was not abandoned to the realm of the dead, nor did his body see decay. 32 **God has raised this Jesus to life**, and we are all witnesses of it. 33 **Exalted to the right hand of God**, he has received from the Father the promised Holy Spirit and has poured out what you now see and hear. 34 For David did not ascend to heaven, and yet he said, "**'The Lord said to my Lord: "Sit at my right hand 35 until I make your enemies a footstool for your feet."'** (quoting Psalm 110:1) 36 "Therefore let all Israel be assured of this: **God has made this Jesus, whom you crucified, both Lord and Messiah."***

David, the greatest king from Israel's prior history, had written Psalm 16 almost a thousand years earlier. David was a king but he was also a prophet and, in line with this, his psalms were *divinely inspired utterances* which foretold the works of God. When David was King of all Israel and had captured the city of Jerusalem, God entered into an unconditional covenant with David through which He promised that one of David's descendants would rule forever on an eternal throne, even though David himself would die just like everyone else. Every Jewish man in Peter's day would have known very well that the Messiah must come through David's lineage in accordance with the Scriptures. Here is a sampling of what they would have been familiar with:

*{2Sa 7:16} 16 [God speaking to David] **Your house and your kingdom will endure forever before me; your throne will be established forever.'** "(see 2 Samuel 7:8-29 for the whole covenant promise)*

*{Psa 132:11} 11 **The LORD swore an oath to David**, a sure oath he will not revoke: "**One of your own descendants I will place on your throne.***

*{Jer 23:5-6} 5 "The days are coming," declares the LORD, "**when I will raise up for David a righteous Branch, a King who will reign wisely and do what is just and right in the land**. 6 In his days Judah will be saved and Israel will live in safety. This is the name by which he will be called: **The LORD Our Righteous Savior**.*

*{Isa 9:7} 7 Of the greatness of his government and peace there will be no end. **He will reign on David's throne and over his kingdom, establishing and upholding it with justice and righteousness from that time on and forever.** The zeal of the LORD Almighty will accomplish this.*

Jesus was a direct descendant of King David, (see Matthew 1:1-17; Luke 3:23-38) and He is the descendant, the Branch, the King, the Savior, and the Messiah that the Scriptures all point to. Peter continued his speech by quoting another Psalm written prophetically by David about the Messiah. This time, Peter used the passage that revealed what happened after Christ's resurrection and ascension to heaven.

*{Psa 110:1} 1 **The LORD says to my lord: "Sit at my right hand until I make your enemies a footstool for your feet."***

Here, the *LORD says to my lord* is not one person but two. The first *LORD* is *Jehovah*, or *God*. The second *lord* is *Adonai*, or *the Lord* who we know to be Jesus. This means that it says, *Jehovah said to Adonai* but it might be easier to think of it as *the Father said to the Son*. Additionally, God's *right hand* speaks symbolically of His power over all things and being *seated at His right hand* denotes having the highest level of authority, second only to God Himself. Therefore, this verse means that, when the resurrected Jesus ascended to heaven and arrived in the throne room of God, God bestowed to Jesus all power and authority in heaven and earth and under the earth, both in this age and the age to come. (see Philippians 2:9-11; Ephesians 1:20-23; Hebrews 2:5-9)

Render Your Heart

Through all of this, Peter had effectively used the Scriptures to prove that Jesus Christ is the King above all kings and the Lord above all lords! Peter then pulled all the pieces of his speech together and explained to the crowd at Pentecost that everything that they were seeing and hearing was the fulfillment of God's prophesies and promises to His people. Peter concluded his speech by making it clear in no uncertain terms that they had killed their King and, this time, instead of tearing their garments, many of the people of Jerusalem and Judea were *cut to the heart*. So Peter pleaded with them, beckoning them, as God's earlier prophets had with a simple message: Repent and turn to God, receive the Holy Spirit, and save yourselves from the ways of this world and from the *day of judgment* to come.

> {Act 2:36-40} 36 **"Therefore let all Israel be assured of this: God has made this Jesus, whom you crucified, both Lord and Messiah."** 37 When the people heard this, **they were cut to the heart** and said to Peter and the other apostles, "Brothers, what shall we do?" 38 Peter replied, "**Repent** and be baptized, every one of you, in the name of Jesus Christ for the forgiveness of your sins. **And you will receive the gift of the Holy Spirit**. 39 The promise is for you and your children and for all who are far off--for all whom the Lord our God will call." 40 **With many other words he warned them; and he pleaded with them, "Save yourselves from this corrupt generation."**

This message remains the cry of God's heart to all people today. This is especially true for His people, Israel, who He still loves because they are the natural descendants of Abraham. (see Romans 11:28) This said, the truth is that the whole world is in rebellion against God, not just Jews who have not recognized Jesus as their Messiah. All of mankind is turned away from God, living lives of sin, error, folly, and complacency, pretending to be good outwardly while plotting selfish schemes inwardly, judging one another relentlessly, and in a word, everyone is a hypocrite. The whole world is in need of Jesus and the Holy Spirit before Christ returns and the *day of judgment* comes because, without faith in Jesus, no one can ever be righteous before God. Anyone who is unwilling to believe the evidence offered by Jesus' miraculous works, particularly His resurrection from the dead, is already condemned because of their unbelief and, without the Holy Spirit, everyone is lost, without hope, and destined for eternal destruction in a place where the fire never goes out and where there is torment, weeping, and gnashing of teeth. (see Matthew 13:42, 50, 25:41; Mark 9:48)

{John 16:8-11} 8 When he [the Holy Spirit] comes, **he will prove the world to be in the wrong about sin and righteousness and judgment**: *9 about sin, because people do not believe in me; 10 about righteousness, because I am going to the Father, where you can see me no longer; 11 and about judgment, because the prince of this world now stands condemned.*

{Jhn 1:10-13} 10 He was in the world, and though the world was made through him, the world did not recognize him. 11 He came to that which was his own, but his own did not receive him. 12 **Yet to all who did receive him, to those who believed in his name, he gave the right to become children of God--** *13* **children born not of natural descent, nor of human decision or a husband's will, but born of God**.

However, when we rend our hearts to God in genuine contrition He leads us to His Son, Jesus Christ. When we believe that Jesus is Lord and that God raised Him from the dead, our faith is *credited to us as righteousness* and we receive the Holy Spirit. When we receive the Holy Spirit, we are marked for salvation from the *day of judgment* and we become the spiritual offspring of Abraham, no matter what our national heritage may be. Through all of this, disciples of Jesus are redeemed out of every nation as the people of Christ, who is our Messiah and King.

CHAPTER 9
Fellowship

In a single day, 3,000 people believed that Jesus Christ is the Messiah of Israel and the Savior of the world. After Peter's Pentecost speech, these new converts were changed forever and joined the 120 existing Christ followers to form a new community, a new group of people who were totally unique and set apart from the rest of the world. As the Church was born and began to grow, Christ followers became known for the first time as Christians. They also demonstrated God's purpose for His people – to love one another as Christ loves us and to manifest His love to the world so that everyone will know that Jesus is Lord. Let's take a look at the fellowship that these early believers shared so that we are encouraged in our relationships with one another as God's people.

A Set Apart People

The new believers in Jerusalem were all filled with the same and singular passion – Jesus. They were consumed with the love of their Savior and couldn't help but to love one another and share everything with one another. Nothing was important to them anymore except Jesus and knowing Him. Possessions that were once the pride of life were now offered for the common good of anyone who had need. No one considered themselves better than anyone else because Jesus had died for them all. They assembled publicly to worship Jesus and they shared communion, or *broke bread*, in their homes as a special privilege reserved only for those who believe. They also ate common meals together, enjoying one another's company, praying together, and praising God.

The first 120 disciples of Christ shared this passion for Jesus even before the Holy Spirit was poured out. They were completely and totally devoted to obeying His commands. Men and women alike were now all of one mind and considered equal as disciples of Christ.

> *{Act 1:14 KJV} 14 These all continued **with one accord in prayer and supplication**, with the women, and Mary the mother of Jesus, and with his brethren.*

The word for *one accord* in Greek is a combination of two words which mean to *rush along* and *in unison*. It is used to describe groups of people who *agree about what is true and what needs to be done*, whether good or bad. It is reminiscent of a *great harmony*, like a *symphony* of many instruments coming together to play a composed melody at the direction of a common conductor. In the case of Christian fellowship, it means that every believer was in harmony with one another because of the love of Jesus. (see Acts 1:14, 2:1, 4:24, 5:12, 15:25) After Pentecost, because the Holy Spirit had been poured out, this natural devotion was raised to a supernatural dimension as 3,120 people were of *one accord*, sharing the same heart and mind. As the Holy Spirit circumcised their hearts in selflessness, they were compelled to share everything that they owned so that everyone had what they needed. They gave their belongings to the apostles to distribute as they saw fit.

> *{Act 2:41-47} 41 Those who accepted his message were baptized, and about **three thousand were added** to their number that day. 42 They **devoted themselves to the apostles' teaching and to fellowship, to the breaking of bread and to prayer**. 43 Everyone was filled with awe at the many wonders and signs performed by the apostles. 44 **All the believers were together and had everything in common**. 45 They sold property and possessions to give to anyone who had need. 46 **Every day they continued to meet together in the temple courts. They broke bread in their homes and ate together with glad and sincere hearts**, 47 **praising God** and enjoying the favor of all the people. And the Lord added to their number daily those who were being saved.*

> *[Act 4:32-37] 32 **All the believers were one in heart and mind. No one claimed that any of their possessions was their own, but they shared everything they had.** 33 With great power the apostles continued to testify to the resurrection of the Lord Jesus. And **God's grace was so powerfully at work in them all** 34 **that there were no needy persons among them. For from time to time those who owned land or houses sold them, brought the money from the sales** 35 **and put it at the apostles' feet, and it was distributed to anyone who had need.** 36 Joseph, a Levite from Cyprus, whom the apostles called Barnabas (which means "son of encouragement"), 37 sold a field he owned and **brought the money and put it at the apostles' feet.***

This type of community was a living demonstration of what God had always intended for society. The Law of God, which He gave to the people of Israel, articulated God's will for His people towards one another. God's Laws clearly outlined His views for restitution for stolen property, moved landmarks, fair treatment of slaves, dealing with a neighbor's stray animal, not pretending that you did not witness a crime, testifying truthfully, deceitful seduction, betrayal, family inheritance, and a whole host of other issues that the people daily faced when dealing with one another. God's Laws for social responsibility, equity, fairness, and the administration of justice placed higher value on human life, dignity, and the care of all creation than any other society in history ever had. Because God is the One who created every person and everything, His statutes and precepts inherently reveal His love for all that He created and His desire for harmony and peace. Moreover, the purpose of God's Laws was to demonstrate His goodness towards His people and then, as His people lived in accordance with His Laws, their kindness towards one another would reveal God's love through them to the whole world.

> *{Deu 4:6-8} 6 Observe them carefully, for **this will show your wisdom and understanding to the nations**, who will hear about all these decrees and say, "**Surely this great nation is a wise and understanding people.**" 7 What other nation is so great as to have their gods near them the way the LORD our God is near us whenever we pray to him? 8 **And what other nation is so great as to have such righteous decrees and laws as this body of laws** I am setting before you today?*

*{Psa 67:1-2} 1 May God be gracious to us and bless us and make his face shine on us-- 2 **so that your ways may be known on earth, your salvation among all nations**.*

Through God's Law, Israelites were instructed to lend freely to their fellow Jews with an open hand, without charging interest, without a tight fist, and without a grudge in their hearts. (see Exodus 22:25; Leviticus 25:36) God also made provision for the poor, the orphan, and the widow who could not provide for themselves, and demanded fair treatment of the foreigner residing among the Israelites. Notably, God's statutes for His people towards one another are slightly different from the rules for His people towards non-Israelites. However, unlike the laws of other nations, foreigners in Israel were never to be abused, mistreated, or oppressed but welcomed and included whenever possible. Israelites were instructed to always remember that they had been horribly mistreated and subjected into slavery when they were foreigners in Egypt so that they would never treat others in the way that they had been treated.

*{Deu 23:19-20} 19 **Do not charge a fellow Israelite interest**, whether on money or food or anything else that may earn interest. 20 **You may charge a foreigner interest, but not a fellow Israelite**, so that the LORD your God may bless you in everything you put your hand to in the land you are entering to possess.*

*{Deu 15:4, 7-8, 10-11} 4 However, **there need be no poor people among you**, for in the land the LORD your God is giving you to possess as your inheritance, he will richly bless you,... 7 **If anyone is poor among your fellow Israelites** in any of the towns of the land the LORD your God is giving you, **do not be hardhearted or tightfisted toward them. 8 Rather, be openhanded and freely lend them whatever they need**... 10 **Give generously to them and do so without a grudging heart**; then because of this the LORD your God will bless you in all your work and in everything you put your hand to. 11 There will always be poor people in the land. Therefore I command you to **be openhanded toward your fellow Israelites who are poor and needy in your land**.*

*{Lev 23:22} 22 " 'When you reap the harvest of your land, do not reap to the very **edges of your field or gather the gleanings of your harvest. Leave them for the poor and for the foreigner residing among you**. I am the LORD your God.' " (see also Leviticus 19:9-10; Deuteronomy 24:18-20,14:29)*

*{Exo 23:9} 9 "**Do not oppress a foreigner; you yourselves know how it feels to be foreigners, because you were foreigners in Egypt.***

After the outpouring of the Holy Spirit on the day of Pentecost, Christian fellowship organically began to line up with God's design for community. Through the guidance of the Holy Spirit, their hearts of devotion to Christ and to one another reflected the heart of God, even in spite of opposition. In fact, a little while after Pentecost, when Peter and John were imprisoned for healing a man in Jesus' name, the persecution which resulted only served to draw the Christian community closer together. After Peter and John were released from prison with a stern warning to stop preaching in the name of Jesus, they returned to the place where the believers were gathered, and they all united in prayer. They understood that the world was against Jesus and, therefore, against them as His followers. Undeterred, they prayed for more boldness to declare the work of Christ and His resurrection. Instead of self-defense or a counter attack, they prayed for God to continue to prove Jesus as Messiah through works including miracles, signs, and wonders – works of love and compassion. (This was also the same way Jesus had proved Himself.) God honored their prayer, and the Holy Spirit filled them afresh with the ability to speak God's word boldly.

> {Act 4:23-31} 23 On their release, Peter and John went back to their own people and reported all that the chief priests and the elders had said to them. 24 When they heard this, **they raised their voices together in prayer to God**. "Sovereign Lord," they said, "you made the heavens and the earth and the sea, and everything in them. 25 You spoke by the Holy Spirit through the mouth of your servant, our father David: "'Why do the nations rage and the peoples plot in vain? 26 **The kings of the earth rise up and the rulers band together against the Lord and against his anointed one.**' (quoting Psalm 2:1-2) 27 Indeed Herod and Pontius Pilate met together with the Gentiles and the people of Israel in this city to **conspire against your holy servant Jesus**, whom you anointed. 28 They did what your power and will had decided beforehand should happen. 29 Now, Lord, **consider their threats and enable your servants to speak your word with great boldness**. 30 **Stretch out your hand to heal and perform signs and wonders through the name of your holy servant Jesus.**" 31 After they prayed, the place where they were meeting was shaken. **And they were all filled with the Holy Spirit and spoke the word of God boldly**.

This said, it had now become abundantly clear that followers of Christ were a unique people, distinct from the world and the established religious system. As we previously discovered, this is called *ekklesia* or the Church. They were "on their own" so to speak but not totally alone because God's grace was with them. As their uniqueness became more prevalent, they became known as followers of *the Way* (Jesus is *the Way*, see John 14:6) and, eventually, they were called *Christians*. (see Acts 9:2, 11:26) Christian community also began to be understood as family. They considered themselves to be brothers and sisters in the bloodline of Christ, or *brethren*, and they depended on one another for the things that they needed. This was particularly true for the first Christians because many of them gave up everything in order to follow Christ or had been disowned by their families for worshipping Jesus. Therefore, they shared everything that they had with each other so that every believer had what they needed. They placed higher priority on taking care of fellow believers so that there would be no lack among them.

> {1Jo 3:16-18} 16 This is how we know what love is: Jesus Christ laid down his life for us. **And we ought to lay down our lives for our brothers and sisters. [fellow believers]** 17 **If anyone has material possessions and sees a brother or sister in need but has no pity on them, how can the love of God be in that person?** 18 Dear children, let us not love with words or speech but with actions and in truth.

> {Jas 2:14-16} 14 What good is it, my brothers and sisters, if someone claims to have faith but has no deeds? Can such faith save them? 15 **Suppose a brother or a sister [fellow believer] is**

without clothes and daily food. 16 If one of you says to them, "Go in peace; keep warm and well fed," but does nothing about their physical needs, what good is it?

{1Jo 4:19-21} 19 **We love because he first loved us.** *20* **Whoever claims to love God yet hates a brother or sister [fellow believer] is a liar.** *For whoever does not love their brother and sister, whom they have seen, cannot love God, whom they have not seen. 21* **And he has given us this command: Anyone who loves God must also love their brother and sister. [fellow believer]**

{Gal 6:10} 10 Therefore, as we have opportunity, let us do good to all people, **especially to those who belong to the family of believers.**

Most significantly, the Holy Spirit empowered *koinonia*, among them which, as we previously learned, stems from the word for *partnership* and emphasizes the significance and contribution of every part to the whole. It was Christ's greatest prayer for His followers to be ONE. This entails each individual contributing and caring for one another selflessly with fairness, equity, justice, and love.

{Rom 12:4-5} 4 For just as each of us has **one body with many members, and these members do not all have the same function,** *5 so* **in Christ we, though many, form one body, and each member belongs to all the others.**

{1Co 12:4-6, 12} 4 There are different kinds of gifts, but **the same Spirit** *distributes them. 5 There are different kinds of service, but* **the same Lord.** *6 There are different kinds of working, but in all of them and in everyone it is* **the same God** *at work... 12* **Just as a body, though one, has many parts, but all its many parts form one body, so it is with Christ.**

{Eph 4:4-6} 4 **There is one body and one Spirit,** *just as you were called to* **one hope** *when you were called; 5* **one Lord, one faith, one baptism;** *6* **one God and Father of all,** *who is over all and through all and in all.*

{Jhn 17:20-23} 20 "My prayer is not for them alone. I pray also for those who will believe in me through their message, 21 **<u>that all of them may be one</u>,** *Father, just as you are in me and I am in you. May they also be in us* **so that the world may believe that you have sent me.** *22 I have given them the glory that you gave me,* **that they may be one as we are one**-- *23 I in them and you in me--so that they may be brought to* **complete unity. Then the world will know that you sent me and have loved them even as you have loved me.**

A little later in the Book of Acts, this heart for each individual contributing to the whole was demonstrated by the early disciples of Christ in a very practical way. God, through the Holy Spirit, issued a prophetic word in order to warn the Church that believers in Jerusalem and Judea were in jeopardy due to an impending famine. Accordingly, Christians from all over united together to care and provide for the believers who were in need.

{Act 11:27-30} 27 During this time some prophets came down from Jerusalem to Antioch. 28 One of them, named Agabus, stood up and **through the Spirit predicted that a severe famine**

would spread over the entire Roman world. (This happened during the reign of Claudius.) 29
The disciples, as each one was able, decided to provide help for the brothers and sisters
[fellow believers] living in Judea. 30 This they did, sending their gift to the elders by Barnabas
and Saul.

Judean Christians who were at risk due to this impending famine were also enduring through great persecution, including expulsion from the Temple and rejection by their families, which left them without many normal means of support. As the prophecy came to pass, the famine did occur in the years that followed and this left everyone in the area pretty much destitute. Other Christians gave willingly from their hearts whatever they were able to give in order to provide relief. In fact, there are references throughout the New Testament writings regarding this offering for the Judean believers because it was treated with utmost importance. (see Galatians 2:10; 1 Corinthians 16:1-4; 2 Corinthians 8–9; Romans 15:25-31) People who had never met each other united and bonded together in familial love for one another to help one another because of their common faith and, mostly, because of their common Savior – Jesus. Notably, they often placed higher priority on service and assistance to fellow Christians abroad than they did to the unbelieving poor in their own cities and nations.

As the Gospel message spread to new territories, Christian communities continued to form. Worshippers of Jesus gathered together as a new faith, a new family, and a new people of God, and God added to their numbers. Believers opened their homes to one another in gracious hospitality, with a special mention for Lydia, Priscilla and Aquila, and a Philippian jailer. (see Acts 8:3, 16:5, 34, 18:3) They gathered together for prayer and fasting, seeking the will of the Lord, manifesting their spiritual gifts, and sharing in communion. (see Acts 12:5, 13:2-3, 15:32, 20:7) Those with more knowledge of the Scriptures taught other believers and strengthened them in their understanding of God and His ways. (see Acts 11:25-26, 15:32, 36, 16:4, 18:24-26, 20:7, 28:23) In cities near and far, Christians opened their hearts and homes for worship, and churches began to spring up and grow. In the same way that the first believers in Jerusalem had grown and multiplied, the Church as we know it today was born by the grace of God and through believer's love for Jesus and for one another.

Thriving Through Conflict

Before the crucifixion, Jesus' disciples were constantly competing to hold the top place of power and authority in His ministry. However, after the resurrection, none of them ever competed for greatness again, and each one of them went on to lay down their lives in the cause of spreading the Gospel.

> *{Mat 20:25-28} 25 Jesus called them together and said, "You know that the rulers of the Gentiles*
> *lord it over them, and their high officials exercise authority over them. 26 **Not so with you.***
> *Instead, **whoever wants to become great among you must be your servant, 27 and***
> ***whoever wants to be first must be your slave**-- 28 just as the Son of Man did not come to be*
> *served, but to serve, and to give his life as a ransom for many." (see also Matthew 23:8-11; Mark*
> *10:35-45; Luke 9:46-48)*

*{Jas 3:16-17} 16 For where you have **envy and selfish ambition, there you find disorder and every evil practice**. 17 But the **wisdom that comes from heaven** is first of all **pure**; then **peace-loving, considerate, submissive, full of mercy and good fruit, impartial and sincere**.*

Along these lines, so far, we've talked about topics that do not offend anyone, namely love and getting along with each other. But, what about when people didn't get along? What happened when there was not unity, harmony, and selflessness? One thing that I love about the Bible is its honesty because Scripture is honest enough to give us real examples of real conflicts between real people. For example:

*{Act 5:1-14} 1 Now a man named Ananias, together with his wife Sapphira, also sold a piece of property. 2 With his wife's full knowledge he **kept back part of the money for himself**, but brought the rest and put it at the apostles' feet. 3 Then Peter said, "Ananias, how is it that satan has so filled your heart that **you have lied to the Holy Spirit** and have kept for yourself some of the money you received for the land? 4 **Didn't it belong to you before it was sold? And after it was sold, wasn't the money at your disposal?** What made you think of doing such a thing? **You have not lied just to human beings but to God.**" 5 **When Ananias heard this, he fell down and died. And great fear seized all who heard what had happened**. 6 Then some young men came forward, wrapped up his body, and carried him out and buried him. 7 About three hours later his wife came in, not knowing what had happened. 8 Peter asked her, "Tell me, is this the price you and Ananias got for the land?" "Yes," she said, "that is the price." 9 Peter said to her, "**How could you conspire to test the Spirit of the Lord?** Listen! The feet of the men who buried your husband are at the door, and they will carry you out also." 10 **At that moment she fell down at his feet and died**. Then the young men came in and, finding her dead, carried her out and buried her beside her husband. 11 **Great fear seized the whole church and all who heard about these events**. 12 The apostles performed many signs and wonders among the people. And all the believers used to meet together in Solomon's Colonnade. 13 No one else dared join them, even though they were highly regarded by the people. 14 **Nevertheless, more and more men and women believed in the Lord and were added to their number**.*

Ananias and Sapphira were free to give or not give according to the Holy Spirit's prompting in their hearts. The issue was not their giving, but their lying. Led with wisdom from the Holy Spirit, Peter called their bluff and said that their act was tantamount to *satan filling your heart, lying to the Holy Spirit*, or *testing the Spirit of the Lord*. We don't know much about why they chose to do what they did, and we don't know if they were phonies who did not truly believe Jesus or real believers who went very far astray. However, Peter emphasized that Christian giving is voluntary, not forced, and that deliberate premeditated hypocrisy, self-aggrandizement, and deception have no place among the people of God. Unfortunately for Ananias and Sapphira, there was no time for Church discipline because, as soon as the truth was revealed to them, they both dropped dead. After this, great awe filled everyone who had heard about these events because God had given them another unique evidence that He was dwelling among them.

Not too long after this, arguments erupted between different types of Christ followers. At this point, all believers were still Jewish in heritage but, in spite of their common ancestry, there were differences that caused strife.

> *{Act 6:1-7} 1 In those days when the number of disciples was increasing, the **Hellenistic Jews among them complained against the Hebraic Jews because their widows were being overlooked in the daily distribution of food**. 2 So the Twelve gathered all the disciples together and said, "It would not be right for us to neglect the ministry of the word of God in order to wait on tables. 3 Brothers and sisters, **choose seven men from among you who are known to be full of the Spirit and wisdom. We will turn this responsibility over to them** 4 and will give our attention to prayer and the ministry of the word." 5 **This proposal pleased the whole group**. They chose Stephen, a man full of faith and of the Holy Spirit; also Philip, Procorus, Nicanor, Timon, Parmenas, and Nicolas from Antioch, a convert to Judaism. 6 They presented these men to the apostles, who prayed and laid their hands on them. 7 **So the word of God spread. The number of disciples in Jerusalem increased rapidly, and a large number of priests became obedient to the faith**.*

Hellenistic Jews were Jews who spoke Greek and lived a more Greek type of lifestyle. They were most likely Jews from other nations who had been converted at Pentecost and remained in Jerusalem. Hebraic Jews were most likely converts who were local to Jerusalem and Judea and who spoke Aramaic and Hebrew. As believers shared their goods with anyone who had need, unfortunately, the widows of the Hellenistic believers suffered neglect in the daily provision of food. This could have been a literal misunderstanding because of language barriers, or it is possible that there could have been some preferential treatment being given to the Hebraic Jews. Either way, it seems unlikely that there was malice involved because of what we know about the genuine love that they had for one another in addition to the quick attention given to resolving the situation. In order to discuss the problem, the apostles gathered everyone together. Functioning in the wisdom of the Holy Spirit, they considered the priorities of the community and the proper role and function of each person within their fellowship. Then, they selected godly men and appointed them to serve the community. Everyone was very pleased with this solution and the news of God's goodness spread so that many more people continued to believe in Jesus and become a part of the greater Christian community.

Several years later, Paul and Barnabas clashed before their second missionary journeys in spite of their common Christ-centered mission.

> *{Act 15:36-41} 36 Some time later Paul said to Barnabas, "Let us go back and visit the believers in all the towns where we preached the word of the Lord and see how they are doing." 37 **Barnabas wanted to take John, also called Mark, with them**, 38 **but Paul did not think it wise to take him, because he had deserted them in Pamphylia and had not continued with them in the work**. 39 They had such a **sharp disagreement that they parted company**. Barnabas took Mark and sailed for Cyprus, 40 but Paul chose Silas and left, commended by the believers to the grace of the Lord. 41 He went through Syria and Cilicia, strengthening the churches.*

Paul and Barnabas were both apostles, (see Acts 14:14) both totally devoted to the Lord Jesus Christ, and they were most likely as close as real brothers. Barnabas was the one person who had believed in Paul when nobody else did. (see Acts 9:26-27) Paul had been such a violent persecutor of Christians that, when he first believed and testified about Jesus as the Messiah, people thought that he was lying in order to deceive them. Barnabas was the first one to accept Paul's faith as genuine and others followed over time. Later on, after this was resolved, Barnabas and Paul taught in Antioch together for a year. (see Acts 11:25-26) Barnabas was also with Paul on his first missionary journey, which means that they had done many great exploits together for the Kingdom of God. (see Acts 13-14) The dispute between them arose when they were about to set out for a second missionary journey. They agreed on their mission of strengthening existing churches and founding new ones but they disagreed about who should go with them. John, who was called Mark (and who eventually went on to be the author of the Book of Mark) had abandoned Paul and Barnabas in the middle of their first missionary journey. We do not know the reason for his desertion, but we can deduct from what we do know that Paul was less than impressed with Mark's courage and commitment to the work of Christ. Barnabas, on the other hand, was known to be encouraging, (see Acts 4:36) and was Mark's biological cousin, (see Colossians 4:10) so he thought that Mark should come with them. Therefore, Paul and Barnabas had a *sharp disagreement*. Digging into the Greek, this means that the two of them were filled with *contentious irritation* and *passionate anger* over the issue. Their intense personalities collided. However, as the Holy Spirit led them, they decided to proceed on two separate missionary journeys with different companions rather than travel together. Even in this separation, God's grace went with all of them. In fact, efforts to spread the Gospel were now doubled. As a side note, over time, Mark redeemed himself in Paul's view, Paul specifically recognized Mark as an asset, and, in his last days, made note that Mark was very helpful to his ministry. (see Colossians 4:10; 2 Timothy 4:11)

Still later in the Book of Acts, another conflict occurred between believers. By this time, Paul was returning to Jerusalem at the end of his third missionary journey. He was convinced that he needed to return to Jerusalem in order to carry out his assignment from the Lord Jesus, no matter the cost or hardship that it would entail. Other believers, however, were concerned about what was ahead for Paul and did not want him to go.

> {Act 21:10-16} 10 *After we had been there a number of days,* **a prophet named Agabus came down from Judea.** 11 *Coming over to us,* **he took Paul's belt, tied his own hands and feet with it and said, "The Holy Spirit says, 'In this way the Jewish leaders in Jerusalem will bind the owner of this belt and will hand him over to the Gentiles.'"** 12 *When we heard this, we and the people there* **pleaded with Paul not to go up to Jerusalem.** 13 *Then Paul answered,* **"Why are you weeping and breaking my heart? I am ready not only to be bound, but also to die in Jerusalem for the name of the Lord Jesus."** 14 *When* **he would not be dissuaded, we gave up and said, "The Lord's will be done."** 15 *After this, we started on our way up to Jerusalem. 16 Some of the* **disciples from Caesarea accompanied us**

and brought us to the home of Mnason, where we were to stay. He was a man from Cyprus and one of the early disciples.

This was a disagreement about interpretation of spiritual things, specifically, prophecy. We are going to dig into prophecy more in a chapter to come, but, needless to say, prophecy can cause conflict. In this example, believers in the churches were dreadfully concerned about Paul, and rightfully so. Paul himself was certain that difficulty was in store for him, but he knew that it was God's will for him to go to Jerusalem. In essence, everyone was hearing the Lord say the same thing about what awaited Paul, but they interpreted the prophetic revelation differently. Nobody wanted to see Paul suffer, but Paul was compelled by something greater than suffering. Paul had already been imprisoned, whipped, beaten, stoned, and left for dead on several occasions on account of Christ and was willing to go through it all again because spreading the Gospel was the only thing that mattered to him. Although he was touched by their sentiment and love for him, Paul remained determined until they relented and entrusted him into the hands of God. From then on, they did everything that they could to help and support Paul. Paul went on to fulfill the will of God for him in Jerusalem and also in Rome. Notably, one of the primary reasons that Paul insisted on going to Jerusalem was to deliver the offering which had been collected for the believers suffering from the famine there. (see Acts 24:17)

There are two additional conflicts that we have not touched on yet and this is because we are going to discuss them in more depth in later chapters of this study. But, for the sake of continuity and emphasis on community, let us not neglect to point them out. After Peter went to Cornelius' house and shared the Gospel with Gentiles, Jewish believers back in Jerusalem criticized him for this unclean and illicit behavior. Up to this point, from their cultural view of things, it was considered vile for a Jew to eat with a Gentile. Peter explained to them how the Holy Spirit had led him through a vision and how God had sovereignly poured the Holy Spirit out upon Gentiles. When they heard Peter's explanation of God's leading and the confirming events, they stopped objecting and instead praised God. (see Acts 11:1-18) Also, there was a disagreement over the requirement of circumcision and obedience to God's Law for believers in the New Covenant. For this, the apostles convened in the Jerusalem Council and, with wisdom from the Holy Spirit, articulated a solution that they put in writing and sent out to followers of Christ everywhere. (see Acts 15:1-35) This solution was so pleasing to believers that they rejoiced, and the Church continued to grow in numbers.

Unity and Maturity

As the Gospel spread and the number of Christ followers multiplied in cities near and far, believers listened to the Holy Spirit to direct their decisions as the Church and the Body of Christ. This included appointing people into their Christ-given callings. The first example of this in the Book of Acts was actually before the Holy Spirit was poured out. The first 120 believers knew the significance of God's sovereign selections, particularly for positions of leadership. In spite of the fact that they sought the Lord's guidance through the old method of casting lots, their approach revealed a certain degree of wisdom. Even without the Holy Spirit, these believers knew that the decision was not theirs to make. They sought the Lord for His decision because they knew that Kingdom life was not a democracy, it was a monarchy, and Christ was their King. Significantly, they would have recalled from their history that the prophet Samuel had been instructed by God to anoint only the leaders whom God indicated to Him. This was because, in spite of what man can see by outward appearances, God looks into people's hearts. (see 1 Samuel 9:15-17, 16:3, 7, 12) Therefore, Christ's first disciples appealed to the Lord to reveal to them the person whom He had selected for the appointment.

> {Act 1:24-26} 24 **Then they prayed, "Lord, you know everyone's heart. Show us which of these two you have chosen** 25 to take over this apostolic ministry, which Judas left to go where he belongs." 26 Then they cast lots, and the lot fell to Matthias; so he was added to the eleven apostles.

Later in the Book of Acts, when arguments broke out between believers and disharmony set in due to inequitable distribution of food, the apostles recognized the seriousness of the problem. Therefore, they appointed deacons to serve God by serving His people. The word for *deacon* is the same word used for a *waiter* and, practically speaking, they served the needs of God's people so that the apostles could continue to devote their time to studying God's Word and to prayer. The men selected as deacons were selected by the people and were already considered exemplary Christ followers. Caution was taken before these men were appointed in order to verify through observation that their actions and behavior demonstrated the genuineness of their faith. (For more about deacons, see 1 Timothy 3:8-13; Titus 1:5-9) This solution pleased everyone, and the Church continued to grow.

> {Act 6:3-7} 3 **Brothers and sisters, choose seven men from among you who are known to be full of the Spirit and wisdom. We will turn this responsibility over to them** 4 **and will give our attention to prayer and the ministry of the word."** 5 **This proposal pleased the whole group.** They chose Stephen, a man full of faith and of the Holy Spirit; also Philip, Procorus, Nicanor, Timon, Parmenas, and Nicolas from Antioch, a convert to Judaism. 6 **They presented these men to the apostles, who prayed and laid their hands on them.** 7 **So the word of God spread.** The number of disciples in Jerusalem increased rapidly, and a large number of priests became obedient to the faith.

As churches were formed and became established in various cities, the apostles selected and appointed *elders* in each church. Then, the apostles prayed and laid hands on the elders in order to share their governing authority over God's people.

> {Act 14:21-23} 21 They preached the gospel in that city and won a large number of disciples. Then they returned to Lystra, Iconium and Antioch, 22 strengthening the disciples and encouraging them to remain true to the faith. "We must go through many hardships to enter the kingdom of God," they said. 23 **Paul and Barnabas appointed elders for them in each church and, with prayer and fasting, committed them to the Lord, in whom they had put their trust.**

An Old Testament example of this was when Moses took his father-in-law's advice and appointed elders of Israel to share the burden of leadership by judging smaller cases in matters of justice. These men had been selected to be Israel's elders because they were already regarded as capable men of integrity who feared the Lord and hated bribes. After these men were selected out of the tribes of Israel, God shared the same Spirit which was upon Moses with them so that they could rule justly the way that Moses did. (see Exodus 18:13-26; Numbers 11:10-29) In the Book of Acts, elders assisted the apostles in presiding over the Church, particularly through determining and implementing the financial and theological matters. This was particularly demonstrated by the elders' handling of the offering for Judean believers and by the elders' participation with the apostles at the Jerusalem Council. (see Acts 11:30, 15, 16:4, 24:17) Later, Paul made a speech to the elders of the church at Ephesus which emphasized the responsibility of overseeing God's flock and protecting God's people from predators and deception. (see Acts 20:17, 28) Most significantly, as the apostles and elders governed the Church, their decisions were always guided by the Holy Spirit. (For more about elders, see 1 Timothy 3:1-7, 5:17-25; Titus 1:5-9)

> *{Act 15:28}* 28 **It seemed good to the Holy Spirit and to us** *not to burden you with anything beyond the following requirements:*

In addition to deacons and elders, the Holy Spirit also revealed to listening believers the foreordained plans of God for individuals within their midst. As this happened, these people were set apart so that God could fulfill His purposes through them for His Church and His Kingdom.

> *{Act 13:1-4}* 1 *Now in the church at Antioch there were prophets and teachers: Barnabas, Simeon called Niger, Lucius of Cyrene, Manaen (who had been brought up with Herod the tetrarch) and Saul. 2 While they were worshiping the Lord and fasting,* **the Holy Spirit said, "Set apart for me Barnabas and Saul for the work to which I have called them."** *3* **So after they had fasted and prayed, they placed their hands on them and sent them off.** *4 The two of them,* **sent on their way by the Holy Spirit***, went down to Seleucia and sailed from there to Cyprus.*

It is noteworthy that God's people did not determine God's call upon anyone's life but, rather, recognized and confirmed God's pre-existing purpose. Examples of this pattern include David, who was anointed to be the King of Israel many years before he was appointed King, (see 1 Samuel 16:13; 2 Samuel 2:11, 5:1-4) Jeremiah, who was called by God as a prophet before Jeremiah was formed in his mother's womb, (Jeremiah 1:5) and Paul, who was chosen as an apostle of God before the foundation of the earth, anointed as an apostle when he first came to faith in Jesus Christ, and appointed as an apostle when the Church at Antioch sent him on his first missionary journey. (Galatians 1:15; Acts 9:15) Once God's purpose was revealed by the Holy Spirit, believers fasted and prayed, laid hands on God's chosen ones and sent them on their way.

As a quick side note, the laying on of hands is also prevalent throughout the Scriptures as a method of transferring blessing, imparting spiritual gifts, and appointing the leaders of God's people. In the Old Testament, Jacob laid hands on the heads of Joseph's sons Ephraim and Manasseh to adopt them as his own children and to bless them, and then he prophesied about their lives and their descendants. (see Genesis 48:1-22) Later, Moses laid his hands on Joshua to impart, or transfer, his anointing of wisdom for leading the people of Israel so that Joshua became his successor. (see Numbers 27:12-23; Deuteronomy 34:9) When the tribe of Levi was selected by God for the work of ministering to Him and to the

Tabernacle, all of Israel gathered together and laid hands on the Levites in order to demonstrate that the Levites served God on their behalf. (see Numbers 8:5-15) Additionally, when God's people offered sacrifices to Him in order to be restored to right standing with Him, they would lay their hands on the head of their offering. This transferred their sin to the offering and the unblemished holiness of the offering to them. (see Exodus 29:10, 15, 19, 33; Leviticus 1:4, 4:4, 15, 24, 8:14, 18, 22, 16:21) Lastly, when the High Priest blessed the people of Israel, he raised his hands with his palms towards the people to symbolize that he was laying his hands on all of them in order to bless them. (see Leviticus 9:22; Numbers 6:22-27) In the New Covenant, the laying on of hands continued and is used to consecrate believers with Christ's perfect righteousness, to fill one another with the Holy Spirit, to impart spiritual gifts, to heal the sick, and to set believers apart for God's special tasks. (see 1 Timothy 4:14; 2 Timothy 1:6; James 5:14; Mark 16:17-18; Romans 1:11) This was demonstrated throughout the Book of Acts.

> {Act 8:17} 17 *Then Peter and John* **placed their hands on them, and they received the Holy Spirit***.*

> {Act 9:12, 17} 12 *In a vision he has seen a man named Ananias come and* **place his hands on him to restore his sight***." ... 17 Then Ananias went to the house and entered it.* **Placing his hands on Saul***, he said, "Brother Saul, the Lord--Jesus, who appeared to you on the road as you were coming here--has sent me* **so that you may see again and be filled with the Holy Spirit***."*

> {Act 19:6} 6 **When Paul placed his hands on them, the Holy Spirit came on them, and they spoke in tongues and prophesied***.*

> {Act 28:8} 8 *His father was sick in bed, suffering from fever and dysentery. Paul went in to see him and, after prayer,* **placed his hands on him and healed him***.*

Through all of this and by the prompting of the Holy Spirit, God's chosen ones were appointed to their God-given tasks. Some people worked within the Church, and some were sent out by the Church. As each person carried out their role, God's purpose was fulfilled in the earth. When those who had been sent out returned home, they all gathered together to hear the report of what God had accomplished. Everyone was greatly encouraged and praised God.

> {Act 14:27} 27 *On arriving there,* **they gathered the church together and reported all that God had done through them** *and how he had opened a door of faith to the Gentiles.*

> {Act 15:4, 12} 4 *When they came to Jerusalem, they were welcomed by the church and the apostles and elders,* **to whom they reported everything God had done through them***. ... 12* **The whole assembly became silent as they listened to Barnabas and Paul telling about the signs and wonders God had done among the Gentiles through them***.*

> {Act 21:18-20a} 18 *The next day Paul and the rest of us went to see James, and all the elders were present. 19 Paul greeted them and* **reported in detail what God had done among the Gentiles through his ministry***. 20 When they heard this,* **they praised God***.*

In fact, throughout the Book of Acts, the Holy Spirit revealed Christ's chosen apostles, prophets, evangelists, shepherds, and teachers. (see Acts 1:2, 5:29, 11:27, 13:1, 15:32, 20:28, 21:8, 10) Indeed, every believer has a unique assignment from Christ which corresponds with one of these types of ministries and each ministry reflects a different aspect of the same purpose. (see Ephesians 4:7) God's purpose for each and every one of His people, no matter how they are gifted and regardless of which way they are called to serve, is to manifest the love of Jesus to the world by being conformed to the image and likeness of Christ. (see Romans 8:29-30)

> *{Eph 4:11-13} 11 So Christ himself gave the apostles, the prophets, the evangelists, the pastors and teachers, 12* ***to equip his people for works of service, so that the body of Christ may be built up*** *13* ***until we all reach unity in the faith*** *and in the knowledge of the Son of God* ***and become mature, attaining to the whole measure of the fullness of Christ.***

God's intent for the Church is for all of His people to be unified as ONE body and to be spiritually mature so that we are a living, breathing, walking, talking demonstration of His kindness and grace through Jesus Christ. Simply put, the aim of the Christian life is *Christlikeness*, both individually and corporately. This is why we live our lives by the promptings of the Holy Spirit, and this is the mission of every believer. God's purpose has always been the building up of His people, both adding new sons and daughters to His family and strengthening His children in our faith and function. We are sons and daughters of one Father, God. We are a holy nation and subjects of one King, Jesus. We are one body, the Body of Christ who is our Head and who directs every part of His Body through the guidance of the Holy Spirit.

> *{Eph 1:22-23} 22 And God placed all things under his feet and appointed him to be head over everything* ***for the church,*** *23* ***which is his body, the fullness of him who fills everything in every way.***

> *{Eph 2:6-7} 6 And God raised us up with Christ and seated us with him in the heavenly realms in Christ Jesus, 7* ***in order that in the coming ages [both now and into the age to come] he might show the incomparable riches of his grace, expressed in his kindness to us [believers] in Christ Jesus.***

> *{Eph 3:10-11} 10* ***His intent was that now, through the church, the manifold wisdom of God should be made known to the rulers and authorities in the heavenly realms,*** *11 according to his eternal purpose that he accomplished in Christ Jesus our Lord.*

Even today, the oneness of Christians is more profound than any other bond in the world. We have a bond with one another that is deeper than flesh and blood, more powerful than family heritage and far surpasses any natural form of partnership or association. What we have in common as Christ followers is not just an intellectual collection of beliefs and a common book. Because of the indwelling Holy Spirit, Christians all have the same heart. We also have the same Father, God, and the same King and brother, Jesus. We are all individual pieces of the same loaf of bread, the Body of Christ which was broken for us.

Not to mention that we have the same home, heaven, and the same mission, to bring heaven to earth and make disciples of all nations, inviting them into the joy of our fellowship.

Practically speaking, giving to one another and serving one another starts in the heart. Do we know that everything that we have has been given to us? Everything from material possessions, to physical and mental abilities, to spiritual capacities, and all other things that we can think of were given to us by the grace of God to share with others. Sometimes, giving and serving is more of an exchange. Everything is equitable and fair as long as everyone is doing their part and keeping their end of the deal. This is common even by worldly standards, or you could call it legalism. Other times, when we give and serve, we try to do so openhandedly but, somehow, we are only comfortable if it seems that, according to our calculation, both parties are even. Or, when we give and serve, we only give to or serve those that we deem are worthy of our charity and then, we consider ourselves to be a philanthropic hero. Or, after we have given and served, even if we have said that we expect nothing in return, we consider the receiver of our "gift" to be indebted to us, and we may even try to use this indebtedness as leverage to manipulate them. This attempt at grace is more like religion which always wears a disguise to mask itself as grace. But when we give and serve freely, without a hint (even in our hearts) of expecting anything in return, we give and serve with true grace. When we truly know that everything that we have is something that we have received freely from the Lord, we share and minister liberally and without judgment. THIS is grace because it is a truly FREE gift.

Of course, this goes much much deeper than material possessions, worldly goods, and acts of kindness. Loving and serving each other entails laying aside our own agendas, preferences, ambitions, and needs in order to live our lives for Jesus. Jesus only gave one command to His disciples: to love one another as He loves us. We cannot do this unless we truly know and have received the love of Jesus for ourselves. On the day of Pentecost, new converts to Christ were *cut to the heart* when they understood the love of God for them. Have we been cut to the heart by His great sacrificial love? To them, everything else seemed trivial by comparison and it was this revelation of the love of Christ for them that made loving one another and sharing everything with one another so effortless.

> {Jhn 15:12-14, 17} 12 **My command is this: Love each other as I have loved you**. 13 *Greater love has no one than this: to **lay down one's life for one's friends**. 14 You are my friends if you do what I command. ... 17 **This is my command: Love each other**.*

If you have a chance sometime, look up the references to *one another* in the New Testament. If you do so, you will see the things that believers are called upon to do for one another, such as *love, submit to, honor, be devoted to, stop passing judgment on, confess your sins to, accept, bear in love with, serve, greet, do not lie to, encourage, and be kind and compassionate to* one another. All of this stems from our own comprehension of Christ's love for us. When we know in our hearts the love of Jesus for us, we naturally have grace for one another, and we overlook each other's faults and failures. When our actions are led by the Holy Spirit, we readily turn the other cheek, go the extra mile, and we step in to assist with our strengths in areas where others are weak. When we trust that God is in control, we give freely, and we receive freely knowing that God is the one who gives every blessing and who makes up for every wrong.

Again, in Christ, believers are one. We are one faith, one people, and one Body. Because of God's grace for us through His Son Jesus Christ, we are blessed by God and we love one another. God reveals His hand of blessing upon our lives so that the whole world can see that He is a good God who blesses people who believe Him. (see Psalm 67; Acts 17:27; Hebrews 11:6) More importantly, God does this so that the whole world will seek Him and may come to know Him for themselves. God loved the world so much that He gave His one and only Son, Jesus Christ and (see John 3:16) Jesus loved all of mankind enough to lay down His life for our sins. (see John 15:13) When we love one another the way that Jesus loves us, we manifest Christ to the world and fulfill God's purpose for His people in the earth.

CHAPTER 10
Miracles

Throughout the Book of Acts, Christ followers were empowered by the Holy Spirit to do the works that Jesus did in the way that He did them. In this chapter, we're going to examine the miracles, signs, and wonders done throughout the Book of Acts so that we are equipped to do the very same ACTS.

Power from Heaven

On the day of Pentecost, miracles started happening among Christ's followers, even though Jesus was physically absent. Jesus had told His disciples that they would receive *power from heaven* to be His witnesses to the ends of the earth, (see Acts 1:8; Luke 24:49) and once the Holy Spirit was poured out, miracles, signs, and wonders became commonplace among believers. By definition, a *miracle* is something which *transcends the common course of nature*, a *sign* is a token mark which *distinguishes, points to, or confirms* something or someone else, and a *wonder* is an *unusual occurrence* that makes people stop and *wonder* how it could have happened. Miracles in the Book of Acts were done when common people testified accurately from the Scriptures, prophesied, spoke in tongues, had God-given dreams and visions, received guidance from the Holy Spirit for daily living, were visited by angels, and selflessly loved one another in the community of believers, all of which we have covered or will cover in more depth in other chapters. The point is that, as soon as believers were filled with the Holy Spirit, they were supernaturally empowered to do the things that Jesus did in the way that He did them.

Healing and Deliverance

After Pentecost, Peter and John continued to witness for Jesus in the Temple area in order to persuade their fellow Jews that Jesus is their Lord and Messiah. A lame man begged for their money, but they had something much better than money to give him. In the name of Jesus they commanded the lame man to do the impossible and stand up – and he did! They used the same approach that they had seen Jesus use many times and that they had probably done themselves when Jesus sent them out previously. And now, a man who was over forty years old and had been lame since birth leapt for joy and praised God!

> *{Act 3:1-10} 1 One day Peter and John were going up to the temple at the time of prayer--at three in the afternoon. 2 Now **a man who was lame from birth** was being carried to the temple gate called Beautiful, where he was put every day to beg from those going into the temple courts. 3 When he saw Peter and John about to enter, he **asked them for money**. 4 Peter looked straight at him, as did John. Then Peter said, "Look at us!" 5 So the man gave them his attention, expecting to get something from them. 6 **Then Peter said, "Silver or gold I do not have, but what I do have I give you. In the name of Jesus Christ of Nazareth, walk." 7 Taking him by the right hand, he helped him up, and instantly the man's feet and unkles became strong**. 8*

He jumped to his feet and began to walk. *Then he went with them into the temple courts,* **walking and jumping, and praising God.** *9 When all the people saw him walking and praising God, 10 they recognized him as the same man who used to sit begging at the temple gate called Beautiful, and* **they were filled with wonder and amazement** *at what had happened to him.*

When Jesus healed people, He gave simple commands in accordance with God's will *on earth as it is in heaven.* For example, He said things such as *Your sins are forgiven* or *Be clean.* (see Matthew 8:3, 9:2) In other cases, He commanded the person to do something they could not previously do because of their condition such as *Take up your mat and walk* to a man who had been lame for thirty-eight years or *Stretch out your hand* to a man with a withered hand. (see John 5:8; Luke 6:10) Jesus spoke to body parts like blind eyes, deaf ears, mute tongues commanding them to *Be opened* and He spoke to the sickness and rebuked it. (see Mark 7:34; Luke 4:39) When Jesus spoke to demons, He addressed them directly saying things such as *Come out of him* or just simply, *Go.* (see Mark 1:25; Matthew 8:32) Sometimes, Jesus did not say anything which obviously pointed out why a miracle had occurred, and other times He acknowledged that the believer's faith had healed them. Sometimes, He touched people, and other times He didn't. Some people were healed even though Jesus was a long distance away. A few people were raised from the dead, which means it was certainly not on account of their great faith. Even though Jesus was totally unpredictable in His approach to each unique situation, we know for certain that whatever He did and said was only what He saw and heard His heavenly Father doing and saying.

As we have discussed, Jesus had the power and the authority to heal and deliver all who came to Him in faith. He did not drone on and on in prayer hoping that maybe God would grant Him what He asked. He did not think things such as, *God heals sometimes but not every time* or *God can heal but He doesn't always.* He did not qualify people through examination of their sins or tell them that they must fix their life first. He did not reference generational hindrances or blocks of unforgiveness. He did not turn people away for any reason whatsoever because, in essence, everyone was already an enemy of God who had a life full of sin and didn't deserve a thing. Every person was already generationally cursed all the way back to Adam and was impossibly filled with bitter unforgiveness. The only hindrances that prevented people from receiving from Jesus were unbelief, which is not being sure that Jesus can or will heal, and religious self-righteousness, which is being qualified or disqualified for blessing through piety or goodness. The only possible exception to this was people who simply did not want to be well or didn't ask to be well. Aside from these things, Jesus did not reckon that there was anything obstructing healing from a person who came to Him in faith because He knew that the answer had nothing to do with their worthiness but that the solution was exclusively in HIM. Healing is not about our great faith but about receiving God's great mercy.

Though we do not have time to go into much depth on this now, let us quickly touch upon how we were healed by the finished work of Jesus. Jesus, through one sacrifice, once and for all took all of our sins upon Himself on the cross, which releases us from every possible Biblical attribution of sickness. As King David noted in Psalm 32, *blessed is the man whose sins are forgiven and whose sins are not counted against him.* Why? Because sin or disobedience, the curse of the Law, and the work of the devil are the reasons why people are sick. In the Book of Exodus, God first revealed Himself to Israel as the *Great Physician* or *God Who Heals* (see Exodus 15: 26) in the context of obedience to His commands. In essence, He said, *If you obey me I'll prevent any disease from touching you.* At this point in time, the Israelites had just been delivered out of Egypt where God had made a distinction between them and the people of Egypt. As we learned in a previous chapter, when massive plagues struck the Egyptians, they did not touch the Israelites. Accordingly, the Israelites would have known that God is fully capable of protecting His people from all sorts of afflictions, and this is what He promised to do for them if they obeyed His commands. This said, as believers in Christ, we do not rely on our obedience but on Christ's obedience. Jesus never sinned, which means that He never disobeyed God. Therefore, legally speaking, through faith in Christ, no disease has a right to touch us due to our sin or disobedience. Moreover, when sins are counted against people, they become subject to the curse of the Law which details God's appointed schedule of retribution for sin. (see Deuteronomy 28, Leviticus 26) Every kind of sickness is accounted for in the curse of the Law, even sicknesses not specifically mentioned by name. (see Deuteronomy 28:61) However, through His death, Jesus became a curse for us and redeemed us from the curse of the Law. Therefore, legally speaking, through faith in Christ, no kind of sickness has any right to afflict us due to the curse. Lastly, certain sicknesses and diseases are due to the devil and demonic oppression. (For an example of this, see Luke 13:16.) The devil has been oppressing mankind through various means since Adam's first sin. However, Jesus overpowered the devil and releases people who have been oppressed by him for far too long. (see Mark 3:27; Matthew 12:29) Through His death and resurrection, Jesus Christ destroyed the work of the devil, namely sin. (1 John 3:7) Therefore, legally speaking, when our faith is in Christ, no disease or demonic oppression has any right to our lives because of the evil one. All of this is to say that, whether sickness is due to sin, disobedience, the curse, or the devil, Jesus took care of it.

As if that is not sufficient, through His suffering and on the cross, Jesus also took all of our sickness upon Himself in addition to all pain, suffering, grief, and sorrow. (see Isaiah 53:4) Jesus drove out all the unclean spirits and healed all the sick to fulfill what the Scriptures had said about Him: *He took our infirmities and carried away our diseases.* (see Matthew 8:16-17-NASB, quoting Isaiah 53:4) During His suffering and crucifixion, all of our infirmities and afflictions were pinned onto Jesus until He died. Through His death, He carried them away and down to the pit of hell. Through resurrection, sin and sickness were left behind and banished from having any power or authority over anyone who believes that Jesus is Lord.

Jesus said it best when He said that *IT IS FINISHED!* In this one statement, He summed up His other healing statements, including *your sins are forgiven, be clean, take up your mat and walk, stretch out your hand,* body parts *be opened,* and demons *be gone.* Now, I know that some of you are wondering, *If it is God's will through the finished work of Christ for everyone to be healed, then why isn't everyone healed?* It is because not everyone receives the free gift of what Christ has done for them. Just like not everyone receives the free gift of salvation through Jesus Christ, even though it is God's will for everyone to be saved, not everyone receives the free gift of healing and deliverance through faith in Christ's finished work, even though it truly is finished. To press into this a little further, again as an example, when we come to salvation through faith in Jesus, we give up all other gods so that our faith rests entirely in Christ. Similarly, when we pursue the Lord for healing and deliverance, we must focus ourselves entirely and exclusively on receiving from Him through the completed work of the cross.

I realize that this was a surface-level crash course in Biblical healing but, the bottom line is this: Because Christ is risen, the blind see, the deaf hear, the lame leap, the mute shout for joy! (Isaiah 35:5-6; Luke 7:22) We pray *Your Kingdom come, Your will be done on earth as it is in heaven.* In heaven *there is no death, mourning, crying, or pain.* (see Revelation 21:4) Blessed are WE who believe Jesus Christ as Lord, Savior, Healer, and Deliverer because our sins are forgiven and not counted against us! When we believe this, miracles happen!

Now that we're up to speed with what the apostles had witnessed and experienced in their time with Jesus, let's proceed. Throughout the Book of Acts, disciples of Christ did the works that Jesus did because they understood the finished work of the cross and resurrection and the power and authority they had through faith in the name of Jesus.

A paralyzed man was healed:

> *{Act 9:32-35} 32 As Peter traveled about the country, he went to visit the Lord's people who lived in Lydda. 33 There he found a man named Aeneas, who was paralyzed and had been bedridden for eight years. 34 "Aeneas," Peter said to him, "Jesus Christ heals you. Get up and roll up your mat." Immediately Aeneas got up. 35 All those who lived in Lydda and Sharon saw him and turned to the Lord.*

A lame man walked:

> *{Act 14:8-10} 8 In Lystra there sat a man who was lame. He had been that way from birth and had never walked. 9 He listened to Paul as he was speaking. Paul looked directly at him, saw that he had faith to be healed 10 and called out, "Stand up on your feet!" At that, the man jumped up and began to walk.*

Men on Malta were healed:

> *{Act 28:7-9} 7 There was an estate nearby that belonged to Publius, the chief official of the island. He welcomed us to his home and showed us generous hospitality for three days. 8 His father was sick in bed, suffering from fever and dysentery. Paul went in to see him and, after prayer, placed his hands on him and healed him. 9 When this had happened, the rest of the sick on the island came and were cured.*

Impure spirits were cast out:

> *{Act 5:15-16} 15 As a result, people brought the sick into the streets and laid them on beds and mats so that at least Peter's shadow might fall on some of them as he passed by. 16 Crowds gathered also from the towns around Jerusalem, bringing their sick and those tormented by impure spirits, and all of them were healed.*

*{Act 8:5-8} 5 **Philip** went down to a city in Samaria and proclaimed the Messiah there. 6 When the crowds heard Philip and saw **the signs he performed**, they all paid close attention to what he said. 7 For with shrieks, **impure spirits came out of many, and many who were paralyzed or lame were healed**. 8 So there was great joy in that city.*

*{Act 19:11-12} 11 **God did extraordinary miracles through Paul**, 12 so that even handkerchiefs and aprons that had touched him were taken to the sick, and **their illnesses were cured and the evil spirits left them**.*

As a quick side note, throughout the Book of Acts, individual cases of healings through deliverance from evil spirits are not recounted in as much detail as they are in the Gospel accounts of Jesus' ministry. Instead, Acts gives a smattering as evidence that no matter what was afflicting people, including sickness, generational curses, demonic oppression, and things like this, believers had authority in the name of Jesus to heal, declare curses null and void, and cast out demons. The same is true for us today.

The dead were raised:

*{Act 9:36-43} 36 In Joppa there was a **disciple named Tabitha** (in Greek her name is Dorcas); she was always doing good and helping the poor. 37 **About that time she became sick and died**, and her body was washed and placed in an upstairs room. 38 Lydda was near Joppa; so when the disciples heard that Peter was in Lydda, they sent two men to him and urged him, "Please come at once!" 39 Peter went with them, and when he arrived he was taken upstairs to the room. All the widows stood around him, crying and showing him the robes and other clothing that Dorcas had made while she was still with them. 40 **Peter sent them all out of the room; then he got down on his knees and prayed. Turning toward the dead woman, he said, "Tabitha, get up." She opened her eyes, and seeing Peter she sat up.** 41 He took her by the hand and helped her to her feet. Then he called for the believers, especially the widows, and **presented her to them alive**. 42 **This became known all over Joppa**, and many people believed in the Lord. 43 Peter stayed in Joppa for some time with a tanner named Simon.*

*{Act 20:7-12} 7 On the first day of the week we came together to break bread. Paul spoke to the people and, because he intended to leave the next day, kept on talking until midnight. 8 There were many lamps in the upstairs room where we were meeting. 9 Seated in a window was a young man named **Eutychus, who was sinking into a deep sleep as Paul talked on and on. When he was sound asleep, he fell to the ground from the third story and was picked up dead.** 10 Paul went down, **threw himself on the young man and put his arms around him. "Don't be alarmed," he said. "He's alive!"** 11 Then he went upstairs again and broke bread and ate. After talking until daylight, he left. 12 The people took the young man home alive and were greatly comforted.*

As another side note, Peter raised Tabitha from the dead in the same way that He had seen Jesus raise Jairus' daughter. (see Matthew 9; Mark 5; Luke 8) Paul, on the other hand, had not been with Jesus during His earthly ministry but he knew the Scriptures better than anyone in the world. He raised Eutychus from the dead in the same way that Elijah and Elisha had raised boys from the dead in the Old Testament. (see 1 Kings 17; 2 Kings 4) This proves that different methods can yield the same results for God as long as we are led by Him. Remember, Jesus rarely did anything in the same way twice because He only did what He saw His Father doing.

Other Kinds of Signs

After Peter and John healed the lame man at the Temple, they were arrested and imprisoned by the religious leaders. When they finally stood before the religious council to explain what had happened, they proclaimed the Gospel of Jesus Christ with great boldness and quoted the Scriptures with the accuracy of trained scholars. Peter and John's *boldness* and *knowledge of the Lord* was in itself a sign, or miracle.

> {Act 4:13-22} 13 **When they saw the courage of Peter and John and realized that they were unschooled, ordinary men, they were astonished and they took note that these men had been with Jesus.** 14 *But since they could see the man who had been healed standing there with them,* **there was nothing they could say.** 15 *So they ordered them to withdraw from the Sanhedrin and then conferred together.* 16 *"What are we going to do with these men?" they asked.* **"Everyone living in Jerusalem knows they have performed a notable sign, and we cannot deny it.** 17 **But to stop this thing from spreading any further among the people,** *we must warn them to speak no longer to anyone in this name."* 18 *Then they called them in again and* **commanded them not to speak or teach at all in the name of Jesus.** 19 **But Peter and John replied, "Which is right in God's eyes: to listen to you, or to him? You be the judges!** 20 **As for us, we cannot help speaking about what we have seen and heard."** 21 *After further threats they let them go. They could not decide how to punish them, because all the people were praising God for what had happened.* 22 *For the man who was miraculously healed was over forty years old.*

The religious leaders took note of Peter and John. Everyone knew that they were ordinary fishermen from Galilee with no special schooling in the Scriptures. (see Luke 5:1-11) The religious leaders, however, were trained experts in the Scriptures but they did not understand the Word of God as well as Peter and John did. Moreover, they could not deny that a man had been miraculously healed and that Peter and John attributed this healing to the fact that Jesus is the One that the Scriptures point to. Furthermore, because everyone knew about the healing, the religious leaders did not want to punish Peter and John and lose the favor of the crowd and so, they ordered Peter and John not to speak about Jesus anymore. However, this only provoked them to even more spirit-filled *boldness*. In fact, after they were released from this ordeal, Peter and John met back up with the other believers, and they all prayed together for more *boldness* than ever!

> {Act 4:29-30 } 29 *Now, Lord,* **consider their threats and enable your servants to speak your word with great boldness.** 30 **Stretch out your hand to heal and perform signs and wonders through the name of your holy servant Jesus."**

A little later in the Book of Acts, the apostles were again entangled with the religious leaders because many miracles, signs, and wonders were being done among followers of Christ and the apostles were again arrested and imprisoned. The religious leaders reprimanded the apostles for not obeying their earlier command not to speak in the name of Jesus anymore.

> *{Act 5:27-42} 27 The apostles were brought in and made to appear before the Sanhedrin to be questioned by the high priest. 28 **"We gave you strict orders not to teach in this name,"** he said. "Yet you have filled Jerusalem with your teaching and are determined to make us guilty of this man's blood." 29 **Peter and the other apostles replied: "We must obey God rather than human beings!** 30 The God of our ancestors raised Jesus from the dead--whom you killed by hanging him on a cross. 31 God exalted him to his own right hand as Prince and Savior that he might bring Israel to repentance and forgive their sins. 32 **We are witnesses of these things, and so is the Holy Spirit, whom God has given to those who obey him."** 33 When they heard this, **they were furious and wanted to put them to death.** 34 **But a Pharisee named Gamaliel, a teacher of the law, who was honored by all the people, stood up** in the Sanhedrin and ordered that the men be put outside for a little while. 35 Then he addressed the Sanhedrin: "Men of Israel, **consider carefully what you intend to do to these men.** 36 Some time ago **Theudas** appeared, claiming to be somebody, and about four hundred men rallied to him. He was killed, **all his followers were dispersed**, and it all came to nothing. 37 After him, **Judas the Galilean** appeared in the days of the census and led a band of people in revolt. He too was killed, and **all his followers were scattered.** 38 **Therefore, in the present case I advise you: Leave these men alone! Let them go! For if their purpose or activity is of human origin, it will fail. 39 But if it is from God, you will not be able to stop these men; you will only find yourselves fighting against God."** 40 His speech persuaded them. They called the apostles in and had them flogged. Then they ordered them not to speak in the name of Jesus, and let them go. 41 The apostles left the Sanhedrin, **rejoicing because they had been counted worthy of suffering disgrace for the Name.** 42 Day after day, in the temple courts and from house to house, **they never stopped teaching and proclaiming the good news that Jesus is the Messiah.***

The apostles would not be silenced. They had seen with their eyes the resurrected Lord Jesus and lived to testify about Him to the ends of the earth. Their *boldness* infuriated the religious leaders so much that they wanted the apostles to be executed. (These were the same people who ordered that Jesus be crucified.) But then, a wise old Pharisee named Gamaliel, who was the most respected Rabbi of his day, (and who had been the apostle Paul's mentor before his conversion to faith in Christ – see Acts 22:3) pointed out that the *persistence* and *longevity* of the apostles would serve to prove the genuineness of their faith and whether or not the hand of God was truly with them. Gamaliel referenced two prior Messiah claimants who had incited the people to follow their leadership while they were alive. One had been a false prophet and the other had led a tax revolt against Rome's authority over Jews. After their deaths, their followers rapidly dispersed and their movements swiftly ended. However, this was not the case with Jesus.

Followers of Jesus, now several months after His crucifixion, were testifying more *boldly* than ever and *persevering* even in the face of opposition against their lives. Gamaliel reasoned that the disciple's *endurance* over the course of time would serve as a sign that God was with them... and it was.

This same kind of supernatural *boldness* and *perseverance* and *knowledge of the Lord* throughout the Book of Acts served as a sign in and of itself. Stephen testified with irrefutable wisdom, believers scattered out of Jerusalem due to persecution persevered in testifying boldly about Jesus everywhere that they went, and Paul continued to fearlessly proclaim the Gospel of Jesus Christ no matter how much hardship and suffering he endured. Christ followers everywhere were only ignited more than ever when they faced persecution and opposition and in fact, they rejoiced all the more that they were considered worthy to suffer for the name of Jesus.

> {Act 6:10} 10 But they **could not stand up against the wisdom the Spirit gave him [Stephen] as he spoke**.

> {Act 8:4} 4 **Those [believers] who had been scattered preached the word wherever they went**.

> {Act 20:18-21} 18 When they arrived, he said to them: "You know how I lived the whole time I was with you, from the first day I came into the province of Asia. 19 **I served the Lord with great humility and with tears and in the midst of severe testing by the plots of my Jewish opponents**. 20 You know **that I have not hesitated to preach anything that would be helpful to you but have taught you publicly and from house to house**. 21 I have declared to both Jews and Greeks that they **must turn to God in repentance and have faith in our Lord Jesus**.

> {Act 21:13} 13 Then Paul answered, "Why are you weeping and breaking my heart? **I am ready not only to be bound, but also to die in Jerusalem for the name of the Lord Jesus**."

Even today, *knowledge of the Lord*, *boldness*, and *perseverance*, especially in the midst of hardship, serve as signs of our faith in Christ and His faithfulness to us. They prove that His supernatural strength is in us and that we are legitimate children of God through faith in Jesus. (see Hebrews 12:7) Just like the first Christ followers of Acts, our response to trials and staying true to our faith in Jesus Christ no matter what we endure is another kind of *wonder* which causes people to take note.

Even More Miracles, Signs, and Wonders

All this said, we're not quite done examining the miracles of the Book of Acts. Many and various miracles, signs, and wonders were performed by Christ's disciples:

> {Act 5:12} 12 The **apostles performed many signs and wonders among the people**. And all the believers used to meet together in Solomon's Colonnade

> {Act 6:8} 8 Now **Stephen**, a man full of God's grace and power, **performed great wonders and signs** among the people.

{Act 14:3} 3 So **Paul and Barnabas** *spent considerable time there, [Iconium] speaking boldly for the Lord,* **who confirmed the message of his grace by enabling them to perform signs and wonders**.

Believers were supernaturally released from prison:

{Act 5:18-25} 18 They **arrested the apostles and put them in the public jail**. *19 But during the night* **an angel of the Lord opened the doors of the jail and brought them out**. *20 "Go, stand in the temple courts," he said, "and tell the people all about this new life." 21 At daybreak they entered the temple courts, as they had been told, and began to teach the people. When the high priest and his associates arrived, they called together the Sanhedrin--the full assembly of the elders of Israel--and sent to the jail for the apostles. 22 But* **on arriving at the jail, the officers did not find them there**. *So they went back and reported,* *23 "We found the jail securely locked, with the guards standing at the doors; but when we opened them, we found no one inside." 24 On hearing this report, the captain of the temple guard and the chief priests were at a loss, wondering what this might lead to. 25 Then someone came and said,* **"Look! The men you put in jail are standing in the temple courts teaching the people."**

{Act 12:5-11} 5 So Peter was kept in prison, **but the church was earnestly praying to God for him**. *6 The night before Herod was to bring him to trial, Peter was sleeping between two soldiers, bound with two chains, and sentries stood guard at the entrance. 7* **Suddenly an angel of the Lord appeared and a light shone in the cell**. *He struck Peter on the side and woke him up. "Quick, get up!" he said, and* **the chains fell off Peter's wrists**. *8 Then the angel said to him, "Put on your clothes and sandals." And Peter did so. "Wrap your cloak around you and follow me," the angel told him. 9* **Peter followed him out of the prison**, *but he had no idea that what the angel was doing was really happening; he thought he was seeing a vision. 10* **They passed the first and second guards and came to the iron gate leading to the city. It opened for them by itself, and they went through it. When they had walked the length of one street, suddenly the angel left him.** *11 Then Peter came to himself and said, "Now I know without a doubt that* **the Lord has sent his angel and rescued me** *from Herod's clutches and from everything the Jewish people were hoping would happen."*

{Act 16:23-26} 23 After they had been severely flogged, **they were thrown into prison, and the jailer was commanded to guard them carefully**. *24 When he received these orders,* **he put them in the inner cell and fastened their feet in the stocks**. *25 About midnight* **Paul and Silas were praying and singing hymns to God**, *and the other prisoners were listening to them. 26 Suddenly there* **was such a violent earthquake that the foundations of the prison were shaken. At once all the prison doors flew open, and everyone's chains came loose**.

Believers experienced supernatural transportation:

{Act 8:39-40} 39 When they came up out of the water, **the Spirit of the Lord suddenly took Philip away**, *and the eunuch did not see him again, but went on his way rejoicing. 40* **Philip,**

> *however,* **appeared at Azotus** *and traveled about, preaching the gospel in all the towns until he reached Caesarea.*

The distance from Gaza to Azotus is a little under 30 miles. The word for *took him away* is better translated *carried him by force* or *snatched* and the word for *appeared* is actually better translated as *found himself* or *discovered.* Philip was at one moment in Gaza and then the next moment realized that he had been transported to another town. He proceeded to preach the Gospel there.

Believers were unharmed by poison:

> *{Act 28:3-6} 3 Paul gathered a pile of brushwood and, as he put it on the fire,* **a viper, driven out by the heat, fastened itself on his hand.** *4 When the islanders* **saw the snake hanging from his hand,** *they said to each other, "This man must be a murderer; for though he escaped from the sea, the goddess Justice has not allowed him to live." 5* **But Paul shook the snake off into the fire and suffered no ill effects. 6 The people expected him to swell up or suddenly fall dead; but after waiting a long time and seeing nothing unusual happen to him, they changed their minds and said he was a god.**

Just because followers of Christ live unharmed, even if we pick up deadly snakes, (see Mark 16:15-18) this does not mean that we need to go around handling snakes in order to prove it. However, we can be unafraid when we eat and drink or have encounters with lethal creatures because our food is made clean by God's word and our prayer (see 1 Timothy 4:5) and poison has no right to afflict us when our faith is in Jesus.

Liars and glory stealers were struck dead, false prophets were struck blind and set free:

> *{Act 5:3-11} 3 Then Peter said, "Ananias, how is it that satan has so filled your heart that you have lied to the Holy Spirit and have kept for yourself some of the money you received for the land? 4 Didn't it belong to you before it was sold? And after it was sold, wasn't the money at your disposal? What made you think of doing such a thing? You have not lied just to human beings but to God." 5* **When Ananias heard this, he fell down and died. And great fear seized all who heard what had happened.** *6 Then some young men came forward, wrapped up his body, and carried him out and buried him. 7 About three hours later his wife came in, not knowing what had happened. 8 Peter asked her, "Tell me, is this the price you and Ananias got for the land?" "Yes," she said, "that is the price." 9 Peter said to her, "How could you conspire to test the Spirit of the Lord? Listen! The feet of the men who buried your husband are at the door, and they will carry you out also." 10* **At that moment she fell down at his feet and died.** *Then the young men came in and, finding her dead, carried her out and buried her beside her husband. 11* **Great fear seized the whole church and all who heard about these events.**

> *{Act 12:21-24} 21 On the appointed day Herod, wearing his royal robes, sat on his throne and delivered a public address to the people. 22 They shouted, "This is the voice of a god, not of a man." 23 Immediately,* **because Herod did not give praise to God, an angel of the Lord**

struck him down, and he was eaten by worms and died. 24 But the word of God continued to spread and flourish.

*{Act 13:6-12} 6 They traveled through the whole island until they came to Paphos. There they met a **Jewish sorcerer and false prophet named Bar-Jesus**, 7 who was an attendant of the proconsul, Sergius Paulus. The proconsul, an intelligent man, sent for Barnabas and Saul because he wanted to hear the word of God. 8 **But Elymas the sorcerer (for that is what his name means) opposed them and tried to turn the proconsul from the faith.** 9 Then Saul, who was also called **Paul, filled with the Holy Spirit, looked straight at Elymas and said**, 10 "You are a child of the devil and an enemy of everything that is right! You are full of all kinds of deceit and trickery. Will you never stop perverting the right ways of the Lord? 11 **Now the hand of the Lord is against you. You are going to be blind for a time, not even able to see the light of the sun." Immediately mist and darkness came over him, and he groped about, seeking someone to lead him by the hand.** 12 When the proconsul saw what had happened, he believed, for he was amazed at the teaching about the Lord.*

*{Act 16:16-18} 16 Once when we were going to the place of prayer, we were met by **a female slave who had a spirit by which she predicted the future.** She earned a great deal of money for her owners by fortune-telling. 17 She followed Paul and the rest of us, shouting, "These men are servants of the Most High God, who are telling you the way to be saved." 18 She kept this up for many days. **Finally Paul became so annoyed that he turned around and said to the spirit, "In the name of Jesus Christ I command you to come out of her!" At that moment the spirit left her.***

It is important for us to note that Ananias, Sapphira, and Herod were struck dead by the sovereign hand of God, not by a person exercising their authority in Christ. Moreover, Paul did not randomly go around using his authority in Christ to curse people by making them blind or by spontaneously casting evil spirits out of people who did not come to him asking to be set free. We will discuss Paul's reasons for blinding Elymas and commanding the spirit of divination out of the Philippian slave girl in another chapter.

People trying to imitate miracles in Jesus' name only served to spread the truth about Jesus all the more.

*{Act 19:13-17} 13 **Some Jews who went around driving out evil spirits tried to invoke the name of the Lord Jesus over those who were demon-possessed.** They would say, "In the name of the Jesus whom Paul preaches, I command you to come out." 14 Seven sons of Sceva, a Jewish chief priest, were doing this. 15 One day the evil spirit answered them, "**Jesus I know, and Paul I know about, but who are you?**" 16 **Then the man who had the evil spirit jumped on them and overpowered them all. He gave them such a beating that they ran out of the house naked and bleeding.** 17 When this became known to the Jews and Greeks living in Ephesus, they were all seized with fear, **and the name of the Lord Jesus was held in high honor.***

The Reason for Miracles

All of the miracles in the Book of Acts served to spread the good news of Jesus Christ like wildfire. This is because miracles prove that Jesus is who He says He is and therefore, miracles draw unbelievers into faith in Jesus Christ. For example, after Peter and John healed the lame man in the Temple area in Jesus' name, the people were amazed and rushed to form a crowd in order to observe what had happened. Then, as the New Living Translation says, *Peter saw his opportunity to address the crowd,* and so he did.

> *{Act 3:12-4:4} 12 When Peter saw this, he said to them: "Fellow Israelites, why does this surprise you? Why do you stare at us* **as if by our own power or godliness we had made this man walk?** *13 The God of Abraham, Isaac and Jacob,* **the God of our fathers, has glorified his servant Jesus**. *You handed him over to be killed, and you disowned him before Pilate, though he had decided to let him go. 14 You disowned the Holy and Righteous One and asked that a murderer be released to you. 15 You killed the author of life,* **but God raised him from the dead. We are witnesses of this**. *16* **By faith in the name of Jesus, this man whom you see and know was made strong. It is Jesus' name and the faith that comes through him that has completely healed him, as you can all see.** *17 "Now, fellow Israelites, I know that you acted in ignorance, as did your leaders. 18 But* **this is how God fulfilled what he had foretold through all the prophets, saying that his Messiah would suffer**. *19* **Repent, then, and turn to God, so that your sins may be wiped out, that times of refreshing may come from the Lord**, *20 and that he may send the Messiah, who has been appointed for you--*even Jesus. *21 Heaven must receive him* **until the time comes for God to restore everything**, *as he promised long ago through his holy prophets. 22 For Moses said, 'The Lord your God will raise up for you a prophet like me from among your own people; you must listen to everything he tells you. 23 Anyone who does not listen to him will be completely cut off from their people.' (quoting Deuteronomy 18:15-19) 24 "Indeed, beginning with Samuel, all the prophets who have spoken have foretold these days. 25 And you are heirs of the prophets and of the covenant God made with your fathers. He said to Abraham, 'Through your offspring all peoples on earth will be blessed.' (quoting Genesis 12:1-3) 26* **When God raised up his servant, he sent him first to you to bless you by turning each of you from your wicked ways**." *4:1 The priests and the captain of the temple guard and the Sadducees came up to Peter and John while they were speaking to the people. 2 They were greatly disturbed because the apostles were teaching the people,* **proclaiming in Jesus the resurrection of the dead**. *3 They seized Peter and John and, because it was evening, they put them in jail until the next day. 4 But many who heard the message believed;* **so the number of men who believed grew to about five thousand**.

In his speech, Peter made it clear that the miracle was not done because he or John had any power in themselves. Rather, Peter emphasized that they were just common men who believed in Jesus. Peter preached the Gospel of Jesus Christ to the crowd using Scriptures that would have been familiar to them, just like he had to the crowd which had gathered on the day of Pentecost. The crowd's astonishment at the miraculous healing of the lame man served the same purpose as divinely inspired speaking in tongues had on Pentecost – it caused the crowd to wonder what had happened and how it had occurred. Again, the sign of the healing proved that Jesus fulfilled the Scriptures pertaining to the Messiah of Israel and Peter specifically highlighted Christ's resurrection from the dead as the explanation for the miracle. Peter again cried out for repentance and returning to God through faith in Jesus before the *day of judgment* comes so that, until Jesus returns to judge the earth and restore all things, believers can experience *times of refreshing* in God's presence. Weary souls who place their faith in Jesus can be relieved of their burden of sin and all of its consequences. This is good news because through Jesus, who came to save, believers have peace with God and access to His unmerited good will towards us. Needless to say, peace with God, time in His presence, and heaven on earth through miracles and healings is quite *refreshing*! Most significantly, because of this speech, a few thousand people became believers in Jesus Christ.

This said, after Peter testified to the crowd, religious leaders arrested Peter and John and had them imprisoned. Then, the next day, Peter and John were brought before the religious leaders and they preached the Gospel to them. These opportunities to witness for Christ, both to the crowd and to significant leaders, came about because of the miracle healing of the lame man.

> *{Act 4:5-12} 5 The next day the rulers, the elders and the teachers of the law met in Jerusalem. 6 Annas the high priest was there, and so were Caiaphas, John, Alexander and others of the high priest's family. 7 They had Peter and John brought before them and began to question them: "**By what power or what name did you do this?**" 8 Then **Peter, filled with the Holy Spirit**, said to them: "Rulers and elders of the people! 9 **If we are being called to account today for an act of kindness shown to a man who was lame and are being asked how he was healed,** 10 then know this, you and all the people of Israel: **It is by the name of Jesus Christ of Nazareth, whom you crucified but whom God raised from the dead, that this man stands before you healed**. 11 Jesus is "'the stone you builders rejected, which has become the cornerstone.' (quoting Psalm 118:22) 12 **Salvation is found in no one else, for there is no other name under heaven given to mankind by which we must be saved**."*

Again, Peter expressed that the miracle, or work of God, pointed to Christ's God-given authority. Peter rebuked the religious leaders for their foolishness because, with their extensive knowledge of the Scriptures, this healing should have been a sign to them that Jesus was the Messiah. However, in spite of all of their so-called knowledge of God, they had crucified their King. So, Peter taught them about the resurrection from the dead by explaining the Scriptures to them. He testified that it was through faith in the power and authority of the name of Jesus that the lame man had been healed and that, in fact, Jesus is the *only* name by which anyone can be saved.

Regardless of the response of the crowd or the religious leaders, the point is that the miracle healing of the lame man had made a way for the Gospel to be proclaimed to those who did not yet know Jesus Christ as their Lord and Savior. In fact, I believe that the true purpose behind all miracles is to procure the greatest miracle of all – the salvation of everyone who will believe. In addition to the temporal benefits received by those who experience God's will *on earth as it is in heaven*, healings, miracles, and wonders are *signs*. Again, a *sign* is something that *points to* something else. For example, when we are traveling down the road and we see a sign saying that our destination is twenty miles away, we do not stop at the sign, but we keep traveling to our destination. The sign is telling us that we are on our way to what really matters. The same is true for miracles. Miracles are *signs*, token marks of approval from God that point to something else that really matters. *Signs* point to Jesus Christ, Messiah of Israel and the King above all kings. Jesus said that the works of God revealed the truth that He is God's Anointed One. Similarly, it is the works of God that *point to* Jesus and prove that we, as His followers, are speaking the word of God's grace. (see Acts 14:3) Sometimes, miracles occur because we preach the Gospel and other times, miracles give us an opportunity to share the Gospel.

Throughout the Book of Acts, as miracles, signs, and wonders abounded, thousands (if not millions) of souls were saved through faith in the name of Jesus.

> *{Act 2:41} 41 Those who accepted his message were baptized, and **about three thousand were added to their number that day**.*

> *{Act 4:4} 4 But many who heard the message believed; **so the number of men who believed grew to about five thousand**.*

> *{Act 5:14} 14 Nevertheless, **more and more men and women believed in the Lord and were added to their number**.*

> *{Act 6:7} 7 So the word of God spread. **The number of disciples in Jerusalem increased rapidly, and a large number of priests became obedient to the faith**.*

> *{Act 9:31} 31 Then the church throughout Judea, Galilee and Samaria enjoyed a time of peace and was strengthened. **Living in the fear of the Lord and encouraged by the Holy Spirit, it increased in numbers**.*

> *{Act 13:48} 48 When the Gentiles heard this, they were glad and honored the word of the Lord; and **all who were appointed for eternal life believed**.*

> *{Act 16:5} 5 **So the churches were strengthened in the faith and grew daily in numbers**.*

> *{Act 17:34} 34 **Some of the people became followers of Paul and believed**. Among them was Dionysius, a member of the Areopagus, also a woman named Damaris, **and a number of others**.*

> *{Act 18:8} 8 Crispus, the synagogue leader, and his entire household believed in the Lord; and **many of the Corinthians who heard Paul believed and were baptized**.*

> *{Act 19:20} 20 In this way **the word of the Lord spread widely and grew in power**.*

> *{Act 26:27-29} 27 King Agrippa, do you believe the prophets? I know you do." 28 Then Agrippa said to Paul, "Do you think that in such a short time you can **persuade me to be a Christian?**" 29 Paul replied, "Short time or long--**I pray to God that not only you but all who are listening to me today may become what I am, except for these chains**."*

God's power and ability to work miracles for us is a great benefit for us personally and for the people we minister to. But let us never forget that there is *more rejoicing in heaven over one sinner who repents.* (see

Luke 15:7, 10) This means that salvation is the most significant miracle ever recorded in the Scripture. Salvation through faith in Christ is the great mystery of godliness which God has now revealed to those who believe. (see 1 Timothy 3:16) Through faith in the Gospel, our sins are forgiven, and nothing has any right to harm, afflict, or oppress us until Jesus calls us home to heaven or until He returns, whichever comes first. When we believe Jesus, the Holy Spirit dwells within us to make us like Him in our character and comes upon us so that we are empowered to do the works that He did. Jesus came as our Anointed One and He empowers us as His anointed ones to proclaim *Repent for the Kingdom of Heaven is at hand!* with miracles, signs, and wonders following.

CHAPTER 11
Persecution

Persecution against Christians is more pervasive throughout the Book of Acts than miracles, signs, and wonders. In fact, chapters in the Book of Acts which contain episodes of persecution or opposition to the Gospel outnumber those that do not. As Jesus had warned His disciples, the world hated Christ followers in the same way that the world had hated Him. (see John 15:18-21) But because of His love, they were ready to face the world. We're going to take a look at the various clashes between Christianity and its opponents throughout the Book of Acts so that we are strengthened for patient endurance when we encounter hostility against our faith.

Background

Events in the Book of Acts took place over a span of more than thirty years. During this entire time, the Roman Empire ruled the known civilized world including all of the various places that we read about in the Book of Acts. Over the passage of these years, there were four different Roman emperors, various provincial governors, and five successive High Priests of the Jewish people. The capital of the Roman Empire was Rome, the Roman capital of the Jewish province was Caesarea Maritima (with a satellite center of justice at Jerusalem) and the religious capital of the Jewish people, the Sanhedrin, the Priesthood was at the Temple in Jerusalem. Due to Jewish subjugation to Roman authority, the High Priests of Israel were appointed by Rome and authorized as the head of the Sanhedrin, which was the Jewish legislative council. The Sanhedrin, which had branches in each city to adjudicate smaller cases among the Jewish people, was held responsible for maintaining order and ensuring that they paid their taxes to Rome. This allowed the Jews great freedom to live in accordance with their religious beliefs while remaining under Roman domination. Notably, Jews also enjoyed exemption from worshiping and bowing down to the Roman emperor as a god.

After the resurrection of Christ, who had been crucified as the King of the Jews, His followers declared more boldly than ever that Jesus is the King of Israel. The movement that the religious and world leaders had tried to suppress through the execution of one man had now multiplied into thousands of followers. To the High Priest, the Sanhedrin, and many common Jews, this was blasphemy against God and the worst form of heresy. In the view of Roman officials, even the hint of any king other than Caesar was problematic and worthy of suspicion. To the average pagan, a foreign god interfered with their ways of life and worship, serving another king was tantamount to treason, and talk of resurrection from the dead was foolish gibberish. On top of all of that, nobody seemed to be clear as to whether Christianity was a sect or denomination of the Jewish faith, which would include them in the Jewish worship exemption, or a whole new and separate faith, or just a group of rebels stirring up revolution.

All of this is significant because, when whittled down to the base, persecution is about power and authority. When believers worship Jesus as the Christ, the Messiah and King of Israel, we worship Him as the King above all kings and the Lord above all lords. (see Revelation 19:6; 1 Timothy 6:15) As Christ followers, this world is not our home even though we still live here in our physical bodies. (see Hebrews 13:14) We are first and foremost spiritual citizens and ambassadors of heaven, even if we have natural citizenship in countries here on the earth. (see 2 Corinthians 5:20; Philippians 3:20) The primary perpetrators for persecution are not regimes, rulers, or societies but *jealousy, suspicion of heresy, protection of the marketplace,* and *denial of the Kingship of Jesus.* As a matter of fact, persecutors often instigate antagonism with false accusations or indictments that spiral out of control and reach way past their point or issue of origin. This is because the real aim of persecution is to separate us from our King, force us to deny our true citizenship, and move us to bow down to another. Persecution is a power play and nothing more than big-time bullying. If we submit and bow down in agreement with our persecutors, then the bully wins. However, if we stand our ground in the truth, no matter the cost, then the bully fails to force our submission. This is of critical importance because, unlike other forms of persecution in the world, when persecution is rendered against us because of our faith in Christ, the consequences can have eternal significance.

Jealousy and Heresy

> *{Act 4:1-7} 1 The priests and the **captain of the temple guard and the Sadducees** came up to Peter and John while they were speaking to the people. 2 **They were greatly disturbed** because the apostles were teaching the people, **proclaiming in Jesus the resurrection of the dead**. 3 **They seized Peter and John and, because it was evening, they put them in jail until the next day**. 4 But many who heard the message believed; so the number of men who believed grew to about five thousand. 5 The next day the rulers, the elders and the teachers of the law met in Jerusalem. 6 Annas the high priest was there, and so were Caiaphas, John, Alexander and others of the high priest's family. 7 **They had Peter and John brought before them and began to question them: "By what power or what name did you do this?"***

Peter and John had just healed the lame man in the Temple area and proclaimed the Gospel of Jesus Christ to the onlooking crowd. The Sadducees in the crowd did not believe in the resurrection from the dead and were deeply offended by what Peter said. In fact, they considered Peter and John's teaching on the resurrection from the dead to be outright *heresy*. They had Peter and John arrested and jailed and then brought them before the Sanhedrin, the High Priest, and his council for questioning. Peter continued to testify about how God raised Jesus from the dead, which fulfilled the Scriptures and declared Jesus to be the only way of salvation.

Unfortunately for the religious leaders, if Peter and John were right, then it meant that they were in error about their beliefs. It also meant that the great and mighty Messiah of Israel that they had been waiting for had been born in a feeding trough to a woman claiming to be a virgin, whom they had rejected because of the gravely suspicious circumstances. (see Matthew 1:22-25; Luke 2:6-7) Moreover, it meant that they had killed the Son of God and their King and so, to admit their error at this point would be profoundly humiliating. Additionally, if what Peter and John were saying was true, then the religious leader's God-given authority had been usurped, the loss of which would nullify their status in Jewish and Roman society. Also, because the Sanhedrin was responsible for keeping the Jewish people under control for Rome, too much stirring of the community put them in danger of appearing to be ill-assigned with their legislative duties. They knew that if they did not keep their people under control, then they as leaders could face exile or execution because even small stirrings about following the King of the Jews were considered to be treason against Caesar. These religious leaders did not want to believe what they were hearing so instead, they were deeply distressed because they could not deny that a man who had been lame since birth had been made well, and everyone in Jerusalem knew about it. Therefore, in order to protect their authority and control over the people, they warned and threatened Peter and John not to speak of Jesus anymore. But, upon their release, Peter and John returned to the believers where they prayed for boldness to speak about Jesus all the more. (see Acts 4:25-30)

> *{Act 4:16-22} 16 "What are we going to do with these men?" they asked. "Everyone living in Jerusalem knows they have performed a notable sign, and we cannot deny it. 17* **But to stop this thing from spreading any further among the people, we must warn them to speak no longer to anyone in this name."** *18 Then they called them in again and commanded them not to speak or teach at all in the name of Jesus. 19 But Peter and John replied, "Which is right in God's eyes: to listen to you, or to him? You be the judges! 20 As for us, we cannot help speaking about what we have seen and heard." 21* **After further threats they let them go. They could not decide how to punish them, because all the people were praising God for what had happened.** *22 For the man who was miraculously healed was over forty years old.*

Not long after this episode, the apostles were doing such great signs and wonders among believers that crowds from all around Jerusalem came, bringing all the sick to be healed of their diseases. The High Priest and the Sanhedrin were filled with *jealousy* which, in the Greek, translates as *punitive zeal, fierce indignation,* or *contentious rivalry.* (see Acts 5:17) They had the apostles arrested and thrown in jail, but an angel of the Lord let them out and told them to keep preaching the Gospel. The next day, the religious leaders were informed that the apostles could not be found in the prison but they found them in the temple courts and brought them in to stand before the council again. (see Acts 5:13-23)

> *{Act 5:24-28} 24* **On hearing this report, the captain of the temple guard and the chief priests were at a loss, wondering what this might lead to.** *25 Then someone came and said, "Look! The men you put in jail are standing in the temple courts teaching the people." 26 At that, the captain went with his officers and brought the apostles.* **They did not use force, because they feared that the people would stone them.** *27 The apostles were brought in and made to appear before the Sanhedrin to be questioned by the high priest. 28* **"We gave you strict orders not to teach in this name,"** *he said.* **"Yet you have filled Jerusalem with your teaching and are determined to make us guilty of this man's blood."**

The two-fold conflict of the religious leaders was laid bare. They placed utmost importance on the approval of the crowd and sought to untruthfully absolve themselves of any guilt regarding Jesus. To demonstrate aggression against the apostles would not have been well-received by the people, so instead, they masked their loathing in gentility while the crowd was watching. However, once they were behind closed doors, they lashed out with self-protective domination and denial of their guilt. Peter plainly reminded them that they *did* kill Jesus and proclaimed again that God had raised Him from the dead. When they heard this, they were all furious and wanted the apostles killed. (see Acts 5:33) However, a wise old Pharisee named Gamaliel convinced them that God's stamp of approval upon Jesus and His followers would be evidenced by their endurance over time. Even though the religious leaders believed the apostles to be heretics, Gamaliel's speech persuaded them to be cautious about placing themselves in a position of fighting against God which, ironically, would make *them* the blasphemers. Therefore, instead of killing them, the council had the apostles flogged, warned them never again to speak in the name of Jesus, and then let them go.

Soon after this, a deacon named Stephen was performing powerful miracles among the people and preaching the Gospel. Some men from the Synagogue of the Freedmen gathered around. These men were descended from Jews who had suffered for their faith under Roman oppression and who, upon their release from this torturous enslavement, had returned to Jerusalem filled with zeal for having endured hardship for their faith. Some believe that Stephen had belonged to this group himself. The apostle Paul, who at this point was a fervent Pharisee called Saul, was also in the crowd. These well educated, totally committed, uncompromising men, who were ready to suffer for their Jewish beliefs, began to debate with Stephen.

> *{Act 6:10-15} 10 But they could not stand up against the wisdom the Spirit gave him as he spoke.*
> *11* ***Then they secretly persuaded some men to say, "We have heard Stephen speak blasphemous words against Moses and against God."*** *12 So they stirred up the people and the elders and the teachers of the law. They seized Stephen and brought him before the Sanhedrin.*
> *13* ***They produced false witnesses, who testified, "This fellow never stops speaking against this holy place and against the law. 14 For we have heard him say that this Jesus of Nazareth will destroy this place and change the customs Moses handed down to us."***
> *15 All who were sitting in the Sanhedrin looked intently at Stephen, and they saw that his face was like the face of an angel.*

These men, including Saul who had the best Scriptural training under the best teachers in the world, could not refute Stephen as the Holy Spirit spoke through him. The Holy Spirit wrote the Scriptures, (see 2 Peter 1:21; 2 Timothy 3:16) so the Holy Spirit can teach God's Word better than even the smartest person on earth. This said, the old-to-new transfer and shift from religious self-righteousness through God's Law and the Temple system to the receipt of God's grace as a free gift through faith in Christ was a humiliating stumbling block, which the crowd could not wrap their minds around. (see 1 Corinthians 1:23) And yet, the wisdom that the Holy Spirit gave Stephen demolished them all in debate. Instead of conceding their defeat, they conspired and enlisted others to do the dirty work of accusing Stephen of heresy. They seized him and brought him before the Sanhedrin. Then, Stephen gave a speech that we're going to dig into in depth in a future chapter in which he connected the dots of the history of Israel.

Essentially, Stephen pointed out in his speech that Israel has a long history of not understanding God's ways and of rejecting God's messengers.

> *{Act 7:51-53} 51* ***"You stiff-necked people! Your hearts and ears are still uncircumcised.*** ***You are just like your ancestors: You always resist the Holy Spirit!*** *52* ***Was there ever a*** ***prophet your ancestors did not persecute?*** *They even killed those who predicted the coming of the Righteous One. And now you have betrayed and murdered him-- 53 you who have received the law that was given through angels but have not obeyed it."*

To translate this into my language, Stephen said, *You knuckleheads! You have totally missed it just like they did!* But in all seriousness, he brought up a valid point. Almost all of the Prophets, whose writings are now the Biblical books that bear their names, were martyred for their faith. Chapter 11 of the Book of Hebrews also gives a historical account of great witnesses of God who suffered on account of His work and calling. In truth, the last person on this list is Jesus. (see Hebrews 12:1-2) Moreover, when Jesus said, *You will be my witnesses*, the word for *witnesses* is the same word used for *martyr*. Jesus told His followers to *count the cost* before following Him and martyrdom was exactly the cost which Stephen proceeded to pay for Christ.

> *{Act 7:54-8:3} 54 When the members of the Sanhedrin heard this,* ***they were furious and*** ***gnashed their teeth at him***. *55 But Stephen, full of the Holy Spirit, looked up to heaven and saw the glory of God, and Jesus standing at the right hand of God. 56 "Look," he said, "I see heaven open and the Son of Man standing at the right hand of God." 57 At this* ***they covered their ears*** ***and, yelling at the top of their voices, they all rushed at him***, *58* ***dragged him out of the*** ***city and began to stone him***. *Meanwhile, the witnesses laid their coats at the feet of a young man named Saul. 59 While they were stoning him, Stephen prayed, "Lord Jesus, receive my spirit." 60* ***Then he fell on his knees and cried out, "Lord, do not hold this sin against*** ***them." When he had said this, he fell asleep.*** *8:1 And Saul approved of their killing him.* ***On that day a great persecution broke out against the church in Jerusalem***, *and all except the apostles were scattered throughout Judea and Samaria. 2 Godly men buried Stephen and mourned deeply for him. 3* ***But Saul began to destroy the church. Going from house to*** ***house, he dragged off both men and women and put them in prison***.

It had become clear again to the Sanhedrin that Christianity was sacrilegiously against their beliefs. According to the Scriptures, witnesses against a blasphemer must be the first ones to throw stones against the accused. (see Leviticus 24:14; Deuteronomy 17:2-7) After the witnesses had thrown stones, everyone else was welcome to join in and they all took off their coats so that their throwing would be unhindered. Stephen's persecutors did what they believed to be right, even though they had used dishonest means and false accusations to procure the "heresy" that they were seeking. Their zeal had boiled over to obsessive fury as they sought to distance and separate themselves publicly and permanently from Christian beliefs. They rejected Jesus as Messiah, and gave a temporal demonstration of some of the eternal consequences for denying Christ when they gnashed their teeth in rage. (see Matthew 8:12) In contrast, Stephen, like Jesus, did not fight, resist, or defend himself but rather prayed for the ones who were killing him. Then, he committed his spirit into the hands of the Lord and *fell asleep* which means that he *died* in faith believing that he will be raised from the dead upon Jesus' return. (see Matthew 9:24; John 11:11-12; 1 Corinthians 11:30, 15:51; 1 Thessalonians 4:14, 5:10) Some believe that Jesus was *standing at the right hand of God* (rather than sitting) to receive His first martyr with comfort and joy. Others believe that He was waiting to sit until the blood of His first martyr proved the substance of the New Covenant by the faith of His followers. Regardless of this, Stephen's blood as the first Christian martyr caused the crowd to go wild and widespread persecution broke out.

Of all of the persecutors, Saul was the most promising enforcer in the whole bunch. His passionate pursuit of excellence and righteousness at any expense was inflamed by the enthusiasm of his cohorts. Starting on the day of Stephen's stoning, Saul was determined to extinguish all Christians from the face of the earth for their horrible heresies against God. The word for *destroy* used to describe Saul's fury is the same word typically used for *wartime torture* and *wreaking havoc*. He was not the only one, but he was certainly an exemplary enemy of the faith. Later in his life, Saul, who became the apostle Paul after a dramatic encounter with the Lord Jesus, described his endeavors as a destroyer of Christians.

> *{Act 22:3-5} 3 "I am a Jew, born in Tarsus of Cilicia, but brought up in this city. I studied under Gamaliel and was thoroughly trained in the law of our ancestors. I was just as **zealous for God** as any of you are today. 4 **I persecuted the followers of this Way [Christians] to their death, arresting both men and women and throwing them into prison**, 5 as the high priest and all the Council can themselves testify. I even obtained letters from them to their associates in Damascus, and went there **to bring these people as prisoners to Jerusalem to be punished**.*

> *{Act 26:9-11} 9 "I too **was convinced that I ought to do all that was possible to oppose the name of Jesus of Nazareth**. 10 And that is just what I did in Jerusalem. On the authority of the chief priests **I put many of the Lord's people in prison, and when they were put to death, I cast my vote against them**. 11 Many a time I went from one synagogue to another **to have them punished, and I tried to force them to blaspheme. I was so obsessed with persecuting them that I even hunted them down in foreign cities**.*

The Book of Hebrews gives us a glance at what this *ravaging* may have looked like for Jews who had believed Jesus as Messiah. This letter to Jewish converts to Christianity encouraged them to remain true to the faith in the same way that they had stood strong and endured hardship and persecution when they had first come to trust Jesus as their Messiah. Incidentally, most people believe that Paul is the writer of Hebrews.

> *{Heb 10:32-35} 32 Remember those earlier days after you had received the light, when you endured in a **great conflict full of suffering**. 33 Sometimes you were **publicly exposed to insult and persecution**; at other times you stood side by side with those who were so treated. 34 You **suffered along with those in prison** and **joyfully accepted the confiscation of your property**, because you knew that you yourselves had better and lasting possessions. 35 So do not throw away your confidence; it will be richly rewarded.*

When a Jew believed in Jesus, they were banished from the Temple, disowned by their family, and treated as if they were dead. They were cut off from their inheritance and everything that they knew of life, family, and friends. Their banishment, if not painful enough, also left them vulnerable as prime targets for being plundered by mobs. Again, the word here for *great conflict* infers *military combat* and is used to describe the *intense struggles of athletes in an open arena display against beasts*. They were beaten, imprisoned, ridiculed, and reproached because their Jewish brothers and sisters believed them to be heretics and blasphemers against the one true God. But, they endured it all patiently and joyfully because they knew that heaven is their home, and Jesus is their King.

Throughout the Book of Acts, there were many other incidents of persecution against Christians due to this type of *jealousy, suspicion of heresy,* and *rejection of Jesus as Messiah.* Religious leaders in Pisidian Antioch were jealous of the large crowd that Paul and Barnabas attracted and therefore, sought to contradict them by inciting wealthy religious women to stir up persecution and banish them from the city. (see Acts 13:13-52) The people of Iconium were divided about the Gospel message until finally, an angry mob plotted to attack and stone Paul and Barnabas who, fortunately, heard about their plan and fled. (see Acts 14:1-7) On another occasion, Paul had to reroute his travel plans because he learned of plots by religious people to kill him. (see Acts 20:3) The people of Lystra were receiving the Gospel message in faith until religious people from Antioch and Iconium came to stir up trouble, after which they stoned Paul and dragged him away thinking that he was dead. (see Acts 14:8-20) A similar thing happened later when the people of Berea were receiving the Gospel until religious people from Thessalonica came to contradict the good news. This time, believers sent Paul away urgently before he could be attacked. (see Acts 17:10-15) The riot which had taken place in Thessalonica had also been started by jealous religious zealots. (see Acts 17:1-9) The philosophers of Athens sneered and snickered at Paul for advocating a God other than their pagan gods, (see Acts 17:16-34) and the people of Ephesus rioted against Christianity because they believed it was robbing their pagan goddess of her majesty. (see Acts 19:23-41) The religious people of Corinth made a united attack against Paul and his companions as heretics but when the governor would not render judgment on matters of religious debate, they stoned the leader of the synagogue instead. (see Acts 18:12-17) Finally, in the last chapters of Acts, Paul's greatest and longest trial was incited by religious zealots accusing him of heresy and defiling the Temple. Though it took a while to get to the heart of the matter, the trial was truly about the Christian belief in the resurrection from the dead which proves that Jesus is Lord, Savior, Messiah, and King. The trial which resulted from this was dragged out over the course of more than four years, placing Paul before the High Priest, the Sanhedrin, two different Roman governors, and a king.

It all started when religious onlookers falsely accused Paul of defiling the Temple for bringing a Gentile into an area where Gentiles were not permitted. The crowd beat Paul until a Roman soldier arrested him without even asking what he had done. The angry mob could not get their story straight aside from agreeing, *Get rid of him!* (see Acts 22:26-36) The Roman commander assumed that Paul was a well-known Egyptian leader of a riot which had taken place earlier who had fled the country but this assumed error was quickly clarified. (see Acts 21:37-40) Paul then spoke to the crowd and gave his testimony by telling the story of his own conversion to Christianity after having been a fully persuaded persecutor of the Church. (see Acts 22:1-22)

> *{Act 22:19-24} 19 " 'Lord,' I replied, 'these people know that I went from one synagogue to another to imprison and beat those who believe in you. 20 And when the blood of your martyr Stephen was shed, I stood there giving my approval and guarding the clothes of those who were killing him.' 21* **"Then the Lord said to me, 'Go; I will send you far away to the Gentiles.'"** *22* **The crowd listened to Paul until he said this. Then they raised their voices and shouted, "Rid the earth of him! He's not fit to live!"** *23 As they were shouting and throwing off their cloaks and flinging dust into the air, 24 the* **commander ordered that Paul be taken into the barracks. He directed that he be flogged and interrogated in order to find out why the people were shouting at him like this.**

As soon as Paul stated that access to God had been made available to Gentiles, his opponents went ballistic. They readied themselves to stone another blasphemer because, in their view, Paul's profanity against God now included defiling the Temple and absolute heresy. The Roman soldiers were not persuaded that they had the whole story, so they initiated torture procedures to procure the truth. As a Roman citizen, Paul invoked his right to a fair trial which put the officers in fear for their jobs (see Acts 22:24-29) so, they brought Paul before the Sanhedrin again. Paul reiterated that the real reason for his trial was his belief in the resurrection from the dead. The council was itself doctrinally divided over this, so their debate escalated to the point that the Romans took Paul away for his own protection. Then, the Lord visited Paul in prison to encourage him to continue to preach the Gospel and that He was sending Paul to Rome. (see Acts 23:1-11) The next morning, over forty Jewish men bound themselves with an oath not to eat until Paul was dead and plotted false pretenses to trap him and kill him. Their plot was discovered, and Paul was sent to appear before Governor Felix in Caesarea protected by a brigade of 200 men, 200 spearmen, and 70 mounted troops. (see Acts 23:12-35) Then, after several days in prison in Caesarea, Paul appeared before Governor Felix while the religious leaders pointed the finger at Paul as a troublemaker, ringleader of a cult, and riot rouser who had desecrated the Temple. Paul denied the charges, explained what really happened, and refocused the dialog on the true issues at hand which was the resurrection from the dead. One day, Felix brought his wife, Drusilla, to the trial, and Paul spoke about righteousness, self-control, and the *day of judgment* until Felix became perturbed and stopped Paul from speaking anymore. Interestingly, Drusilla had been another man's wife, so Felix may have had a guilty conscience or may have wanted to prevent Paul from saying something along the lines of what John the Baptist had said to Herod, which had resulted in John's beheading. (see Matthew 14:1-12; Mark 6:14-29; Luke 9:7-9) Felix sent Paul off to prison hoping that Paul would offer him a bribe to be released. Additionally, Felix left Paul in prison indefinitely because he wanted to gain favor with the religious leaders to strengthen their political alliance. (see Acts 24:1-27)

Two years later, Paul was still in prison when the new governor, Festus, took office. Governor Festus was immediately confronted by the religious leaders whose wish for Paul's execution had not waned a bit with the passage of time. When the trial was resumed in Caesarea, they resumed their false accusations against Paul. (see Acts 25:1-7) Festus wanted to please the religious council in order to secure good relations as their new governor, so he suggested that Paul be taken back to Jerusalem. Paul appealed to his right as a Roman citizen to appear before the highest courts in the land. Before heading to Caesar's court, King Agrippa II and his sister Bernice happened to be passing through town, and Festus discussed Paul's case with him. Paul then appeared before Agrippa, gave the testimony of his transformation, and spoke about the resurrection from the dead. (see Acts 25:8-26:32) Then, Paul was sent to Caesar. Upon his arrival in Rome, Paul lived under house arrest for two more years and proclaimed the Gospel of Jesus Christ to everyone who came to visit him. (see Acts 28:30-31) Paul's trial before Caesar is not recorded in the Book of Acts. He was eventually martyred for Christ under Roman Emperor Nero and was beheaded only because it was against the law to crucify a Roman citizen.

Marketplace and King

Religious resentment and doctrinal disagreements are not the only culprits for persecution. In fact, one of the reasons why the resurrection from the dead through faith in Christ is so controversial is because it proves Jesus to be the King above all kings. The Jews who rejected Jesus are the ones that said, *We have no king but Caesar,* (see John 19:15) which clearly articulated their rejection of Jesus as their *King*. In addition to religious reasons for rejecting Christ, there were non-religious reasons for denying His Lordship including the protection of their careers, their status in society, and their authority over the Jewish people. This said, the religious leaders and their system were not the only ones persecuting Christians. In fact, common people and world leaders also made anti-Christian decisions in order to protect their livelihoods and the *marketplace*, to maintain relations with the religious system, or in hopes of a payoff. The rulers of this world went head to head with followers of another King.

> *{Act 12:1-5} 1 It was about this time that **King Herod arrested some who belonged to the church, intending to persecute them.** 2 **He had James, the brother of John, put to death with the sword.** 3 **When he saw that this met with approval among the Jews, he proceeded to seize Peter also**. This happened during the Festival of Unleavened Bread. 4 **After arresting him, he put him in prison**, handing him over to be guarded by four squads of four soldiers each. **Herod intended to bring him out for public trial after the Passover.** 5 So Peter was kept in prison, but the church was earnestly praying to God for him.*

King Herod (Agrippa I) knew that persecuting Christians would solidify good relations with the religious leaders and that this would give additional security to his Rome-appointed position of authority over them. Therefore, with deliberate intent of violence against Christians, he ordered many church members to be arrested, and James, the son of Zebedee, to be beheaded. This was about ten years after Stephen was stoned to death and was another high profile Christian being martyred for his faith in Christ. This James (there were two prominent ones) was one of the twelve disciples who walked with Jesus and he was also one of the disciples who, before Jesus' crucifixion and resurrection, competed for high ranking position in the Kingdom.

*{Mar 10:38-39, 42-45} 38 "You don't know what you are asking," Jesus said. "**Can you drink the cup I drink or be baptized with the baptism I am baptized with?**" 39 "We can," they answered. Jesus said to them, "**You will drink the cup I drink and be baptized with the baptism I am baptized with**," ... 42 Jesus called them together and said, "You know that those who are regarded as **rulers of the Gentiles lord it over them**, and their high officials exercise authority over them. 43 **Not so with you. Instead, whoever wants to become great among you must be your servant**, 44 **and whoever wants to be first must be slave of all.** 45 **For even the Son of Man did not come to be served, but to serve, and to give his life as a ransom for many**." (see also Matthew 20:20-28)*

James did indeed *drink the cup* of suffering and enter into the *baptism* of a martyr's death like Jesus. His execution pleased the religious leaders so much that Herod had the apostle Peter arrested and imprisoned as well. Notably, after an angel released Peter from prison, Herod ordered that the guards responsible for keeping Peter in prison be executed. (see Acts 12:19)

In another incident, during the course of Paul's first missionary journey, there was a Jewish sorcerer and false prophet named Elymas or Bar-Jesus at Paphos who had become a spiritual advisor to the proconsul, or governor. The proconsul was the highest ranking Roman official in the territory, and it was not uncommon for men of such rank to maintain prophets as part of their paid counselors. When Paul and Barnabas came through town, Elymas did everything that he could to prevent the proconsul from believing the Gospel of Jesus Christ. If the proconsul believed the apostles, Elymas would be unemployed. We don't know exactly how Elymas interfered with Kingdom work, but it was sufficient to cause Paul to strike him blind. (see Acts 13:6-12) Before this seems inappropriately cruel, take into consideration the importance of clearly delineating the truth of the Gospel and the Holy Spirit from false prophecy and works of sorcery. To not censure Elymas and his methods could have been perceived as condoning them, so a distinction had to be made between God's truth and spiritual error.

Later, on Paul's second missionary journey at Philippi, there was a slave girl with a fortune-telling spirit who worked as a psychic to earn money for her masters. She discerned before anyone else in town that Paul and his companions were servants of the Most High God, and she followed them around day after day shouting prophetic statements about them. Finally, Paul commanded the evil spirit to come out of her. Even though the false spirit revealed the truth, the unholy source had to be addressed to make a distinction between those working by the power of the Holy Spirit versus an unclean spirit of divination.

*{Act 16:19-24} 19 **When her owners realized that their hope of making money was gone, they seized Paul and Silas and dragged them into the marketplace to face the authorities**. 20 They brought them before the magistrates and said, "These men are Jews, and are throwing our city into an uproar 21 by advocating customs unlawful for us Romans to accept or practice." 22 **The crowd joined in the attack against Paul and Silas**, and the **magistrates ordered them to be stripped and beaten with rods**. 23 **After they had been severely flogged, they were thrown into prison**, and the jailer was commanded to guard them carefully. 24 When he received these orders, he put them in the inner cell and fastened their feet in the stocks.*

After this, the owners of the Philippian slave girl accused Paul and his companions of introducing a new religion that was unauthorized by the Roman government. However, the real reason behind their attack was because their business and money-making scheme had been crushed because the girl could no larger charge for her psychic services. Fortunately, as Paul and Silas sang songs of praise in prison, a great earthquake shook off their shackles and opened the prison doors which led to their jailer (and his whole family) to believe the Gospel of Jesus Christ. After this, the city officials of Philippi sent the police to tell the jailer to tell Paul and his companions that they could leave town. However, Paul insisted on his rights as a Roman citizen to speak to the city leaders directly. When the Rome-appointed city leaders learned that Roman citizens had been illegally beaten without a fair trial, which could cost them their jobs, they went to visit Paul, apologized, and begged him to leave their city. Paul first returned to the other Christians in Philippi to encourage and strengthen them in their faith, and then he left Philippi. (see Acts 16:16-40)

Thessalonica was the next city on their journey and many prominent and wealthy Jews and Gentiles placed their faith in Jesus. The religious leaders became jealous of Paul's popularity and were, most likely, upset about losing wealthy contributors to their synagogues. So, they rounded up a mob from the marketplace to start a riot against Paul and his companions and took them before the city council. They accused the Christians of treason against Caesar for their profession of allegiance to another King, namely Jesus. The whole city was thrown into a turmoil over the rumors of such a rebellion. A believer named Jason posted bond for himself and the other Christians, and then they were released by the city council. (see Acts 17:1-9) However, believers in Thessalonica continued to endure harsh and brutal persecution from their fellow countrymen for years. Paul later wrote to encourage them:

> {2Th 1:4-8} 4 *Therefore, among God's churches* **we boast about your perseverance and faith in all the persecutions and trials you are enduring.** *5 All this is evidence that God's judgment is right, and as a result you will be* **counted worthy of the kingdom of God, for which you are suffering.** *6 God is just:* **He will pay back trouble to those who trouble you** *7 and* **give relief to you who are troubled,** *and to us as well. This will happen when the Lord Jesus is revealed from heaven in blazing fire with his powerful angels. 8 He will punish those who do not know God and do not obey the gospel of our Lord Jesus.*

In Athens, Paul preached a message to prominent citizens, philosophers, and the most well regarded council of justice in the world. In a city that prided itself on its philosophical wisdom and which was full of idols, Paul said that it was ignorant to believe that God lived in man-made temples or was represented by man-made idols made of stone, silver and gold. Moreover, Paul told them about how the one true God was in control of all the nations and their appointed times in history and how this God had appointed a servant, who is the King above all kings and who will judge the world at an appointed time in the future after the resurrection from the dead. The people of Athens laughed at Paul and his God though a few people did become believers. (see Acts 17:16-34)

Lastly, during Paul's third missionary journey, a huge riot was brought about in Ephesus because of the impact of the Gospel on the marketplace. In particular, those selling spiritual things that Christians no longer purchased were inflamed because of their diminishing businesses. In the months leading up to this riot, some Jewish exorcists had tried to cast an evil spirit out of a man using the name of Jesus, even though they were not Christians. Because they were not true believers, the evil spirit did not obey them and instead beat them up unmercifully, sending them away naked and battered. The news of this had spread all over Ephesus.

> *{Act 19:17-20} 17 When this became known to the Jews and Greeks living in Ephesus, **they were all seized with fear, and the name of the Lord Jesus was held in high honor**. 18 Many of those who believed now came and openly confessed what they had done. 19 **A number who had practiced sorcery brought their scrolls together and burned them publicly. When they calculated the value of the scrolls, the total came to fifty thousand drachmas.** 20 In this way the word of the Lord spread widely and grew in power.*

A drachma was a silver piece which was also one day's wage in that day. In modern estimated equivalents, fifty thousand drachmas is worth about six million dollars. This means that a six million dollar bonfire of spiritual propaganda burned in Ephesus as people abandoned false spirituality. This demonstrated their repentance which we can safely assume means that they had no intention of repurchasing godless spiritual things. Needless to say for merchants selling these items, this was not good for business.

> *{Act 19:23-34} 23 About that time there arose a great disturbance about the Way. 24 **A silversmith named Demetrius, who made silver shrines of Artemis, brought in a lot of business for the craftsmen there**. 25 He called them together, along with the workers in related trades, and said: "You know, my friends, that we receive a good income from this business. 26 And you see and hear how **this fellow Paul has convinced and led astray large numbers of people here** in Ephesus and in practically the whole province of Asia. **He says that gods made by human hands are no gods at all**. 27 **There is danger not only that our trade will lose its good name**, but also that the temple of the great goddess Artemis will be discredited; and the goddess herself, who is worshiped throughout the province of Asia and the world, will be robbed of her divine majesty." 28 When they heard this, they were furious and began shouting: "Great is Artemis of the Ephesians!" 29 **Soon the whole city was in an uproar. The people seized Gaius and Aristarchus, Paul's traveling companions from Macedonia, and all of them rushed into the theater together. 30 Paul wanted to appear before the crowd, but the disciples would not let him**. 31 Even some of the officials of the province, friends of Paul, sent him a message begging him not to venture into the theater. 32 The assembly was in confusion: Some were shouting one thing, some another. **Most of the people did not even know why they were there**. 33 The Jews in the crowd pushed Alexander to the front, and they shouted instructions to him. He motioned for silence in order to make a defense before the people. 34 But when they realized he was a Jew, **they all shouted in unison for about two hours: "Great is Artemis of the Ephesians!"***

The merchants of Ephesus cloaked their financial motivation with patriotism and pagan worship of their goddess. As the riot escalated, many people were swept into the frenzy, not even knowing why. Additionally, the mob became anti-Jewish and anti-Christian because both rejected the worship of their pagan gods. Paul desired to use this opportunity to preach the Gospel, but the crowd was too dangerously out of control. Finally, the city clerk of Ephesus quieted the crowd and called for order and true justice. He pointed out that, in truth, there was no valid case against anyone and that the courts were open if anyone wanted to submit legitimate charges. The town clerk was also concerned for his job because he would have to report to the Roman authorities who were over him about what had happened in the city that he presided over, so he dismissed the crowd and sent them home. Paul, however, encouraged the Christians of Ephesus and continued on his journey.

All of this is to say that the spread of Christianity impacted the culture of the day in more ways than we can discuss fully right now. To some, it was received as the good news of eternal life. To others, it was a message of death to their beliefs and way of life, (see 2 Corinthians 2:16) so they fought it with all their strength and every scheme imaginable.

Conduct in Persecution

When Jesus walked on the earth, He was surrounded by suspicion and controversy as He ushered in the Kingdom of God. We can see clearly from the examples that we just examined that, as His followers did the works that He did while spreading the Gospel, they were confronted with the same antagonism. We previously discussed Jesus' conduct in trials, but now let us glance at the example set for us by the believers in the Book of Acts.

For starters, it is worth mentioning again that persecution and suffering for righteousness sake is not the same as suffering for doing wrong. None of the episodes that we see believers in Acts enduring were due to their erroneous conduct, and most of the incidents were perpetrated by false accusations. While it does not always prevent attacks from coming, there is a certain level of security in being innocent.

> {Act 25:8} *8 Then Paul made his defense: "**I have done nothing wrong against the Jewish law or against the temple or against Caesar.**"*

> {Act 24:16} *16 So I **strive always to keep my conscience clear before God and man**.*

> {Act 26:30-31} *30 The king rose, and with him the governor and Bernice and those sitting with them. 31 After they left the room, they began saying to one another, "**This man is not doing anything that deserves death or imprisonment.**"*

The believers in Acts knew the signs of the times and were expecting Jesus to return based on what He had taught them. We can find and familiarize ourselves with Jesus' teachings about this in Matthew 24, Mark 13, and Luke 12 and 21 in addition to the prophecies from the Old Testament, which point to the *day of the Lord*. They were not paranoid about being persecuted, but they were prepared for it because they were familiar with Jesus' teachings. Therefore, persecution served to ignite their faith all the more, and they rejoiced in their suffering for Christ.

{Act 4:29-30} 29 Now, Lord, **consider their threats and enable your servants to speak your word with great boldness**. 30 **Stretch out your hand to heal and perform signs and wonders** *through the name of your holy servant Jesus.*"

{Act 5:41-42 } 41 The apostles left the Sanhedrin, **rejoicing because they had been counted worthy of suffering disgrace for the Name**. 42 Day after day, in the temple courts and from house to house, **they never stopped teaching and proclaiming the good news that Jesus is the Messiah**.

{Act 16:25} 25 [In prison] About midnight Paul **and Silas were praying and singing hymns to God**, and the other prisoners were listening to them.

They knew their rights as citizens of their country of origin.

{Act 16:37} 37 But Paul said to the officers: "They beat us publicly without a trial, **even though we are Roman citizens**, and threw us into prison. And now do they want to get rid of us quietly? No! Let them come themselves and escort us out."

{Act 22:25} 25 As they stretched him out to flog him, Paul said to the centurion standing there, **"Is it legal for you to flog a Roman citizen who hasn't even been found guilty?"**

{Act 25:10-11} 10 Paul answered: **"I am now standing before Caesar's court, where I ought to be tried.** I have not done any wrong to the Jews, as you yourself know very well. 11 If, however, I am guilty of doing anything deserving death, I do not refuse to die. But if the charges brought against me by these Jews are not true, no one has the right to hand me over to them. **I appeal to Caesar!"**

They viewed every conflict as an opportunity to share the Gospel. (see Matthew 10:18; Mark 13:9; Luke 21:13)

{Act 3:12 NLT} 12 **Peter saw his opportunity and addressed the crowd**. "People of Israel," he said, "what is so surprising about this? And why stare at us as though we had made this man walk by our own power or godliness?

{Act 8:4} 4 Those who had been scattered **preached the word wherever they went**.

{Act 19:30-31} 30 **Paul wanted to appear before the crowd**, but the disciples would not let him. 31 Even some of the officials of the province, friends of Paul, sent him a message begging him not to venture into the theater.

{Act 26:1-3} 1 Then Agrippa said to Paul, "You have permission to speak for yourself." So Paul motioned with his hand and began his defense: 2 **"King Agrippa, I consider myself fortunate to stand before you today** as I make my defense against all the accusations of the Jews, 3 and especially so because you are well acquainted with all the Jewish customs and controversies. Therefore, **I beg you to listen to me patiently**.

They allowed the Holy Spirit to do the talking and expected supernatural revelation to help them. (see Matthew 10:19-20; Mark 13:9-11; Luke 12:11-12)

> *{Act 4:8} 8 Then Peter,* **filled with the Holy Spirit,** *said to them: "Rulers and elders of the people!*

> *{Act 6:9-10} 9 Opposition arose, however, from members of the Synagogue of the Freedmen (as it was called)--Jews of Cyrene and Alexandria as well as the provinces of Cilicia and Asia--who began to argue with Stephen. 10* **But they could not stand up against the wisdom the Spirit gave him as he spoke.**

> *{Act 23:6 KJV} 6 But* **when Paul perceived** *that the one part were Sadducees, and the other Pharisees,* **he cried out in the council,** *Men [and] brethren, I am a Pharisee, the son of a Pharisee: of the hope and resurrection of the dead I am called in question.*

They submit themselves to the governing religious and civil authorities up to the point of denying Jesus or disobeying God.

> *{Act 4:19} 19 But Peter and John replied,* **"Which is right in God's eyes: to listen to you, or to him?** *You be the judges!*

> *{Act 5:29} 29 Peter and the other apostles replied:* **"We must obey God rather than human beings!**

> *{Act 23:2-5} 2 At this the high priest Ananias ordered those standing near Paul to strike him on the mouth. 3 Then Paul said to him, "God will strike you, you whitewashed wall!* **You sit there to judge me according to the law, yet you yourself violate the law by commanding that I be struck!"** *4 Those who were standing near Paul said, "How dare you insult God's high priest!" 5 Paul replied,* **"Brothers, I did not realize that he was the high priest; for it is written: 'Do not speak evil about the ruler of your people.'"**

Notably, Paul sharply rebuked the religious leaders for their insolent aggression against him and against God's Law. However, as soon as he learned that he had spoken to the high priest who was the one in authority, Paul apologized and acknowledged the high priest's authority before proceeding.

They forgave and blessed their enemies.

> *{Act 7:59-60} 59 While they were stoning him, Stephen prayed, "Lord Jesus, receive my spirit." 60 Then he fell on his knees and cried out,* **"Lord, do not hold this sin against them."** *When he had said this, he fell asleep.*

Through all of this, they were encouraged by the Lord and His angels as they endured the great trials of their faith.

> *{Act 5:19-20} 19 But during the night* **an angel of the Lord opened the doors of the jail** *and brought them out. 20* **"Go, stand in the temple courts,"** *he said,* **"and tell the people all about this new life."**

*{Act 12:11} 11 Then Peter came to himself and said, "Now I know without a doubt that **the Lord has sent his angel and rescued me** from Herod's clutches and from everything the Jewish people were hoping would happen."*

*{Act 18:9-10} 9 One night **the Lord spoke to Paul in a vision: "Do not be afraid; keep on speaking, do not be silent. 10 For I am with you, and no one is going to attack and harm you**, because I have many people in this city."*

*{Act 23:11} 11 The following night **the Lord stood near Paul and said, "Take courage!** As you have testified about me in Jerusalem, so you must also testify in Rome."*

A Call for Endurance

Jesus prepared His followers for antagonism and for persecution. We live in perilous times just as the believers did in the Book of Acts. There are places in the world today where Christians are experiencing intense persecution and even dying as martyrs for Christ. The reasons for today's antagonism and persecution are no different than the reasons were for the early followers of Christ: *jealousy, suspicion of heresy, protection of the marketplace,* and *denial of the Kingship of Jesus.* Before Christ returns, we can expect the religious system and the world to become increasingly hostile against the Christian faith, and we must be prepared for this in our hearts.

In His High Priestly prayer, Jesus did not pray that we would be taken out of the world because it is our job to be His witnesses to the world. Rather, He prayed that God would *protect us from the evil one.* (see John 17:5) Additionally, He instructed us to pray, *Lead us not into temptation but deliver us from evil.* (see Matthew 6:13) When Paul wrote to the persecuted Thessalonians, he was concerned that the *tempter,* who is the evil one, had tempted them away from their faith in Jesus Christ. (see 1 Thessalonians 3:5) In fact, most of the letters written by the apostles to believers at the inception of Christianity (which we know of as the New Testament epistles) include some form of encouragement for staying true to the faith in the midst of trials, opposition, and persecution. The next time that you read through these letters read them with an outlook which gives weight to the type of suffering the early believers were experiencing. This said, the Book of Revelation contains prophetic descriptions of the times immediately preceding Christ's return, and paints a picture of hardship on the earth in epic proportions. At some point before God's wrath is poured out, those who believe Jesus will be gathered up out of the earth. (see 1 Thessalonians 4:13-18) However, before this, we can anticipate false prophets, false Messiahs, wars, famines, plagues, and unprecedented earthquakes, and bizarre events in the stars and the seas. Additionally, we will face increasing cultural, religious, and political pressures and, eventually, segregation in the commercial system. No matter what happens, we as Christ followers are called upon to endure, to continue to stay true to our faith, and to continue to proclaim the Gospel of Jesus Christ boldly and unashamedly.

*{Rev 13:10} 10 "If anyone is to go into captivity, into captivity they will go. If anyone is to be killed with the sword, with the sword they will be killed." **This calls for patient endurance and faithfulness on the part of God's people.***

> *{Rev 14:12} 12 This calls for **patient endurance** on the part of the people of God who **keep his commands and remain faithful to Jesus**.*

Jesus said that *if you love your life that you will lose it, but if you lose your life, you will gain it*. (see Matthew 10:39; Mark 8:35; Luke 9:24, 17:33; John 12:25) We can look to the example set by Old Testament heroes of the faith in Chapter 11 of the Book of Hebrews. They lived their lives on earth, but kept their eyes on the heavenly home that God had prepared for them. This is faith. Our faith is revealed by what we do when we truly believe what Jesus has done. Let us never forget that because of Jesus, heaven is our born-again birthright as sons and daughters of God. He is worthy of our worship, our sacrifice, and our lives.

> *{Heb 11:13, 16} 13 All these people were **still living by faith when they died**. They did not receive the things promised; they only saw them and welcomed them from a distance, **admitting that they were foreigners and strangers on earth**. ... 16 Instead, **they were longing for a better country--a heavenly one. Therefore God is not ashamed to be called their God, for he has prepared a city for them**.*

As a side note, let me make a quick comment about the Jews. Although the Jews were known to be some of the primary persecutors against Christians in the Book of Acts, they are still beloved of God on account of their forefathers and it is God's will for all Israel to be saved in the end. (see Romans 11:26-28) We will discuss this a bit more in a future chapter. In truth, the Jews are the most persecuted people in the history of humanity largely for the same reasons that Christians are persecuted, namely the worship of the one true God as a distinct and set apart people. The Jews have far more experience at being culturally distinct while living in and among the unbelievers of the world. They, too, have set an example of endurance in their faith as a witness and testimony of our common God.

As for me, when the Lord first called me to serve Him, He made it abundantly clear that it may cost me my life. He pointed me to this verse:

> *{Rev 6:9-10} 9 When he opened the fifth seal, I saw under the altar the souls of those **who had been slain because of the word of God and the testimony they had maintained**. 10 They called out in a loud voice, "How long, Sovereign Lord, holy and true, until you judge the inhabitants of the earth and avenge our blood?"*

I accepted this and continued in my walk with Him. A little bit further in my walk of faith, I was worshipping the Lord in a church service, and I said to Him, *Lord, I'll do anything for you,* and I knew in my heart that I truly meant *anything,* even the ultimate price. I will never forget His response. He said to me, *Wendy, I know, and I will do anything for you. In fact, I already have*. Out of love, Jesus already paid the ultimate price for me. For this, He is my Lord, Savior, and King both now and forever more.

Jesus endured the cross and the pit of hell for us so that we could inherit heaven and be with Him forever. He won the victory for us and included us in the greatest triumph of all eternity – the resurrection from the dead. Jesus Christ came to set us free, but persecutors seek to enslave us again. We will bow down to no one else if we have both of our knees bowed to Jesus. We must choose today whom we will serve. (see Joshua 24:15)

{Rev 12:11} *11 They triumphed over him by the blood of the Lamb and by the word of their testimony;* **they did not love their lives so much as to shrink from death**.

CHAPTER 12
Devotion

Believers in the Book of Acts were singularly devoted to the Lord Jesus Christ and their lives were consumed with worship for their eternal King. Nothing else mattered. They devoted their lives to prayer and eagerly waited for His prompting through the Holy Spirit to direct their hearts and their lives. They willingly fasted to humble themselves before Him, increase their sensitivity to His Spirit, and to become vessels of His power. They studied the Scriptures night and day to receive new revelation of all that He had accomplished for them. They took communion together to celebrate their bond with one another in Him as a special people of God. Let's take a look at the worship, prayer, fasting, study, and communion that they exhibited in the Book of Acts so that we can be encouraged in our devotion to Jesus.

Worship

Right before the Book of Acts began, a few things took place in the lives of Jesus' disciples which are noteworthy. After the resurrection but before the Great Commission and ascension, the majority of Jesus' disciples decided to return to ordinary life as they had known before walking with Jesus. They were fishermen, so they went back to fishing. At daybreak one morning, Jesus appeared on the shore of the sea where they were fishing and called out to them. They proceeded to have a miraculous breakfast and serious conversation with Jesus that would alter the course of their lives forever. (see John 21:1-14) For at least four of them, this whole episode was extremely reminiscent of how Jesus had called them to walk with Him in the first place.

> {Mat 4:18-22} 18 *As Jesus was walking beside the Sea of Galilee, he saw two brothers, Simon called Peter and his brother Andrew. They were casting a net into the lake, for they were fishermen. 19* **"Come, follow me," Jesus said, "and I will send you out to fish for people."** *20* **At once they left their nets and followed him.** *21 Going on from there, he saw two other brothers, James son of Zebedee and his brother John. They were in a boat with their father Zebedee, preparing their nets.* **Jesus called them,** *22* **and immediately they left the boat and their father and followed him**. *(see also Mark 1:16-20)*

When Jesus first began His earthly ministry, He called His disciples to *follow Him* and they had dropped everything, even right in the middle of their work day. Without *ifs, ands,* or *buts,* their lives changed in an instant as they received a new purpose. After three years of walking with Jesus, and after His crucifixion and resurrection, during their sea-side breakfast with the Lord, the disciples were re-commissioned into their Kingdom purpose. Jesus again called them out of their fishing boats and sat down with Peter to ask him three times, *Do you love me more than these?* (see John 21:15-17) Peter had previously boasted that he loved Jesus more than the other disciples (see Matthew 26:33) but now, each time that Peter responded affirmatively to Jesus' question of his love and devotion, Jesus directed Peter to care for His people like a shepherd cares for his sheep. Essentially, Jesus called upon His disciples, once again, to give up everything that they had ever known in order to follow Him and to be fishers of men for the Kingdom of God.

This is our form of worship as Christ followers. We are called to lay down our lives for Jesus and to live in accordance with our changed hearts. Sometimes, like the first disciples, this means dropping everything that we are doing and leaving behind life as we know it in order to follow Him fully. The first believers recognized that nothing on earth could possibly compare in significance, value, or appeal to the privilege of knowing Jesus and walking with Him. The same is still true for us today because Jesus is worthy of our worship, our devotion, our love, and our lives.

> *{Rom 12:1-2} 1 Therefore, I urge you, brothers and sisters,* **in view of God's mercy, to offer your bodies as a living sacrifice, holy and pleasing to God--this is your true and proper worship.** *2* **Do not conform to the pattern of this world,** *but be transformed by the renewing of your mind. Then you will be able to test and approve what God's will is--his good, pleasing and perfect will.*

In this verse, *worship* is defined as *service rendered for hire* including *ministry in service to God* and *sacred services according to His will*. In the Old Testament, worship very literally consisted of priestly service in the Tabernacle or Temple of God which fulfilled God's regulations for sacrifice and consecration. In those days, only specially designated people were anointed to serve God, enter into His presence, and hear His voice. Priests were set apart from everyone else and dedicated exclusively to their God-assigned duties. In this form of worship, they were not serving the people but ministering to God. Another word for *worship* means *to kiss the hand in token of reverence* or *to kneel or prostrate oneself to express respect*. When we worship Jesus, we worship our King as we would a king on earth, except that our King is in heaven. We pay our respects to Him out of reverence for His majesty and we willingly serve Him as New Covenant priests by serving Him with the temples which are our bodies. We offer our King songs of praise and adoration while we are on earth and when we arrive in heaven, our worship will sound like this:

> *{Rev 4:8b} 8b Day and night they never stop saying: "* **'Holy, holy, holy is the Lord God Almighty,' who was, and is, and is to come.** *"*

> *{Rev 4:11} 11 "* **You are worthy,** *our Lord and God,* **to receive glory and honor and power,** *for you created all things, and by your will they were created and have their being."*

> *{Rev 5:9} 9 And they sang a new song, saying: "* **You are worthy** *to take the scroll and to open its seals,* **because you were slain, and with your blood you purchased for God persons from every tribe and language and people and nation.**

> *{Rev 5:12} 12 In a loud voice they were saying: "* **Worthy is the Lamb, who was slain, to receive power and wealth and wisdom and strength and honor and glory and praise!** *"*

> *{Rev 5:13} 13 Then I heard every creature in heaven and on earth and under the earth and on the sea, and all that is in them, saying:* **"To him who sits on the throne and to the Lamb be praise and honor and glory and power, for ever and ever!"**

A heart positioned towards God in adoration, ready and willing to do whatever He may ask of us is the very heart that God has been seeking from the beginning of mankind. Unfortunately, this was impossible for any human to achieve until the Holy Spirit was poured out. Adam had bowed his knee to the deceiver by eating from the wrong tree, and all of his descendants followed his example. Even the love of the Old Testament priests grew cold because they focused more on ritual and duty than their relationship with God. Jesus, however, never bowed His knee to the tempter, and His love never grew cold because He willingly offered all of Himself in obedience to God. This was His form of worship, even unto death.

> *{Hos 6:6} 6 For I desire mercy, not sacrifice, and* **acknowledgment of God rather than burnt offerings**. *(see also Proverbs 21:3; 1 Samuel 15:22; Isaiah 1:11)*

> *{Heb 10:5-7} 5 Therefore, when Christ came into the world, he said: "Sacrifice and offering you did not desire,* **but a body you prepared for me***; 6 with burnt offerings and sin offerings you were not pleased. 7* **Then I said, 'Here I am***--it is written about me in the scroll--* **I have come to do your will, my God.'"** *(quoting Psalm 40:6-8)*

Now that we are indwelt with the same Spirit that Jesus had, we can worship God the way that Jesus did. Each one of us is a priest rendering service to God, and each one of us is consecrated to worship Him, stand in His presence, and hear His voice. (see 1 Peter 2:9; Revelation 5:10; Hebrews 4:16, 8, 9) As the Psalm referenced above says, *Sacrifice and offering you did not desire, but my ears you have opened.* Our ears have been opened so that we can listen to the Holy Spirit and obey God's guidance for our lives. (see Hebrews 3:7, 15) We offer Him our bodies to be obedient to His ways because we know that we are not our own and that we have been bought with the price of the precious blood of Jesus. (see Romans 6:13; 1 Corinthians 6:19-20)

This said, worshipping Jesus in heaven and serving His Body on earth are inextricably intertwined. When we affirm our love for Christ the way that Peter did that morning at breakfast, Jesus will direct us just as He directed Peter: To care for His people like a shepherd cares for His sheep. One of the significant duties of the Old Covenant priesthood was to keep the people of Israel in right relationship with God through the sacrificial system, through teaching them God's ways, and through interceding and blessing them in His name. (see Hebrews 10:11; Leviticus 10:11; Numbers 6:24-26) Jesus came as our High Priest to do these things for us and establish the New Covenant. (see Hebrews 10:10; Philippians 2:5-8; Matthew 5-7; Hebrews 7:25, 8:12) Now, when we offer our lives to God in worship as His New Covenant priests, He, undoubtedly, leads us to care for and love others in the same way that He loves us all. Every disciple of Christ is commissioned to find Jesus' lost sheep and to feed and nourish His lambs. All believers are able to pray for one another and bless one another in the name of Jesus so that all of His people grow to spiritual maturity.

The first followers of Christ in the Book of Acts displayed this type of total dedication to Jesus and to one another through the supernatural selflessness within the Christian community.

> *{Act 1:14} 14 They all **joined together constantly in prayer**, along with the women and Mary the mother of Jesus, and with his brothers.*

> *{Act 2:41-42} 41 Those who accepted his message were baptized, and about three thousand were added to their number that day. 42 **They devoted themselves to the apostles' teaching and to fellowship, to the breaking of bread and to prayer**.*

> *{Act 4:32} 32 **All the believers were one in heart and mind. No one claimed that any of their possessions was their own**, but they shared everything they had.*

Additionally, Saul dropped his life's purpose as a Pharisee and persecutor of Christians and, in a dramatic turnaround, became the apostle Paul and the most passionate advocate of Christianity the world has ever known. Now, that's a life change! Another dramatic conversion was the jailer in Philippi who guarded Paul and Silas in prison and was transformed in his heart when he believed the word of Christ. The jailer then risked his job to show compassion.

> *{Act 16:30-34} 30 He then brought them out and asked, "Sirs, what must I do to be saved?" 31 They replied, "Believe in the Lord Jesus, and you will be saved--you and your household." 32 Then they spoke the word of the Lord to him and to all the others in his house. 33 **At that hour of the night the jailer took them and washed their wounds**; then immediately he and all his household were baptized. 34 **The jailer brought them into his house and set a meal before them; he was filled with joy because he had come to believe in God--he and his whole household**.*

In my walk with the Lord, I made a decision one January to commit the entire year to Jesus and to do whatever He said, no matter what. By the end of that year, my life was more filled with His presence and His joy than ever before, and my commitment has not waned since. As I pressed further into my dedication and He asked me to give away everything I own, He used the *breakfast by the sea* passage to guide me from time to time. Though His conversation with me was slightly different than the one He had with Peter, when a possession of mine would be a little more challenging for me to part with, I would hear the Lord say, *Do you love me more than this?* and quickly my decision was made simple. Also, as I interacted with people with differing priorities or in disagreements over things large and small, the Lord would ask me about the issue at hand, *Do you love me more than this?* and I would be able to let go of my pride or my need to be right. For this reason and many others, I have come to the conclusion that being singularly devoted to Jesus makes sorting through the issues of life a whole lot simpler. And, in truth, nothing else really matters. I think the believers in the Book of Acts felt this way, too.

Prayer

From the first chapter of the Book of Acts, prayer steps into the position of top priority among believers. Prayer is prevalent in almost every chapter of Acts, and there are several different types of prayer exhibited. The New Covenant, sealed with the shed blood of Jesus Christ, changed every believer's position before God and, when the Holy Spirit was poured out, a whole new world of prayer and communing with God was opened up because the dialog between man and God became two-way. Christ's disciples devoted themselves to God's Kingdom purpose through lives of prayer and the apostles, in particular, viewed it as their highest responsibility.

> *{Act 2:42} 42 **They [all believers] devoted themselves** to the apostles' teaching and to fellowship, to the breaking of bread and **to prayer**.*

> *{Act 6:3-4} 3 Brothers and sisters, choose seven men from among you who are known to be full of the Spirit and wisdom. **We [apostles]** will turn this responsibility over to them 4 and **will give our attention to prayer** and the ministry of the word."*

One type of prayer to point out from the Book of Acts is what I call a *poor in spirit* prayer. Before the Holy Spirit had been poured out, Jesus told His disciples to wait in Jerusalem until they received power from heaven to be His witnesses in the earth. Obediently, 120 of them gathered together in prayer.

> *{Act 1:14} 14 **They all joined together constantly in prayer**, along with the women and Mary the mother of Jesus, and with his brothers.*

Jesus said, *Blessed are the poor in spirit, for theirs is the Kingdom of Heaven.* (see Matthew 5:3) Jesus also talked about our spiritual poverty through a parable about a Tax Collector who approached God from a position of destitution compared to a who Pharisee boasted about his own worthiness. The Tax Collector gained right standing with God while the Pharisee did not.

> *{Luk 18:9-14} 9 To some who were **confident of their own righteousness** and looked down on everyone else, Jesus told this parable: 10 "Two men went up to the temple to pray, one a Pharisee and the other a tax collector. 11 The Pharisee stood by himself and prayed: '**God, I thank you that I am not like other people**--robbers, evildoers, adulterers--or even like this tax collector. 12 I fast twice a week and give a tenth of all I get.' 13 "**But the tax collector stood at a distance. He would not even look up to heaven, but beat his breast and said, 'God, have mercy on me, a sinner.'** 14 "I tell you that this man, **rather than the other, went home justified before God.** For all those who exalt themselves will be humbled, and those who humble themselves will be exalted."*

At this point in the first 120 believer's lives, they were definitely *poor in spirit* because the Holy Spirit had not been poured out yet and so, they were waiting for the Kingdom of Heaven. Additionally, the Gentile Centurion, Cornelius, demonstrated this *poor in spirit* approach to prayer before Peter was sent to tell Him about Christ. The word for *prayer* in the following passage about Cornelius below translates as *asking or begging from a place of need*. In short, Cornelius understood his need for God. His family was the first Gentile family to receive the Holy Spirit.

*{Act 10:1-2} 1 At Caesarea there was a man named Cornelius, a centurion in what was known as the Italian Regiment. 2 **He and all his family were devout and God-fearing;** he gave generously to those in need and **<u>prayed</u> to God regularly**.*

In spite of the fact that the Holy Spirit has been poured out to believers today, we are just as *poor in spirit* as the first disciples and Cornelius were. Therefore, we humble ourselves before God by acknowledging Christ's righteousness and not our own because only Jesus gives us right standing with God and access to His grace. Without Jesus, we are destitute in spirit, and our righteousness is nothing but filth. (see Romans 5:1-2; John 6:63; Isaiah 64:6) Moreover, as we realize all that Christ has done for us, we recognize all the more just how *poor in spirit* we really are. Accordingly, we pray *poor in spirit* prayers when we are in desperate need of what God has for us, and when we commit ourselves to waiting for God to speak, to move, and to do what He has promised. We pray *poor in spirit* prayers when we know that we are powerless to do anything without Him, or that if we stepped out that it would be entirely our own doing and not His prompting, or that He has told us to wait for Him to bring about what He has promised. We submit and surrender ourselves and our lives to God's ways, God's plan, and God's timing because we know that, without Him, we are nothing. Sometimes, it's as simple as saying, *Come Holy Spirit*.

Psalms for Prayer of Lowliness and Humility Before God
14, 19, 25, 39, 49, 90, 147

Another example of a *poor in spirit* prayer in the Book of Acts was when a believer named Simon had gone astray in his heart and needed to return to proper alignment with God and God's purposes. Peter urged Simon to pray a prayer of deep contrition and to humble himself afresh before God through faith in Christ. Simon's *fear of the Lord* returned to Him swiftly as he saw the error of his ways. (see Acts 8:9-24)

*{Act 8:22-24} 22 **Repent of this wickedness and pray to the Lord** in the hope that he may forgive you for having such a thought in your heart. 23 For I see that you are full of bitterness and captive to sin." 24 Then Simon answered, "**Pray to the Lord for me so that nothing you have said may happen to me.**"*

In the event that we have royally messed up in our lives or gone astray from God's path for us, we can humble ourselves afresh before God through *poor in spirit* prayers. However, as New Covenant believers, we should not get stuck too long in this type of prayer. Why? Because Christ has changed our position to one of a right standing with God through faith in Jesus so that we do not have to become ensnared by believing that Christ's sacrifice was not sufficient for us. When we genuinely and earnestly approach God seeking His forgiveness, we can receive it thankfully through faith and move on to the other things God has for us.

Psalms for Prayer of Contrition and Forgiveness
5, 6, 14, 31, 32, 38, 41, 44, 51, 66, 74, 102, 120, 130, 137, 143

Along these lines, New Covenant prayer has become an exchange of giving to God the bad stuff on earth and receiving from Him the goodness of heaven. We bring Him mourning and receive comfort and blessing, we bring Him ashes and receive a crown of beauty, we bring Him heaviness and receive a garment of praise. (see Isaiah 61:1-3) Disciples of Jesus petition and praise God for justice in our favor through the cross of Christ because our status has changed from being beggars to being receivers, from being impoverished to having great riches in Christ, and from being God's enemies to being His children. We come with thankful hearts believing Jesus when He said, *It is finished!*

> *{Heb 4:16} 16 Let us then **approach God's throne of grace with confidence [boldly]**, so that we may **receive mercy and find grace to help us in our time of need**.*

Let's do a quick refresher on what Jesus accomplished for us so that we don't pray for what we already have in Christ. Because of the shed blood of Jesus, our sins have been forgiven, and God remembers them no more. (see Hebrews 10:14-20) Because of the cross of Christ, all of the charges of guilt against us for sin and error have been satisfied and paid in full. (see Colossians 2:11-12) Because Jesus became a curse, the curse of the Law has no power in our lives. (see Galatians 3:13) Because Jesus conquered sin and death, the devil has no authority over our lives. (see Hebrews 2:14; 1 John 3:8) Because Jesus became God's enemy, took our place as sinners, and became sin for us, we have become friends with God, have right standing with God, and we are the righteousness of God. (see John 5:15; Romans 5:1-2, 8:1; 2 Corinthians 5:21) Plus, all of this is not to mention that we have been spared from eternal damnation and have been granted eternal life with Him. Practically speaking, this means that we do not have to ask God for what we already have and, instead, we can praise and thank God for what He has already done. Accordingly, when we enter into our times of prayer through faith in Jesus Christ, we come forgiven, blameless, righteous, and justified as if we had never sinned. In fact, this is what coming *boldly to the throne of grace* is all about. In the Old Testament, the High Priest could only enter behind the veil into the Most Holy Place of God's presence once per year on the Day of Atonement. Even then, there were many rules to follow and rituals to carry out before he could approach the mercy seat of God on behalf of the people. After all of these rituals were performed, he was still not assured of God's favor, and there was a chance that he may die when he entered into God's presence. (see Hebrews 9:1-8; Leviticus 16:2) Therefore, the other priests would tie a rope around the High Priest's ankle in case that he dropped dead so that, if the priest took too long coming back out, they could drag him out of God's presence without going in and dropping dead themselves. But now, because of the life, death, and the resurrection of Jesus Christ, we enter into God's presence through prayer completely confident, knowing that we will not be struck dead and that God will hear us and help us. We do not need to be fearful or ashamed in God's presence and we no longer need a safety rope! We enter into prayer and God's presence knowing that, because of Jesus, we have a right to be there.

Therefore, we enter into *every* prayer with praise and thanksgiving in our hearts for who God is and what He has done for us. The all powerful God who created and knows everything has entered into relationship with us. How cool is that? Through faith in Christ, God has become our *Provider*, our *Shepherd*, our *Healer*, our *Friend*, and our *loving heavenly Father*. Because of Jesus, we are assured of the victory, often temporally, but always eternally and God delights to bless us so that, when we come to commune with Him, we do not have to beg but we can simply accept and receive these blessings. (see Jeremiah 32:40-41) On top of all of that, we thank Him because we know that He is busy working everything out for our good, no matter how bad it may appear on earth. (see Romans 8:28) Therefore, whether our prayers are answered or seem unheard, and no matter what our circumstances may look like, we enter into prayer with praise and thankfulness. (see Philippians 4:4, 6; 1 Thessalonians 5:18; Ephesians 5:20; 2 Corinthians 2:14; 1 Corinthians 15:57)

Psalms for Prayer of Praise
8, 19, 30, 65, 84, 96, 97, 100, 103, 107, 113, 136, 145, 150

Another form of prayer in the Book of Acts was demonstrated when believers positioned themselves to focus entirely on God's presence and receiving from Him. For those who had literally walked with Jesus during His years of ministry, I imagine that they entered into His spiritual presence in a way that evoked memories and, sometimes, even sensations of His physical presence. Some people today call this *soaking in His presence* but in the Book of Acts, they called it a *trance*.

> *{Act 10:9-10} 9 About noon the following day as they were on their journey and approaching the city, **Peter went up on the roof to pray**. 10 He became hungry and wanted something to eat, and while the meal was being prepared, **he fell into a trance**. (He then proceeded to receive a vision from the Lord.)*

> *{Act 22:17-18} 17 "When I returned to Jerusalem and was **praying at the temple, I fell into a trance** 18 and saw the Lord speaking to me. 'Quick!' he said. 'Leave Jerusalem immediately, because the people here will not accept your testimony about me.'*

A *trance* is defined (paraphrasing) as *an altered state of mind where, though the person is awake, their mind is wholly fixed on divine things so that they perceive the things revealed to them by God*. In these examples, Peter and Paul both entered into the presence of the Lord to receive wisdom from God, to seek deeper revelation of truth in the Scriptures, to be recharged by the Holy Spirit's power and to receive direction about their next steps in serving Jesus. In fact, the purpose of this form of prayer is to allow Jesus to speak to us through the Holy Spirit. This form of prayer is something totally unique to Christians because we have the privilege of hearing God's voice and living in His presence. In fact, without the Holy Spirit's guidance, all prayer is typically blind begging for God to do something, praising Him because He did it, or groaning before Him because He didn't do it. But now, Christ's righteousness allows believers to enter into the presence of God boldly to receive His mercy, grace, and direction. Moreover, as we live more and more by submitting to this guidance from the Holy Spirit in prayer, our minds become renewed and alert to God's heart and His purposes. We are transformed from glory to glory in His presence, we receive the mind of Christ, and we can test and approve the perfect and pleasing will of God. (see 2 Corinthians 3:18; 1 Corinthians 2:16; Romans 12:2) God, who is the source of all the wisdom that we need, is just a prayer away. It's time for us to allow HIM to do the talking.

For me, one of the first things that I do when praying this way is to cast my cares on Jesus. I very literally, write down on a piece of paper the things that are weighing me down or troubling me and the things that I need right now, meaning today. Most times, I try to sum up the issue or need in one word or a simple phrase because He already knows what I mean. Other times, I talk through the whole thing with Him the same way that I would talk to a friend in the room with me because, truthfully speaking, He *is* in the room with me. Then, I let everything go and leave it in God's hands, trusting that He will take care of it. He has been God for a very long time, so I do not need to tell Him how to do His job.

As a side note and as I mentioned earlier, quite a few years ago, the Lord asked me to give everything that I owned away, and I did. Then, God also asked me not to ask other people for anything that I needed but to only ask Him in prayer to meet my needs, and I have remained obedient to that, even up to today. Because of this, I have realized the value of *TODAY* being the primary focus of the petitions that I present to Him. More importantly, I have come to know and trust that God does not desire for me to be anxious or worried about anything because He is always faithful and He knows what we need before we even ask Him. (see Matthew 6:8)

> {1Pe 5:7} 7 **Cast all your anxiety [cares] on him because he cares for you**. *(quoting Psalm 55:22)*

> {Phl 4:6} 6 **Do not be anxious about anything**, *but in every situation, by prayer and petition, with thanksgiving,* **present your requests to God**.

> {Mat 6:31-34} 31 **So do not worry,** *saying, 'What shall we eat?' or 'What shall we drink?' or 'What shall we wear?' 32 For the pagans run after all these things, and* **your heavenly Father knows that you need them. 33 But seek first his kingdom and his righteousness, and all these things will be given to you as well.** *34 Therefore* **do not worry about tomorrow,** *for tomorrow will worry about itself. Each day has enough trouble of its own. (see also Luke 12:22-34)*

After I have written my cares, anxieties, and needs on the paper, I draw a line underneath my list and put my pen down. Now that God has my list for Him, it's time for me to receive His list for me. I simply open myself up to receiving from Him anything that He wants to say to me or instruct me to do. Oftentimes, right away the Holy Spirit will speak a few things to me, and I write them down. I always have my Bible at hand in case that He points me to certain Scriptures or passages. Sometimes, I pray out loud whether in my native language or praying in tongues, but mostly I maintain a posture of waiting for the Lord to speak to me. I try to let Him do most of the talking while I listen closely to what He is saying. Sometimes, I close my eyes and lay down while I allow the Lord to minister to me through the Holy Spirit in whatever way He sees fit. Usually, I listen to music or worship while I wait and while I pray but other times I wait in absolute silence. What the Lord speaks to me during these times may be the answer to one of my petitions, wisdom about something which He desires for me to do that day, a Scripture verse to encourage me or a prophetic word or promise for my life. He may silently reveal wounds and minister healing to me, or He may give me a vision from heaven.

Psalms for Prayer for Fellowship with God, Wisdom, and Worship
1, 5, 8, 11, 16, 19, 23, 25, 27, 29, 37, 64, 96, 100, 111, 133, 150

Another type of prayer in the Book of Acts is one of a petition for an urgent or pressing need. When the first believers endured persecution for their faith in Jesus, they prayed for God to come NOW into their situation. Similarly, when Paul and Silas were in prison because of their faith, they prayed to God and praised Him with songs hoping that He would deliver them expediently – and He did. The persecuted disciples in Jerusalem and imprisoned Paul and Silas did not cower before their oppressors or before God. They knew what Christ had accomplished for them, and they praised God even in their urgent need.

> {Act 4:31} 31 **After they [persecuted believers] prayed**, *the place where they were meeting was shaken. And they were all filled with the Holy Spirit and spoke the word of God boldly.*

> {Act 16:25} 25 *About midnight[in prison]* **Paul and Silas were praying and singing hymns to God**, *and the other prisoners were listening to them.*

Because of the cross of Jesus Christ, justice for believers is *as it is in heaven, NOW*. Because of the resurrection, no sin, curse, or an attack of the enemy has any legal right to our lives. Since Jesus has already obtained justice for us through the cross, we enter into this type of prayer believing that the verdict is already in for Christ followers, and God's justice is always in our favor. (see Mark 11:24) Jesus, the *Innocent One*, was declared by God to be *Guilty* of all of our sins and received our punishment on the cross. He was sentenced to death and sent to the prison known as Hell. Then, through resurrection, Jesus proved that the prison sentence which He served in Hell on our behalf had been fulfilled. The Judge declared all believers to be *Not Guilty*, not because we are innocent but because our sentence of condemnation had been satisfied by Jesus. There is no double jeopardy in God's court. Praise God! Therefore, when we find ourselves under attack or in a high pressure situation where we need God to do something for us NOW, we have the right to cry out to God for justice in the name of Jesus. This could include persecution, oppression, sickness, lack, depression, defeat, or any other curse of the Law that may be illegally manifesting itself in our lives. Sometimes, all we can say in prayer is, *Help!* or it is also wise to simply cry out, *Jesus!* and, oftentimes, these are perfect situations for praying in tongues or wordless groaning from our inmost being. (see Romans 8:26) This type of prayer also applies to promises or prophecies which God has spoken to us in accordance with His will. Because of Jesus, God says, *Yes* to all of His promises of blessing for our lives, and we have a legal right to receive them freely from Him. (see 2 Corinthians 1:20)

Jesus talked about persistent prayer for urgent justice in another parable about prayer:

> {Luk 18:1-8} 1 *Then Jesus told his disciples a parable to show them that* **they should always pray and not give up.** *2 He said: "In a certain town there was a judge who neither feared God nor cared what people thought. 3 And there was a widow in that town who kept coming to him with the plea,* **'Grant me justice against my adversary.'** *4 "For some time he refused. But finally he said to himself, 'Even though I don't fear God or care what people think, 5 yet* **because this widow keeps bothering me, I will see that she gets justice**, *so that she won't eventually come and attack me!' " 6 And the Lord said, "Listen to what the unjust judge says. 7* **And will not God bring about justice for his chosen ones, who cry out to him day and night?** *Will he keep putting them off? 8* **I tell you, he will see that they get justice, and quickly.** *However, when the Son of Man comes, will he find faith on the earth?"*

The Persistent Widow knew that she had been wronged by an enemy and, therefore, she relentlessly and shamelessly bombarded the Judge with her requests. No matter how long it took for the Judge to hear her, she did not back down from what she knew was right, and she kept her sights on receiving justice from the Judge. Notably, she did not try to bring about justice herself in her own way but submitted herself to the authority of the Judge to legally give her the justice that she knew was due her. Most significantly, she did not give up or allow anything to convince her that she would never receive her justice or that she should quit harassing the Judge.

Again, because of Jesus, we have the right to receive the victory that Christ has attained for us, and we have the right to stand in faith and in prayer until we receive it. Therefore, when God has truly spoken a promise to us, nothing has the right to keep us from receiving it and we should pray believing that this is true. Like the Persistent Widow, it may take time for us to see the answer to our prayers, but we can rest assured that God hears us and will answer us. The question is are we willing to believe and stand in faith and keep asking no matter how long it takes?

Psalms to Cry Out for God's Help
3, 4, 25, 27, 31, 34, 35, 37, 40, 41, 46, 49, 55, 56, 59, 86, 91, 102, 107, 118, 142, 145

Another form of prayer that we see in the Book of Acts is *intercession* or *praying for one another*. When Peter was thrown in prison by Herod, the whole church interceded for him.

> {Act 12:5, 12} 5 So Peter was kept in prison, but **the church was earnestly praying to God for him**. ... 12 When this had dawned on him, he went to the house of Mary the mother of John, also called Mark, **where many people had gathered and were praying**.

Simply put, *intercession* is *praying for someone else the way that we would pray for ourselves*. It literally means *to have a conversation or consultation with God about someone else*. Again, because of the Holy Spirit, prayer conversation will be two-way. For me, I simply bring the person up in conversation with God. I present any known needs, anxieties, and situations in the person's life in addition to any known promises or prophecies which that person is expecting to receive from God. I also speak blessing over them in the name of Jesus based on the Word of God and the finished work of the cross and praise God for victory in their lives through Christ. Then, I listen for God's response. If God speaks anything to me that may direct or encourage them then, most times, I share it with them, unless God tells me to keep it in private prayer between the two of us or until a later date.

Intercession in the Book of Acts also takes on various forms of ministry. One type of ministering intercession is when believers pray for someone else who is present. For example, on Paul's journey back to Jerusalem, Christians gathered together to pray for him. Believers may have prayed something along the lines of, *God, bless Paul on his journey back to Jerusalem and prevent him from being beat up too badly so that he can fulfill Your purpose in the earth*. They probably presented any of Paul's needs to God, spoke anything else that the Holy Spirit revealed to them, and blessed Paul and his journey in the name of Jesus.

> {Act 20:36} 36 When Paul had finished speaking, **he knelt down with all of them and prayed**.

*{Act 21:5} 5 When it was time to leave, we left and continued on our way. **All of them, including wives and children**, accompanied us out of the city, **and there on the beach we knelt to pray**.*

Of course, the most notable type of ministering intercession is when a believer exercises their power and authority in Christ to do the works that Jesus did. For example, Peter prayed to seek the Lord for instructions on how to raise a girl from the dead and, once he had his instructions, he carried out God's purpose in the power and authority of the name of Jesus. Similarly, Paul prayed to receive his instructions from the Lord and then laid his hands on the men on Malta, who were healed. Because the anointing of the Holy Spirit was with both Peter and Paul, it was as if Jesus Himself were laying His hands on the people being ministered to.

*{Act 9:40} 40 Peter sent them all out of the room; then **he got down on his knees and prayed. Turning toward the dead woman, he said, "Tabitha, get up."** She opened her eyes, and seeing Peter she sat up.*

*{Act 28:8-9} 8 His father was sick in bed, suffering from fever and dysentery. **Paul went in to see him and, after prayer, placed his hands on him and healed him**. 9 When this had happened, **the rest of the sick on the island came and were cured**.*

As we enter into this type of ministry, particularly healing and deliverance, God will remind us of episodes in the Gospels where Jesus addressed a certain situation, like Peter with Tabitha. Or, He will tell us or show us in our mind's eye how or where we are to lay our hands on the person that we are ministering to in addition to anything else He may want us to say or to do while we are with them, like Paul with the men of Malta. No matter how God reveals what He wants us to do or say, in this type of ministry, we ARE Jesus' Body, and we do the works that He did in the power of Jesus' name.

Lastly, in the Book of Acts, believers prayed for the nations. Even when the world raged against them, they prayed for boldness to proclaim the Gospel.

*{Act 4:24-31} 24 When they heard this, **they raised their voices together in prayer to God**. "Sovereign Lord," they said, "you made the heavens and the earth and the sea, and everything in them. 25 You spoke by the Holy Spirit through the mouth of your servant, our father David: " **'Why do the nations rage and the peoples plot in vain? 26 The kings of the earth rise up and the rulers band together against the Lord and against his anointed one.'** (quoting Psalm 2:1-2) 27 Indeed Herod and Pontius Pilate met together with the Gentiles and the people of Israel in this city to conspire against your holy servant Jesus, whom you anointed. 28 **They did what your power and will had decided beforehand should happen**. 29 Now, Lord, consider their threats and enable your servants to speak your word with great boldness. 30 Stretch out your hand to heal and perform signs and wonders through the name of your holy servant Jesus." 31 After they prayed, the place where they were meeting was shaken. And they were all filled with the Holy Spirit and spoke the word of God boldly.*

Interestingly, they did not pray for the nations to change, but they prayed for themselves and one another to fulfill God's purposes in the nations. Additionally, they recognized the prophetic fulfillment of what was happening in the nations in their times, but they did not allow this to divert their focus from their Christ-given assignment in the earth before His return. This is all somewhat reminiscent of the way that Jesus prayed to God for His disciples and all believers as our High Priest. (see John 17) He did not pray for nations but *for His people* whom He redeemed *out of every nation.* (see Revelation 5:9) Jesus prayed for those who will believe in Him to be *sanctified in the truth*, to be *protected from the evil one*, to be *drawn into complete unity as one Body*, and to be *sent out as His witnesses* in the earth so that the world may come to know Him. This said, Jesus died because of His love for all people, and it is God's desire that everyone is saved through faith in Him. As Christ's Body in the earth, we adopt the same heart towards every individual person, no matter what nation they are from. We pray for all people from all nations to be saved through faith in Jesus Christ.

> *{Act 26:28-29} 28 Then Agrippa said to Paul, "Do you think that in such a short time you can* **persuade me to be a Christian?**" *29 Paul replied, "Short time or long--**I pray to God that not only you but all who are listening to me today may become what I am**, except for these chains."*

> *{1Ti 2:1-6} 1 I urge, then, first of all,* **that petitions, prayers, intercession and thanksgiving be made for all people-- 2 for kings and all those in authority, that we may live peaceful and quiet lives in all godliness and holiness.** *3 This is good, and pleases God our Savior, 4* **who wants all people to be saved and to come to a knowledge of the truth.** *5 For there is one God and one mediator between God and mankind, the man* **Christ Jesus**, *6* **who gave himself as a ransom for all people.** *This has now been witnessed to at the proper time.*

Additionally, in the Book of Acts, a prophet named Agabus received prophetic revelation about an upcoming event, namely a famine in Jerusalem and Judea. It was this prophecy that allowed the Church to prepare for and serve other believers who would be affected when the famine came. The prophetic word was not issued for the purpose of judging the nations but for the purpose of building up and strengthening followers of Christ so that God's purpose through them could be fulfilled. (see Acts 11:27-29) Similarly, as we watch what is happening in the nations of the world, it is important that we know the signs of the times from the teachings of Jesus, the prophecies of the Old Testament about the *day of the Lord* when Jesus will return, and current prophetic revelation given by the Holy Spirit for our times, cities, and nations. This way we can strengthen and encourage fellow believers, no matter how dark the world becomes or how much antagonism we face as followers of Christ. Our focus and purpose is to fulfill His commission in the earth, making disciples from all the nations. Only when we accomplish this will He return, and *The Spirit and the Bride say, "Come!"* (see Matthew 24:14; Revelation 22:17)

Psalms for Prayer for Wisdom About the Nations
2, 9, 46 & 47, 66 & 67, 79, 83, 96-100, 114 & 115, 117

The point is this, just like the believers in the Book of Acts, as followers of Jesus, we are all called to lives of prayer. We who believe Jesus are *God's house,* and God's house is called a house of prayer. (see

Hebrews 3:6; Matthew 21:13; Mark 11:17; Luke 19:46, quoting Isaiah 56:7) This said, with all of these various forms of prayer, it would seem like prayer is the most stress-free thing in the world. However, though it is simple, it is not always easy or painless. In fact, at one point in time in my walk with Jesus, I became intensely frustrated because it didn't seem like any of my prayers were being answered. I finally went brashly to God and said something along the lines of, *Clearly, I don't know how to pray so from now on, I'm not praying anything unless I know it is your will!* (see 1 John 5:14) God, in mercy and with great patience, took the opportunity to teach me how to pray. Largely this was in tandem with learning about His ways, which are so different and so much better than our own way of doing things. (see Isaiah 55; Exodus 33:13) He renewed and continues to renew my mind so that I can discern His perfect will and come into agreement with it. He revealed and continues to reveal the Scriptures and the depth of what they mean to us in Christ so that my confidence and boldness in my petitions and my actions is ever increasing. As I continue to grow in the knowledge of His ways and pray them into existence in the earth, my prayers are answered, and I expectantly stand in faith for those that have not been answered yet.

Fasting

Fasting was another common practice among the first followers of Christ. Believers fasted to humble themselves before God, to petition Him for their needs, to increase their awareness of His presence with them, to implore Him for answers to their prayers, to intercede for others, to increase their power in ministry, and to receive prophetic revelation for the present times and for the times to come. In the Book of Acts, the examples of fasting occurred most prevalently when the Church was earnestly seeking God to appoint and send leaders for ministry, which we covered in another chapter. However, the point of their fasting was to humble themselves before God in order to hear very clearly from God about a very important decision.

> {Act 13:2-3} 2 **While they were worshiping the Lord and fasting, the Holy Spirit said,** "Set apart for me Barnabas and Saul for the work to which I have called them." 3 **So after they had fasted and prayed, they placed their hands on them and sent them off.**

> {Act 14:23} 23 Paul and Barnabas **appointed elders** for them in each church and, **with prayer and fasting, committed them to the Lord**, in whom they had put their trust.

Essentially, fasting turns up the volume and intensifies all of the various forms of prayer that we just discussed, all of which are rooted and grounded in the finished work of Christ's resurrection. Fasting is defined as *willingly abstaining from food and nourishment, either entirely or in part, for a set period of time as an act of devotion to God.* By abstaining from that which sustains us – food – we rely more heavily on the One Who sustains us – Jesus. Non-food "fasting" is technically abstinence or refraining from any other type of activity, and this is a different spiritual discipline altogether. Fasting is specific to food and our bodies as we adopt a position of greater dependence on God and His power in our lives. This is significant because, instead of eating and drinking in the natural, we replace it by *eating the bread of life* and *drinking of the living waters.* (see John 6:35; Revelation 22:17; Isaiah 55:1) As our natural and carnal desires are re-directed towards God, our spiritual hunger and thirst is magnified and satisfied through Jesus Christ. Through fasting, we willingly subject our flesh to weakness so that the Holy Spirit within us can move in our lives more powerfully and more profoundly – in the same way that we see Him working in the lives of believers in the Book of Acts.

Study of the Word of God

The word *disciple* means *student, pupil,* or *learner* and disciples of Christ in the Book of Acts set their hearts upon learning God's Word and growing in their knowledge of Him.

> *{Act 2:42}* 42 **They [all believers] devoted themselves** to the **apostles' teaching** and to *fellowship, to the breaking of bread and to prayer.*

> *{Act 6:3-4}* 3 *Brothers and sisters, choose seven men from among you who are known to be full of the Spirit and wisdom.* **We [apostles]** *will turn this responsibility over to them* 4 *and* **will give our attention to** *prayer and the* **ministry of the word.***"*

It is God's desire to be known by His people. In Eden, God was known by Adam and could have taught Adam everything that he needed to know in order to carry out God's purpose in the earth. Unfortunately, Adam chose to eat from a tree of knowledge instead of valuing true knowledge of God, and mankind has suffered the consequences ever since. Later, God's people, Israel, were instructed to meditate on the Word of God day and night, to write God's statutes on their doorposts, tie them on their hands and foreheads, and teach them to their children day after day after day (Deuteronomy 6 and 11) so that, through their knowledge of God, they could obey Him, be blessed, and not fall into deception by worshiping other gods. Unfortunately, God's people did not learn His ways from Him, and they suffered the consequences. Knowledge of God is important because, even God's people *perish for a lack of knowledge,* and even God's people can be *sent into exile for lack of understanding.* (see Hosea 4:6; Isaiah 5:13) This is why Jesus spent most of His time teaching God's people the Word and ways of God. (see Acts 1:1) During His earthly ministry, Jesus explained to His disciples as much as they were able to grasp and some things that they did not understand until later. Then, after the resurrection, He revealed the Scriptures to them as He had never before by teaching them about Himself using the Old Testament Scriptures.

> *{Luk 24:44-47}* 44 *He said to them, "This is what I told you while I was still with you:* **Everything must be fulfilled that is written about me in the Law of Moses, the Prophets and the Psalms.***"* 45 **Then he opened their minds so they could understand the Scriptures.** 46 *He told them, "This is what is written: The Messiah will suffer and rise from the dead on the third day,* 47 *and repentance for the forgiveness of sins will be preached in his name to all nations, beginning at Jerusalem.*

Then, Jesus commanded His disciples to go and make disciples by teaching the people all that they had learned from Him. (see Matthew 28:19-20) The *apostle's teaching* referred to in the Book of Acts was largely what we know of today as the New Testament. These letters to the early Church explain how Christ fulfilled the Old Testament Scriptures and include some practical counsel for living as His followers. Accordingly, each and every portion of the Scriptures, both in the Old Testament and New Testament, is relevant and significant for us to learn about God, His ways, and to know what Jesus has done for us. We learn so that we know Jesus for ourselves, and we learn so that we can teach others about Him. In the same way that we have to receive His love before we can love others the way He loves us, we need to learn from Him so that we can teach others what He has taught us.

In fact, the whole reason that Jesus Christ died for us is so that we may know God for ourselves through the indwelling Holy Spirit. The Holy Spirit is our Teacher, like Jesus is personally instructing us and giving us revelation in the Word and ways of God. The word *revelation* is *apokalypsis* from which we get the word *apocalypse*. When the Holy Spirit teaches us something from God's Word, it is like a mini apocalypse in our minds, which is forever seared on our hearts. Through the Holy Spirit, Jesus is still teaching His disciples as much as we can handle and some things that we won't understand until later. By the power of the Holy Spirit, who is the Spirit of truth, we study God's Word, which is the truth, so that, through our knowledge of God, we can receive the blessings that Christ has obtained for us and so that we do not fall into deception. (see 1 John 2:27) Therefore, let us not waste the privilege we have been given but be good *disciples, students, pupils,* and *learners* as we devote ourselves to the knowledge of God and our Lord Jesus Christ.

Communion

Lastly, in the Book of Acts, believers devoted themselves to Jesus and to one another through taking communion together. When Jesus taught His disciples how to partake of His Body, He broke the bread and handed it out to everyone present. When believers take communion together, we emulate Him in this. The expression *breaking bread* originated from this practice and, among Christ's first disciples, *breaking bread* was considered different than regular meals.

> *{Act 2:42, 46} 42 They devoted themselves to the apostles' teaching and to fellowship, to the* **breaking of bread** *and to prayer. ... 46 Every day they continued to meet together in the temple courts. They* **broke bread** *in their homes and ate together with glad and sincere hearts,*

> *{Act 20:7, 11} 7 On the first day of the week we came together to* **break bread***. Paul spoke to the people and, because he intended to leave the next day, kept on talking until midnight. ... 11 Then he went upstairs again and* **broke bread** *and ate. After talking until daylight, he left.*

After Jesus taught His disciples about communion on Passover night, they sang hymns together in praise to God. (see Matthew 26:30; Mark 14:26) In accordance with Jewish tradition, we can safely assume that they sang Psalms 113–118 which is called the great *Hallel*, or *praise*, from which we get the word *Hallelujah*. We have already covered communion in depth, but it is significant that communion is a sacred act of mutual devotion: Christ's devotion to us, our devotion to Him, and our covenant devotion to one another as His special, set apart people. The first believers knew that they were a new nation of priests who were totally devoted to the Lord Jesus Christ, and today we are no different. So, let us say, *Hallelujah!* in the same way that they did.

The Purpose of Devotion

The purpose of devotion is to worship God with our lives and the fruit of enduring devotion is spiritual maturity, or *Christlikeness*. Spiritual maturity is reflected by a life that is consecrated to God, a heart that is conformed to Jesus' heart, and works of the Holy Spirit for the building up of His Church.

> *{2Co 3:18} 18 And we all, who with unveiled faces contemplate the Lord's glory, **are being transformed into his image with ever-increasing glory**, which comes from the Lord, who is the Spirit.*

Let each of us press onwards in our devotion to Jesus and to His Body so that we may become like Him, receive everything that He died to give us, and accomplish all the works that He has prepared for us to do.

SELECTION OF NEW TESTAMENT PRAYERS	
Matthew 6:9-13	The Lord's prayer, aka the disciple's prayer because it is for us
Ephesians 3:14-21	To grow in comprehension of God's love for us in Christ
Colossians 1:9-14	To grow in the knowledge of God's will and then be able to do it
Philippians 1:9-11	To increase depth of insight and discernment
Ephesians 1:15-23	To increase revelation of our inheritance and authority in Christ

CHAPTER 13

Types & Shadows

History has a way of repeating itself, and there is nothing new under the sun. (see Ecclesiastes 1:9-10) But did you ever stop to consider that the One who wrote history may be speaking through it? In fact, the historical accounts that we see in the Old Testament Scriptures serve as shadows, types, and prophetic pictures of Jesus and God's plan of redemption through Christ. (see Colossians 2:17; Hebrews 8:5, 10:1; Romans 5:14; John 5:39) Jesus came the first time to fulfill these types and shadows and is coming again to finalize them and restore all things.

Stephen, a deacon of the church at Jerusalem, proclaimed the Gospel of Jesus Christ with miracles, signs, and wonders following. The Holy Spirit gave wisdom to Stephen that even the best trained religious scholars in the world could not refute, including Saul who later became the apostle Paul. For this, false accusers stirred up allegations against Stephen which were the same allegations made against Jesus, namely, blasphemy against the Temple and the Law of Moses. Jesus had been found guilty as a blasphemer and sentenced to death by crucifixion. When Stephen was brought before the same religious judiciary council to deliver his speech as a follower of Christ, they gnashed their teeth, covered their ears, found him guilty of blasphemy, and stoned him to death as the first Christian martyr. The whole scene was exceptionally reminiscent of how they had responded to Jesus. (see Matthew 26:57-68; Mark 14:53-65)

Interestingly, Stephen's speech to the Sanhedrin was about history repeating itself. What we're going to do in this chapter is use Stephen's speech as a guideline to dig into the Old Testament stories, highlighting certain significant aspects which are shadows, types, and prophetic pictures from Israel's history. Then, we'll tie those stories together by revealing Jesus as their fulfillment and what this means to us as His followers.

Abraham

Stephen's speech:

> *{Act 7:2-8} 2 To this he replied: "Brothers and fathers, listen to me!* **The God of glory appeared to our father Abraham while he was still in Mesopotamia,** *before he lived in Harran. 3* **'Leave your country and your people,'** *God said,* **'and go to the land I will show you.'** *4 "So he left the land of the Chaldeans and settled in Harran. After the death of his father, God sent him to this land where you are now living. 5* **He gave him no inheritance here, not even enough ground to set his foot on.** *But God promised him that he and his descendants after him would possess the land, even though* **at that time Abraham had no child.** *6 God spoke to him in this way:* **'For four hundred years your descendants will be strangers in a country not their own, and they will be enslaved and mistreated.** *7 But I will punish the nation they*

> *serve as slaves,' God said, 'and afterward they will come out of that country and*
> *worship me in this place.' 8 Then he **gave Abraham the covenant of circumcision**. And*
> *Abraham became the father of **Isaac** and circumcised him eight days after his birth. Later Isaac*
> *became the father of **Jacob**, and Jacob became the father of the **twelve patriarchs**.*

In a time when no one in the earth worshipped the one true God and mankind's relationship with God seemed totally doomed to failure and beyond repair, God appeared to a man named Abram and called him to a new life. God promised to give Abram a great name, to make him very fruitful by multiplying his descendants into a great nation, and to give him a land which we know of today as the land of Israel. Abram was a wealthy man who lived in Ur of the Chaldeans but God called upon him to leave Ur in faith believing that God would bless him with land of his own and with many descendants who would then bless the whole world. God gave Abram some general direction but, in truth, He didn't really tell Abram where he was going. God just said, essentially, *I'll tell you when you get there*. Abram was a normal guy and he had done nothing to deserve this type of favor from God because he worshipped the sun, moon, and stars just like every other Chaldean. Moreover, because Abram's wife, Sarai, was barren, from a human perspective, the whole thing looked ridiculously hopeless. Nevertheless, Abram believed God and went by faith toward Canaan, where God had told him to go, but he made a stop along the way in Haran. Abram settled for a while in Haran and set up life there which looked mostly like life in Ur except that he now worshiped the one true God instead of the sun, moon, and stars. After a while, God beckoned Abram again and he proceeded onwards to Canaan as God had originally instructed. Once Abram arrived in Canaan, he set up camp as a sojourner on someone else's land. God had told Abram, *I'll tell you when you get there*, and now God appeared to Abram again and said, *You're here*. Abram looked to the north, south, east, and west and believed that he and his descendants would inherit the land as a free gift from God. (see Genesis 12)

Several years later, Abram still had no son (or any offspring or descendants) through his barren wife, Sarai. However, God reassured Abram that he and Sarai would indeed have a son and Abram continued to believe God. This time, God entered into a blood covenant with Abram, reaffirming His solemn oath that Abram would have a whole nation of descendants through the promised son in addition to the promised land. At the same time, God spoke prophetically to Abram about what was to come before His promise was fulfilled. God told Abram that, in spite of His selection of Abram and his descendants and His promise to give them a land of their own, Abram's descendants would first suffer as strangers in another land as slaves. They would be abused and mistreated until the time came for their oppressors to be punished, at which point, God would deliver them. At the same time that this was happening, the sin and wickedness of the people occupying the land promised to Abram's descendants would accrue and escalate until God's mercy had reached its limit. Then, when it came to be time for God's vengeance to be executed upon the wickedness of the people occupying the promised land, God would send Abram's descendants to conquer them and take over their land. (see Genesis 15)

> {Gen 15:13-16} 13 Then the LORD said to him, "**Know for certain that for four hundred**
> **years your descendants will be strangers in a country not their own** and that **they will be**

> *enslaved and mistreated* there. 14 ***But I will punish the nation they serve as slaves***, *and afterward they will come out with great possessions. 15 You, however, will go to your ancestors in peace and be buried at a good old age. 16* ***In the fourth generation your descendants will come back here***, *for the sin of the Amorites has not yet reached its full measure."*

Alas, several more years passed, and Abram's situation looked more and more unpromising because he still had no child from his barren wife Sarai. Moreover, Abram was almost 100 years old and Sarai was 90 and had stopped menstruating. A child born to them at this point would be an absolute miracle. But, Abram continued to believe God. Then, God appeared to Abram again and, this time, He expanded His covenant promise to include a multitude of nations as Abram's descendants while reaffirming the bestowment of the promised land and promising to always be God to Abram's people. In this exchange, God changed Abram's name, which means *father*, to Abraham, which means *father of the multitude*, and He changed Sarai's name to Sarah, both of which mean *princess*. Without going into too much detail, in Hebrew, the change of both Abra*h*am and Sara*h*'s names to include what we see as the added *"h"* indicates that the *breath of life* had been added to both of them. At this time, God also required Abraham to symbolically agree to the terms of the covenant through another act of faith by circumcising himself and every male in his household for the rest of time. Circumcision was the sign of inclusion in this special set apart people of God, God's chosen people out of all mankind. (see Genesis 17)

Some more time passed (still no son) and God appeared to Abraham again. This time, He said that Sarah would have a son within a year. (see Genesis 18) God was faithful to His promise and, within that year, Sarah gave birth to Isaac, the one and only son of Abraham who would inherit the covenant promises of God. (see Genesis 21) As time passed, Isaac had a son named Jacob, and Jacob, whose name God changed to Israel, had twelve sons. Later on, when Sarah died, Abraham purchased a tomb from a Hittite who owned the land. The Hittite had offered to give it to him, but Abraham insisted on paying for it, even at a price which was set prohibitively high. A grave was the only piece of the promised land Abraham ever owned, and he bought it himself. (see Genesis 23) But, he still believed God.

For Abraham's complete story, see Genesis 11:27–25:11 and Hebrews 11:8-12, 17–19

Joseph

Stephen's speech continued:

> *{Act 7:9-16} 9 "Because the **patriarchs were jealous of Joseph, they sold him as a slave into Egypt. But God was with him** 10 **and rescued him from all his troubles**. He gave Joseph wisdom and enabled him to gain the goodwill of Pharaoh king of Egypt. So **Pharaoh made him ruler over Egypt and all his palace**. 11 "**Then a famine struck** all Egypt and Canaan, bringing great suffering, **and our ancestors could not find food**. 12 When Jacob heard that there was grain in Egypt, he sent our forefathers on their first visit. 13 **On their second visit, Joseph told his brothers who he was**, and Pharaoh learned about Joseph's family. 14 After this, **Joseph sent for his father Jacob and his whole family, seventy-five in all**. 15 Then Jacob went down to Egypt, where he and our ancestors died. 16 Their bodies were brought back to*

*Shechem and placed in **the tomb that Abraham had bought** from the sons of Hamor at Shechem for a certain sum of money.*

Joseph was his father Jacob's favorite child, and his brothers knew it and hated him for it. Then, God gave Joseph a prophetic dream about his brother's wheat sheaves bowing down to his wheat sheaf and another dream about the sun, moon, and eleven stars all bowing down to a single, more glorious, star. Joseph, and everyone else around, interpreted this to mean that Joseph was saying that, someday, his father, mother, and brothers would be subject to his authority and bowing down to him. Jacob, who was also called Israel, raised an eyebrow but took note of the dream whereas Joseph's brothers loathed him all the more for it and mocked him relentlessly. Then one day, Joseph's brothers plotted to kill him and tell their father, Jacob, that a wild animal had eaten him. But, they thought the better of it, so instead they threw him in a pit and then sold him as a slave for twenty pieces of silver to a band of traders passing by on their way to Egypt. Then, they spilled blood all over his clothes and brought his garments back to their father with the whole wild animal story. At the news of his favorite son's death, Jacob could not be comforted.

No matter what happened, God was with Joseph as he went through many trials as a slave in the land of Egypt. Joseph was even raised up to a position of authority over a powerful household but was then falsely accused and thrown into prison for a few years. Then, because of Joseph's God-given ability to interpret Pharaoh's dreams, Joseph was raised up to the position of second in command to Pharaoh himself, and the Pharaoh of Egypt was the most powerful man in the world in that day. God enabled Joseph to accurately predict a famine and execute a strategy which caused Egypt to be the only nation with any grain when the famine came. Meanwhile, when the famine hit the land of Canaan, Jacob commanded ten of Joseph's brothers to go to Egypt in order to buy grain for them all. They did not know anything about what had happened to Joseph and therefore, they did not recognize him when they bowed down to him as the one in the position of authority over all of the grain in Egypt. Of course, when they bowed down to Joseph, they fulfilled the dream that God had given Joseph all those years earlier. Joseph recognized them the first time but did not reveal who he was to them until the second time that they came. He insisted that all of his brothers be there and, when all eleven of them appeared before him, he revealed who he truly was. Then, Jacob and the twelve tribes of Israel all came down to live in Egypt as well. Joseph's entire family did bow down to him, and he showed them mercy and tender forgiveness.

Later on, after Jacob died, they all went back to the land of Canaan to bury their father in the tomb that Abraham had purchased, and then they all returned to their homes in Egypt again. The same tomb that Abram had purchased now contained the bodies of Sarah, Abraham, Isaac, Rebekah, and Jacob. Before Joseph died, he made his brothers promise to take his bones back to this tomb when the nation of Israel inherited the Promised Land from God because they all still wholeheartedly believed God's covenant promises to them as Abraham's descendants. Hundreds of years later when the nation of Israel left Egypt forever, they did faithfully carry Joseph's bones with them. (see Exodus 13:19) (Jewish tradition states that they carried all of Joseph's brother's bones, too.) Nevertheless, until this happened, a tomb was still the only piece of land owned by God's people.

For Joseph's complete story, see Genesis 37, 39–50 and Hebrews 11:22

Moses

Stephen's speech continued:

> *{Act 7:17-19} 17* **"As the time drew near for God to fulfill his promise** *to Abraham, the number of our people in Egypt had greatly increased. 18 Then* **'a new king,** *to whom Joseph meant nothing, came to power in Egypt.' 19 He* **dealt treacherously with our people and oppressed our ancestors** *by forcing them to* **throw out their newborn babies so that they would die.**

Just as God had told Abraham, his descendants were oppressed in a foreign land for four hundred years. Joseph and his brothers died, but their children and grandchildren continued to multiply and become powerful in Egypt until the Egyptians saw them as a threat and forced them into slave labor to keep them under control. Their slave drivers tried to crush their spirits with brutality and they were forced to build great cities in Egypt for Pharaoh. As time passed and God's appointed time for delivering His people drew near, the situation grew worse and worse. The people of Israel, God's chosen people, still believed the covenant promises of God, even though their circumstances were bleak at best. They groaned out to God in prayer.

Stephen's speech continued:

> *{Act 7:20-44} 20* **"At that time Moses was born,** *and he was* **no ordinary child.** *For three months he was cared for by his family. 21 When he was placed outside, Pharaoh's daughter took him and brought him up as her own son. 22 Moses was educated in all the wisdom of the Egyptians and was powerful in speech and action. 23 "When Moses was forty years old, he decided to visit his own people, the Israelites. 24 He saw one of them being mistreated by an Egyptian, so he went to his defense and* **avenged him** *by killing the Egyptian. 25* **Moses thought that his own people would realize that God was using him to rescue them, but they did not.** *26 The next day Moses came upon two Israelites who were fighting. He tried to reconcile them by saying,* **'Men, you are brothers;** *why do you want to hurt each other?' 27 "But the man who was mistreating the other pushed Moses aside and said,* **'Who made you ruler and judge over us? 28 Are you thinking of killing me as you killed the Egyptian yesterday?'** *29 When Moses heard this,* **he fled to Midian,** *where he settled as a foreigner and had two sons. 30 "After forty years had passed, an angel appeared to Moses in the flames of a burning bush in the desert near Mount Sinai. 31 When he saw this, he was amazed at the sight. As he went over to get a closer look, he heard the Lord say: 32 'I am the God of your fathers, the God of Abraham, Isaac and Jacob.' Moses trembled with fear and did not dare to look. 33 "Then the Lord said to him, 'Take off your sandals, for the place where you are standing is holy ground.* **34 I have indeed seen the oppression of my people in Egypt. I have heard their groaning and have come down to set them free. Now come, I will send you back to Egypt.'** *35* **"This is the same Moses they had rejected with the words, 'Who made you ruler and judge?'** *He was*

sent to be their ruler and deliverer by God himself, *through the angel who appeared to him in the bush.* 36 **He led them out of Egypt and performed wonders and signs** *in Egypt, at the Red Sea and for forty years in the wilderness.* 37 *"This is the Moses who told the Israelites,* **'God will raise up for you a prophet like me from your own people.'** 38 *He was in the assembly in the wilderness, with the angel who spoke to him on Mount Sinai, and with our ancestors; and he* **received living words to pass on to us.** 39 *"But our ancestors refused to obey him. Instead, they rejected him and in their hearts turned back to Egypt.* 40 *They told Aaron, 'Make us gods who will go before us. As for this fellow Moses who led us out of Egypt--we don't know what has happened to him!'* 41 **That was the time they made an idol in the form of a calf.** *They brought sacrifices to it and reveled in what their own hands had made.* 42 **But God turned away from them and gave them over to the worship of the sun, moon and stars.** *This agrees with what is written in the book of the prophets: " 'Did you bring me sacrifices and offerings forty years in the wilderness, people of Israel?* 43 *You have taken up the* **tabernacle of Molek and the star of your god Rephan, the idols you made to worship. Therefore I will send you into exile'** *beyond Babylon.* 44 *"Our ancestors had the* **tabernacle of the covenant law with them in the wilderness.** *It had been made as God directed Moses, according to the pattern he had seen.*

Moses was born at just the right time to be murdered at birth by the Egyptians because of their paranoid desire to suppress the Israelites. Fortunately, Moses wasn't killed at birth. Instead, he grew up in Pharaoh's palace with all the riches of Egypt and became very powerful. But somehow, he knew in his heart that God had chosen him to be the leader of the people of Israel at this very important time. He left Pharaoh's palace to be among his people, thinking that they would understand God's call on his life. But they didn't. When he avenged them, they perceived it as aggression and when he tried to make peace between them, they saw him as a busybody. They completely rejected him, and he fled to the wilderness to be a shepherd. Egyptians looked down on shepherds so much so that being a shepherd would have been the lowest, most despicable, and most shameful vocation of all. Moses was in a state of total disgrace.

Forty years later, God appeared to Moses in the burning bush because the time had come for Moses to fulfill God's call upon his life. God had seen and heard the suffering of His people, so He came down to send Moses to lead them. Moses tried to refuse God's calling and asked God how the people of Israel would know that God had sent him. God promised to confirm Moses with miracles, signs, and wonders so that the people of Israel would believe and follow him. God sent Moses to confront Pharaoh, demanding the release of God's people from slavery so that they could worship God freely in the wilderness and God was faithful to His promise of miraculous proof that He was with Moses. Then, Moses went on to lead the people of Israel out of Egyptian slavery, through the supernaturally parted waters of the Red Sea, and into the wilderness to worship God freely.

While they were in the wilderness, Moses went up on Mount Sinai to talk with God. Even though this was less than two months since God had walked the Israelites through a parted sea, they grew impatient waiting for Moses to return from his chat with God. They decided instead to have Moses' right hand man, Aaron, who was also Moses' brother, make a golden calf so that they could worship it as the god who had brought them out of Egypt. Additionally, they worshipped Molech, who was a Cannanite diety associated with child sacrifice, and Rephan, who was an Egyptian god, as well as other images, gods, and the work of their own hands. In fact, they degraded themselves to worshiping the sun, moon, and stars again, the very things which God had called their ancestor Abraham to stop worshipping. In general, their hearts had become worldly and they longed for Egypt more than they did for the Promised Land, even though they had been slaves there. Finally, Moses came down from the mountain and *put the kabash* on the whole thing.

Then, in spite of their egregious error, God's mercy prevailed and He gave them the design for His Tabernacle so that they could build it, and so that He could dwell with them as His people. For the next forty years in the wilderness, they resisted and rejected Moses' leadership with much grumbling, fickle hearts, and stubborn and stiff-necked refusal of God's ways of leading them. But Moses told them that, in the days to come, God would raise up a prophet like him whom they *must* listen to because He would speak the very words of God. Even though they often rejected and did not listen to Moses, anyone who did not listen to the prophet to come would be held to account by God Himself.

For Moses' complete story, see Exodus 1–Deuteronomy 34, Hebrews 11:23-29

The Time from Joshua to David

Stephen's speech continued:

> {Act 7:45-47} 45 *After receiving the tabernacle, our ancestors* **under Joshua brought it with them when they took the land from the nations God drove out before them**. *It remained in the land* **until the time of David**, 46 *who enjoyed God's favor and asked that he might* **provide a dwelling place for the God of Jacob**. 47 **But it was Solomon who built a house for him**.

After Moses died, Joshua took over as the leader of a whole new generation of Israelites. Once they crossed over the Jordan River into the land which God had promised to give to them as descendants of Abraham, the first thing that they did was to reaffirm their covenant agreement with God by mass-circumcising all the men of Israel. The place where they did this is called *Gilgal* which means *to roll* because, at this special time and through this act of faith, the reproach of their slavery in Egypt was *rolled away* forever. As Joshua stayed under God's guiding hand, seven enemy nations much larger and mightier than Israel were pushed back and conquered, bit by bit. However, the Israelites did not fully expel all of their enemies from the Promised Land, and these remaining enemies became a *thorn in their flesh*. (see Numbers 33:51-66; Joshua 23:13; Judges 2:3; Ezekiel 28:24; Micah 7:2-8)

For the next several hundred years, Israel waxed and waned in faithfulness to God. Then, Israel requested a king in order to be like other nations, and God granted them their request. God appointed Saul, a tall and handsome kingly looking guy who started out well as the leader of Israel but, under pressure, became more focused on protecting his image and authority than obeying God. Therefore, God anointed David to be King of Israel. David was a mighty warrior for God and His people, and Saul became so jealous of David that he went bonkers trying to kill him. So, David spent several years living in caves and hiding from Saul until Saul finally died. During Saul's life, David never attempted to kill Saul, even though he had several opportunities to do so. But after Saul died, David took his rightful position as God's anointed King of Israel.

Once David was reigning as king in Jerusalem, he longed in his heart to build a Temple for God. To this, God essentially said, *I've never complained about living in a tent, and I have never left My people.* God granted David victory and peace from all his enemies and an everlasting dynasty but denied him the right of building a Temple because David was a man of war and had shed too much blood. However, David's son, Solomon, whose very name means *peace*, would build God's Temple. By the end of David's life, all of the enemies of God's people in the Promised Land had been defeated because God had granted peace to His people under David's authority. At the same time, David had made all of the necessary preparations so that Solomon could build God's Temple. After David's death, Solomon built the glorious Temple of God in Jerusalem and became the most famous king in the whole world. He had unsurpassed wealth, majesty, and wisdom while kings and commoners from nations near and far came to honor him.

Joshua's complete story, see Joshua 1–24

For David's complete story, see 1 Samuel 16 – 1 Kings 1 and 1 Chronicles 10:1-29:30

For Solomon's complete story, see 1 Kings 1–11 and 2 Chronicles 1:1-9:31

The Tabernacle of Moses and the Temple of Solomon

Stephen's speech continued:

> {Act 7:48-50} 48 "However, **the Most High does not live in houses made by human hands.** As the prophet says: 49 " 'Heaven is my throne, and the earth is my footstool. **What kind of house will you build for me?** says the Lord. Or where will my resting place be? 50 Has not my hand made all these things?'

After God delivered the Israelites from their Egyptian oppressors by walking them through the parted waters of the Red Sea, He gave Moses instructions for building the Tabernacle, the place where His presence would dwell with His people. Once it was built in accordance with these intricate instructions, a flame was kept burning within the Tabernacle night and day as a symbol of God's presence, and God's glory filled the Tabernacle so that all Israel could see that God was with them as a cloud by day and a pillar of fire by night. (see Exodus 40:34-38) After God's glory filled the Tabernacle, no one, including Moses, was allowed to enter into the Most Holy Place where God's presence dwelt, or they would die. The only exception to this was the High Priest who could only enter the Most Holy Place once per year on the Day of Atonement. Then, on that day, the High Priest entered behind the veil to where the Ark of the Covenant and the mercy seat of God were, and this was only after certain ritual and blood sacrifices had been completed. If God approved of the High Priest's offering, then the people would be blessed but if not, then the High Priest would drop dead in God's presence and the people of Israel could anticipate a bad year.

Later, when Solomon built the Temple in Jerusalem, he followed the same exact pattern for the Temple which God had given to Moses for the Tabernacle, in addition to some further instructions that God had given to David for the Temple and the area surrounding it. (see 1 Chronicles 28:11-21) The requirements for the Most Holy Place and the High Priest remained intact. When Solomon dedicated the Temple to the Lord, the presence of God's glory filled the Temple so powerfully that the priests could not stay standing on their feet. (see 2 Chronicles 5:13)

For the pattern of the Tabernacle/Temple, see Exodus 25–30, 1 Kings 5–8, and 2 Chronicles 2–7

Jesus

The stories of Abraham, Joseph, Moses, David, Solomon, and the Temple were shadows pointing to Jesus and God's purposes for Him in the earth. Jesus fulfilled certain aspects of the stories that we just reviewed.

Like Abraham: In a time when no one in the earth truly worshipped God, God called upon Jesus. God promised to make Him fruitful and multiply His descendants in the earth, to give Him a great name, a great nation, a land of His own, and that all the nations of the earth would be blessed through Him. God called upon Jesus to leave everything He knew, including all the splendor and riches of heaven, in order to head towards the land which God had promised Him. He went by faith, trusting in God's promises. God promised Him offspring who would live by faith, but, there was a stop along the way called the Law. The Law, given to the people of Israel, created followers who looked mostly like everyone else in the world except that their God was the one true God. But this was not the full measure of what God had said. Jesus continued to believe God's promises even though the situation continued to look more and more hopeless. God required Jesus to symbolically agree to the terms of the New Covenant by spiritually circumcising Himself through death and resurrection which *rolled away* the old nature of man. A grave was the only piece of land on earth that Jesus ever occupied. All of His true followers, or members of His household, are included in His covenant when they are *circumcised* through faith in Christ and only those who are included in this covenant will receive the eternal Promised Land of the new heavens and the new earth. God had said to Jesus, *I'll tell you when you get there* and, after the resurrection, Jesus looked around knowing that, in due time, He and His followers would inherit eternal life on the new earth just as God promised. However, before this happens, Christ's followers will suffer and endure under the oppression of the world for many many years, until the sin of the world reaches a sufficient level for God's righteous vengeance. At that appointed time, Jesus will return to punish our oppressors and to judge the world and we who believe will live in our promised land with Jesus forevermore.

Like Joseph: Jesus, God's favorite and one and only Son, came to His brothers, the people of Israel, and told them that God had appointed Him to be their King. His brothers were jealous of Him and, therefore, they plotted to kill Him. They threw Him in a pit (called the grave) and sold Him into slavery (under the oppressive rule in the evil one's domain of the pit of hell.) But God was with Jesus and prospered Him in everything that He did. God raised Jesus up out of the prison of hell to the position of utmost authority over all creation, second only to God Himself. Jesus did not reveal Himself to all of His brothers the first time that they met with Him but the second time that He comes, He will have mercy on all true Jews who fear God. (see Romans 11:26) They will bow down to Jesus as their King, just as He knew all along, along with everyone else destined for eternal life.

Like Moses: When the appointed time drew near for the Messiah and deliverer of God's people to be born, the harsh oppression of the world grew worse and worse. Jesus was born at just the right time to be murdered by world rulers who were fearful of the arrival of the promised King of Israel but, fortunately, He was not killed then. With all of His heart, Jesus knew that He was God's chosen Savior of His people, who should have understood who He was, but they didn't. He was there to avenge them and put them back in right standing with God, but they took it as aggression against them. He called them to a standard of love and peace, but they called Him a drunkard and a heretic. They completely rejected Him and crucified Him with a criminal's death, the lowest form of shame and disgrace, and sent Him to the barren wilderness of the grave. But God called Jesus out of the grave through resurrection, the greatest sign and wonder of all time which confirmed that God had sent Him as their Savior who delivered everyone who believes out of bondage forever.

Like Moses: Jesus had all the riches of heaven but gave them up to come to the world in order to save His people. When the time came for His ministry to take place in the earth, God demonstrated that Jesus was the Messiah through miracles, signs, and wonders so that people would believe Him and follow Him. Jesus leads His people out of slavery through the waters of baptism (like the Red Sea) so that we can worship God freely while we are still here on this wilderness called the earth. While Jesus is ascended in the heavens and in the throne room of God, some people will grow impatient waiting for Him to return and will even let their hearts go astray to other gods, saying that those gods are the ones who delivered them from bondage. Others will become rebellious and turn their hearts back to worldly ways, longing more for worldly promises (even though they were slaves to them) than for the promise of heaven. Between now and when Jesus returns, many resist and reject Jesus' leadership with much grumbling, fickle hearts, and stubborn and stiff-necked refusal of God's ways of leading them. This said, Jesus IS the prophet like Moses who spoke the very words of God and, at the appointed time, God will hold everyone accountable who has not listened to Him.

Like the time from Joshua to David: Ever since Jesus ascended into heaven as the first of the resurrection to reach the eternal Promised Land, God has been pushing back Jesus' enemies, bit by bit, making them a footstool under His feet. When the stone of His grave was *rolled away*, Jesus rolled away the reproach of sin, death, and the world forever. However, Jesus' enemies have not been fully expelled from this world and have been a *thorn in the flesh* to believers who are still here on the earth. (see 2 Corinthians 12:7) But, He will return to Jerusalem as a mighty warrior of vengeance and God will grant Him peace from all of His enemies, the last enemy being death. (see 1 Corinthians 15:26)

Like David: The God-appointed religious leaders of Jesus' day made a good show of piety but had become more focused on protecting their image and authority than obeying God. This said, they were still technically in charge, so Jesus honored their God-given authority in spite of the fact that He was God's Anointed One. The religious leaders became so jealous of Jesus that they went bonkers and killed him.

Jesus spent three days in a cave called the grave before emerging again as the true and rightful King of Israel, having defeated all of the enemies of mankind. God granted Jesus peace from His enemies and an everlasting dynasty but Jesus was not yet allowed to stay and dwell forever with His people, which is the desire of His heart. This will happen when He returns.

Like Solomon: After the final enemy of mankind (death) has been conquered once and for all through believer's resurrection from the dead, a new Jerusalem will be established on a new earth which has not seen any war. The Lord will dwell among His people as the one and only King and Lord with unsurpassed wealth, majesty, and wisdom. Everyone on earth, near and far, will come to worship and adore Him. (see Revelation 21)

Like the Temple: The true and eternal Tabernacle, Most Holy Place, and throne room of God are in Heaven. Since Adam's wrong tree incident, no man has been able to enter into or access God's presence. But Jesus, our great High Priest, offered a sufficient unblemished sacrifice and sprinkled the heavenly tabernacle with His own blood, and God accepted our High Priest's offering. Therefore, by grace through faith, we who believe Jesus can enter into God's presence and access all of His blessings for our lives. (see Hebrews 9–10) Moreover, when the new heavens and the new earth will come, we who believe Jesus will dwell forever in the new Jerusalem which has no Temple because we will access God as freely as Adam and his wife did. Then, God's glory will fill the whole earth, and everyone will joyfully worship Him for eternity in a time of unsurpassed peace.

Like the Temple: Jesus' physical body on earth carried the New Covenant in the same way that the Tabernacle/Temple contained the Ark of the Old Covenant. (see John 1:14) Jesus carried the glory of God, and the fire of the Holy Spirit dwelt in His inmost being as He, God Himself, dwelt among men as *Emmanuel*, which means *God with us*. (see Isaiah 7:14; Matthew 1:23) When Jesus said to the religious leaders that they would *destroy this temple* and that He would raise it in three days, He meant His own body. (see John 2:19-22) In fact, when the Roman soldiers came to arrest Jesus on the night of His crucifixion, the glory of God was emanating so powerfully from Him that the soldiers could not stay standing on their feet. (see John 18:6) Now that the Holy Spirit has been poured out, God's Temple is being built in the hearts of everyone who believes that Jesus is Lord.

Like Moses/the Tabernacle: God sent Jesus to confront the *prince of this world*, who is the devil, demanding the release of God's people from slavery to sin and death so that we can worship God freely. We, the Church, *are* the Tabernacle of God where His presence dwells in us through faith in Jesus Christ. (see 1 Corinthians 3:16) We are the house of God, being built together according to His exact specifications. He fills our hearts with the fire of the Holy Spirit and His glory dwells among us for all to see that He is with us.

The Evil Farmers

In spite of all the apparent déjà vu and the fact that Jesus fulfilled the symbols, types, and prophetic pictures pertaining to the Messiah of Israel throughout the Scriptures, the religious leaders rejected Him. Jesus knew that this was going to happen and, during His life, He told a parable about a vineyard which was rented to certain farmers who rejected all of the servants sent by the owner in attempts to take over the vineyard for themselves.

> *{Luk 20:9-19} 9 He went on to tell the people this parable:* "A man planted a vineyard, **rented it to some farmers and went away for a long time.** *10 At harvest time he* **sent a servant** *to the tenants so they would give him some of the* **fruit of the vineyard.** *But the tenants* **beat him and sent him away empty-handed.** *11 He* **sent another servant,** *but that one also they* **beat and treated shamefully and sent away empty-handed.** *12 He* **sent still a third,** *and they* **wounded him and threw him out.** *13* "Then the owner of the vineyard said, 'What shall I do? **I will send my son, whom I love; perhaps they will respect him.'** *14* "But when the tenants saw him, they talked the matter over. 'This is the heir,' they said. **'Let's kill him, and the inheritance will be ours.'** *15 So they* **threw him out of the vineyard and killed him.** "What then will the owner of the vineyard do to them? *16 He will come and kill those tenants and* **give the vineyard to others."** *When the people heard this, they said, "God forbid!" 17 Jesus looked directly at them and asked, "Then what is the meaning of that which is written:* " **'The stone the builders rejected has become the cornerstone'?** *18* **Everyone who falls on that stone will be broken to pieces; anyone on whom it falls will be crushed."** *19 The teachers of the law and the chief priests looked for a way to arrest him immediately, because they knew he had spoken this parable against them. But they were afraid of the people. (see also Matthew 21:33-46; Mark 12:1-12)*

Through Stephen's speech, he addressed literally what Jesus had spoken of figuratively through this parable. Stephen covered the history of Israel from the call of Abram out of Ur, to Israel's jealous rejection of Joseph, their rebellion against Moses, their many years of incomplete obedience and compromise with worldliness, their demand for human leadership in order to blend in with the nations of the world, and how even David had been loathed for being God's anointed one. Moreover, Stephen's speech did not include the many years of Israel's history when God sent prophets whom the leaders of Israel had persecuted and executed for speaking God's truth. Jesus knew that these *farmers* and *builders* were about to kill Him, just as their ancestors had done to God's messengers before Him, and with even more vehemence because the eternal inheritance was on the line since He was God's one and only Son. Indeed, after Jesus told this parable, the religious leaders knew that they had to kill Him because the parable was against them. And, eventually, they did exactly as He had said.

Stephen

Stephen, after tying together all the pieces of Israel's history, made it clear in no uncertain terms that these leaders of Israel had killed their King and the very Son of God in the same way that their ancestors had resisted and rejected God's chosen servants and messengers throughout their history. But the religious leaders didn't want to hear it.

> *{Act 7:51-60} 51* "**You stiff-necked people!** *Your hearts and ears are still uncircumcised.* **You are just like your ancestors: You always resist the Holy Spirit!** *52 Was there ever a*

*prophet your ancestors did not persecute? They even killed those who predicted the coming of the Righteous One. **And now you have betrayed and murdered him [Jesus]**-- 53 you who have received the law that was given through angels but have not obeyed it."   54 **When the members of the Sanhedrin heard this, they were furious and gnashed their teeth at him.** 55 But Stephen, full of the Holy Spirit, looked up to heaven and saw the glory of God, and Jesus standing at the right hand of God. 56 **"Look," he said, "I see heaven open and the Son of Man standing at the right hand of God."** 57 At this **they covered their ears and, yelling at the top of their voices, they all rushed at him,** 58 **dragged him out of the city and began to stone him.** Meanwhile, the witnesses laid their coats at the feet of a young man named Saul. 59 While they were stoning him, Stephen prayed, "Lord Jesus, receive my spirit." 60 Then he fell on his knees and cried out, "Lord, do not hold this sin against them." When he had said this, he fell asleep.*

In response to Stephen's speech, the religious leaders covered their ears, gnashed their teeth and proceeded to stone Stephen to death. However, Stephen looked up to the heavens and saw Jesus *standing at the right hand of God*. Jesus' place at God's right hand was something which had previously sent the religious leaders over the edge because it was an unquestionable and absolute assertion of Jesus' deity and God-given authority as His Son. (see Matthew 26:64; Mark 14:62; Luke 22:69) Notably, Stephen said that he saw Jesus *standing at the right hand of God*, not sitting. There is no definite reason given for this difference and, in spite of this phrase being quoted often throughout the New Testament, nowhere else is Jesus standing rather than sitting. What we do know is that Jesus was looking for *farmers* who would produce the proper fruit. Spiritually speaking, fruit is character in keeping with devotion to God through faith in Jesus Christ, a heart fixed on heaven and eternal rewards over temporal earthly things, and standing in His righteousness through faith even unto death. Stephen's unswerving devotion, empowered by the Holy Spirit, proved that a Christ follower had produced the proper fruit of righteousness through faith. Perhaps, Jesus was standing until this happened. Perhaps, Jesus was standing to receive His first martyr home to heaven with open arms. No matter why Jesus was standing, we do know that Stephen and all of Christ's martyrs since him are in heaven with Him asking the Lord, *How long until you avenge my blood?* (see Revelation 6:10) and, someday soon, He will.

The Promised Son

These historical accounts have been entirely centered on the Jewish people because, ever since the call of Abram and because of God's original covenant with him, they are special to God as Abraham's descendants. The people of Israel are still God's chosen people and are loved by Him. (see Romans 11:28) Their relationship with God has not always been pretty, but this is not because of any unfaithfulness on God's part. However, before we go trouncing on the Jewish people for their errors, let us be diligently aware that, as God's chosen people, Israel's relationship with God is a display for all the world to see. God is speaking through their history and through His relationship with them. In fact, Israel's history reflects not only their own faulted faithfulness towards God but is itself a shadow, type, and prophetic picture of the faithlessness of all of mankind towards God in spite of God's great mercy towards us. The Jewish people are chosen by God but not always choosing Him. Couldn't the same be said of all of us?

Like Abraham: Way back in the beginning, when no one on the earth worshipped the one true God because Adam and his wife had eaten from the wrong tree, God promised that a Son would be born who would crush the head of the serpent forever. (see Genesis 3:15) Years and years went by and, still no son, the situation looked more and more hopeless. Then, God promised that this righteous Son would come through the nation of Israel, His chosen people, even though the people were barren of their own righteousness. More years continued to pass without a Son, but God continued to reaffirm His covenant that His promised Son would be born through Israel who, like a barren wife, was still totally unable to produce righteous followers who lived by faith. As the time came for the Son to be born, a forerunner named John the Baptist was sent by God to announce that the Son was coming soon. Finally, as God had promised, Jesus was born by the power of a miraculous conception. God changed the name of His offering a relationship with Him from *Israel*, which means *strives with God*, to *Jesus*, which means *God is salvation*. God breathed the breath of life into Jesus when He was born again out of death and God breathed the breath of life into Christ's offspring by pouring out the Holy Spirit. God's covenant of righteousness was expanded from being exclusively one nation of people to including a multitude from all nations, available to everyone who believes Jesus and receives His righteousness through faith.

Since our first ancestor Adam, we have all been guilty of resisting the Holy Spirit, covering our ears, and hardening our hearts to a personal relationship with God. We are all barren of any ability to produce our own righteousness, and we are all guilty of crucifying the Messenger whom God sent to save us. We all want the eternal inheritance for ourselves, and we all try to sidestep God's appointed way of attaining it by worshipping other gods, primarily because we find God to be offensive and His ways to be unpalatable. Therefore, just as Stephen revealed Israel's long history of resisting God, let us examine our own personal history. Are we resisting God and repeating the errors of the past, or are we receiving the free gift offered to us through God's promised Son? Are we abusing the fact that God has chosen us as His people by living selfishly, or are we living with top priority placed on God's eternal purposes? Are we the ones standing in the truth of Christ, or are we the ones throwing stones?

CHAPTER 14
My Witnesses

After Stephen's speech, a great wave of persecution against Christians broke out and believers were scattered out of Jerusalem. (see Acts 8:1) From this point forward, Christianity spread like wildfire and was on its way to the ends of the earth. Everywhere Christ followers went, they preached the Gospel of the Kingdom of God and changed the world. Christians were witnesses of what God had done through the resurrection of Jesus Christ, and they testified about Jesus so that everyone who would listen and believe could be saved. Some people believed them, and their lives were changed forever. Others did not believe, and riots broke out. Regardless of how they were received, Christ followers kept on witnessing. Let's examine the example set for us by the believers in the Book of Acts so that we are empowered as Christ's witnesses today.

You Will Be My Witnesses

Every single one of the first 120 believers in Jerusalem was someone whose life had been dramatically changed by Jesus Christ. This group contained ordinary fishermen who had walked with Jesus while He performed miracles, men and women whom Christ had healed from sickness and freed from demonic oppression, Jesus' mother Mary, who still remembered Jesus' divine conception by the power of the Holy Spirit, Jesus' half-brothers who had not previously believed that Jesus was the Christ, and other disciples who had seen and heard the resurrected Jesus with their own eyes and ears. (see Acts 1:13-15, 2:1, 10:41)

> *{Luk 24:46-48} 46 He told them, "This is what is written: The Messiah will suffer and rise from the dead on the third day, 47 **and repentance for the forgiveness of sins will be preached in his name to all nations, beginning at Jerusalem**. 48 **You are witnesses of these things**.*

> *{1Co 15:3-7} 3 For what I received I passed on to you as of first importance: that Christ died for our sins according to the Scriptures, 4 that he was buried, that he was raised on the third day according to the Scriptures, 5 **and that he appeared to Cephas, and then to the Twelve. 6 After that, he appeared to more than five hundred of the brothers and sisters at the same time, most of whom are still living, though some have fallen asleep.** [died] 7 **Then he appeared to James, then to all the apostles**,*

These believers could not return to life as usual after the resurrection of Christ and their purpose in life was permanently altered. Their short-term instructions from King Jesus were to go to Jerusalem and wait for the Holy Spirit. (see Acts 1:4-5) Jesus' last words on earth before ascending to heaven were:

> *{Act 1:8} 8 But you will receive power when the Holy Spirit comes on you; **and you will be my witnesses in Jerusalem, and in all Judea and Samaria, and to the ends of the earth**."*

In a legal sense, a *witness* is *one who affirms what they have seen, heard, or experienced*. In a court of Law, a *witness* testifies for or against someone or something based on what they know about that person or situation. Additionally, as we learned in a prior chapter, the word for *witness* can also be translated as *martyr*. The Book of Hebrews, chapter 11 lists God's faithful *witnesses* throughout history, including men and women who took God at His Word and lived lives which demonstrated what they believed about God and all that He had promised them. Many of them had great victories on earth while they were still alive, and many of them suffered hardship, persecution, and martyrdom because people would not receive their message. Interestingly, the final person on the list of God's witnesses is Jesus. (see Hebrew 12:1-2) Jesus left His home in heaven as God's witness in order to testify about what He had seen, heard, and experienced of the Kingdom of God and the love of His heavenly Father. He suffered a martyr's death at the hands of men because He would not deny what He believed so that we could be saved. Now, by sending His followers out as His witnesses, disciples everywhere are commissioned to go and do as He did so that everyone can believe and be saved.

This said, not everyone will receive the Gospel message. During His ministry years, when Jesus sent His disciples to testify about Him, He told them to *shake the dust off of their feet* when people rejected the message of the Kingdom of God. Historically, when a Jew left a Gentile town or city, they would *shake the dust off their feet* and their clothing to symbolically demonstrate how they were separating themselves from the error of the Gentile's worldly ways. Similarly, after giving people ample time to hear the Gospel and receive salvation through faith in Jesus, Christ's disciples would *shake the dust off of their feet* in order to visibly express the rejecter's error. This was a very serious matter, denoting eternal damnation due to their rejection of Christ. This was not taken lightly because, as ambassadors of Jesus, who came not to judge but to save, the foremost objective of witnessing is washing people's feet of the dust of this world, not shaking dust back at them. (see John 13:1-20)

> {Mat 10:14-15} 14 **If anyone will not welcome you or listen to your words**, *leave that home or town and* **shake the dust off your feet**. *15 Truly I tell you,* **it will be more bearable for Sodom and Gomorrah on the day of judgment** *than for that town. (see also Mark 6:10-11; Luke 9:5)*

Witnessing is the primary theme of the Book of Acts from start to finish. From the first 120 believers on the day of Pentecost to the people of Rome whom Paul taught while under house arrest, Acts is a chronology of how Christianity spread throughout the known world in that day. Starting on the day of Pentecost, Peter testified to onlookers from every nation under heaven that Jesus is the Messiah of Israel and 3,000 people believed and were baptized into the faith. After that, more and more people continued to believe the Gospel and become witnesses for Christ. (see Acts 2:14-47)

> {Act 2:47b} 47b And **the Lord added to their number daily** *those who were being saved.*

Shortly after that, onlookers at the Temple were eyewitnesses to Peter and John healing a man who had been lame since birth by the power of the name of Jesus, and the number of believers totaled 5,000 men, not including women and children. However, the religious officials became incensed by their preaching and put them in prison. They were released from prison with a strict warning not to preach in the name of Jesus anymore, but they refused to obey this order. (see Acts 3:1-4:4)

> *{Act 4:19-20} 19 But Peter and John replied, "Which is right in God's eyes: to listen to you, or to him? You be the judges! 20 As for us, **we cannot help speaking about what we have seen and heard**."*

Later, as more and more people were placing their faith in Jesus, the apostles were arrested and imprisoned for testifying about Jesus and performing miracles in His name, but an angel released them and told them to keep witnessing. When the religious authorities warned them against testifying for Christ, they refused to submit. (see Acts 5:12-42)

> *{Act 5:19-20} 19 But during the night an angel of the Lord opened the doors of the jail and brought them out. 20 "**Go, stand in the temple courts**," he said, "**and tell the people all about this new life**."*

> *{Act 5:30-32} 30 **The God of our ancestors raised Jesus from the dead**--whom you killed by hanging him on a cross. 31 God exalted him to his own right hand as Prince and Savior that he might bring Israel to repentance and forgive their sins. 32 **We are witnesses of these things**, and so is the Holy Spirit, whom God has given to those who obey him."*

> *{Act 6:7} 7 **So the word of God spread. The number of disciples in Jerusalem increased rapidly**, and a large number of priests became obedient to the faith.*

Not too long after that, Stephen gave his speech and became the first Christian martyr. This was followed by the great persecution that scattered believers out of Jerusalem and onwards into Judea and Samaria and to the uttermost ends of the earth. Because of this, Philip the evangelist went to Samaria and preached the Gospel of Jesus Christ to people who received the message with great joy. Peter and John also traveled to Samaria and stopped in various towns along the way, witnessing for Christ. (see Acts 8:4-25) On his way towards Gaza, Philip used the Scriptures to teach an Ethiopian about Jesus, and the man believed, was baptized, and went back to his home country to share the Gospel. After that, Philip was supernaturally transported to Azotus and continued to proclaim the Kingdom of God. (see Acts 8:26-40) Paul, after his dramatic conversion, immediately began to testify in Damascus that Jesus is the Messiah of Israel and shocked onlookers who couldn't believe that he had become a Christ follower. (see Acts 9:20-25) Then, Peter was led by the Holy Spirit to go to Caesarea and proclaim the Gospel to Cornelius and his family who believed the message of Jesus and received the Holy Spirit and eternal life. (see Acts 9:32-10:48)

> *{Act 11:18} 18 When they heard this, they had no further objections and praised God, saying, "So then, **even to Gentiles God has granted repentance that leads to life**."*

Believers who had been scattered by the persecution in Jerusalem preached the Word of God to Jews and Gentiles everywhere that they went and churches began to be formed and established. Barnabas was sent by the Jerusalem church to Antioch to encourage the believers there, and even more people came to know

Jesus as Lord. He fetched Paul to help him teach the new believers and they taught together for about a year so that everyone's faith was strengthened. (see Acts 11:19-26) Back in Jerusalem, James the brother of John was martyred for his faith, and Peter was thrown in prison for being a Christ follower but, after an angel released Peter from prison, he continued to preach the Gospel wherever he went. (see Acts 12:1-19) When the Church at Antioch sent Paul and Barnabas to Jerusalem with a love offering because of a prophetic word that had predicted a famine, many new believers put their faith in Jesus. (see Acts 12:24-25)

> *{Act 12:24} 24 But the **word of God continued to spread and flourish**.*

On Paul's first missionary journey, he was accompanied by Barnabas and John Mark, and he traveled around the regions of Syria, Cyprus, Lycia, Galatia, and people were converted to Christianity in every town that they visited. However, persecution drove them out of Pisidian Antioch, and they *shook the dust off of their feet*. They fled out of Iconium due to the plots against their lives after they witnessed for Jesus and performed signs and wonders in His name. A riot broke out in Lystra after Paul and Barnabas refused to be worshiped as gods, and then persecutors from other towns persuaded the crowd to stone Paul until they thought he was dead. After that, they went to Derbe and made many disciples of Christ there. Upon their return to Antioch, they told all the believers who had sent them on their journey about all that God had done through their witnessing and how the Gentiles were unquestionably included in the faith. (see Acts 13:1-14:28)

> *{Act 13:48-49} 48 When the Gentiles heard this, they were glad and honored the word of the Lord; and **all who were appointed for eternal life believed**. 49 **The word of the Lord spread through the whole region**.*

After the Jerusalem Council and a sharp disagreement between Paul and Barnabas, Barnabas and John Mark went to witness for Christ in Cyprus. Paul, Silas, Timothy, and Luke (the author of the Book of Luke and the Book of Acts) went to revisit the churches in Galatia and traveled through Asia (which we know of today as Turkey), Macedonia, Achaia, and Palestine, testifying of Jesus everywhere that they went, and the churches grew in number. Then, the Lord spoke to Paul in a vision of a Macedonian man pleading for them to come preach the Gospel to them, so they set their course according to the direction of the Lord. In Philippi, the Lord opened the heart of an influential woman named Lydia, and she believed and was baptized, along with all of her household. A commotion was stirred after Paul expelled an evil fortunetelling spirit out of a girl whose owners were profiting from her oppression. Paul and Silas were mobbed, beaten, and thrown in prison. But an earthquake broke off their prison shackles which created the opportunity for them to testify about Jesus to their jailer. (see Acts 15:36-16:40)

> *{Act 16:31} 31 They replied, "**Believe in the Lord Jesus, and you will be saved--you and your household**."*

Later, another riot broke out in Thessalonica after they preached about King Jesus and were accused of treason against Caesar. They paid bond to the city council and were released. The people of Berea were more open-minded and studied the Scriptures to confirm or deny what Paul and his team were teaching about Jesus. But then, troublemakers plotted against Paul, and he hurried out of town. Paul witnessed for Christ to philosophers in Athens, and some of them received his message with curiosity while others laughed at him. Paul went on to Corinth where Jews at the synagogue opposed and insulted him for testifying that Jesus is the Messiah, so he *shook the dust off of his feet*. However, the Lord wanted Paul to stay in Corinth and continue to proclaim the Gospel there. (see Acts 17:1-18:8)

> *{Act 18:9-10} 9 One night the Lord spoke to Paul in a vision:* "**Do not be afraid; keep on speaking, do not be silent**. *10 For I am with you, and no one is going to attack and harm you, because* **I have many people in this city**."

Paul stayed in Corinth for about a year and a half and the religious people persisted in starting an uprising against him by accusing him of teaching contrary forms of worship. Fortunately, the governor of Corinth didn't want to hear about the accusations and threw them all out of court. Paul then went to Ephesus where they received the message of Jesus gladly and asked him to come back, which he promised to do if the Lord allowed. (see Acts 18:11-23) Around this time, because of all the disturbances that were erupting in various cities, Roman Emperor Claudius issued a decree in 49AD that evicted all Jews out of Rome. He knew that the various riots had started in his territories because of a man claiming to be the King of the Jews named *Chrestus*. Most historians believe that this was a mispronunciation of *Christos,* the Greek word for *Christ*. To prevent a similar riot from breaking out in Rome, he banned Jews from the city. Due to this, Priscilla and Aquila moved to Ephesus, became Christians (if they had not yet believed) and partnered up with the apostle Paul. They would never have moved to Ephesus if they had not been ordered out of their homes by the change in Roman law. This beautifully proved that nothing could stop the spreading of the Gospel to those who would believe, no matter how things changed in the world or its laws. (see Acts 18:1-2) While they were in Ephesus, a disciple named Apollos taught about Jesus but needed some further instruction to teach more accurately. Priscilla and Aquila taught Apollos about Jesus more accurately and then he went on his own missionary journeys to preach the Gospel in Athens and Corinth. (see Acts 18:24-19:1)

> *{Act 18:27-28} 27 When Apollos wanted to go to Achaia, the brothers and sisters encouraged him and wrote to the disciples there to welcome him. When he arrived, he was a great help* **to those who by grace had believed**. *28 For he vigorously refuted his Jewish opponents in public debate,* **proving from the Scriptures that Jesus was the Messiah**.

After a short visit to Jerusalem and regrouping in Antioch, Paul, Timothy, Erastus, and Luke set out on Paul's third missionary journey. They first returned to Ephesus (as Paul had promised if the Lord allowed) and instructed them in the Scriptures for about two years. While he was there, some unbelieving exorcists tried to use the name of Jesus without believing in Him for themselves and were beaten up by the demon that they were attempting to expel. Consequently, a great wave of repentance came upon the people of Ephesus, and they put their faith in the Lord Jesus Christ. After this, a riot broke out when an Ephesian merchant stirred up trouble because his idol making business was dried up due to people's repentance from false spirituality. (see Acts 19:2-21:14)

{Act 19:20} 20 *In this way **the word of the Lord spread widely and grew in power**.*

After that, Paul and his team continued to travel to the churches to encourage them in the faith as he set his course towards Jerusalem in spite of prophetic warnings about the suffering that awaited him. When he arrived in Jerusalem, Paul was falsely accused of blaspheming against the Temple of God and the Law of Moses. The whole city was thrown into an uproar and Paul used this opportunity to give his personal testimony to the crowd, which threw them into even greater pandemonium and caused them to demand Paul's execution. Paul then appeared before the religious leaders who became so violent that the Roman soldiers knew Paul would be safer in prison. Then, the Lord encouraged Paul as His faithful witness. (see Acts 19:15-23:22)

{Act 23:11} 11 *The following night the Lord stood near Paul and said, "**Take courage! As you have testified about me in Jerusalem, so you must also testify in Rome.**"*

Paul was then sent to Caesarea to appear before Governor Felix and testified about Jesus Christ, the resurrection from the dead, and holy living. Felix became uncomfortable and stopped Paul from speaking any further. After two years in prison, Paul witnessed for Christ to the new Governor, Festus, and King Agrippa who was passing through town. Paul shared his personal testimony and taught about how Jesus fulfilled the Scriptures pointing to the Messiah of Israel. Festus thought Paul had lost his mind, and Agrippa cynically disbelieved the Gospel message. Nevertheless, Paul had appealed to Caesar and, therefore, journeyed onward to Rome as a prisoner. On his way, his ship wrecked on the island of Malta, and he had the opportunity to preach the Gospel there. The people of Malta thought that he was a god because he did not die after being bitten by a poisonous snake but Paul told them about Jesus and healed the sick of their diseases in Jesus' name. Finally, Paul arrived in Rome and was placed under house arrest. He invited the Jewish leaders in town to visit him so that he could testify to them about Jesus as the Christ. They were curious about Christianity because they had heard that it was being denounced all over the Roman Empire. (see Acts 28:22) Paul testified to them from the Scriptures about the Kingdom of God and some were persuaded while others did not believe. For the next two years, he continued to witness for Christ to anyone and everyone who came to visit him while he was still under house arrest. (see Acts 23:23-28:31)

This is how the Book of Acts concludes, even though Christ's faithful witnesses have never stopped testifying about God's grace through faith in Jesus.

Teach, Preach, Testify

Throughout the Book of Acts, the Gospel message was shared in various ways depending on who was speaking and who was listening. Believers everywhere testified about the resurrection of Jesus Christ as their main point and as the foundational truth of the Christian faith. (see Acts 2:24, 3:15, 4:2, 10, 5:30, 10:40, 13:30, 17:31, 23:6)

{Act 2:32} 32 ***God has raised this Jesus to life, and we are all witnesses of it.***

Primarily, the word of Christ was communicated by *teaching* from the Scriptures, *preaching* the good news, and *testifying* of personal encounters with Jesus. Simply put, *teaching* is instruction from the Scriptures in the knowledge of God through Jesus Christ, *preaching* is sharing the good news of Christ's salvation, and *testifying* is sharing a personal story of the transformative power of the Gospel of Jesus Christ. By the power of the Holy Spirit, believers in the Book of Acts tailored their message as Christ's witnesses everywhere that they went, sharing the Gospel with Jews, who typically wanted evidence from the Scriptures or a miraculous sign as proof of God's power, and Gentiles who mostly sought after wisdom and higher understanding so that their lives could be improved. (see 1 Corinthians 1:22)

Peter *preached* to Jews from the Scriptures and to Gentiles referencing the work of Jesus' ministry on earth, which we have already covered in depth. (see Acts 2, 3, 10) Stephen addressed Jews by *teaching* them from the Scriptures about the signs pointing to Christ as the Messiah, which we have also already discussed. (see Acts 7) Philip the evangelist *preached* the Kingdom of God to Samaritans and *taught* an Ethiopian from the Scriptures. (see Acts 8) Believers scattered by the persecution in Jerusalem *preached* the Gospel wherever they went. Priscilla and Aquila were *taught* by Paul and then *taught* Apollos who went on to *preach* and *teach* powerfully for the Lord Jesus, refuting the Jews from the Scriptures. (see Acts 18) The apostle Paul *taught* from the Scriptures, *preached* the Gospel of salvation, and *testified* to kings and commoners alike.

As an example of Paul's *teaching*, in Pisidian Antioch, after the customary Scripture reading in the synagogue, Paul taught from the Scriptures that Jesus is the Christ. His discourse was largely similar to the speeches given by Peter and Stephen when they addressed a mostly Jewish audience. Like Peter, Paul explained that Jesus is the promised Messiah through the line of David, and he emphasized the resurrection from the dead as his main point and pivotal truth. Like Stephen, Paul reminded Jews of their history, warning them not to be like their ancestors who had rejected Jesus as the Christ.

> {Act 13:16-41} 16 *Standing up, Paul motioned with his hand and said: "Fellow Israelites and you Gentiles who worship God, listen to me! 17* **The God of the people of Israel chose our ancestors**; *he made the people prosper during their stay in Egypt; with mighty power he led them out of that country; 18 for about forty years he endured their conduct in the wilderness; 19 and he overthrew seven nations in Canaan, giving their land to his people as their inheritance. 20 All this took about 450 years. "After this, God gave them judges until the time of Samuel the prophet. 21 Then the people asked for a king, and he gave them Saul son of Kish, of the tribe of Benjamin, who ruled forty years. 22 After removing Saul, he made David their king. God testified concerning him: 'I have found David son of Jesse, a man after my own heart; he will do everything I want him to do.' (quoting 1 Samuel 13:14) 23* **"From this man's descendants God has brought to Israel the Savior Jesus, as he promised.** *24* **Before the coming of Jesus, John preached repentance and baptism to all the people of Israel.** *25 As John was completing his work, he said: 'Who do you suppose I am? I am not the one you are looking for. But there is one coming after me whose sandals I am not worthy to untie.' 26 "Fellow children of Abraham and you God-fearing Gentiles,* **it is to us that this message of salvation has been sent.** *27* **The people**

*of Jerusalem and their rulers did not recognize Jesus, yet in condemning him they fulfilled the words of the prophets that are read every Sabbath. 28 Though they found no proper ground for a death sentence, they asked Pilate to have him executed. 29 When they had carried out all that was written about him, they took him down from the cross and laid him in a tomb. 30 **But God raised him from the dead,** 31 **and for many days he was seen by those who had traveled with him from Galilee to Jerusalem. They are now his witnesses to our people.** 32 "We tell you the good news: What God promised our ancestors 33 he has fulfilled for us, their children, by raising up Jesus. As it is written in the second Psalm: " 'You are my son; today I have become your father.' (quoting Psalm 2:7) 34 **God raised him from the dead so that he will never be subject to decay.** As God has said, " 'I will give you the holy and sure blessings promised to David.' (quoting Isaiah 55:3) 35 So it is also stated elsewhere: " 'You will not let your holy one see decay.' (quoting Psalm 16:10) 36 "Now when David had served God's purpose in his own generation, he fell asleep; he was buried with his ancestors and his body decayed. 37 **But the one whom God raised from the dead did not see decay.** 38 "Therefore, my friends, **I want you to know that through Jesus the forgiveness of sins is proclaimed to you.** 39 **Through him everyone who believes is set free from every sin, a justification you were not able to obtain under the law of Moses.** 40 **Take care that what the prophets have said does not happen to you**: 41 " 'Look, you scoffers, wonder and perish, for I am going to do something in your days that you would never believe, even if someone told you.' " (quoting Habakkuk 1:5)*

Paul addressed his fellow Israelites as children of Abraham who had been included in God's special people by birth. From the Scriptures, He refreshed their memory about the Egyptian slavery of their ancestors and how God had delivered them from bondage on the night of Passover. He reminded them of the forty years their ancestors spent in the wilderness under Moses' leadership until it was time for Joshua to lead them into the Promised Land. He discussed the time from Joshua to David and God's covenant promise to David that the Messiah of Israel would come from his descendants, would never see decay, and would rule on God's throne for all eternity with an everlasting dynasty. Then, Paul pointed to John the Baptist as Jesus' forerunner, (see Isaiah 40:3) who announced the coming of the King and the Kingdom of God and Paul told the story of how the Jewish leaders in Jerusalem had rejected Jesus as the Christ and had, in fulfillment of all the prophecies, crucified Him. But God, by His power, had raised Jesus from the dead giving irrefutable proof that Jesus is the Messiah of Israel, the descendant of David, and the King above all kings who reigns forever. This was good news! The Messiah that all Israel had been waiting for had come and, through faith in Him they could have a right relationship with God, something that they had never been able to attain through obedience to the Law. Therefore, Paul begged them to repent and believe Jesus. The following week, almost the entire city showed up to hear the Gospel. Some believed, and some did not. Subsequently, he was run out of town by angry religious people, but the good news of Jesus Christ continued to spread throughout the region. It is safe to assume that this reflects Paul's teaching to Jews in the synagogues in every city that he visited. (see Acts 13:5, 14-49, 14:1, 16:13, 16, 17:1-3, 10, 17, 18:4-5, 19)

As an example of Paul's *preaching*, in both Lystra and Athens, Paul spoke to Gentiles who did not have any Scriptural knowledge of the one true God. By the power of the name of Jesus, Paul had healed a man in Lystra who had not been able to use his feet, and the crowd began to worship him and Barnabas like Roman gods. Legend had it that Zeus and Hermes had visited Lystra previously and killed everyone in the city because no one had offered them hospitality. Therefore, when the people of Lystra saw Paul and Barnabas operating in God's miracle power, they assumed that their gods had returned, so they rushed to be as gracious as possible. The chief priest of the temple of Zeus even brought animals to offer as sacrifices to them with wreaths of flowers to pay homage. Dismayed by this, Paul and Barnabas refused to allow themselves to be worshiped and instead used this as an opportunity to preach the Gospel.

> *{Act 14:15-18} 15 "Friends, why are you doing this?* **We too are only human, like you***. We are bringing you good news, telling you to* **turn from these worthless things to the living God, who made the heavens and the earth and the sea and everything in them***. 16 In the past,* **he let all nations go their own way***. 17 Yet he has not left himself without testimony: He has shown kindness by giving you rain from heaven and crops in their seasons***; he provides you with plenty of food and fills your hearts with joy." 18 Even with these words, they had difficulty keeping the crowd from sacrificing to them.*

In Athens, Paul preached to Epicurean and Stoic philosophers. Epicureans were materialists who believed that the world was ruled by chance and, accordingly, their approach to life was, *eat, drink, and be merry*. Stoics believed that the world was ruled by fate which was out of their control and, therefore, their aim was to live with minimal emotion and in alignment with the laws of nature while their mindset was, *what will be will be*. After testifying about Jesus in the public square of Athens, Paul was taken (not by force) to Mars Hill and to the Areopagus, the center of justice which was situated on a hill named after the Greek god of war. Paul preached about Jesus to some of the most highly respected and brightest minds in the world. They were curious about Paul's teachings and wanted to philosophize over it.

> *{Act 17:22-33} 22 Paul then stood up in the meeting of the Areopagus and said: "People of Athens!* **I see that in every way you are very religious***. 23 For as I walked around and looked carefully at your objects of worship,* **I even found an altar with this inscription: to an unknown god. So you are ignorant of the very thing you worship--and this is what I am going to proclaim to you***. 24 "***The God who made the world and everything in it is the Lord of heaven and earth*** and does not live in temples built by human hands. 25 And he is not served by human hands, as if he needed anything. Rather, he himself gives everyone life and breath and everything else. 26* **From one man he made all the nations, that they should inhabit the whole earth; and he marked out their appointed times in history and the boundaries of their lands***. 27* **God did this so that they would seek him and perhaps reach out for him and find him, though he is not far from any one of us***. 28 'For in him we live and move and have our being.'(quoting a Greek philosopher)* **As some of your own poets have said, 'We are his offspring.'** *(quoting a Greek poet) 29 "Therefore since we are God's offspring, we should not think that the divine being is like gold or silver or stone--an image made by human design and*

*skill. 30 **In the past God overlooked such ignorance, but now he commands all people everywhere to repent. 31 For he has set a day when he will judge the world with justice by the man he has appointed. He has given proof of this to everyone by raising him from the dead.*** 32 When they heard about the resurrection of the dead, some of them sneered, but others said, "We want to hear you again on this subject." 33 At that, Paul left the Council.*

In his preaching to both the people of Lystra and Athens, Paul emphasized God as the one true God who created heaven and earth and pardoned their ignorance of Him with great mercy. By accentuating God as Creator, to the spiritual men of Lystra, Paul indicated a God more powerful and mighty than any of their gods. Paul also presented God as Creator as the explanation for creation to the intellectual men of Athens who knew that all standards of logic demand a genesis for the cause and effect of all things. In both instances, Paul highlighted God's provision of rain, crops, sustenance, and life to everything living as the obvious sign of God's existence and of His goodness towards all that He created. (see also Romans 1:19-20; Matthew 5:43-48) Paul informed them of how every person in every nation on earth is descended from Adam, whom God had created, and how God loves all people in spite of the fact that they do not know Him or worship Him. Paul acknowledged that the philosophers and poets of Athens had sensed and expressed this through their own poetry, which Paul even quoted. To the great judges of the Areopagus, Paul stressed God's authority and control over all the nations of the earth throughout the entire course of history, indicating that God is the true eternal Judge of all. Paul preached the resurrection as proof that God has appointed Jesus Christ as the eternal Judge of all, and that He will return to administer everlasting justice, including wrath to those who have not believed. Notably, Paul did not bash the people of Lystra or Athens or their beliefs. He used what they believed to be true as a segue into revealing the superiority of Jesus Christ as the one true God's Chosen One and only Son. Some people believed, and some did not.

Lastly, in addition to teaching and preaching, Paul *gave his testimony* as a witness of how Jesus Christ had changed his life. As an example of this, he spoke to the riotous crowd in Jerusalem after his arrest at the Temple.

*{Act 22:3-21} 3 "**I am a Jew**, born in Tarsus of Cilicia, but brought up in this city. **I studied under Gamaliel and was thoroughly trained in the law of our ancestors. I was just as zealous for God as any of you are today. 4 I persecuted the followers of this Way to their death, arresting both men and women and throwing them into prison**, 5 as the high priest and all the Council can themselves testify. I even obtained letters from them to their associates in Damascus, and went there to bring these people as prisoners to Jerusalem to be punished. 6 "About noon as I came near Damascus, **suddenly a bright light from heaven flashed around me**. 7 I fell to the ground and heard a voice say to me, 'Saul! Saul! Why do you persecute me?' 8 " 'Who are you, Lord?' I asked. " '**I am Jesus of Nazareth, whom you are persecuting**,' he replied. 9 My companions saw the light, but they did not understand the voice of him who was speaking to me. 10 " 'What shall I do, Lord?' I asked. " 'Get up,' the Lord said, 'and go into Damascus. **There you will be told all that you have been assigned to do.**' 11 My*

companions led me by the hand into Damascus, because the brilliance of the light had blinded me. 12 "A man named Ananias came to see me. He was a devout observer of the law and highly respected by all the Jews living there. 13 **He stood beside me and said, 'Brother Saul, receive your sight!' And at that very moment I was able to see him.** *14 "Then he said: 'The God of our ancestors has chosen you to know his will and to see the Righteous One and to hear words from his mouth. 15* **You will be his witness to all people of what you have seen and heard.** *16 And now what are you waiting for?* **Get up, be baptized and wash your sins away, calling on his name.'** *17 "When I returned to Jerusalem and was praying at the temple, I fell into a trance 18 and saw the Lord speaking to me. 'Quick!' he said. 'Leave Jerusalem immediately, because the people here will not accept your testimony about me.'* 19 " **'Lord,' I replied, 'these people know that I went from one synagogue to another to imprison and beat those who believe in you. 20 And when the blood of your martyr Stephen was shed, I stood there giving my approval and guarding the clothes of those who were killing him.'** *21 "Then* **the Lord said to me, 'Go; I will send you far away to the Gentiles.' "** *(For other tellings of Paul's story, see Acts 9:3-19, 26:1-23)*

Paul did not shrink back from sharing the full testimony of how Jesus Christ had transformed his life and that he had been the worst of sinners. (see 1 Timothy 1:16) He had rejected Jesus and persecuted Christ followers with a passion and deserved God's punishment and wrath. But God, in His great mercy, intervened in Paul's life and, in an instant, Paul was forever changed. Paul thought that he was beyond hope or might be unusable by God because of his past, but God had other plans for him and commissioned him as a witness for Christ to the nations. From that day forward, he lived to teach, preach, and testify about Jesus Christ and the Kingdom of God.

Cut to the Heart

Paul's transformation story is probably the most dramatic conversion in the Book of Acts. Interestingly, Paul, who had been called Saul, did not receive the Gospel message the first time that he heard about Jesus. Quite the contrary, it infuriated him. He had been the most aggressive religious zealot in his day against Jesus and all of His claims of Lordship and had persecuted Christians, approved of their assassinations, and tried to force Christ's witnesses to deny that Jesus is the Messiah. But then, when Paul was on his way to Damascus on a mission to find, imprison, and kill more Christians, he had an encounter with the Jesus, and his life was changed forever.

> *{Act 26:14-15} 14 We all fell to the ground, and I heard a voice saying to me in Aramaic,'* **Saul, Saul, why do you persecute me? It is hard for you to kick against the goads.'** *15 "Then I asked, 'Who are you, Lord?' " 'I am Jesus, whom you are persecuting,' the Lord replied. (see also Acts 9:3-5, 22:8-9)*

A *goad* is an iron tool used to prod cattle along in the way that their masters want them to go and *kicking against the goads* was a proverbial expression for *resisting the obvious to the point of self-destruction.* Paul knew the Scriptures and prophecies about the Messiah of Israel as well as or better than anyone in the world, and they all pointed to Jesus like a master's *goad* directing his path. Everything Paul thought that he believed about Jesus was rebuked in an instant as Jesus spoke the truth in love to him. After this dramatic encounter, Paul received the Holy Spirit, was baptized, and went on to be the greatest witness for Jesus Christ that the world has ever known. (For Paul's complete transformation story, see Acts 7:58, 8:1, 3, 9:1-21, 22:1-21, 26:1-29.)

> *{Act 26:16-18} 16 'Now get up and stand on your feet.* **I have appeared to you to appoint you as a servant and as a witness of what you have seen and will see of me.** *17 I will rescue you from your own people and from the Gentiles. I am sending you to them 18* **to open their eyes and turn them from darkness to light, and from the power of satan to God, so that they may receive forgiveness of sins and a place among those who are sanctified by faith in me.'**

All true witnessing begins and ends with a person who has been *cut to the heart* by the Gospel of Jesus Christ. In fact, once the Holy Spirit was poured out, people near and far were *cut to the heart* by the word of the Lord Jesus. Some, like the 3,000 people who repented after hearing Peter's Pentecost day speech, were *cut to the heart* and became believers. Others, like the religious people listening to Stephen's speech, were *cut to the heart* in anger and indignation.

> *{Act 2:37} 37 When the people heard this, they were* **cut to the heart** *and said to Peter and the other apostles,* **"Brothers, what shall we do?"**

> *{Act 7:51 , 54 KJV} 51 "You stiff-necked people!* **Your hearts and ears are still uncircumcised.** *You are just like your ancestors:* **You always resist the Holy Spirit!**... *54 When they heard these things, they were* **cut to the heart**, *and they gnashed on him with [their] teeth.*

The truth is that God's desire has always been for a people who will worship Him in Spirit and in truth, not because of outward circumcision through religious observance but because of *circumcision of the heart.* (see Deuteronomy 10:14-16, 30:6; Jeremiah 4:4, 9:25-26; John 4:24; Romans 2:28-29; Philippians 3:3) In the past, when the time came for judgment on the city of Jerusalem because of the sin of the people, the Lord showed the prophet Ezekiel a vision of a man dressed in white linen who placed the mark of God on the people who were *cut to the heart* as evidenced by the fact that they wept, sighed, and grieved over the horrendous lack of regard for God in the city. Only the people who were genuinely moved in their hearts were marked to be saved from the destruction to come. God's prophet Jeremiah was so deeply *cut to the heart* for God's people that he is commonly called *the weeping prophet.* When Jesus walked on earth, He wept so much with compassion for people because of His *circumcised heart* that some thought that He might be Jeremiah reincarnated. (see Matthew 16:14; Luke 9:8, 19:41; John 11:33-35) After Jesus ascended to heaven, the Holy Spirit was poured out so that everyone who believes Jesus could receive His *circumcised heart.* This change of heart would be revealed in the same way that it had been in times past – genuine care and concern for all people and dismay over their separation from God and His ways. For example, when the apostle Paul was in Athens, he was *deeply disturbed* about all the idols that he saw (see Acts 17:16) which, in the Greek, means that he was *suddenly filled with a poignant combination of grief and anger*. He had tremendous compassion for the people who did not know God and was incensed at their false worship. Later, in Corinth, Paul was *pressed in his spirit,* meaning that he felt an *unshakable pressure, compulsion, or urgency* about sharing Jesus with them. (see Acts 18:5 KJV; 2 Corinthians 5:14) Paul, who had been completely opposed to Christ and His followers was now totally *cut to the heart* and wanted everyone to know Jesus and to receive all the benefits of His salvation. The way he lived his life clearly demonstrated this.

When we are *cut to the heart* for Christ, it is because we have received revelation from God that Jesus is who He says He is. It is exhilarating and humiliating at the same time because it is like realizing with full assurance that something that we have been in denial about for a long time is actually true. It is like something that has been veiled or blurry is now crystal clear and completely obvious. It is like recognizing that we have been wrong all along about Jesus and that we do not deserve the grace that He has never stopped extending to us. This said, being *cut to the heart* does not always happen the first time that we hear the Gospel. Even the apostle Paul had shaken his fists and gnashed his teeth when Stephen testified of Jesus. But later, Stephen's execution became one of the most memorable and impactful events in Paul's life because he had been permanently *cut to the heart* by the Gospel of Jesus Christ. When we are *cut to the heart* like this, all of a sudden, our hearts are changed. We desire to the depths of our being to be pleasing to God and this desire grows stronger and stronger the more we walk with Christ. At first, like the apostle Paul, we may think that we are unworthy of Jesus because of all the ways that we have denied Him or because of the things that we have done in our lives. But this doesn't hinder God at all. He ignores our resistance and calls us to a Kingdom purpose as His witnesses because He knows what He designed us for since before the foundation of the earth. (see Ephesians 2:8-10) Have you been *cut to the heart* yet?

First to the Jew

As Paul traveled near and far to spread the Gospel message, his practice was to preach and teach first in the Jewish synagogues in every new territory. This reflected what Jesus had done when He was on the earth. Jesus came to testify about Himself as the King of the Jews to the people of Israel, those who are outwardly circumcised as an expression of their covenant with God. (see Matthew 10:5-6, 15:24) As God's chosen people, Jews were given the first opportunity to believe in Jesus and receive Him as their King. They rejected Him and crucified Him but then, after Christ's resurrection and ascension, this "first right of refusal" continued. In fact, through the first seven chapters of the Book of Acts, the Gospel was proclaimed only to the Jews (see Acts 3:26) and almost all believers were of Jewish descent. It was only after the Jews of Jerusalem demonstrated their rejection of the Gospel by the stoning of Stephen that God extended the invitation of salvation through faith in Jesus Christ to Samaritans and Gentiles. (see Matthew 8:10-12, 22:1-14)

In line with this pattern, Paul always gave the Jews of each city the first opportunity to believe Jesus before he moved on to preaching to Gentiles. (see Acts 13:46, 17:2) On his first journey, Paul first preached the Gospel to the Jews in the synagogues in Cyprus, Pisidian Antioch, and Iconium. (see Acts 13:5, 14-49, 14:1) On his second journey, in Philippi, Paul preached at the Jewish place of prayer which was customarily found by the river in cities without a synagogue. (see Acts 16:13, 16) Then, he preached in the synagogues of Thessalonica, Berea, Athens, Corinth, and Ephesus in order to give the Jews the first opportunity to hear the good news. (see Acts 17:1-3, 10, 17, 18:4-5, 19) Notably, in two instances, at Pisidian Antioch and at Corinth, Jews rejected the message of Jesus as the Christ and deemed themselves to be unworthy of eternal life. Paul *shook the dust off of his feet* and announced that he would preach only to the Gentiles. (see Acts 13:46, 18:6)

> *{Act 18:6 NLT}* 6 *But when they opposed and insulted him,* **Paul shook the dust from his clothes and said, "Your blood is upon your own heads--I am innocent.** *From now on I will go preach to the Gentiles."*

> *{Act 13:46, 51}* 46 *Then Paul and Barnabas answered them boldly:* **"We had to speak the word of God to you first. Since you reject it and do not consider yourselves worthy of eternal life, we now turn to the Gentiles.** *...* 51 **So they shook the dust off their feet as a warning to them** *and went to Iconium.*

Nevertheless, as soon as Paul arrived in the next city, he again began in the Jewish synagogue teaching, preaching, and testifying about Christ. (see Acts 14:1, 19:19) By his third missionary journey, Paul was largely revisiting the churches that had been established and was preaching and teaching to the Jews and the Gentiles alike. Later on, when Paul arrived in Rome as a prisoner, while he was under house arrest and able to receive guests, he called first for the Jewish leaders to come and visit him so that he could teach them about Jesus as the Messiah of Israel. After Jews had been given the first right of refusal to hear and believe the message of Christ, Paul received and witnessed to anyone who came to visit him. (see Acts 28:17-28)

God has not rejected the Jewish people, and they are still a priority to Him today. Jews were chosen by God first, loved by God first, and will be judged first when Christ returns. (see Romans 2:9-10) Jews are still loved by God because of the covenant promises He made to Abraham, Isaac, and Jacob. This said, when it comes to the Gospel of Jesus Christ, they are enemies because, simply put, they are *kicking against the goads*. However, their hearts were hardened to the Gospel message so that the Gentiles, who are enemies of God because of sin, could come to know Jesus and be saved. (see Acts 11:18-20, 13:47, 15:17, 22:21, 26:23, 28:25-28) If you were not Jewish at birth, then this means you! Therefore, let us not be conceited but grateful regarding the Jewish heritage of our faith and merciful to God's chosen people by giving them top priority as we witness for Christ. (For more on this subject, see Romans 9–11.)

> *{Rom 1:16}* 16 *For I am not ashamed of the gospel, because it is the power of God that brings salvation to everyone who believes:* **first to the Jew, then to the Gentile.**

And Then the End Will Come

Ever since Adam's error, God has employed witnesses to testify about who He is, what He has done, and what He will do in times to come. Adam and Eve, eyewitnesses to Eden, testified about God, being in relationship with Him, and about the promise of a Son who would crush the head of the serpent. (see Genesis 2–3) Enoch walked with God, prophesied, and his supernatural life was, in itself, a testimony.

(see Genesis 5:21-23) Noah was a preacher of righteousness who built an ark because of what he believed God had told him about the judgment that was to come. (see Genesis 6:9-22; 2 Peter 2:5) Later, when it seemed that all hope was lost and no one in the world worshipped or acknowledged God, God called upon Abraham to live a life of faith as a witness and testament of redemption by faith in the one true God. (see Genesis 12:1-4) Later, when God led the nation of Israel out of slavery, the miracles, signs, and wonders done in Egypt and the parted waters of the Red Sea testified to all the surrounding nations that the most powerful God of all creation was with His chosen people. This continued to speak loudly, even forty years later. (see Exodus 15:14-16, 18:1; Joshua 2:10) The Laws of God were given to Israel to govern them so that they would be a living testimony of God's holiness, character, purity, justice, fairness, and care for all people. Israelites were instructed to constantly remember what they had seen, heard, and experienced of God's goodness so that they would live in alignment with His ways as His witnesses to the world. (see Exodus 19:4-6; Deuteronomy 4:5-6, 33-35) As time progressed, God reminded His people of their role as His witnesses to all the nations of the earth. (see Isaiah 43:10, 12, 44:8) Similarly, for New Covenant believers, after Jesus' resurrection, He gave His disciples the Great Commission as His witnesses to all the nations of the earth.

> *{Mat 28:18-20} 18 Then Jesus came to them and said, "All authority in heaven and on earth has been given to me. 19 **Therefore go and make disciples of all nations**, baptizing them in the name of the Father and of the Son and of the Holy Spirit, 20 and teaching them to obey everything I have commanded you. And surely I am with you always, to the very end of the age."*

Witnessing for Christ starts with being *cut to the heart* by Jesus Christ and living to tell what Christ has done. As we allow the Holy Spirit to work in our hearts to make us like Christ, we reveal God's character, goodness, and love, and our lives become a living testimony even when we are not teaching, preaching, or sharing our testimony. A true witness for Christ does not consider the Great Commission to be a work assignment or intolerable burden of responsibility. When our lives have been changed by Jesus Christ, we are always prepared to share the story of how Jesus Christ has changed our lives by His salvation, (see 1 Peter 3:15) and we stand firm in our testimony in the face of hardship, persecution, and even possibly death so that everyone who will believe can come to know Jesus and be saved. (see 2 Timothy 2:10) No matter what happens to them, a transformed person simply can't help but tell everyone about Jesus!

Importantly, there is also a responsibility to witnessing for Christ. As an example, in the Old Testament, God called upon the prophet Ezekiel to declare a message of hope through repentance from sin. Prior to this assignment, Ezekiel had only pronounced judgment upon people because they were in rebellion against God, but now God gave Ezekiel a message of good news and life through repentance and returning to God. Ezekiel was held accountable by God for sharing the message but not for how people responded to it. If Ezekiel shared the message with people and they did not repent of their sin, then the people's sin was on their own head because they had been given the opportunity to believe and chose not to. However, if Ezekiel did not share the message with the people, then God held their sin against Ezekiel. (see Ezekiel 33:1-9) As disciples of Christ, we have this same type of responsibility for proclaiming the Gospel. The apostle Paul alluded to the connection between Ezekiel's accountability to

God the responsibility of witnessing for Christ when he declared himself to be innocent of everyone's guilt because he had faithfully preached the full Gospel to them, meaning that he had been obedient in delivering God's message. (see Acts 20:26-27) Similarly, each and every one of Christ's disciples has been commissioned by Jesus to declare a message of hope through repentance from sin and believing in Jesus so that everyone can hear the word of Christ and believe. (see Romans 10:8-17) We have a responsibility to deliver God's message and, significantly, Jesus will not return until we have accomplished our task as His witnesses to the ends of the earth.

> *{Mat 24:14} 14 And this* **gospel of the kingdom will be preached** *in the whole world* **as a testimony to all nations, and then the end will come**.

MY TESTIMONY

Hello, my name is Wendy, the worst of sinners. I used to be completely focused on worldly success, measured by money, power, status, and the approval of important people. This made me a workaholic, a control-freak, and a perfectionist who didn't trust God at all. I used my intelligence and skill to dominate people, used innuendo and sensuality to manipulate, cussed like a sailor, looked down on lazy people, and thought Christianity was for wimps. I never seemed to have enough of what I wanted, so I settled for less and strived for more. Inwardly I was prideful, insecure, and never felt like I measured up. I worked and fought to attain as much as I could in an attempt to prove my worth to myself and to the world. My life always felt like it was a precariously balanced house of cards.

In March of 2004, a voice in my head kept continually prompting me to *go get a Bible*. Over and over again, I heard *go get a Bible, go get a Bible*. It sounded a lot like the same voice that tells me to go get some chocolate (which I usually act upon) so I obeyed it, purchased a Bible, and began to read it. About six months later, I was in the park on a Sunday, knowing that it was the Lord's day, and I prayed to God for the first time in Jesus' name. I said something to the effect of, "God, if you're really out there, I need you to give me a sign." As if God needed my further instructions, I added, "And make it really obvious because I am new at this." Even though it didn't make sense to me at all, I just knew, accepted, and believed that God heard me because I had prayed this prayer through faith in Jesus. In God's absolute and amazing grace, within 24 hours of my prayer and through a series of supernatural events, God gave me an undeniable sign. My life was permanently changed.

At this point, I did not understand anything about God or His ways, about Jesus or the Holy Spirit, or what I was supposed to do next. For a while, I proceeded to live according to my own agenda even though going to church had become an important part of my life. But God in His infinite wisdom and patience continued to speak to me and guide me. After a few years of ignorance and half-hearted devotion, I realized that God had so much more for me and I was willing to do anything that it took to attain it. In 2009, God asked me to leave everything that I knew behind and give away everything that I owned, and I did. In 2010, He told me not to ask anyone for anything that I need but to simply trust Him in prayer and obey His voice. It's been a wild adventure!

God is good. My life today is evidence of His love, His faithfulness, His provision, and His goodness. Jesus is exactly who He says He is. May His name be praised forever and ever!

CHAPTER 15
Yeast

As Christianity spread throughout the known world, people from various backgrounds began to follow Christ. There were Jews with deep roots in the requirements of God's Law and Gentiles who were unfamiliar with God's standards of purity and respect for life. There were those who sought to enforce religious requirements, which contradicted the freedom that Christ attained for believers, and there were those who abused Christian freedom to continue living lives of sin, which contrasted the holiness of being God's special people. Additionally, false teachers arose seeking money and acclaim for themselves while distorting the truth and the aim of the Christian life. Jesus had compared their false teachings to *yeast* which spreads quickly throughout the whole to cause corruption. In other words, wrong beliefs are a deadly threat to our faith. Let's take a look at how Christ followers in the Book of Acts encountered false teaching and how we can keep our faith free of *yeast*.

As a quick side note before we begin, this chapter addresses some highly sensitive subjects of sin and error. Please know that it is not my aim to offend, exclude, or condemn anyone. God's grace through faith in Jesus is bigger and more powerful than any sin. If you are struggling in any of the areas that are spoken of in this chapter, God's grace is available to you through faith in Jesus Christ to forgive your offenses and to strengthen you to overcome beliefs and behaviors which are not aligned with God's will. Nothing is eternally unforgivable except rejecting Jesus as Lord. He came and died for you, for me, and for everyone because all of us stumble in many ways. (see James 3:2) If any of us were capable of perfection, Jesus could have spared Himself the trip to earth, to the cross, and to the pit of hell on our behalf. This said, we are not ignorant of God's design for our lives because the Scriptures reveal His will and His holiness. The Word of God from the Book of Genesis to the Book of Revelation clearly articulates beliefs and behaviors that are in line with God's ways and those which are contrary to them. Disciples of Jesus live according to God's ways willingly from the heart because they are empowered by the Holy Spirit, the very nature of Christ dwelling within them. (see 1 Timothy 3:9-11; Romans 8:1-4; Galatians 5:22-25)

Jerusalem Council

While Paul and Barnabas were teaching Jewish and Gentile Christians at the church at Antioch, some men arrived and began to teach that Gentile converts to Christianity must be circumcised in order to be included in God's people. Paul and Barnabas adamantly disagreed with them. Their dispute escalated to the point that the church at Antioch sent Paul, Barnabas, and a company of believers to Jerusalem to speak to the apostles and elders there about the issue. (see Acts 15:1-3) Upon their arrival in Jerusalem, additional believers stood to argue the case for the requirement of circumcision. In fairness to these sincere believers, recall that ever since Abraham, circumcision has been the outward symbol of inclusion in God's covenant with the Jewish people as His special people out of all the earth, and therefore, every Jewish male was to be circumcised on their eighth day of life. (see Genesis 17:9-14; Leviticus 12:3) These men perceived very well that Christianity had been birthed out of Judaism and that Christians were now God's special set apart people who worshipped Christ, the King of the Jews, as their King. (see John 4:22; Romans 9:4, 11:18; 1 Peter 2:9 quoting Exodus 19:5-6) They also understood correctly that the Gentiles were being adopted into God's family. Under the Old Covenant, this "adoption" into God's family or inclusion in His people, was outwardly displayed by Gentile converts when they submitted themselves to circumcision. (see Exodus 12:43-49) The believers arguing the case for circumcision were not rejecting the inclusion of Gentiles into the faith but, rather, were trying to include Gentiles according to the old rules. In contrast, under the New Covenant, adoption into God's family is by grace through faith in Jesus Christ. This is outwardly displayed through the "circumcision" of baptism by which believers *roll away* the old Adamic nature to become a new creation in Christ. (see Colossians 2:11-12; Romans 6:4) Moreover, we have already discussed that what God is looking for is *circumcision of the heart*. This said, with these two contrasting sides in debate, a council of the apostles and church elders was gathered together to settle the matter once and for all. This meeting is now commonly known as the Jerusalem Council.

> *{Act 15:7-11} 7 After much discussion, Peter got up and addressed them: "Brothers, you know that some time ago God made a choice among you that the Gentiles might hear from my lips the message of the gospel and believe. 8* **God, who knows the heart, showed that he accepted them by giving the Holy Spirit to them, just as he did to us.** *9* **He did not discriminate between us and them, for he purified their hearts by faith.** *10 Now then, why do you try to* **test God by putting on the necks of Gentiles a yoke that neither we nor our ancestors have been able to bear?** *11* **No! We believe it is through the grace of our Lord Jesus that we are saved, just as they are."**

Years earlier, Peter had explained to believers at Jerusalem how God had poured out the Holy Spirit on Gentiles when he preached the Gospel in the home of Cornelius. This had been done spontaneously and sovereignly by God without any prerequisite except that they believed what Peter told them about Jesus. It had been very reminiscent of the day of Pentecost when Jewish believers received the Holy Spirit and therefore, Peter concluded that this demonstrated that God sees no difference between Jew and Gentile when their faith is in Christ. (see Romans 10:12; Galatians 3:28; Ephesians 2:14-15) Peter now repeated this story to the Jerusalem Council, making it clear that salvation is by God's grace through faith in Jesus Christ and not through obedience to the Old Covenant. In fact, Cornelius and his household were water baptized in Jesus' name *after* receiving the Holy Spirit, so even the New Covenant outward display of "circumcision" through baptism was not a prerequisite for salvation. (see Acts 10:44-48) All of this is to say that, to require circumcision in accordance with the Old Covenant standard was tantamount to not believing that Christ completely fulfilled the Law in order for His followers to receive righteousness as a free gift through faith in Him, which Peter called *testing God*. Therefore, Peter declared circumcision to be an undue and unbearable load to place on the new Gentile converts. (For more about circumcision in the New Testament, see Romans 2:25-29; Galatians 5:1-12; 6:12-16; 1 Corinthians 7:17-19; Colossians 3:11; James 2:10)

> *{Act 15:13-19} 13 When they finished, James spoke up. "Brothers," he said, "listen to me. 14 Simon has described to us how **God first intervened to choose a people for his name from the Gentiles**. 15 **The words of the prophets are in agreement with this**, as it is written: 16 " 'After this **I will return and rebuild David's fallen tent**. Its ruins I will rebuild, and I will restore it, 17 **that the rest of mankind may seek the Lord, even all the Gentiles who bear my name, says the Lord, who does these things'**-- 18 things known from long ago. (quoting Amos 9:11-12, Isaiah 45:21) 19 "It is my judgment, therefore, that **we should not make it difficult for the Gentiles who are turning to God**."*

In short, James agreed with Peter. Interestingly, this James was Jesus' biological half-brother, the natural son of Mary and Joseph, the head of the Jerusalem Church, and the author of the Book of James. James articulated that God's desire, as expressed in the Scriptures, is for a people who bear His name and live by faith in Him, including Jews and Gentiles alike. He also agreed that Christ followers are not subject to the burden of the Laws of the Old Covenant. However, because the Scriptures had been taught to the Jews since birth, certain conduct would be particularly offensive to Jewish followers of Christ and to unconverted Jews who would find such conduct to be in sharp contrast with the purity of God's holiness. Therefore, James proposed that all believers willingly abstain from these things so as not to cause offense or hinder their witness for Christ.

> *{Act 15:20-21} 20 Instead we should write to them, telling them to **abstain from food polluted by idols, from sexual immorality, from the meat of strangled animals and from blood**. 21 For the law of Moses has been preached in every city from the earliest times and is read in the synagogues on every Sabbath."*

First, James proposed that Christians willingly abstain from eating food offered to idols. In those days, feasts offered to other gods in their temples were a commonplace form of worship, and the consecrated meat was sold in the Gentile marketplaces. To a knowledgeable Jew, eating food offered to a rival god would directly contrast the first commandment of *You shall have no other gods before me* and the understanding that God is not in pagan temples, nor is His likeness represented by idols of silver or gold. (Exodus 20:3, 22-23) Moreover, meat offered to idols would not have been butchered in accordance with kosher laws and, therefore, all such food would be considered unclean and polluted with idolatry. The point is not that the gods are actually gods because they are not, just like the golden calf was not the god who brought Israel out of Egypt when they had erroneously worshiped it. (see 1 Corinthians 10:7; Exodus 32) However, to a Jew, eating the food offered to an idol would be regarded as just about the same thing as worshipping the false god, and everyone knew that this was punishable by death. (see Deuteronomy 17:2-5; Leviticus 24:14) An exceptional Old Testament demonstrator of adherence to this standard was Daniel, who refused to eat the meat and luscious food of the Babylonian king in order to keep himself undefiled. (see Daniel 1:8) With this said, for Christians who claim to follow the King of the Jews to treat eating food offered to idols lightly would be regarded by faithful Jews as a negation of God's holiness and worthiness of all worship. Also, it created a slippery slope of temptation for Gentile converts to Christianity who had previously worshipped these gods to renounce their faith in Christ and return to their old way of life. (For more about this topic in the New Testament, see 1 Corinthians 8, 10:14-33; Revelation 2:14, 20)

Second, James proposed that Christians abstain from sexual immorality. The shortest way to express the definition of sexual immorality is *any sex outside of a marriage between one man and one woman.* Marriage was created to give man a helper to carry out God's purposes in the earth and the purpose of sex is for a man and his wife to *produce godly offspring* so that the world is filled with a people dedicated to God. (see Genesis 1:26-28, 2:18, 23-25; Malachi 2:15-16) A Jew who knew God's standard of holiness would know that the Book of Leviticus, Chapter 18, clearly defines sexual practices which were strictly forbidden by God's Law. Addressed to an adult male, these practices are: sex with any close relative, your mother, your father's wife, your sister or half-sister, your granddaughter, your step sister, your aunt, your daughter-in-law, your brother's wife, both a woman and her daughter or granddaughter, your wife's sister, anyone else's wife, aka adultery, and sex during a woman's menstruation. All of these practices are out of line with God's design for sex which has the capacity to create life. In the event that children were born through such practices, they and their descendants were disbarred from the assembly of God's people until the tenth generation. (see Deuteronomy 32:2) The next forbidden act in this passage about sexual immorality pertains to offering any offspring to a pagan god, Molech. Quite clearly, a child deliberately dedicated to any other god would be the opposite of having children dedicated to God Himself. (see Leviticus 20:2) Lastly, this passage covers two forms of forbidden sexuality which have no hope of producing offspring and which are not at all God's design for sex, namely, homosexuality and bestiality. (For additional Old Testament Laws pertaining to sex outside of marriage and rape, see Exodus 22:16-17, 19; Leviticus 19:20-22; Deuteronomy 22:13-30, 27:20-23) The sexual standards of the people of Israel were designed by God to protect the dignity of all people and were the highest legal standards in the world for the protection of women. It was one of the things that most set Jews apart from all other nations who participated in all of the practices above in addition to wild orgies, sexual rites offered at temples to their deities, and a whole host of other perverse and exploitive acts. Indeed, worldly culture throughout history has considered sexual purity to be an unreasonable restriction on human fleshly need. However, to a Jew, for followers of the Messiah of Israel to dismiss or ignore God's standard of sexuality would be an abominable form of ungodliness and would have been a repugnant rejection of His ways. Moreover, sexual sin is against our own bodies meaning that it reveals a certain level of self-loathing while also dishonoring the dwelling place of the Holy Spirit, which is the Spirit of Christ who loved us enough to die for us. (For more about this topic in the New Testament, see Romans 1:26-27; 1 Corinthians 6:13-7:40; Galatians 5:19; Ephesians 5:3; 1 Thessalonians 4:3; Revelation 2:14, 20)

Third and fourth, James proposed that Christians willingly abstain from eating the meat of a strangled animal and from eating blood. We have previously discussed the importance and value which God places on blood and on life. God created everything, and therefore He values all that He created. To eat an animal which had been strangled meant that the blood had not been properly drained out and was still in the animal. Out of respect for the animal's life, eating this was against God's Law and made a person unclean. (see Genesis 9:4; Leviticus 17:11-16, 19:26) Similarly, to eat blood, animal or human, whether drinking it raw or cooking it into a pudding or other dish, which have been common pagan practices throughout history, was equally disrespectful to life. Additionally, by God's Law, any blood sacrifice offered outside of God's standards was considered equal to murder, and the person who did this was to be permanently cut off from God's people. (see Leviticus 17:3-4) Every Jew knew the value that God placed on life and blood and, therefore, willing abstention from strangled meat and blood were the only dietary guidelines introduced for the Church. (For more about this topic in the New Testament, see Mark 7:19; Acts 10:9-16; Romans 14; Colossians 2:16-17, 21; 1 Corinthians 8:13)

Significantly, the weightiness of all of the issues addressed at the Jerusalem Council is discovered in how they each pertain to inclusion in God's people and His covenant promises. Circumcision is all about inclusion. However, to obligate circumcision would have been a rejection of God's grace through Jesus Christ because to require obedience to one Law according to the old standard is equal to necessitating compliance with the entirety of the old standard. (see James 2:10) Any requirement other than belief that Jesus is Lord and that God raised Him from the dead is not the New Covenant which was sealed with the blood of Christ. This said, idol worship, sexual immorality, and disregard for life are all about inclusion or, rather, expulsion. According to God's Law, these practices were all punishable by death or expulsion from God's people and, if allowed to pervade and accrue throughout the community, would result in the eviction of God's people from the Promised Land. (see Leviticus 18:24-30; Deuteronomy 18:9-14) In fact, these are the reasons why nations throughout history have been *spit out* of their lands. (see Genesis 15:16, 18:20-21, 19:12-13; Deuteronomy 9:4-5) These practices reveal a condition of heart that is not turned to God in faith, is not revering His holiness, and is not respecting life, which He authors. (see Acts 3:15; James 2:14-26) Lukewarm believers who profess to know Christ but who reveal their indifference through their actions will be *spit out* of His mouth just like the nations were spit out of their lands. (see Revelation 3:16) At the Jerusalem Council, the apostles and elders established these regulations, not to require obedience to the Old Covenant in any way but, to keep believers in the New Covenant aligned with God's will for their lives so that everyone who believes can receive all that has been promised through faith in Christ, both in this age and in the age to come.

Along these lines, the Jerusalem Council is a good example of the Church functioning as a set apart, self-governing group of people of God, or *ekklesia*, and of exercising their Christ-given authority for *binding* and *loosing*. Binding and loosing are legal terms for establishing that which is *forbidden* and that which is *permitted*. To *impose a requirement* is to render it *binding* but to *allow a behavior* is to *loose* people from obligation. At the Jerusalem Council, the apostles and elders concurred with Peter and James that believers are *loosed* from the requirement of circumcision but are *bound* to abstaining from idol worship, sexual immorality, and eating strangled meat and blood. Disregard for these regulations could result in expulsion from the Church.

Jesus spoke to His disciples (who became the apostles) about *binding* and *loosing* after Peter first acknowledged Him as the Son of God and Messiah of Israel. It is upon this revelation of Jesus as the Christ that the Church is established and from which the Church derives authority to govern the people of God. (see Matthew 16:13-20) In another passage, Jesus taught His disciples about *binding* and *loosing* in the context of conflict resolution between fellow believers. According to this teaching, Christian conflicts should respectfully escalate step-by-step from the offended parties privately, to the inclusion of other believers as witnesses, to the authority of the church for a verdict. Then, if the offender will not heed the decision of the church, they are to be expelled and treated like an unbeliever and traitor. (see Matthew 18:10-18) The Church at Corinth experienced this when a believer was caught continually having sexual relations with his father's wife and was expelled from the church. (see 1 Corinthians 5:1-5, 9-13) But before we get too haughty, let us consider something. How do we treat unbelievers and enemies of God? We proclaim the Gospel of Jesus Christ and salvation by grace through faith for all sinners who repent. Therefore, if we are to treat the expelled like an unbeliever, there is no reason not to reinstate a sincerely repentant person back into the Church. As a further demonstration, the repentant and sorrowful Corinthian man was welcomed back and comforted by God's people and God's grace. (see 2 Corinthians 2:5-11) Additionally, as Jesus taught about *binding* and *loosing*, He explained that offenses between believers are minor by comparison to the way that all of us have sinned against God. In modern day equivalents, God, through Jesus' death in our place, paid our multi-billion dollar debt (10,000 talents) and so, therefore, releasing a fellow believer from a debt of several thousand dollars (100 denarii) is a disproportionately low expectation. (see Matthew 18:21-35) In fact, the ability of believers to forgive others is another way in which the condition of our heart is revealed. If we find it difficult to forgive others then, perhaps, it is because we have not fully received God's forgiveness through Christ for ourselves.

Finally, God-given authority to *bind* and to *loose* would have been understood as essentially synonymous with possessing the *keys to the Kingdom of Heaven*. Under the Old Covenant, scribes, religious leaders, and experts in God's Law held the *keys to the Kingdom of Heaven* because they had the God-given right to determine what was allowed and what was forbidden. The aim of the Law was righteousness and access to God so that God's people could know Him. Unfortunately, the religious authorities enforced so many of their own binding regulations that made it impossible for anyone to enter, including themselves. (see Matthew 23:13) By doing so, they lost their own knowledge of God and impeded everyone else's ability to know Him. (see Luke 11:52) Under the New Covenant, the Church has the *keys to the Kingdom of Heaven* through Christ-given authority to *bind* and to *loose*. For Christians, righteousness and access to God is attained by grace through faith in Jesus Christ as a free gift not because of what we do or do not do. (see Ephesians 2:8) Understanding God's mercy and grace to its depths, unlike the religious leaders of the old system, the apostles and elders at the Jerusalem Council did not make it difficult for believers to enter into the Kingdom of Heaven. Praise God!

After much discussion and prayer and by the power of the Holy Spirit, the apostles and elders at the Jerusalem Council were in complete unity and agreement. They decided to write a letter to Christ followers everywhere announcing their decision. Everyone was greatly encouraged.

> *{Act 15:30-31} 30 So the men were sent off and went down to Antioch, where they gathered the church together and delivered the letter. 31* **The people read it and were glad for its encouraging message.**

As a quick side note, later in the Book of Acts while Paul and his traveling team were sharing the news about the apostles' decision that circumcision was not required for New Covenant believers, Paul had Timothy circumcised, which would seem to be a contradiction. Timothy's mother was Jewish which qualified him as an Israelite (Jewishness passes through the mother because paternity was impossible to prove in those days) but his father was Gentile, which was why he had not been circumcised previously. In order to not cause a big fuss among the unbelieving Jews and new converts to Christianity in the cities on their itinerary, Paul exercised willing deference so that Jesus Christ could be the primary focus of conversation, not circumcision. In contrast, a little later in the course of time, a man named Titus, who had been born 100% Gentile, utterly refused to be circumcised in order to be accepted into the faith. Paul absolutely agreed with Titus, and God continued to use Titus mightily. (see Acts 16:1-3; Galatians 2:3; Book of Titus)

Savage Wolves

Many years later when Paul was on his way back to Jerusalem, knowing that prison chains and suffering had been predicted for him, he called for a meeting with the elders from the church at Ephesus, and they travelled to meet him at Miletus. They all knew that this was the last time that they would ever see each other, so Paul's speech had a special weight to it.

> *{Act 20:18-24} 18 When they arrived, he said to them:* **"You know how I lived the whole time I was with you***, from the first day I came into the province of Asia. 19* **I served the Lord with great humility and with tears and in the midst of severe testing by the plots of my Jewish opponents***. 20 You know that I* **have not hesitated to preach anything that would be helpful to you** *but have taught you publicly and from house to house. 21* **I have declared to both Jews and Greeks that they must turn to God in repentance and have faith in our Lord Jesus***. 22 "And now, compelled by the Spirit, I am going to Jerusalem, not knowing what will happen to me there. 23 I only know that in every city the Holy Spirit warns me that prison and hardships are facing me. 24 However,* **I consider my life worth nothing to me; my only aim is to finish the race and complete the task the Lord Jesus has given me--the task of testifying to the good news of God's grace***.*

Paul used his own life of service to God as an example to be followed. In spite of severe persecution, opposition, and plots against his life, Paul diligently taught everyone all that they needed to know in order to live godly lives as Christ followers. The singular aim of his existence was to proclaim the Kingdom of God and to fulfill the call of God upon his life. He tirelessly and relentlessly taught God's grace through faith in Jesus Christ and lived his life as a demonstration of Christlike humility, liberty, and love. Then, Paul's speech to the Ephesian elders took a tone of warning. He urged them to guard themselves and the flock from predators as responsible shepherds of God's precious people. Paul urged these leaders to keep watch over themselves and their own lives in order to effectively guard and lead God's people because *savage wolves* and predators with deceptive teaching would arise out of the ranks of the Church. These false teachers and false prophets would pervert the truth in order to plunder the vulnerable, create a following for themselves, and lead people away from God's grace through faith in Christ.

> *{Act 20:28-35} 28* **Keep watch over yourselves and all the flock** *of which the Holy Spirit has made you overseers. Be shepherds of the church of God,* **which he bought with his own blood.** *29 I know that after I leave,* **savage wolves will come in among you and will not spare the flock.** *30 Even* **from your own number men will arise and distort the truth in order to draw away disciples after them.** *31* **So be on your guard!** *Remember that for three years* **I never stopped warning each of you** *night and day with tears. 32 "Now I* **commit you to God and to the word of his grace, which can build you up and give you an inheritance among all those who are sanctified.** *33* **I have not coveted anyone's silver or gold or clothing.** *34 You yourselves know that these hands of mine have supplied my own needs and the needs of my companions. 35 In everything I did, I showed you that by this kind of hard work we must help the weak, remembering the words the Lord Jesus himself said: 'It is more blessed to give than to receive.' "*

Truth be told, false prophets and teachers have been a challenger of God's people throughout history. The first false prophet was satan in the Garden of Eden who told Adam's wife a lie about what she would gain for herself if she disregarded God's command. Later, the people of Israel are instructed to identify false prophets as anyone who pointed to a god other than the Lord, even if their prophetic words and miraculous signs came to pass, or anyone who spoke presumptuously in the name of the Lord, as evidence by what they spoke not coming to pass. Notably, false prophets and their teachings were a tool that God used to test the hearts of His people in order to reveal if they would remain faithful to Him or turn away to follow other gods. (see Deuteronomy 13:1-5, 18:15-22) Throughout Israel's history, false prophets, teachers, and shepherds (or leaders) lied to God's people by encouraging them to overindulge God's mercy through godless living and heartless religious observance rather than wholehearted devotion and true worship. (see Isaiah 28:7, 56:10-12, 58:1-14; Jeremiah 6:13-15, 8:4-17, 23:9-40; Ezekiel 11:1-13, 13:1-23, 14:1-11; Hosea 5:1-15; Micah 2:6-13, 3:1-12; Zechariah 11:4-17; Malachi 1:6-2:9) This testing of heart continued when, for forty days in the wilderness, the devil relentlessly attempted to entice Jesus to worship him instead of God but Jesus did not succumb to his false promises. (see Matthew 4:9; Luke 4:7) Later, Jesus taught His disciples to beware of false prophets, aka *ferocious wolves*, who would come disguised as sheep but who do not produce the proper fruit of *Christlikeness*. He also warned His disciples that many false prophets and false Messiahs will come attempting to deceive God's people, particularly in the times imminently preceding His return. (see Matthew 7:15, 24; Mark 13:22; Luke 6:26) In fact, in the final days before the return of Christ, believers will be put to the ultimate test as the *man of lawlessness* is raised into power with false signs and wonders, even calling fire down from heaven as he proclaims himself to be god and demands worship from everyone on earth. (see 2 Thessalonians 2:1-12; Matthew 24:15; Revelation 13:13; Daniel 7:25, 9:27)

Shepherds who are not fully devoted to the Lord themselves devour and discard God's people without the slightest consideration for their welfare. These leaders are really only in it for the paycheck and the allegiance of men. (see John 10:11-13; Romans 16:17-18; 2 Corinthians 11:1-15; Philippians 1:15, 17-18; 1 Timothy 6:3-10) Presumptuous religious teachers quarrel over words and rules which require strict adherence and incite fearful obedience. (see Colossians 2:4, 16-23; 1 Timothy 1:3-11, 4:1-5, 7; 2 Timothy 2:23) False prophets and apostles authorize immorality, indulge their own worldly and fleshly lusts, and spout off false dreams, visions, and counterfeit miracles like the magicians of Pharaoh's court in the days of Moses. (see 2 Timothy 3:1-9; 2 Peter 2:1-22; Jude 1:3-16; Exodus 7:11-12, 22, 8:7, 18-19) In contrast to this, Paul again used himself as an example to the elders of Ephesus. Though he had at one time been the supreme religious zealot who persecuted Christians and approved of their execution, Paul declared himself innocent of the bloodshed of all men. Paul understood God's grace through Jesus Christ to its depths, and he had received it for himself. He never used or abused anyone but put his own life in danger for the benefit of God's people. (see 2 Corinthians 11:16-33) Paul did not use his God-given authority for personal gain or worship and even refused it. (see Acts 14:11-15; 1 Corinthians 3:4-11, 4:1-13, 9:1-18) He did not teach any religious conformity at all other than the grace of God through faith in Jesus Christ. This is evidenced through conduct which reveals a purified heart.

Paul taught what he refers to in this speech as the *whole counsel of God*. He had been professionally trained in the Scriptures but had been personally transformed by revelation of Jesus Christ. Then, in Christ's service, Paul taught every part of God's eternal redemptive plan as the Scriptures reveal it. In Paul's day, the *whole counsel of God* was what we know of today as the Old Testament which tells of God's plan and promise of redemption. Today, the *whole counsel of God* includes the New Testament which reveals how God accomplished what He promised in the Old Testament through the life, death, and resurrection of Jesus Christ and speaks about Christ's return. There is no part of the Word of God that is insignificant, and there is no part of the *whole counsel of God* that does not point to Jesus Christ as Lord, Savior, and promised Messiah of Israel. Paul knew better than anyone in the world that the *whole counsel of God* is the message of unmerited favor and eternal life through faith in Jesus Christ. Anything added to or subtracted from that is a distortion and a lie. Accordingly, similar to what we saw as the result of the Jerusalem Council, Paul's only desire was for believers to know God's grace *(not religion)* and to be built up *(not overburdened)* in the righteousness of Christ so that we receive our eternal inheritance *(inclusion in the New Covenant)* with those whose hearts have been purified *(not disregarding God's ways)* through faith in Jesus as our Lord and Savior. If anyone is teaching something contrary to this, be on guard.

Types of Yeast

False teaching is no different today than it has been since the beginning. For example, Adam and his wife were made in God's image to *be like God*. Then, the evil one came along with a lie that if they disobeyed

God's command, they would *be like God*. Similarly, Jesus is the creator, owner, and King of *all the kingdoms of the world*. Then, the devil came along with a lie that if Jesus disobeyed God and worshipped him instead, Jesus would receive *all the kingdoms of the world*. In both instances, the devil's deception promised what they already had through a false path which would subject them to the enemy and, ultimately, lead them to death. This said, there are three main types of false teachings which Jesus referred to as *yeast* when He taught His disciples to watch out for them.

> *{Mat 16:11-12} 11 How is it you don't understand that I was not talking to you about bread?* **But be on your guard against the yeast of the <u>Pharisees and Sadducees</u>."** *12 Then they understood that he was not telling them to guard against the yeast used in bread,* **but against the teaching [doctrine] of the Pharisees and Sadducees.** *(see also Luke 12:1)*

> *{Mar 8:15} 15 "Be careful," Jesus warned them.* **"Watch out for the yeast of the Pharisees and that of <u>Herod</u>."**

Literally, yeast is a *self-reproducing fungus which spreads aggressively throughout whatever it is added to and changes its character through fermentation and decay*. In the Scriptures, *yeast* (which is also called *leaven*) is symbolic of *sin, wickedness,* or *gain attained unjustly through wrongdoing or violence*. For example, on the night of the original Passover when God liberated Israel out of Egyptian slavery, every Israelite was instructed to remove all traces of yeast from their homes as an act of purification by faith. Notably, God delivered the Israelites on the night of Passover by grace through faith in His covenant promise to them. They demonstrated this faith by painting the blood of the Passover Lamb on their doorposts and by purifying their lives from *yeast*. Every year, Jews remove all yeast from their homes for seven days to celebrate the Festival of Unleavened Bread in order to remember this most significant turning point in their history. (see Exodus 12:8, 15-20, 39; Leviticus 23:5-8; Deuteronomy 16:1-8) Additionally, under the Old Covenant, or God's Law, no offerings presented on the altar were to be made with yeast or honey which symbolized the sweetness of luxurious fancies and which also causes rot. (see Leviticus 2:11; Exodus 23:18, 34:25) In the New Testament, yeast also symbolizes false teachings of *religion, unbelief,* and *worldliness* which have the potential to spread through believers and draw us away from the truth of Christ.

The *yeast of the Pharisees* is *religion* which also, inevitably, results in hypocrisy. The Pharisees were a sect of Judaism that was divided into various schools or denominations ranging from highly conservative to extremely liberal in their interpretation of the Scriptures. Each school interpreted the Scriptures for pragmatic application to modern living and considered their interpreted rules and traditions to be equal with the Laws of God. At times, their requirements were excessively *binding* and required more than God had originally intended. For example, they had over 39 different classes of work forbidden on the Sabbath, they tithed even their garden herbs and spices, and they required fasting twice a week. Other times, their regulations were excessively *loosing* by releasing people from Laws that God had intended to be obeyed. For example, they made divorce easy to obtain for any reason whatsoever, they disregarded God's policies for finances, and they loop-holed their way out of showing mercy to others. (see Matthew 23:1-33; Mark 12:38-40; Luke 10:25-37, 20:45-47) The Pharisee approach to the Scriptures was often metaphoric, not for its prophetic value in foreshadowing the Messiah but for its practical value for living in their times. This meant that passages of Scripture were often taken out of their original context and that their rules often neglected to take the *whole counsel of God* into consideration. Regardless of this, Pharisees considered themselves blameless before God because of their principles of personal piety and their pursuit of holiness through good works. They condemned anyone who did not adhere to their way of thinking and they anticipated that the resurrection from the dead would be their greatest triumph while everyone who did not adhere to their standards burned in hell for eternity. In further hypocrisy, when push came to shove, they aligned themselves with worldly powers when their authority was threatened. Pharisee "righteousness" was entirely self-righteousness based on self-effort because of the things that they did or did not do and, while they were at it, they made a big show of all the things that they were so busy doing or not doing so that everyone could see how devoted they were.

In fact, the basis for all *religious* teaching is that our standing before God is contingent upon what we do or do not do. Religion teaches that our self-effort and our works or abstinence are the reasons why we receive and maintain blessing from God. This reveals a *get what you deserve* attitude. In contrast, *the Gospel is the power of God unto salvation* which includes salvation, healing, deliverance, sustenance, redemption from the curse of the Law, and victory over the evil one. Through faith in the life, death, and resurrection of Jesus Christ, all of God's blessings are a free gift, and we receive from God what we could never deserve. With the exception of renouncing Christ, nothing that we do or do not do will ever change our status with God. Religion is not worship. Religion is hypocrisy because it causes us to feel superior based on things that have no eternal boasting value. (see Ephesians 2:8-9) Religion places us back in bondage to the fear of God's punishment and, ultimately, death. This freedom from the fear of death (which is the root of all other fears) is exactly why Christ died and was raised again for us. (see Hebrews 2:14-15; 1 John 4:18) Religion is a lie which offers us what God has already given us freely in Christ Jesus through the false path of obedience to rules rather than obedience to the Holy Spirit. (see Romans 8:1-4) If we are working to earn God's goodness and blessings, then we are not actually doing good works for Christ.

Technically speaking, the *yeast of the Pharisees*, including all forms of religion and legalism, is *falling from grace*. (see Galatians 5:1-4) We do not *fall from grace* when we stumble in sin because grace was designed to cover over all sin. You could even say that when we sin, we fall *into* grace. On the other hand, we *fall from grace* when we dive-bomb from relying on Christ's perfect record through faith to relying on our completely imperfect record through piety, no matter how many religious regulations we follow or how holy we think our actions are. The *yeast of the Pharisees* moves believers backwards and out of the grace of the New Covenant by subjecting us to the old standard of Law or any type thereof. Notably, converted Christians from the party of the Pharisees were the ones who proposed that Gentiles must submit themselves to circumcision in order to be included in God's people. However, Peter correctly reiterated that God's grace purifies hearts with Christ's righteousness through faith alone. (see Acts 15:5, 9)

Let me make a quick side note about faith. Among Christians, some false teachings have arisen which over-emphasize faith as the way to access God's blessings. It is true that we access God's grace through faith. However, these teachings condemn believers for their lack of faith when it appears that they are not blessed. These teachings are false because they have turned faith into a work of piety which earns or deserves God's favor. Any teaching which condemns, aggrandizes, or takes a *get what you deserve* attitude towards a Christ follower based on their performance or lack thereof, is error. Grace is never a matter of our performance because we cannot merit unmerited favor. Grace is always a matter of who God is and what He accomplished for us through Jesus Christ. Faith is never a matter of our performance because that would lead us into self-righteousness, and we have no righteousness of our own to offer God. Christ followers receive every blessing from God by grace through faith. (see Ephesians 2:8)

The second type of yeast is the *yeast of the Sadducees*, which is *unbelief*. The Sadducees were another prominent sect of Judaism who believed only the first five books of the Bible. Clearly, this resulted in their interpretations of Scripture being negligent of the *whole counsel of* God because they denied the relevance or applicability of significant portions of God's Word. They did not believe in the resurrection from the dead, angels, spirits, or eternal life, and they did not believe that God's power still functioned in their day the way that it had in the days of their ancestors. (see Mark 12:18; Acts 23:6-8) Their views placed prominence on living according to God's Law and personal responsibility for upstanding conduct, even though they often compromised these standards in order to maintain their influence and affluence among *the powers that be* in the world. They believed that death was the end of the line for all people and that there was no eternal hope.

False teachings rooted in *unbelief* emphasize manpower while denying or doubting God's power. Unbelief places all responsibility for our lives in our own hands and this, inevitably, keeps us in constant fear of death. Unbelief teaches us that *it's all up to me*, and to *try really hard*, *be good*, and *do the right thing*, as if any of us were capable of being good or knowing the right thing to do apart from Christ and His guidance through the Holy Spirit. Unbelief is a lie that Jesus isn't really who He says He is and that He didn't really do what He said He did or, even if He did, then He probably didn't do it for me. Unbelief rejects and or denies God's ability or willingness to forgive our sin completely and not hold it against us, or doubts God's delight in blessing us in our day according to His promises throughout the Scriptures. Another form of unbelief is just a lack of knowledge of the *whole counsel of God* or, in a word, ignorance. How can any of us believe what we have not been taught?

In contrast, and just in case you don't know, Jesus Christ was born as God in the flesh by an act of God's power. Then, by another act of God's power, He was crucified and, on the cross, took upon Himself all of the responsibility for our lives in addition to all of our sin, every punishment for ungodliness, and all sickness, curse, and oppression of the evil one. Next, in the greatest display of God's power that the world has ever known, God raised Jesus from the dead to eternal life. Because of this, we who believe are already saved, healed, freed from the curse, and are no longer subject to the devil's reign. When we believe that Jesus is Lord and that God raised Him from the dead, we already have every blessing of God. (see Ephesians 1:3; 2 Corinthians 1:20) To top it off, Jesus ascended to heaven and poured the Holy Spirit into our hearts so that He can guide us in what to do and give us power to do it according to His will. Our only job is to believe Him, (see John 6:29) and the rest is all up to Him. Moreover, if we find ourselves unintentionally ignorant, then we can devote ourselves to the study of the *whole counsel of God* and live our lives by the direction of the Holy Spirit so that we have revelation knowledge of God, through which grace and peace are multiplied. (see 2 Peter 1:2) In case you think this is not for you, Jesus did this for all mankind so that anyone who believes in Him can receive every benefit and blessing of God from here to eternity. (see 2 Corinthians 5:15; John 1:12, 3:16) If Jesus Christ did not do any part of this for us, then Christians are the most pathetic and deluded people on planet earth. (see 1 Corinthians 15:1-20)

Teaching that has been affected by the *yeast of the Sadducees* is not really about Jesus and does not fully express all that has been accomplished by God through Christ's resurrection from the dead. Sometimes, this is because the one teaching denies that God's power is for us today and sometimes, this is because the message of the cross has been compromised in order to be appealing to a worldly audience. For example, the Sadducees were greatly distressed that the apostles were teaching that Jesus Christ had been raised from the dead and that the hope of eternal life came through faith in Him. They did not want to lose their Rome-appointed governing authority due to an uprising among the people and, therefore, they urged the apostles not to teach in the name of Jesus anymore. (see Acts 4:1-2, 18, 5:40) But, the apostles did not comply with the Sadducees' demand because any teaching (even "Biblical" teaching) which is not firmly rooted in Jesus Christ and His resurrection from the dead is not Christianity. These teachings may be capable of producing self-controlled or "good people," but they have utterly missed the point of Christ's work of redemption. Oftentimes, sadly, false teaching is the result of teachers who themselves do not know the full Gospel, and therefore, they cannot teach it. For example, a man named Apollos taught powerfully about Jesus in Ephesus, but for a while, he only knew about the Baptism of John and had no knowledge of the outpouring of the Holy Spirit. Fortunately, he was willing to be taught and went on to be a powerful preacher and accurate teacher. (see Acts 18:24-28, 19:1-6)

As a side note, there are two ways in which believers *test God*. As we have discussed before, there is *negative testing* with expectation of failure and *positive testing* with expectation of proving genuine. Unbelief is a way of *negatively testing God* because it is from a heart that expects Him to fail. Israel was guilty of this throughout their history when they doubted God's power, ability, or willingness to fulfill all or any part of what He had promised. (see Exodus 17:2; Deuteronomy 16:6; Psalm 78, 95:9, 106:14) Peter also referred to enforcing circumcision on Gentile believers as *testing God* because it negated and disbelieved the fullness of God's grace through faith in Jesus Christ alone. (see Acts 15:10) In contrast, as we continually place our faith in Christ and allow God to renew our minds, we are encouraged to *positively test* God's perfect and pleasing will for our lives, which is His will being done *on earth as it is in heaven*, by believing that Jesus Christ is the same yesterday, today, and forever. (see Romans 12:2; Hebrews 13:8)

The third type of yeast is the *yeast of Herod*, which is *worldliness* and returning to our old Adamic nature of *sin and wickedness*. In Jesus' day, there was a political sect of Judaism called the Herodians who believed that the best aim of their religious pursuits was through worldly influence. They regarded the authority of Herod as a type of God-appointed Messiahship and sought to combine their God-given authority with the Roman governing structures. They blurred the lines between believers and nonbelievers and missed the point of being a set apart people. This said, Jesus did not warn against the yeast of the Herodians but the *yeast of Herod*. I take this to include *worldliness* in general that stresses luxury, domination, being served, and self-indulgence as the highest aims and marks of success in life and the condoning of immorality and compromised integrity as an accepted means to an end. Herod considered himself to be god and lived his life paranoid of losing his authority and status. He even indulged in murder and forbidden marriage just because he wanted to and because he could. People bowed down to him, and he liked it that way.

False teachings rooted in *worldliness* stress the aims of the world as the pursuit of the Christian life and marks of Christian success. Worldly teaching distorts things like *church building* or *expansion* to bear a closer resemblance to the people of old building the Tower of Babel in order to make a *name for themselves.* (see Genesis 11:1-9) Worldly teaching attempts to use the Church's God-given authority to regulate the conduct of unbelievers or to extend the influence of the Church by mingling with world governments. Worldly teachings include messages of common sense, also known as the ways of the world, logic, reasonings, intellect, self-empowerment, and self-improvement. Worldly teachings consent to carnality and gluttony in all its forms, to excessive hard work for security or self-aggrandizement, and to immorality, particularly sexual sin, in the name of grace or tolerance. Spiritually speaking, worldly teaching drifts away from the Holy Spirit and God's guidance to alternative spirits which are not of God. These teachings consider all forms of spirituality to be equal with Christianity and incorporate or permit things such as horoscopes, karma, secret knowledge, visualizations, witchcraft which is manipulation, and sorcery which does not derive its power from God. These teachings may also emphasize eating, drinking, and being merry because life on earth is so short, or that luxury and lavish lifestyle is evidence of God's blessing or proves a believer's great faith. Paul called all of this the *old yeast of malice and wickedness* and begged people to turn from these worthless things and to place their faith in the one true God. (see Acts 14:15, 17:30; 1 Corinthians 5:8) Additionally, false teachers who purport these kinds of teachings will often charge huge sums of money for their ministry services rather than preaching the Gospel free of charge. (see 1 Corinthians 9:18; Matthew 10:8) Their dogma is also known as the *doctrine of Balaam* who is commonly called *a prophet for profit.* (2 Peter 2:15; Jude 1:11; Revelation 2:14; Numbers 22-24) Ironically, Balaam's very name means *not of the people,* or *a foreigner,* or *perhaps,* indicating both his worldliness and willingness to compromise his beliefs for the right price.

The *yeast of Herod* is probably the closest metaphor to *honey,* which was not permitted by God's Law to be offered on the altar of sacrifice because honey represented the sweetness of the fancies of life. Notably, God gave Israel a land *flowing with milk and honey* and *every good thing* which demonstrates that God desires to bestow His richest blessings upon His people. (Exodus 3:8, 17, 33:3; Ezekiel 20:6) However, honey which has been obtained through wrong motives, via destructive paths which have neglected faith in God's ways, timing, and ability to bless, does not honor God at all. Besides that, to believe that we can earn and offer something to God as a sweet sacrifice that He did not give to us in the first place is a twisted delusion.

God's purpose for us is not to blend in with the world but to stand out. Peter called this *saving ourselves from a corrupt generation*, and Paul called this being the *unleavened bread of sincerity and truth*. (see Acts 2:40; 1 Corinthians 5:8) The word *holy* means *set apart*, which can also simply mean *different for God's reasons*. When Israel was formed, it was the one and only nation out of all the nations on the earth that was chosen by God to know Him, which made them very special and very different – they were inherently *holy*. Their purpose was not to tell other nations how to govern themselves but to demonstrate God's holiness to all the nations of the world by obeying His Laws and maintain His holy standards. (see Exodus 19:5-6; Leviticus 11:44, 19:2, 20:26; Deuteronomy 7:6, 14:2, 26:18-19; Psalm 67) Along these lines, Jesus came as the Holy One of God who, in stark contrast to the ways of the world, demonstrated sacrifice, submission, service, and purity as an example of God's *holiness*. Additionally, Jesus was born as the King of God's people to rule over them, and He respectfully paid His taxes to Caesar without attempting to overthrow, rule through, or blend in with Rome's worldly authority. (see Matthew 22:21; Mark 12:17; Luke 20:25) Jesus' aim was love, His nature was pure, and His triumph was surrender. As Christ followers, we are chosen by God to be a set apart, self-governing, *holy* people, and our purpose is to know God and to be like Christ in order to manifest the character and love of Jesus to the world. (see 1 Peter 1:16, 2:9; Romans 8:29)

Spiritual Warfare

The purpose of knowing the various types of false beliefs and the roots of their deception is to assist us in discerning the spirit behind what we hear and believe and to accurately assess what is motivating our own actions. A good way to do this is to ask ourselves, *Who or what is the god of this thought?* If the aim, emphasis, or ultimate result is self-effort, fear of condemnation, earning blessing, doing the right thing, being a good person, following a person other than Christ, logic, common sense, intellect, money, security, status, being followed or admired by people, me myself and I, what I want right now, or getting what I deserve (good or bad) because of what I have done or not done, then be on guard because you might have a yeast infection. Ew.

> {1Jo 4:1-3} 1 *Dear friends,* **do not believe every spirit, but test the spirits to see whether they are from God,** *because many false prophets have gone out into the world.* 2 **This is how you can recognize the Spirit of God: Every spirit that acknowledges that Jesus Christ has come in the flesh is from God,** 3 **but every spirit that does not acknowledge Jesus is not from God. This is the spirit of the antichrist,** *which you have heard is coming and even now is already in the world.*

> {1Jo 4:1 NLT} 1 *Dear friends,* **do not believe everyone who claims to speak by the Spirit. You must test them to see if the spirit they have comes from God.** *For there are many false prophets in the world.*

The dominant spirit behind every deceptive belief is the *antichrist spirit*. The antichrist spirit is exactly what it is called – *against Christ*. It is not anti-Jesus, not anti-God, not anti-spirit or spirituality because most people think that Jesus was a good guy, believe in God, and subscribe to some form of spirituality.

This said, the rubber meets the road when Jesus is proclaimed to be the Christ because this means that He is King of all creation and has the right to be the Lord of our lives. Any teaching that says that Jesus is not God, was not born in the flesh, did not die, or was not raised from the dead is a lie from the pit of hell. Being born in the flesh made Jesus the King of the world. The resurrection confirmed that He is the King above all kings and Lord above all lords. (see Romans 1:4)

This is of utmost importance because it is the very basis and foundation of our Christian faith and of the Church. When Peter recognized Jesus as the Christ, Jesus responded that His Church would be built upon this revelation and that *the gates of hell would not prevail against it*. (see Matthew 16:18) Gates represent the power of a city, palace, or prison that have the ability to lock out or lock in. Through death, Jesus entered into the gates of hell, and the evil one locked the gates believing that Christ had been conquered. However, death and hell could not hold Him. On the third day, when Jesus Christ rose from the dead, He busted through the gates of hell, and the Church was with Him when He did. (see Acts 2:32, 24, 3:15, 4:10, 5:30, 10:40, 13:30, 17:31; 1 Corinthians 6:14; Ephesians 1:10; Colossians 2:12; 1 Peter 1:21) Therefore, the gates of hell *DID NOT prevail* against Christ or His Church. Jesus is ALIVE, and Christ is KING. It is finished! Hallelujah!

Again, the only work which Jesus requires of us is to believe Him. (see John 6:29) This said, with all the false ideas and beliefs lurking around every corner, we have our work cut out for us. In fact, our work is warfare. Therefore, the apostle Paul supplied us with the *Armor of God* so that we are able to stand our ground and hold firmly to the truth of what Christ accomplished for us.

> *{Eph 6:10-18} 10 Finally,* **be strong in the Lord and in his mighty power**. *11 Put on* **the full armor of God**, *so that you can take your stand* **against the devil's schemes**. *12 For* **our struggle is not against flesh and blood, but against the rulers, against the authorities, against the powers of this dark world and against the spiritual forces of evil in the heavenly realms**. *13 Therefore* **put on the full armor of God**, *so that when the day of evil comes,* **you may be able to stand your ground**, *and after you have done everything, to stand. 14 Stand firm then, with the* **belt of truth** *buckled around your waist, with the* **breastplate of righteousness** *in place, 15 and with your* **feet fitted with the readiness that comes from the gospel of peace**. *16 In addition to all this, take up the* **shield of faith**, *with which you can extinguish all the flaming arrows of the evil one. 17 Take the* **helmet of salvation** *and the* **sword of the Spirit, which is the word of God**. *18 And pray in the Spirit on all occasions with all kinds of prayers and requests. With this in mind, be alert and always keep on praying for all the Lord's people. (see also Romans 13:12; 2 Corinthians 6:7; 1 Thessalonians 5:8)*

As we learned previously, Jesus gave all believers authority to trample *snakes and scorpions* and to overcome all the power of the enemy. (see Luke 10:19) While we do have authority over literal snakes and scorpions, *snakes* represent the serpent of old who is the father of all lies and who has been sinning from the beginning, and *scorpions* represent the stings of unbelief, oppression, religion, the words of our persecutors, and the fear of death. (see John 8:44; Revelation 20:2; 1 John 3:8; Ezekiel 2:6; 1 Kings 12:11; 1

Corinthians 15:55-56; Revelation 9:3) Our warfare is never against people, including ourselves. Our battle is to combat ideas, beliefs, and lies that deny Christ and what He has done for us.

> *{2Co 10:3-5} 3 For though we live in the world, **we do not wage war as the world does.** 4 The weapons we fight with are **not the weapons of the world.** On the contrary, they have **divine power to demolish strongholds.** 5 **We demolish arguments and every pretension that sets itself up against the knowledge of God,** and we take captive every thought to make it obedient to Christ.*

> *{2Co 10:5 KJV} 5 **Casting down imaginations, [vain ideas] and every high thing that exalteth itself against the knowledge of God,** and **bringing into captivity every thought to the obedience of Christ;***

As a quick side note, in my opinion, the King James translation of this verse is the best because our aim is to focus our thoughts on *Christ's obedience* on our behalf, which always succeeds in demolishing lies. Otherwise, we may become a self-righteous Pharisee because of the superior obedience of our thoughts, which is really not the point. God's grace is always about what Jesus did for us through His life, death, and resurrection. But I digress...

In the Old Testament, *strongholds* were literally a *fortified tower* in the center of a town or city. When the city was under enemy attack, everyone ran to the stronghold to be safe. What was literal in the Old Testament is now spiritual in the New Testament. A *spiritual stronghold* is anything other than Christ, including beliefs and behaviors, which we run to for comfort or security. Similarly, in the Old Testament, *high places* were the places where people of the world would go to set up altars to their gods to offer sacrifices and worship. (see Exodus 23:24 and many other references, particularly throughout 1 Kings and 2 Kings) Spiritually speaking, *high things* are the altars in our minds of spiritual beliefs or traditions of men that are not rooted in Jesus Christ. Arguments, imaginations, pretensions, and vain ideas are our own worldly fantasies, carnal lusts, and prideful motives that lead us into sin and error. (see James 1:14) Lastly, the rulers, authorities, powers of this dark world, and spiritual forces of evil are the servants of satan, who is *the prince of this world,* its ways, and its evil spirits. They are assigned by the evil one with dominion or territory over our lives, our families, our cities, and our nations to oppress us in whatever way possible to prevent us from worshipping Christ freely. (see John 12:31, 14:30; 2 Corinthians 4:4; Ephesians 2:2; 1 John 5:19; Daniel 10:13) In short, satan's schemes are all clever deceptions attempting to lure us back into the darkness behind the gates of hell and to return us to the torment of his oppressive rule.

However, for believers, the name of Jesus is our stronghold and the fortified tower that we run to God for safety from every enemy attack. (see Proverbs 18:10; Psalm 18:2, 61:3-4, 91, 144:2) We allow God to renew our minds through revelation of Jesus Christ so that we can discern the perfect and pleasing will of God. (see Romans 12:2) We, the Church, declare the finished work of Jesus Christ as the manifold wisdom of God to refute every false belief and to expel every evil spirit that harasses or torments us. (see Ephesians 3:10-11) We say, *It is finished in Jesus' name!* and know that the enemy is already under our feet. (see

Ephesians 1:19-23) Our work and warfare is to continue, persevere, and hold fast in faith and in the truth of Christ until He returns. (see Colossians 1:23; 1 Timothy 4:16; 1 Corinthians 11:2, 15:2; Romans 11:22; 1 Thessalonians 5:21; Hebrews 3:6, 14, 4:14, 6:11, 10:23)

The True Aim

Jesus set us free from the evil one's power and authority so that we can know God and worship Him freely. God's will for our lives is for us to know Him, to be like Christ, and to make disciples of all nations through spreading the Gospel. Teachings that reveal God's grace through the life, death, and resurrection of Jesus Christ, deepen our understanding of the freedom and victory that we have in Jesus, and call us to lives of *holiness* and *Christlikeness* are teachings that accurately point to the true aim of the Christian life.

> *{1Ti 1:5 NLT} 5 The **purpose of my instruction** is that all believers would be filled with **love that comes from a pure heart, a clear conscience, and genuine faith**.*

> *{Gal 5:6b} 6b **The only thing that counts is faith expressing itself through love**.*

> *{Rom 14:17} 17 For the **kingdom of God** is not a matter of eating and drinking, but of **righteousness, peace and joy in the Holy Spirit**,*

> *{1Co 2:2, 5} 2 For I resolved to **know nothing while I was with you except Jesus Christ and him crucified**. ... 5 **so that your faith might not rest on human wisdom, but on God's power**.*

This brings us back to *yeast*. Truth be told, not every Old Testament offering prohibited the use of yeast. The peace offering of thanksgiving to God included a loaf of bread made with yeast and the offering for the Feast of Weeks (or Pentecost) included breads baked with yeast. (see Leviticus 7:13, 23:17) These offerings were not burned on the altar to God because they had no atoning value so, instead, they were offered to the High Priest for his enjoyment. They were always offered with rejoicing over what God had done and the harvest that He promised for the future. Similarly, in spite of the fact that all of us have been polluted by the yeast of sin or erroneous beliefs, we can always offer ourselves to Jesus as our High Priest for His enjoyment, even though our offering has no atoning value. We express our humble gratitude for all that He has done for us, and we wait expectantly for all that He has promised us. Additionally and finally, Jesus told a parable comparing the Kingdom of God to yeast which spreads until the whole batch of dough is leavened. (see Matthew 13:33; Luke 13:21) Christians change the character of the world by destroying and demolishing lies of the evil one and false beliefs with the grace and truth of Jesus Christ. Disciples of Christ make disciples of all nations by spreading the Kingdom of God, just like self-replicating *yeast*.

CHAPTER 16
God's Guidance

The first 120 Christ followers were commissioned by Jesus to take the Gospel to the ends of the earth. However, before they could do even one thing of value for Christ and His Kingdom, their first instruction was to wait for the Holy Spirit. Jesus gave them this command when He was physically with them in His resurrection body, and they took His orders as seriously as obedient subjects of a King. Then, after the Holy Spirit was poured out, Christ's disciples did not do anything without God's guidance because they regarded direction from the Holy Spirit as equal in value to Jesus being there with them. In fact, throughout the Book of Acts, Christ followers were guided into their Kingdom tasks moment by moment through prophecy, dreams, visions, and angels so that the Gospel of Jesus Christ spread through His witnesses to manifest His love to the ends of the earth. Let's dig into these things so that we can live for Christ by God's guidance through the Holy Spirit in the same way that they did.

Life Led by the Holy Spirit

Without the Holy Spirit, even disciples who had walked with Jesus were stuck flipping a coin for divine guidance. (see Acts 1:26) They were totally without the ability to hear from God for themselves regarding what they were supposed to do next. In this condition, Jesus did not want them to do a thing for Him or in His name. The disciples still thought that it was time for the Messiah to come and conquer all of Israel's enemies in the final and catastrophic *day of the Lord* which they knew about from the Scriptures. (see Acts 1:6) They were most likely expecting Jesus to come back imminently to lead them as His army in slaying all of their enemies. They were, indeed, entering into war. But this was a war for the hearts and souls of men, and this war would only be won by doing the things that Jesus did in the way that He did them. They needed the Holy Spirit so that they could receive direction from the Lord Himself and therefore, His final marching orders to His disciples were:

> *{Luk 24:49} 49 I am going to send you what my Father has promised;* **but stay in the city until you have been clothed with power from on high.***"*

> *{Act 1:4-5} 4 On one occasion, while he was eating with them, he gave them this command:* **"Do not leave Jerusalem, but wait** *for the gift my Father promised, which you have heard me speak about. 5 For John baptized with water, but in a few days you will* **be baptized with the Holy Spirit.***"*

All of their plans for the future were replaced with a higher calling to the Kingdom of God. Anything less would have been disobedient. For ten days, they waited in prayer. Then finally, Pentecost! Immediately, they became animated by the Spirit of the Lord, and their war against evil began through the words of their mouths. They made known the completed work of the cross, they declared the enemy's defeat, and they proclaimed the love of God through the Gospel of Jesus Christ in every language under heaven. (see

Acts 2:7-11) Only after Christ's followers had received the Holy Spirit were their hearts transformed to be the softened and circumcised hearts which were compassionate rather than conquering. From this day forward, Jesus would be leading them as if He were there in person and the disciples were ambassadors of heaven who extended offers of peace to sinners, religious rebels, and enemies of God.

In the Book of Acts, believer's plans were subject to the Lord's discretion and they followed the promptings of the indwelling Holy Spirit. Sometimes, the Holy Spirit said *go* and other times *stay*. Sometimes, the Holy Spirit prevented believers from going where they desired to go and other times compelled them to go even in the face of great suffering.

> *{Act 8:29-30}* 29 **The Spirit told Philip, "Go to that chariot and stay near it."** 30 **Then Philip ran up to the chariot** *and heard the man reading Isaiah the prophet. "Do you understand what you are reading?" Philip asked.*

> *{Act 10:19-21}* 19 *While Peter was still thinking about the vision,* **the Spirit said to him, "Simon, three men are looking for you.** 20 **So get up and go downstairs. Do not hesitate to go with them, for I have sent them."** 21 **Peter went down** *and said to the men, "I'm the one you're looking for. Why have you come?"*

> *{Act 16:6-7}* 6 *Paul and his companions traveled throughout the region of Phrygia and Galatia,* **having been kept by the Holy Spirit** *from preaching the word in the province of Asia.* 7 *When they came to the border of Mysia, they tried to enter Bithynia,* **but the Spirit of Jesus would not allow them to***.*

> *{Act 16:9-10}* 9 *During the night* **Paul had a vision of a man of Macedonia standing and begging him, "Come over to Macedonia and help us."** 10 *After Paul had seen the vision,* **we got ready at once to leave for Macedonia, concluding that God had called us to preach the gospel to them***.*

> *{Act 18:9-11}* 9 *One night the Lord spoke to Paul in a vision:* **"Do not be afraid; keep on speaking**, *do not be silent.* 10 *For I am with you, and no one is going to attack and harm you,* **because I have many people in this city."** 11 **So Paul stayed in Corinth for a year and a half**, *teaching them the word of God.*

> *{Act 18:21}* 21 *But as he left, he promised,* **"I will come back if it is God's will**.*"* *Then he set sail from Ephesus.*

> *{Act 20:22-24}* 22 *"And now,* **compelled by the Spirit, I am going to Jerusalem**, *not knowing what will happen to me there.* 23 *I only know that* **in every city the Holy Spirit warns me that prison and hardships are facing me**. 24 *However, I consider my life worth nothing to me;* **my only aim is to finish the race and complete the task the Lord Jesus has given me--the task of testifying to the good news of God's grace***.*

> *{Act 22:18}* 18 **and saw the Lord speaking to me. 'Quick!' he said. 'Leave Jerusalem immediately**, *because the people here will not accept your testimony about me.'*

The Holy Spirit supernaturally transported Philip from one town to another so that He could proclaim the Gospel there:

> *{Act 8:39-40} 39 When they came up out of the water, **the Spirit of the Lord suddenly took Philip away**, and the eunuch did not see him again, but went on his way rejoicing. 40 **Philip, however, appeared at Azotus and traveled about, preaching the gospel** in all the towns until he reached Caesarea.*

All of this is to say that Christ followers no longer made decisions for themselves based on their own logic or way of thinking about things. They lived their lives by literally *following Christ*, allowing themselves to be guided by His promptings through the Holy Spirit and doing nothing except what Jesus directed them to do.

Angels

God also sent His angels to guide believers in the Book of Acts. Throughout the Old Testament, God sent angels to His people to bring words of encouragement, to assist with dramatic escapes, to fight battles with them and for God's people, and to reveal heaven's agenda. (see Genesis 18:2, 19:1-22, 32:1; Joshua 5:13-15; 2 Kings 6:17; Isaiah 6:5, etc.) Jesus Christ is the *Lord of Hosts* which means that He is the captain and commander of God's army of angels who carry out His commands. This is one of God's most commonly used names in the Scriptures, mentioned over 250 times. Angels can take the form of human beings who supernaturally appear and disappear, or they may be seen only through eyes which God has granted to see in the spiritual realm.

Angels were responsible for releasing Peter from prison on two occasions, once with John and once on his own. The second time that it happened, it was so surreal that Peter thought it was a vision, but it wasn't.

> *{Act 5:19-20} 19 But during the night **an angel of the Lord opened the doors of the jail and brought them out.** 20 "Go, stand in the temple courts," he said, "and tell the people all about this new life."*

> *{Act 12:7-11} 7 **Suddenly an angel of the Lord appeared and a light shone in the cell.** He struck Peter on the side and woke him up. "Quick, get up!" he said, and the chains fell off Peter's wrists. 8 Then the angel said to him, "Put on your clothes and sandals." And Peter did so. "Wrap your cloak around you and follow me," the angel told him. 9 **Peter followed him out of the prison, but he had no idea that what the angel was doing was really happening; he thought he was seeing a vision.** 10 They passed the first and second guards and came to the iron gate leading to the city. It opened for them by itself, and they went through it. When they had walked the length of one street, **suddenly the angel left him.** 11 Then Peter came to himself and said, "**Now I know without a doubt that the Lord has sent his angel and rescued me** from Herod's clutches and from everything the Jewish people were hoping would happen."*

An angel of the Lord told Philip to take a certain road to his next divine appointment:

> *{Act 8:26-27} 26 Now **an angel of the Lord said to Philip**, "Go south to the road--the desert road--that goes down from Jerusalem to Gaza." 27 So he started out, and on his way he met an Ethiopian eunuch, an important official in charge of all the treasury of the Kandake (which means "queen of the Ethiopians"). This man had gone to Jerusalem to worship,*

God sent an angel to Cornelius so that he would send for Peter and hear the Gospel of Jesus Christ:

> *{Act 10:3-8} 3 One day at about three in the afternoon he had a vision. **He distinctly saw an angel of God, who came to him** and said, "Cornelius!" 4 Cornelius stared at him in fear. "What is it, Lord?" he asked. **The angel answered**, "Your prayers and gifts to the poor have come up as a memorial offering before God. 5 Now send men to Joppa to bring back a man named Simon who is called Peter. 6 He is staying with Simon the tanner, whose house is by the sea." 7 **When the angel who spoke to him had gone**, Cornelius called two of his servants and a devout soldier who was one of his attendants. 8 He told them everything that had happened and sent them to Joppa.*

> *{Act 10:21-22} 21 Peter went down and said to the men, "I'm the one you're looking for. Why have you come?" 22 The men replied, "We have come from Cornelius the centurion. He is a righteous and God-fearing man, who is respected by all the Jewish people. **A holy angel told him to ask you to come to his house so that he could hear what you have to say**." (see also Acts 11:13)*

An angel appeared to Paul to encourage and reassure him in spite of impending shipwreck:

> *{Act 27:21-26} 21 After they had gone a long time without food, Paul stood up before them and said: "Men, you should have taken my advice not to sail from Crete; then you would have spared yourselves this damage and loss. 22 But now I urge you to keep up your courage, because not one of you will be lost; only the ship will be destroyed. 23 **Last night an angel of the God to whom I belong and whom I serve stood beside me** 24 and said, 'Do not be afraid, Paul. You must stand trial before Caesar; and God has graciously given you the lives of all who sail with you.' 25 So keep up your courage, men, for I have faith in God that it will happen just as he told me. 26 Nevertheless, we must run aground on some island."*

An angel of the Lord struck Herod down dead when he did not give glory to God. This instilled the fear of God in many people, and they placed their faith in Jesus.

> *{Act 12:23-24} 23 Immediately, **because Herod did not give praise to God, an angel of the Lord struck him down, and he was eaten by worms and died**. 24 But the word of God continued to spread and flourish.*

Angels ministered to believers constantly and are sent to care for God's people. (see Hebrews 1:14; Psalm 34:7, 91:4, 11-12) Sometimes they were seen and sometimes they were not but, nevertheless, they were there carrying out God's commands.

Prophecy, Dreams & Visions

From the outset of the outpouring of the Holy Spirit, God revealed that He would be speaking to and through His people in various ways. In the same way that all believers have the ability to hear Jesus' voice, all believers have the ability to prophesy, dream dreams and see visions.

> {Act 2:17-18} 17 " 'In the last days, God says, I will pour out my Spirit on all people. **Your sons and daughters will prophesy**, your young men will **see visions**, your old men will **dream dreams**. 18 Even on my servants, both men and women, I will pour out my Spirit in those days, and **they will prophesy**. (quoting Joel 2:28-32)

Technically speaking, to *prophesy* is *to speak by divine inspiration, to foretell future events pertaining to the Kingdom of God, to speak things which can only be known by divine revelation*. In other words, it is to share with others the things that God is speaking to you. In its simplest form, a person who prophesies speaks from the heart of God about His love and the grace available to everyone through faith in Christ. (see Revelation 19:10) Practically speaking, to *prophesy* is to hear God saying something through the Holy Spirit and then to speak what He is revealing to you for yourself, for another person, or about a situation. As we mature in our prophesying, we find ourselves listening and speaking at the same time as the words of the Lord *flow* out of our mouths like living water. Prophetic revelation is given to believers for ourselves and for one another in order to comfort us in our trials, encourage us into our Kingdom purpose, and build up our faith in Jesus Christ. (see 1 Corinthians 14:3, 12) It can include *gentle* rebukes (as the Holy Spirit reveals them) for the purpose of helping one another stay on track in our walk of faith and holiness. God uses prophecy to reveal His omniscience by disclosing the secrets of our hearts and by accurately foretelling the things which are to come. (see 1 Corinthians 14:24-25) Moreover, all believers are encouraged to eagerly desire to *prophesy* so that they may build up the Church. (see 1 Corinthians 14:1, 39)

Dreams and *visions* are similar to prophecy, except revelation from God is given through images or motion pictures instead of words. A picture speaks a thousand words, so these images can be a highly impactful way that God uses to guide us. *Dreams* come when we are asleep, and *visions* come when we are awake or are in a meditative state. The Holy Spirit will place an image in our minds eye, which may include items of Biblical or spiritual significance, or may be images, people, places, or things which hold metaphoric value in our lives or the life of the person we are ministering to. The majority of the time, prophecy, dreams, and visions are subject to interpretation. Sometimes, the Holy Spirit will give us the interpretation, but other times He will not, and we must receive by faith what the Lord has revealed to us the way that He has given it to us. This said, revelation, which the Holy Spirit gives us no matter which form it takes, will always be aligned with the *whole counsel of God*, His character, and the completed work of Christ, which helps us to *test the spirit* and discern that God is speaking. Sometimes, God's message is crystal clear but, most often, it seems as if we are seeing imperfectly like puzzling reflections in a dimly lit mirror. (see 1 Corinthians 13:12; Numbers 12:6-8) This is by design and keeps us dependent on Christ and the Holy Spirit.

Examples of prophecy, dreams, and visions are prevalent throughout the Book of Acts. Starting with its simplest form, the Holy Spirit reminded disciples of the teachings of Jesus and gave them divine inspiration of the right words to say to specific groups of people. This included Peter, who had been a commonplace fisherman, Stephen, to whom the Spirit gave such wisdom that even trained scholars could not refute him, and regular believers who had been scattered by the persecution and testified about Jesus everywhere they went. (see Acts 2:14-41, 3:12-26, 4:8-13, 6:10, 8:4) In fact, once a believer received the Holy Spirit, it was normal for ordinary men and women to *prophesy*.

*{Act 15:32} 32 Judas and Silas, **who themselves were prophets, said much to encourage and strengthen the believers**.*

*{Act 19:6} 6 When Paul placed his hands on them, the Holy Spirit came on them, and **they spoke in tongues and prophesied**.*

*{Act 21:8-9} 8 Leaving the next day, we reached Caesarea and stayed at the house of Philip the evangelist, one of the Seven. 9 **He had four unmarried daughters who prophesied**.*

God spoke to a disciple named Ananias through a *vision* and he was instructed to go find and lay hands on the apostle Paul.

*{Act 9:10-17} 10 In Damascus there **was a disciple named Ananias. The Lord called to him in a vision**, "Ananias!" "Yes, Lord," he answered. 11 The Lord told him, "Go to the house of Judas on Straight Street and ask for a man from Tarsus named Saul, for he is praying. 12 **In a vision he [Saul/Paul] has seen a man named Ananias come and place his hands on him to restore his sight**." 13 "Lord," Ananias answered, "I have heard many reports about this man and all the harm he has done to your holy people in Jerusalem. 14 And he has come here with authority from the chief priests to arrest all who call on your name." 15 But the Lord said to Ananias, "Go! This man is my chosen instrument to proclaim my name to the Gentiles and their kings and to the people of Israel. 16 I will show him how much he must suffer for my name." 17 Then Ananias went to the house and entered it. Placing his hands on Saul, he said, "Brother Saul, the Lord--Jesus, who appeared to you on the road as you were coming here--has sent me so that you may see again and be filled with the Holy Spirit."*

God spoke to Peter through a *vision* in order to relay the message that all foods and all people were made clean in the New Covenant.

*{Act 10:9-20} 9 About noon the following day as they were on their journey and approaching the city, **Peter went up on the roof to pray**. 10 He became hungry and wanted something to eat, and while the meal was being prepared, **he fell into a trance**. 11 **He saw heaven opened and something like a large sheet being let down to earth by its four corners.** 12 It contained all kinds of four-footed animals, as well as reptiles and birds. 13 **Then a voice told him, "Get up, Peter. Kill and eat." 14 "Surely not, Lord!" Peter replied.** "I have never eaten anything impure or unclean." 15 **The voice spoke to him a second time, "Do not call anything impure that God has made clean." 16 This happened three times, and immediately the***

> *sheet was taken back to heaven. 17 **While Peter was wondering about the meaning of the** **vision,** the men sent by Cornelius found out where Simon's house was and stopped at the gate. 18 They called out, asking if Simon who was known as Peter was staying there. 19 **While Peter was** **still thinking about the vision, the Spirit said to him,** "Simon, three men are looking for you. 20 So get up and go downstairs. Do not hesitate to go with them, for I have sent them."*

Notice from this a few things: The Lord spoke through the vision and then after the vision, the Holy Spirit gave Peter direction on what to do, demonstrating two different forms of communication. Additionally, Peter and the Lord had a conversation during the vision but, in spite of this dialog, Peter did not fully grasp the interpretation of the vision and wondered what it meant. It was not until after God confirmed the inclusion of Gentiles by pouring out the Holy Spirit on Cornelius' household that Peter understood what the vision had truly meant. (see Acts 11:4-18) Sometimes, this is how it happens with us today. We will receive a vision that is metaphorically significant, but we do not fully understand how to interpret what we see so we talk to the Lord about it until He gives us all that will be revealed in that moment. Then as the Holy Spirit guides our steps, we watch the Lord orchestrate events to bring the vision to pass. Finally, after it's all done, we realize that God told us exactly what He was doing before it even happened and we understand what He was communicating through the prophetic word, dream, or vision.

God gave Peter *prophetic revelation* about the inner workings of Ananias and Sapphira's hearts.

> *{Act 5:3-4, 8-9} 3 **Then Peter said, "Ananias, how is it that satan has so filled your heart** **that you have lied** to the Holy Spirit and have kept for yourself some of the money you received for the land? 4 Didn't it belong to you before it was sold? And after it was sold, wasn't the money at your disposal? What made you think of doing such a thing? You have not lied just to human beings but to God." ... 8 **Peter asked her,** "Tell me, is this the price you and Ananias got for the land?" "Yes," she said, "that is the price." 9 **Peter said to her, "How could you conspire to** **test the Spirit of the Lord?** Listen! The feet of the men who buried your husband are at the door, and they will carry you out also."*

God also gave *prophetic revelation* to speak warnings to His listening people regarding the things that were to come in the world.

> *{Act 11:27-29} 27 During this time some prophets came down from Jerusalem to Antioch. 28 One of them, named Agabus, stood up and **through the Spirit predicted that a severe famine** **would spread over the entire Roman world. (This happened during the reign of Claudius.)** 29 The disciples, as each one was able, decided to provide help for the brothers and sisters living in Judea.*

Notice that Agabus' prophecy of famine was not given as a proclamation of judgment against the Roman world. Instead, it was interpreted as a grace of God for the preparation of His people because they perceived that the prophecy was given for the building up of the Church. To dig into this a little bit, no matter what Jesus taught, His resounding underlying message was always *repent for the Kingdom of Heaven is at hand.* When Jesus was asked about disasters and calamities happening in the world, this message remained the same. Essentially, Jesus instructed His followers not to consider those who experience catastrophe or misfortune to be worse sinners who were more deserving of God's apparent judgment. Rather, Jesus conveyed that disasters speak warnings that anyone who does not repent and place their faith in Him as Lord and Savior will suffer the ultimate calamity on the *day of judgment* which is to come. (see Luke 13:1-5) Jesus never went on sin hunts to expose the reasons why bad things were happening in the world but steadfastly continued proclaiming *repent for the Kingdom of Heaven is at hand* so that everyone could come to know Him and be saved. Throughout the Old Testament, God often gave conditional prophetic warnings of what would happen if people would not repent. This said, in most cases, God was clear that if people repented, He would relent of the impending calamity. (see Jeremiah 7:3, 18:8, 26:13, 36:3; Ezekiel 18:21; Joel 2:14; Jonah 3:10) However, other times, God reached the limit of His mercy, and the sin of the people attained to full measure. By then, repentance would profit the people nothing because it was too late. Jesus prophesied about the coming *day of judgment* as an appointed time that has been set, which only God (not even Jesus and definitely none of us) knows, when God's vengeance will be poured out on the earth because the sin of all mankind has reached its full measure. (see Matthew 24:1-51; Mark 13:1-37; Luke 12:35-59, 21:5-38) God's judgment and wrath was satisfied when He poured it out on Christ on the cross, and therefore, for everyone who has repented and placed their faith in Jesus, God relents of the judgment that we deserve. This is why the message of *repent for the Kingdom of Heaven is at hand* is of utmost importance and is the loving tone of all true prophecy.

In the meantime, the purpose of revelation for cities or nations is not to decree judgment but to inspire faithfulness to the Lord and invite unbelievers into God's grace through faith in Jesus Christ. According to the apostle Paul, God marked out the boundary lines of all the nations and the appointed times when they would rise and fall since before the creation of the earth. His purpose was that everyone in all nations would seek Him and try to find Him or, in other words, that they would *repent for the Kingdom of Heaven is at hand*. (see Acts 17:26-27) As God's foreordained plans are fulfilled in the earth, He reveals them to His people through prophetic revelation. (see Amos 3:7) This encourages God's people and is a testimony to unbelievers of God's omniscience and that Christ is King. The Old Testament is filled with examples of this type of prophecy. For example, the books of 1 and 2 Kings, written for the purpose of encouraging the people of Israel in their faithfulness to God, are both packed full of historical accounts of God speaking through a person and then *it came to pass just as the man of God had said*. As a smattering of other examples, the prophet Isaiah prophesied the events of the reign of Cyrus of Persia approximately 150 years before it came to pass, Jeremiah accurately predicted that the people of Israel would be in Babylonian exile for 70 years, 20 years before the 70 years began, and Daniel accurately foretold the events in the lives of the kings of Babylon whom he served while he was in exile. (Isaiah 44:28; Jeremiah 25:11-12; Daniel 2:29-45, 4:19-33, 5:13-31) Interestingly, all of these prophets also prophesied things which are still yet to come. For us today, when believers prophesy about the things going on in the world and they come to pass, we are encouraged by knowing that God already knows the end from the beginning, and our faith is built up so that we are able to stand firm in Christ no matter what happens between now and when He returns. (see Isaiah 46:10; Revelation 1:8, 21:6, 22:13)

Paul *prophetically* warned the Ephesian elders of false teachers who would spring up out of the ranks of the Church. They also prophetically knew that they would never see each other again.

> {Act 20:25-32} 25 *"Now I know that **none of you among whom I have gone about preaching the kingdom will ever see me again**. 26 Therefore, I declare to you today that I am innocent of the blood of any of you. 27 For I have not hesitated to proclaim to you the whole will of God. 28 **Keep watch over yourselves and all the flock of which the Holy Spirit has made you overseers**. Be shepherds of the church of God, which he bought with his own blood. 29 **I know that after I leave, savage wolves will come in among you and will not spare the flock**. 30 **Even from your own number men will arise and distort the truth in order to draw away disciples after them**. 31 **So be on your guard!** Remember that for three years I never stopped warning each of you night and day with tears. 32 "Now **I commit you to God and to the word of his grace, which can build you up and give you an inheritance among all those who are sanctified**.*

Believers in every city received *prophetic insight* about the suffering that lay ahead for Paul as he journeyed onwards towards Jerusalem. Agabus even acted it out.

> {Act 20:22-23} 22 *"And now, compelled by the Spirit, I am going to Jerusalem, not knowing what will happen to me there. 23 **I only know that in every city the Holy Spirit warns me that prison and hardships are facing me**.*

> {Act 21:4b} 4 ***Through the Spirit they urged Paul not to go** on to Jerusalem.*

> {Act 21:10-15} 10 *After we had been there a number of days, **a prophet named Agabus came down from Judea**. 11 **Coming over to us, he took Paul's belt, tied his own hands and feet with it and said, "The Holy Spirit says, 'In this way the Jewish leaders in Jerusalem will bind the owner of this belt and will hand him over to the Gentiles.' "** 12 When we heard this, we and the people there pleaded with Paul not to go up to Jerusalem. 13 Then Paul answered, "Why are you weeping and breaking my heart? I am ready not only to be bound, but also to die in Jerusalem for the name of the Lord Jesus." 14 **When he would not be dissuaded, we gave up and said, "The Lord's will be done."** 15 After this, we started on our way up to Jerusalem.*

What these believers spiritually discerned was all true, but God's will in the matter was subject to interpretation. Everyone listening to the Holy Spirit knew that suffering awaited Paul if he went to Jerusalem, so they urged him not to go but Paul knew that it was God's will for him to go, in spite of the suffering that was in store. This is somewhat reminiscent of Jesus' encounter with Peter when Peter admonished Jesus that He would not have to suffer and die on a cross. (see Matthew 16:21-23; Mark 8:31-33) Jesus had on His mind the ways of God and the necessity of what lay ahead for Him. Peter couldn't quite make sense of it and responded as an advocate of the ways of the world, the flesh, and the devil. In fairness, Peter loved Jesus and it could seem that his perspective on the situation best represented the love of God for His Son. But in fact, Jesus was not functioning from a human perception of the love of God but from true knowledge of the love of God. Therefore, He proceeded to demonstrate the love of the

Son for the Father through His obedience and sacrifice. Similarly, the believers prophesying to Paul heard the Holy Spirit correctly, but their interpretation was carnal and selfish. On the other hand, Paul had already been imprisoned, whipped, beaten, stoned, and left for dead on account of the Gospel, and he was willing to go through it all again because the love of Christ compelled him in selflessness. He was ready to pay the ultimate price for Christ, and nothing would deter him from obeying the call of God on his life.

This type of thing still happens in the Church today. Prophetic revelation occasionally comes with clear divine instruction but, most times, it is subject to the interpretation of the one being prophesied to. Therefore, as we steward the gift of prophecy, we must all do our best to communicate exactly what the Holy Spirit is saying through us to others without interpretation before we proceed to presume what it means. Particularly when God speaks symbolically through dreams, visions, pictures, or specific phrases, certain things may have significance to the person being prophesied to which hold no importance to us. God may be speaking encouragement even if we think it is impending doom. Each one of us is responsible for our own obedience to the Lord. If we are the one delivering the prophetic word, or conveying the dream or vision, then our responsibility is to communicate the message of the Lord the way that He is revealing it to us. If we are the beneficiary of prophetic revelation, then we are responsible for seeking the Lord's will for its application to our lives.

Manifesting Christ

We have the same assignment today that the first believers did – to manifest the love of Jesus as His representatives in the earth until He returns. God places His Spirit in us and changes our hearts today, just like He did for Christ's first disciples. Jesus calls us to Kingdom work and the Holy Spirit guides us step by step, moment by moment into our Kingdom tasks. We have the opportunity as believers to offer ourselves as Christ's willing and obedient subjects.

> *{Rom 12:1-2} 1 Therefore, I urge you, brothers and sisters, in view of God's mercy,* **to offer your bodies as a living sacrifice, holy and pleasing to God--this is your true and proper worship.** *2 Do not conform to the pattern of this world, but be transformed by the renewing of your mind.* **Then you will be able to test and approve what God's will is**--*his good, pleasing and perfect will.*

> *{1Co 6:19-20} 19 Do you not know that your bodies are temples of the Holy Spirit, who is in you, whom you have received from God?* **You are not your own;** *20* **you were bought at a price.** *Therefore honor God with your bodies.*

When we live according to the Holy Spirit, we are peaceable, merciful, loving, and pure and the results of this are ever increasing love, joy, peace, patience, kindness, goodness, faithfulness, gentleness, and self-control. (see James 3:17; Galatians 5:22-23) In a word, we are more *Christlike*, which makes us suitable ambassadors of the Kingdom of Heaven. Works that we do for Christ, as He prompts us through the Holy Spirit, are symbolized by *fine linen, silver, gold,* and *precious stones.* These good works yield eternal rewards for us because they are motivated from a heart emanating faith, hope, and love. (see 1

Corinthians 3:12-15, 13:13; Revelation 19:8) Unfortunately, just like the first 120 believers, if left to ourselves without the Holy Spirit, we may as well be tossing a coin. Even "righteous" deeds are nothing but *filthy rags* before God when they are done without the leading of the Holy Spirit. (see Isaiah 64:6) These works, no matter how good they may be, are eternally profitless, made of *wood, hay,* and *straw,* and will burn in the final *day of judgment.* (see again 1 Corinthians 3:12-15) More significantly, in the same way that Jesus' disciples pre-Holy Spirit constantly argued with one another over who was the greatest (see Matthew 18:1; Mark 9:34; Luke 9:46, 22:23-24) believers today who are functioning from the flesh will strive against one another. Unrestrained, our sinful nature is jealous, selfishly ambitious, greedy, competitive, and lusty. To live from this operating system results in: impurity, corruption, idolatry, manipulation, discord, rage, drunkenness, sexual immorality, and every evil thing. (see James 3:16; 1 John 2:16; Galatians 5:19-21) Basically, when we do not obey the Holy Spirit, then we are really no different than the people of the world. (see Romans 8; 1 Corinthians 2; Galatians 5:16-26; Colossians 3:1-17)

> {Gal 5:17} 17 **For the flesh desires what is contrary to the Spirit, and the Spirit what is contrary to the flesh. They are in conflict with each other,** *so that you are not to do whatever you want.*

> {Rom 8:12-14} 12 *Therefore, brothers and sisters,* **we have an obligation--but it is not to the flesh, to live according to it.** *13 For if you live according to the flesh, you will die; but if by the Spirit you put to death the misdeeds of the body, you will live. 14 For* **those who are led by the Spirit of God are the children of God.**

To view it from different angles, to a certain extent, we receive the benefits of our salvation because we were included with Jesus in His death which we discussed previously. Since we are dead with Christ in His death, we are blameless from sin because nobody takes a dead person to court or is able to hold charges against them. For this, Jesus is worthy of our worship, our service, and our lives. On the flip side, Jesus derives benefits from our inclusion in His death because when we know that we are dead to our own desires we are free to live our lives at the direction of the Holy Spirit. We are not crucifying our flesh – we *are crucified with Christ.* We are not dying to ourselves – we are already *dead in Christ.* No matter which way we look at it, *it is finished* so that we can align ourselves with heaven's agenda rather than our own.

> {Col 3:2-3} 2 *Set your minds on things above, not on earthly things. 3* **For you died, and your life is now hidden with Christ** *in God.*

> {1Pe 4:1-2 NLT} 1 *So then, since Christ suffered physical pain,* **you must arm yourselves with the same attitude he had,** *and be ready to suffer, too. For if you have suffered physically for Christ, you have finished with sin. 2* **You won't spend the rest of your lives chasing your own desires, but you will be anxious to do the will of God.**

The Christian life is not a democracy, it is a monarchy, and Christ is our King. Therefore, we do not ask Jesus to co-labor with us in our goals, dreams, and desires, rather, we co-labor with Christ to do the Kingdom works that He has designed for us. (see 1 Corinthians 3:9) Additionally, as we progress in the

Christian life towards spiritual maturity, we do not become LESS dependent on the Holy Spirit, we become MORE dependent on Jesus and His guidance. We realize that we are not only dead in His death, but we are totally useless without Him. The more we do the things that Jesus did, which are completely out of the realm of human capacity, the more we NEED Him to guide, lead, and empower us for our Kingdom tasks. Even more so if we undergo hardship, trials, and opposition, we NEED His comfort and strength in order to endure. Therefore, no matter what is happening in our lives, we NEED Jesus and God's guidance through the Holy Spirit.

Oftentimes, this means that, just like the first 120 disciples who eagerly and expectantly waited to hear from Jesus about what they were supposed to do next, we have to wait for the Holy Spirit to give us our divine marching orders. Waiting is hard to do because we naturally want to do what we want to do…and we want to do it now. Moreover, we have so much of our own ability to procure what we want and "make things happen" or "use our God-given gifts and skills" that, sometimes, waiting for God seems irresponsible. Other times, we simply grow impatient. This said, waiting is the token mark of submission to a higher authority because waiting silently communicates, *I report to someone else.*

An example of this in the Old Testament was the first King of Israel, a man named Saul. He was anointed by the prophet Samuel who told Saul that after the Spirit of the Lord had changed his heart, he could do whatever he found fit to do. However, when it came to the important matters, Saul was told to wait for his next instructions from Samuel, who was God's representative at the time. (see 1 Samuel 9:15-8) For a while, Saul experienced victory because the Spirit of the Lord was with him. Unfortunately, Saul eventually grew impatient and found it difficult to wait for Samuel to come and give him his next instructions. He started looking at his circumstances as they seemed to slip out of his control and look formidable for his people. So, he decided to override Samuel's orders with his own will. He did what he thought that he should do according to his own way of seeing things and, simply put, protect his ego. It cost Saul his kingship. (see 1 Samuel 13:7-14, 15:23; 1 Chronicles 10:13-14) Similarly, for us, even though we are indwelt with the Holy Spirit, we retain great liberty in Christ to do whatever we see fit to do without fear of punishment or condemnation from God. Unlike Saul, we have the Lord's representative with us at all times to speak to us and tell us what to do next. This said, sometimes, the Holy Spirit instructs us to do something that we do not want to do or stops us from doing what we do want to do and other times, the Holy Spirit is silent and we have to wait for further instructions even if it seems like our circumstances are slipping beyond our control. This is where we have a choice: to live for ourselves or to live for Christ.

> {Gal 2:20} 20 *I have been crucified with Christ and **I no longer live, but Christ lives in me. The life I now live in the body, I live by faith in the Son of God,** who loved me and gave himself for me.*

> {Gal 5:24-25} 24 *Those who belong to Christ Jesus **have crucified the flesh with its passions and desires**. 25 **Since we live by the Spirit, let us keep in step with the Spirit**.*

Early disciples of Christ experienced this type of pressure when persecution grew fierce against them and they were under tremendous pressure to reject Jesus as their Messiah. Frankly, in the short term, their circumstances were so horrendous that life would have been much easier for them if they did reject the guidance of the Holy Spirit and deny Christ. However, to do so would mean renouncing their salvation and condemning themselves for all eternity. Day after day, the temptation that they faced was to harden their hearts to the whisper of the Holy Spirit and cave into the agenda of the evil one instead. The writer of the Book of Hebrews encouraged them to remain true to Christ by obeying the Holy Spirit.

> *{Heb 3:7-8, 12-15} 7 So,* **as the Holy Spirit says: "Today, if you hear his voice,** *8* **do not harden your hearts** *as you did in the rebellion, during the time of testing in the wilderness, (quoting Psalm 95:7-11) ... 12 See to it, brothers and sisters, that none of you has a sinful, unbelieving heart that turns away from the living God. 13* **But encourage one another daily, as long as it is called "Today," so that none of you may be hardened by sin's deceitfulness.** *14 We have come to share in Christ, if indeed we hold our original conviction firmly to the very end. 15 As has just been said:* **"Today, if you hear his voice, do not harden your hearts** *as you did in the rebellion."*

This is serious stuff. God gave us His Spirit within us, but we retain our free will to obey the Spirit of the Lord or not. Renouncing Christ doesn't happen all at once, it starts with how we are responding day by day to the whispers of the Holy Spirit as we face the pressures of life. Trials reveal which voice we are truly listening to: the Holy Spirit, the world, our flesh, or the devil. (see James 3:13-18) Selfish people, like Ananias and Sapphira, put on a good show as professing believers but inwardly their hearts were in error. (see Acts 5:1-11) Religious people, like Stephen's accusers, resist the Holy Spirit and gnash their teeth when things do not go their way. (see Acts 7:51) Even those who believe and have been baptized, like Simon in Samaria, can be led astray by flare ups of their old nature's desires. (see Acts 8:18-23) The only way that we will be able to *fight the good fight of faith* (see 1 Timothy 6:12; 2 Timothy 4:7) and endure through the trials of life is to listen to and obey the Holy Spirit and to constantly encourage one another in living our lives by the direction of the Holy Spirit.

Fortunately, as our loving Heavenly Father, God knows what is best for us which means that we can trust Him as He guides us by the promptings of the Holy Spirit. We do not have to fear obeying the Holy Spirit or being punished by God if we mess up because, as long as our hearts are positioned as willing and obedient children, He will guide us every step of the way. If we have been guilty of ignoring Him from time to time, He does not hold it against us when we return to Him, and in fact, He brings us right back on track. Jesus is our King and has a right to be the Lord of our life. However, we are not slaves and, in fact, He calls us His friends and His brothers and sisters. (see John 15:15; Romans 8:29) He lovingly teaches us everything that we need to know, and He guides us like a Shepherd who cares for His sheep so that we can receive all that He has promised us both now and in the age to come. (see Psalm 23; John 10:1-15)

*{Rom 8:15} 15 **The Spirit you received does not make you slaves, so that you live in fear again**; rather, the **Spirit you received brought about your adoption to sonship**. And by him we cry, "Abba, Father." (see also Galatians 4:6)*

*{1Jo 2:27 NLT} 27 **But you have received the Holy Spirit, and he lives within you**, so you don't need anyone to teach you what is true. For **the Spirit teaches you everything you need to know**, and what he teaches is true--it is not a lie. So just as he has taught you, remain [abide] in fellowship with Christ.*

*{Jhn 10:27} 27 **My sheep listen to my voice; I know them, and they follow me**.*

Without overstating it, living life according to the Holy Spirit is the occupation of the Christian life here on earth. God's purpose in sending Jesus was to restore us to right relationship with Himself so that every believer can walk with Him in intimate fellowship and hear His voice. Old Testament examples that foreshadow walking with God include Enoch, Noah, Abraham, Moses, and David who lived in *close fellowship with God*, were called a *friend of God*, who *spoke with God face to face*, and who were *men after God's own heart*. (see Genesis 5:21-24, 6:9, 17:1, 24:40; Exodus 33:11; Numbers 12:8; 1 Samuel 13:14; 2 Chronicles 20:7; James 2:23; Isaiah 41:8; Acts 13:22; Hebrews 11) Each of these men were consumed with God's heart and His purposes. They were willing to look foolish by worldly standards in order to maintain close fellowship with the Lord and follow His instructions. They discarded their own plans in order to keep their minds on the Kingdom of Heaven and, therefore, God was not ashamed to be called their God. Additionally, a life of fellowship with the Lord and speaking with and for God go hand in hand. Significantly, each of the people mentioned above as those who shared close fellowship with God were also called *prophets*. Enoch prophesied about the things to come, Noah proclaimed God's impending judgment of the world, Abraham was called a prophet of God, and so were Moses and David. (see Jude 1:14; 2 Peter 2:5; Genesis 20:7; Deuteronomy 18:18, 34:10; Acts 2:30) As New Covenant believers, we live in even more intimate fellowship then these men from of God from the Old Testament because the Spirit of the Lord has come to dwell within us. This means that we walk in close fellowship with Jesus and, as we listen and obey, He will speak through us as His representatives in the earth.

Keep it simple, listen to Jesus and do what He says. Stay available to the Lord and be flexible when He sends you in a different direction than what you were expecting, which He often does. When we do this, our lives become something altogether supernatural, just like it did for the believers in the Book of Acts. When we offer ourselves to God as living sacrifices and live our lives by following God's guidance, we walk among angels, in spiritual gifts, callings, miracles and, yes, we prophesy, dream dreams, and see visions. But much *much* more significantly, we live lives of LOVE. Through this, *only through this*, we manifest Christ to the world and fulfill God's purpose in the earth.

{1Co 13:1-3, 8-13} 1 If I speak in the tongues of men or of angels, but do not have love, I am only a resounding gong or a clanging cymbal. 2 If I have the gift of prophecy and can fathom all mysteries and all knowledge, and if I have a faith that can move mountains, but do not have love, I am nothing. 3 If I give all I possess to the poor and give over my body to hardship that I may boast,

*but do not have love, I gain nothing...   8 Love never fails. But where there are prophecies, they will cease; where there are tongues, they will be stilled; where there is knowledge, it will pass away. 9 For we know in part and we prophesy in part, 10 but when completeness comes, what is in part disappears. 11 When I was a child, I talked like a child, I thought like a child, I reasoned like a child. When I became a man, I put the ways of childhood behind me. 12 For now we see only a reflection as in a mirror; then we shall see face to face. Now I know in part; then I shall know fully, even as I am fully known.   13 And now these three remain: faith, hope and love. **But the greatest of these is love**.*

Religion, rules, spiritual gifts, sacrifice, knowledge, and piety are childish things that cause division if they absorb our attention. Our truest aim is to see Jesus face to face and to know His friendship. The true Christian life of spiritual maturity is a life that is yielded to God, a heart that is consumed with Christ's purpose, and works by the power of the Holy Spirit which manifest the love of Jesus to all mankind. This is LOVE in action and this is the only thing that truly matters.

May each one of us offer ourselves in absolute surrender to following God's guidance through the indwelling Holy Spirit.

{Rom 12:1-2} 1 Therefore, I urge you, brothers and sisters, in view of God's mercy, to offer your bodies as a living sacrifice, holy and pleasing to God--this is your true and proper worship. 2 Do not conform to the pattern of this world, but be transformed by the renewing of your mind. Then you will be able to test and approve what God's will is--his good, pleasing and perfect will.

May each one of us press onwards in our devotion to Jesus so that we become mature in Christ, accomplish all that He has prepared for us, and receive everything that He died to give us.

{Phl 3:12-16} 12 Not that I have already obtained all this, or have already arrived at my goal, but I press on to take hold of that for which Christ Jesus took hold of me. 13 Brothers and sisters, I do not consider myself yet to have taken hold of it. But one thing I do: Forgetting what is behind and straining toward what is ahead, 14 I press on toward the goal to win the prize for which God has called me heavenward in Christ Jesus. 15 All of us, then, who are mature should take such a view of things. And if on some point you think differently, that too God will make clear to you. 16 Only let us live up to what we have already attained.

May each one of us grow in our revelation knowledge of our inheritance in Christ Jesus, the power of God, and His purpose for us as His Church.

{Eph 1:17-23} 17 I keep asking that the God of our Lord Jesus Christ, the glorious Father, may give you the Spirit of wisdom and revelation, so that you may know him better. 18 I pray that the eyes of your heart may be enlightened in order that you may know the hope to which he has called you, the riches of his glorious inheritance in his holy people, 19 and his incomparably great power for us who believe. That power is the same as the mighty strength 20 he exerted when he raised Christ from the dead and seated him at his right hand in the heavenly realms, 21 far above all rule and authority, power and dominion, and every name that is invoked, not only in the present age but also in the one to come. 22 And God placed all things under his feet and appointed him to be head over everything for the church, 23 which is his body, the fullness of him who fills everything in every way.

May we as the Church, including all of Christ's disciples from every nation in the earth, be united as ONE so that we reveal the love of Jesus to the world.

{Jhn 17:20-23} 20 [Jesus praying] "My prayer is not for them alone. I pray also for those who will believe in me through their message, 21 that all of them may be one, Father, just as you are in me and I am in you. May they also be in us so that the world may believe that you have sent me. 22 I

have given them the glory that you gave me, that they may be one as we are one-- 23 I in them and you in me--so that they may be brought to complete unity. Then the world will know that you sent me and have loved them even as you have loved me.

May each one of us be living examples of ACTS because we have been <u>A</u>ctivated as the <u>C</u>hurch with the <u>T</u>rue gospel and <u>S</u>piritual power. Hallelujah!!

ABOUT THE AUTHOR

Wendy Bowen was the ultimate Type A, workaholic, overachiever, and control-freak until she had a dramatic encounter with the Lord Jesus Christ. Since then, the Lord called Wendy to give away all of her possessions and live by faith, prayer, and obedience to His voice. She lives for the purpose of proclaiming the Gospel and building up the Church by teaching the Word of God, helping believers experience Jesus through the Holy Spirit, and equipping disciples in their Kingdom purpose. The Lord blesses her ministry with His manifest presence and with miracles, signs, and wonders.

www.activatedchurch.com

www.ingramcontent.com/pod-product-compliance
Lightning Source LLC
LaVergne TN
LVHW081327060426
835513LV00012B/1214